Genesis Reloaded
Questioning a Literal
Interpretation of the Bible

Professor Fred Galves

This edition published by
Dog Ear Publishing
4010 W. 86th Street, Ste H
Indianapolis, IN 46268

www.dogearpublishing.net

ISBN: 978-145751-364-0
This book is printed on acid-free paper.

Printed in the United States of America

TABLE OF CONTENTS

TABLE OF CONTENTS

TABLE OF CONTENTS

TABLE OF CONTENTS

TABLE OF CONTENTS

INTRODUCTION

I have been a law professor at Pacific McGeorge School of Law in Sacramento, California, for the past nineteen years. I teach Civil Procedure, Evidence, Computer-Assisted Litigation, and Street Law and have taught a range of other law courses such as Banking Law & Regulation, Federal Courts, Civil Pre-Trial Litigation, and Securities Law. In addition, I have taught various undergraduate courses, including Diversity, Discrimination, and the Law; Principles of Economics (EC 10); and Law & Social Justice. I have written many law review articles in most of the areas in which I teach, as well as a textbook for evidence students and other legal books. I say all of this only to emphasize the fact that I have no scientific or theological expertise that would otherwise qualify me to write this book.

I do, however, have a great deal of experience in closely and critically analyzing legal text, rhetoric, and argumentation, as well as a very keen interest in the subjects of faith and atheism. Moreover, I have a heart and a mind (which I believe were given to me by God) which respect and believe in God enough to at least try to *understand* His Word (if it is, in fact, His Word) for my relationship with Him to grow, and to figure out what my faith means to me and what it may require of me.

Recently, I have been very intrigued by the popularity of the books by atheist and scientist Richard Dawkins, *The God Delusion* and *The Greatest Show on Earth*, as well as by the book by Christopher Hitchens, *God Is Not Great*, and by the authors' various interviews and debates with theologians and others. I also have always been intrigued by fire-and-brimstone evangelist Christians such as Billy Graham, Oral Roberts, and Jerry Falwell and by their very passionate and literal interpretations of the Bible, as well as by such historical figures as Mother Teresa, Martin Luther, and Mahatma Gandhi. I also appreciate the modern perspective of comedian Bill Maher on all of these various issues, including in his movie, *Religulous*, in addition to Sam Harris's *The End of Faith* and his other books. Religious faith, science, and philosophy are often very different and seemingly irreconcilable, yet I find their paradoxical overlapping interplay utterly fascinating.

My wife and I attend a Catholic church and our two boys attend Catholic schools. I often, however, find myself questioning many teachings of the Catholic Church while strongly embracing others. I take my faith and my belief in God very seriously, and this has required me to make an important decision about how literally I should take the Bible. To believe in God, must I also believe in some strict literal interpretation of the Bible? If so, according to whose strict literal interpretation? Is it even possible for there to be just one true, literal interpretation of a text as amorphous and multilayered as the Bible?

INTRODUCTION

My wife, Christine, and I often discuss these concerns, and we enjoy debating various sides of the issue. Because Christine is a very skilled and formidable attorney, it is often enlightening for me to debate her. We do this to explore the topics and to consider our own faith. We both believe in God, but, again, we often find ourselves questioning the Bible and the Catholic Church and, for that matter, all religions. We question whether humans would even matter all that much to a supreme being of the universe. After all, what makes *us* so special—other than our own big human egos?

For instance, my wife and I have a real problem with the fact that women are not allowed to become priests in the Catholic Church. We wonder whether this ban means that God is sexist, that the men who wrote the Bible were sexist, that Catholic traditions are sexist, or all of the above. On an even more sexist level, why do we even assume that God is necessarily a *male*? Does God really have male genitals, male hormones, and male chromosomes like a male human being? On Earth, Jesus may have possessed such characteristics, but does God in Heaven really have male genitals? Why? If it would be to have sex, then with whom would He have sex? If not—that is, if God does not have male genitals, hormones, or chromosomes—why should He be considered a he, clearly more like one half of humanity, which He supposedly created, than the other half?

These troubling concerns of sexism also bring me to the personal quandary of writing this book using the pronoun "He" when referring to God. Shouldn't I be using the pronoun "She" at least half the time when referring to God? I was tempted to use the pronoun "It" when referring to God to be non-sexist and fair; but somehow, it seemed awkward to use It, even when I capitalized It out of respect. So, reluctantly, just for the sake of ease, I have chosen to use the pronoun He when referring to God in this book. I have done this simply to avoid using pronouns in a way that would be confusing to religious or other readers who have become accustomed to the presumptuous and sexist use of the pronoun He when referring to God; however, I remain fully cognizant of the fact that my decision, at a core level, is still a sexist, though convenient, copout, so I apologize for not being more disciplined in insisting on gender neutrality.

That said, on the issue of women not being able to become Catholic priests, we have been told that because no woman was ever allowed to be one of the original twelve disciples of Jesus, women cannot now become priests or the leaders of churches. Of course, this brings up the controversy of Mary Magdalene (which inspired the movie *The Da Vinci Code*, based on the book). Officially, Mary Magdalene was not a disciple, but she loved Jesus very much and appeared more consistently devoted to Him than did Thomas, certainly more so than did Judas, and even more than did Peter. There is a least some evidence (much of it outside of the canon, for obvious reasons), however, that Jesus and Mary were lovers, if not married, so Mary Magdalene is often seen as an embarrassment and inconvenience for Christianity in many ways and therefore is often marginalized. Although she appears to be very devoted and a disciple of Jesus in many ways, she officially is not considered to be a disciple, and even the thought of it is considered heresy by many. Moving forward from that argument, if no woman was ever an official disciple, then for certain church leaders, there is no contradiction in the "biblical" belief that a woman should never become a priest.

Although no disciple may have ever been a woman, neither were any of Jesus's original disciples in the Middle East during the 1st century African, Latino, Asian, or Anglo. Why is there no similar exclusion of men from these various racial and ethnic backgrounds prohibiting them from now becoming priests? I am not advocating such racism, but it seems odd that priests can be of a particular *race* or *ethnicity* different from that of the original twelve disciples, which does not disqualify them from being priests, but they cannot be of a different *gender* from that of the original twelve disciples because that would disqualify them. Such appears to be an unfair and sexist double standard, but to admit it as such also would be to admit the fallibility of these Church teachings. Also, if there are gay or bisexual priests, albeit supposedly celibate ones, that too would be a difference, unless any disciple were gay or bisexual, which of course never could have been acknowledged.

Mostly, however, my wife and I wonder why her increased hormonal level of estrogen, along with her God-given female genitalia, should necessarily disqualify her from being a spiritual leader in our church. Does my wife's femininity, which God Himself bestowed upon her, somehow offend God or otherwise render Him unable to work through her other than in a subservient role to other men in the Church? We get awfully concerned when we read, "And if they [women] will learn anything, let them ask their husbands at home: for it is a shame for women to speak in the church" (1 Corinthians 14:35). Did God actually write that? Would God ever write such a thing, or was that the exclusive work of Paul in a letter to the Corinthians almost 2,000 years ago? Could any calling that my wife might feel be only a strange and improper daydream, probably concocted by Satan himself, the great deceiver, because by creating my wife as a female, God was saying to her, "I would never call *you*, or anyone of your kind, to the very important position of being a priest in the church"?

It would be quite alarming and, I suppose, wholly unacceptable if God reportedly said that only white people could become priests and leaders in the Church while ethnic and racial minorities were to be relegated to subservient roles more "befitting" of their nonwhite, non-leading, intellectually inferior racial or ethnic background! But of course, that was the belief of the Church earlier in our early US history—and those believers had a biblical basis to support the inferiority of the "Negro, as well as of "heathen" Native Americans and perhaps of South or Central American Latinos (although many of the latter derived from Catholic Spanish Conquistadors, so perhaps the judgment against them was not as pronounced). Fortunately, the US Supreme Court has said otherwise, at least with respect to official state racial discrimination. At the time, however, many such racist views *were* attributed to the God of the universe according to what He supposedly said in his own divinely inspired Word. Second Corinthians 6:14 says, "Be ye not unequally yoked together with unbelievers: for what fellowship hath righteousness with unrighteousness? And what communion hath light with darkness?" This verse was used by some to justify racial segregation, even though it involves discrimination based on one's belief, not on one's race. Still, most of us probably would not tolerate such racist interpretations today anyway, but at the very least, wouldn't we call into question whether such racist teachings actually came directly from the God who created all humans? Would God write such a thing in light of the fact that we are all supposed to be the children of God and thus all equal brothers—and sisters?

She makes good arguments, my wife. That's why I try not to cross her. Whenever I do, I jokingly appeal to the part of the Bible where it says that women should submit to their husbands: "Wives, submit yourselves unto your own husbands, as unto the Lord" (Ephesians 5:22). Or to Proverbs 21:19: "It is better to dwell in the wilderness, than with a contentious and an angry woman." Although these may not be the most persuasive arguments, at least they occasionally can produce a smile from my wife as she deconstructs my arguments. I might as well also admit that my wife is a better writer and lawyer than I am, not to mention that she keeps better track of the bills and the homestead, etc. She also usually has much better judgment than me, with the exception of my excellent judgment when it comes to the selection of a mate!

An interesting response from some conservative literalists—who believe that this kind of gender-based discrimination is biblically supported—is to suggest that the high divorce rate in American society in recent decades is a direct result of women demanding equality in their marriages, in the law, and in society. In other words, they believe that the feminist movement of the 1960s is responsible for our high divorce rates because many women have refused and continue to refuse to fulfill their subservient biblical roles. Of course, when this kind of religious fundamentalism goes "too far," such as when strict Muslims suggest that women must wear a head-to-toe burqa, or should marry the man their fathers have chosen for them, or should not be formally educated, then Christian fundamentalists finally get concerned. Only then, when a non-Christian religion is at issue, do they seem to recognize such practices as sexist evils of a radical and misguided religion enforced by the likes of the Taliban or Al-Qaeda. Apparently, Christian fundamentalists can only see "obvious" sexism when it is Muslim-based; but when any kind of sexism is Christian-based, it is "of God." And who are we to question God?

Maybe we should just admit that all sexism, including religiously based sexism, is wrong, period, regardless of whether it is Christian-based sexism or Muslim-based sexism. Perhaps we also should recognize that it is wrong to blame the victims of such inequality for any resulting disharmony when those victims have the courage to demand equality. For example, when former slaves demanded their freedom, that action certainly upset the then-existing "harmony" in racial relations, as it partially resulted in the US Civil War. Similarly, when the inhabitants of the original thirteen colonies declared their independence from England, that action also upset British–American relations and resulted in the American Revolutionary War. Accordingly, blaming former slaves and former colonists for demanding justice and equality and for thus "causing" the resulting disharmony with their oppressors completely misses the mark. Certainly, God should be above blaming the victim for any resulting disharmony when an oppressed group has the courage to demand equality.

INTRODUCTION

Most importantly, however, divorces occur for many reasons that have nothing to do with the fulfillment of biblical roles or with the lack of such fulfillment. If the lack of women fulfilling their "Biblical roles" is what caused divorces, then there should never be any divorces in Christian households, but there are. Perhaps former United Farm Worker and civil rights leader Cesar Chavez captured this sentiment best when he said: "Once social change begins, it cannot be reversed. You cannot un-educate the person who has learned to read. You cannot humiliate the person who feels pride. You cannot oppress the people who are not afraid anymore. We have seen the future, and the future is ours." http://www.worldofquotes.com/author/Cesar+Chavez/1/index.html

When it comes to exploring my faith, it helps me to talk to people with views different from my own. Ever since high school, I have had very long and interesting discussions with my father, who is a pastor of a fundamentalist church. We often discuss the Bible and his conservative political views. I thank him for these discussions. I certainly appreciate his incredible patience in dealing with my incessant questioning over the years. I know I have thoroughly exhausted a subject with him when we get to a point in the conversation at which my dad finds it necessary to leave and go pray for his poor misguided son. My dad really thinks that when we debate, I am arguing against God Himself; really, though, I am just arguing against the biblical interpretation my father uses. I have always marveled at people like my father who profess to have achieved a literal interpretation of the Bible that is unaffected by their own backgrounds or preconceived notions. For my dad, it is as though the King James Version of the Bible is the only version, or at least the official version, of the Bible, without anything lost in translation, from oral history to oral history, from language to language, or from handwritten version to handwritten version over thousands of years—and he has figured out exactly what it means because he just reads what it says.

Muslims believe that one cannot truly understand the Qur'an unless one reads it in the original Arabic because all translations are necessarily inferior. The same could apply to the Christian Bible. The Bible translated into Spanish, French, Norwegian, etc. all might be necessarily inferior to the King James Version, but if so, wouldn't that make the Latin Vulgate superior to the English King James Version? And if that is true, then why wouldn't the original Hebrew and Greek manuscripts be superior to the Latin Vulgate (ignoring the fact that none of the true originals exist anymore)? And why should we be fussing with Greek and Hebrew anyway? Jesus likely spoke Aramaic. If we are trying to tease out the original meaning of Jesus's ancient words in ancient tongues, all is lost because we simply do not have transcripts of his teachings in the original Aramaic.

My dad sure does give a literal reading of the Bible a good try, though, often consulting Greek and Hebrew dictionaries to obtain the "authentic" meanings of various words and terms used in earlier translations of the Bible from other languages (as if the meanings of words in other languages never evolve over time). As he preaches, he often reads the text in Early Modern English from the King James Version and then further explains some of the English words used by referring to the foreign-language definitions and roots from which they were translated. He considers this to be a purer interpretation because it is closer to the original meaning. Although his method is certainly a noble attempt to interpret the text more literally and as close to the original meanings from earlier texts as possible, the need to consult foreign-language dictionaries in the first place underscores the fact that the linguistic and conceptual journey of the text is wrought with different meanings, interpretations, and translations that need to be further explored and explained.

If God truly wrote the Bible or divinely inspired it without error because He is God, then why wouldn't God have been able to make sure that the Bible got translated correctly all along the way over the years from language to language? Why didn't God make it so that there would never be any need for people to consult foreign-language dictionaries to obtain the missing "correct" or "authentic" meanings of the words used in the King James Version or in any translation? If the writers of the Bible were divinely inspired by God, why weren't the interpreters of the Bible also divinely inspired by God? Indeed, aren't pastors, by consulting dictionaries so they can translate, interpret, and explain the arcane text, really making an admission that the overall translation and interpretation of the Bible is a large problem? Doesn't their use of these various dictionaries actually expose their noble, but still flawed, attempt to "fix" an interpretation problem that they claim does not exist?

This book is the written record of my intellectual, philosophical, and spiritual journey through some basic foundations of the Christian religion, at least as conceived of by traditional fundamentalists who proclaim to follow a very strict and literal interpretation of the King James Version of the Bible. The process of asking unrelenting questions, with respect to any topic, is as important as the substance of this book, which together constitute a new and honest attempt to view the fascinating paradox of faith and rationality. Perhaps the virtue for me has simply been in the struggle of considering hard questions, and exploring possible solutions—and perhaps as you read and consider this book, that might also be the case for you.

PART ONE

WHO AM I TO QUESTION A LITERAL INTERPRETATION OF THE BIBLE?

As the history of inquiries in many fields plainly shows, genuine inquiry presupposes a certain amount of skepticism, a willingness to ask pointed, embarrassing questions, concerning the established order. Good universities are awash with skepticism, which explains their historically precarious position in society. Unless investigators are free to question existing assumptions, they are not likely to make any fundamental contributions.

Thomas Nickles, "*Questioning and Problems in Philosophy of Science*," in Questions and Questioning, Michel Meyer, Ed., Walter de Gruyter (Jan 1, 1988).

Chapter One

The Nerve and Audacity to Question God and the Bible

I was born a working-class Mexican-American kid who made it to Harvard Law School. After graduation, I clerked for a federal judge, worked at a big law firm, and then became a law professor, a legal scholar, and an occasional guest legal commentator on television and radio. What made my progression from an especially challenged background to a successful professional career was my intellectual curiosity to question everything—and tenaciously so. I have never really stopped asking deep, hard, and often unique questions, including philosophical and spiritual ones that are outside of my area of legal expertise. Even more importantly, I have never stopped searching for answers (which admittedly, often has led to still more questions). But perhaps most importantly, nothing arrests my unrelenting quest to know things; or at least, to wonder, even wildly, about them—I do not have the roadblocks of embarrassment, fear of offending others, or eventual apathy that might lead others to just let well enough alone.

Before launching into my questioning of the text of Genesis, I should briefly address whether such a presumptuous enterprise is itself a form of blasphemy that perhaps should not even be attempted by someone professing to believe in God. More than 2,000 years ago, a Greek philosopher wondered what would possess an otherwise powerful and loving God to create a universe with evil in it. After all, everything we know could have been so very different had we lived in a universe without the option for us to choose and pursue evil. So much human pain and suffering could have been avoided if there had never been any evil. So why did God create evil *as an option* for us? Why does God continue to allow evil? And what can and should God now do about it, if anything?

If God is willing to prevent evil, but not able,
Then He is not omnipotent;
If He is able, but not willing,
Then He is malevolent;
If He is both willing and able,
Then from whence cometh evil?
If He is neither willing nor able,
Then why call him God?

- Epicurus (341–271 BC)

The reason for pondering Epicurus's questions is to consider whether these types of questions are legitimate questions for us to ask or whether such questioning is nothing more than the action of arrogant humans wrongly challenging, even mocking, God. Consider for a moment, however, that it might be perfectly appropriate to ask such questions. Even if such questions might at first appear to be irreverent, they still might be worth pondering deeply, especially if some helpful answers to them can be developed.

Of course, turnabout is fair play, so it may be valid to rhetorically ask a skeptic, like Epicurus, "Who are you to question God?" But if engaging in a personal attack on a questioner is the entire response to that person's question, then such a response is really no answer to the question posed. Instead, attacking the nerve and audacity of the questioner amounts to nothing more than a dodge and an attempt at misdirection, perhaps to mask the facts that: (1) the original question is conveniently being ignored in an attempt to focus solely on the haughty character of the questioner instead of on the question itself; and, (2) even if the attack on the questioner is valid, the original question is still pending and remains unanswered (possibly because it cannot logically or credibly be answered with deficient religious, supernatural, or superstitious explanations). In sum, we should not "shoot the messenger" just because we may not like the message; therefore, attacking a questioner is no answer to the question posed but is simply an attempt to change the subject to something much more trivial.

Chapter Two

My First Question Was about Hair

I am a Christian, and I believe in God. You might have very serious doubts about those bold claims as you read this book, however. I am not a theologian, nor am I a religious expert of any kind. I am not a creationist, and I am certainly not a scientist. As I have already conceded, my expertise in all of these areas is quite limited; however, I always have been extremely interested in the classic debate between believers and nonbelievers, and in the notion that the Bible can and should be interpreted literally, to the extent that a strict literal interpretation is even possible.

Before we get to that discussion, however, a little personal history on my upbringing and perspective would be helpful. I am from Pueblo, Colorado. As a young boy, I took my first Holy Communion at Holy Family Parish and attended catechism, which, for Catholic children, is the Saturday-morning equivalent of Sunday school. Traditionally, the Catholic Church considered divorce a mortal sin and would not allow one to get remarried in the church unless one could obtain an annulment of that first marriage, so it was a profound disappointment when my parents divorced in 1967; I was six.

A few years later, in the early 1970s, my father became a born-again Baptist fundamentalist. Because I was fascinated by their following the Bible so closely as the literal word of God, I joined him, and we attended Park Hill Baptist Church together on Wednesday evenings and twice on Sundays (Sunday morning and Sunday night). I "took Jesus as my savior" when I was about ten years old, and I attended Park Hill Baptist for many years before going away to college. During that time, I would witness to strangers by going to various neighborhoods, knocking on doors, and then asking people if they were saved; if they were not, I would ask whether I could lead them to Jesus or at least leave a tract with them—a cartoon story pamphlet showing them how they could be saved.

In the seventh grade, I went to live full-time with my dad up in Colorado Springs, a mostly conservative military, "family values" kind of town located fifty miles north of Pueblo. He put me in a fundamentalist Christian school. This proved to be very difficult for me at the time, especially having to cut off all of my shoulder-length hair. I did not understand why fundamentalist Christians objected to my hair being as long as that of Jesus, at least as portrayed in paintings, although it may have been that people in Jesus's time kept short hair to deter lice infestations. This would be the beginning of many such questions for me.

It did not help my self-esteem when my dad's wife at the time left him because I had come to live with them. It was hard for me to be at least a partial cause (or so it seemed) of my dad's second divorce. It was also very hard for my dad, who was losing his second wife because of me, although he was willing to do so for me if I wanted to live with him. Feeling guilty and being only twelve, I soon returned to Pueblo to live with my mother. My dad eventually got back with his wife after I left, but it was difficult for him, and things were never quite the same between us after that—I had disappointed him greatly.

Back in Pueblo, I finished middle school and then high school, sometimes attending a Catholic church, sometimes attending a Baptist church, and sometimes not attending church at all. I then went away to college, and later to law school. I was still a Catholic–Baptist Christian hybrid of some sort, but in light of the liberal arts undergraduate program and then the legal education I was receiving, I could not help but to begin really questioning everything. This included not only the formal subjects in the courses I was taking but also what I had grown up with: the literal stories of the Bible. I was fortunate to be receiving a great education, and most people thought it was a wonderful opportunity for me, but according to some, it was only great as long as I did not allow Satan to deceive me with logic, science, and evidence whenever they did not seem to comport with the literal stories of the Bible. After I became a lawyer, from my mid-twenties through my late forties, I flirted with various belief systems and non-belief systems such as agnosticism, theism, atheism, and Christianity, and even with occasional returns to Christian fundamentalism. Currently, my wife and I attend a very liberal Catholic church whenever we can, but I would hardly fit into any traditional religion at this point.

Many of my perspectives have been informed by various influential family members throughout my life. I have a very interesting and eclectic immediate and extended family. My grandfather on my mother's side, Anthony, was illiterate and never attended any school, but became an accomplished machinist and worked on the railroad all of his life. My grandmother on that side, Andrea, raised eight kids from the pre-Depression era through the early 1960s. My grandfather on my father's side, Fred, was a WWII veteran and a union boss. My grandmother on that side, Ernestine ("Ernie") worked at a meat-packing plant. That my grandparents were very hard-working is quite the understatement. My tenacity comes from them.

Over the years, my dad and I have always discussed and argued religious and political issues. My dad has remained a staunchly conservative pastor of a small fundamentalist church for more than thirty-five years. My mother is a mystic Catholic who will pray a Rosary for me just as readily as she will read me my horoscope as well as try to interpret my dreams. She is the epitome of hard work, faith, and love. As for my parents, I can definitely see from whom I mostly got my left brain and from whom I mostly got my right brain.

My dear Uncle Ernest was an electrician, who originally had wanted to become a priest, but he later would be blacklisted in the 1950s as a member of the Communist Party. He also was an atheist who taught me much throughout my life, probably most of all to explore and to question everything. I had another uncle, Kurt (my maternal aunt's husband), who was a German Jew who had escaped the Holocaust and came to this country in the late 1930s as a young boy with nothing. He persevered and grew up to become an extremely successful businessman in New

York City. (He owned Paxton Sportswear.) He taught me much about the greatness of our country, and the land of opportunity that it can be if one works hard enough. Listening to Uncle Kurt and Uncle Ernest argue about communism and capitalism as a young boy whenever they were visiting from New York was an incredibly valuable learning experience for me.

Other family members were as influential, if only for being who they were in the world. My uncle George was a gifted musician and sketch artist and always would comment to me on the news of the day from various interesting perspectives. He would continually point out to me the numerous abuses of power in our society. My aunt Shawnee (Delores is her real name) was a Broadway dancer and a Radio City Music Hall Rockette in the late 1950s. I always admired her determination so much because she had the courage to leave Pueblo as a young girl and to go to New York City with nothing but her ambition and desire to become a dancer. One aunt, Viola, followed suit and had bit parts as an actress in New York. Another aunt, Virginia, was an insurance executive in New York. Virginia was always very savvy about the world and is now an extremely gifted painter. Yet another aunt, Theresa, was a kindergarten school teacher, and my aunt Anita is one of the kindest and sweetest people I know. Many family members were attracted to New York City, perhaps because early on, my aunt Shawnee succeeded there so spectacularly under the bright neon lights of Broadway. My mother, however, stayed in Pueblo, and at the age of seventeen, she married my father, who was eighteen.

I have two older siblings. The oldest is my sister, Viki, who was born soon after my parents married. Viki always has been an artist in every sense of the word. She is extremely well-read, and a true counterculture hippie who helped to manage a recording studio in New York. Among many other things, she is quite knowledgeable about Native American culture and religion and all things in society that are avante guard. My brother, Ken, was also a product of the 1960s and is particularly knowledgeable about various traditional and New Age religious constructs as well as being a talented contractor-carpenter, a martial arts and weapons instructor, and a Harley-riding, amply tattooed biker.

I, however, pursued a more traditional route by becoming an attorney. Although, given my socioeconomic and ethnic background, it was very intimidating for me at the time to pursue higher education. As smart and creative as they are and were, not everyone in my family graduated from high school, and even fewer went to college; but they were always extremely supportive of me. After graduating from law school in 1986, I clerked for a federal judge, the Honorable John L. Kane Jr., and then I worked as a lawyer in the litigation department of a large, prestigious law firm in Denver (Holland & Hart) for five years before becoming a full-time law professor. I have been a law professor at Pacific McGeorge School of Law in Sacramento, California, now for almost twenty years.

Chapter Three

From Legal Concepts to Religious Ones

If one wants to discuss law, politics, and religion in America, an interesting place to begin is the Establishment Clause in the 1st Amendment to the US Constitution which prohibits the government from establishing an official government religion for US citizens. The Constitution leaves matters of religion regarding how to legally worship, should we decide to do so, to personal choice. In contrast, the Free Exercise Clause, also in the 1st Amendment, provides that the government cannot interfere with our personal choices about how we may or may not legally choose to worship. In fact, escaping state-run religions and religious persecution from governments formed the basis of one of this country's most important founding constitutional principles enshrined in the 1st Amendment. The competing tension between the 1st Amendment's Establishment Clause and Free Exercise Clause has been a great cornerstone of our religious-political history. One need only read the headlines for interesting examples of how that competing tension, as played out in church-state and religious liberty issues, is still alive and well in various contemporary social, political, and legal contexts.

Even more fundamentally, however, like most human beings, I also have long wondered why we are all here and how we could exist if there is no supreme being making life and the universe possible. Without such a supreme being, our lives might otherwise appear to be relatively short and meaningless. It is perhaps the deepest of all philosophical, scientific, and religious questions: Why is there something instead of nothing? Could life as we know it really be a result of mere happenstance? From the opposite viewpoint, could it be anything but that? Is there a God? Do I have a soul? Or am I just longing for an easy and comforting explanation, like a god of some sort, which allows my existence in this universe to somehow all make cosmic sense to me?

I think God exists; at least I want to believe that He does. I want to believe in God because it seems that there must be some kind of greater power than just me—than all of us—so that our purpose in life has more meaning than just survival and reproduction as complex organisms. That, of course, is not to say that a higher purpose in life is impossible without a god of some sort. People can, and often do, find moral foundations and personal meanings for their lives in various internal or external non-deity sources. As George Bernard Shaw once said, "I want to be thoroughly used up when I die. The harder I work, the more I live. I rejoice in life for its own sake. Life is no short candle for me. It is, instead, a splendid torch, which I have in my hands for this one moment in time. I must make it burn as brightly as possible before handing it to the future." This is truly a great thought about life that requires no belief in a god, but still, I *want* to believe that there is more out there for me and us, something like a god entity beyond my and our limited ability to contemplate the metaphysical.

WHO AM I TO QUESTION A LITERAL INTEPRETATION OF THE BIBLE?

It feels rather arrogant and foolish not to believe in God, especially when I really ponder the infinite complexity and splendor of the earth, the universe, and life itself. Paradoxically, however, it feels just as arrogant and foolish to think that I can know for sure who and what God is, based merely on: (1) a collection of translations of old books written by various men in the Middle East thousands of years ago (and selectively added to while other contemporaneous writings were purged, isolated, or destroyed by church leaders); and, (2) the interpretations of those ancient texts by either myself or others. Because my assumption that there must be a God might be nothing more than just a hopeful supposition based on my superstitions and/or my fear that there is nothing more than this short life, it again feels rather arrogant and foolish to ignore the possibility that my very hopeful assumption about the existence of God ... might just be wrong.

Even assuming that there is a god (or gods or goddesses), how would we go about knowing God in an honest and objective way? When one considers the plethora of religious texts and the numerous ancient and current deities that have been worshipped by various peoples of the world throughout the ages, it certainly seems myopic to think that the Bible is the exclusive, correct, and official text of the one and only true God. It also seems very narrow-minded to deem all alternate texts and interpretations describing other gods as mere fakes, or at best, hopelessly misguided attempts to find the one true, yet elusive, God. For a sampling of hundreds and even thousands of various worldwide gods and myths, see John Bowker, *God: A Brief History* (DK Publishings) (May 1, 2002).

Similarly, focusing on the Bible as the one and only sourcebook of truth begs the question of why any *current* version of the Bible should be considered to be the *actual* Bible. As alluded to earlier, so many other similar ancient Judeo-Christian books that could have been a part of the Bible were simply voted out by Christian church leaders in the 3rd century, when the Bible was officially canonized. Is all of past, present, and future humanity really supposed to believe that the current Bible is indisputably the only true text of the one and only authentic God? Are we also supposed to believe that anything and everything else is a hopeless fairytale concocted by evil or seriously mistaken human beings who were probably negatively influenced by Satan? What an ethnocentric and self-absorbed assumption on our part that would be.

Accepting for the moment that such an assumption is true, however, consider how incredibly fortunate I would be to have been born in the United States, a country where the majority of people just happen to generally follow the one correct version of God—Christianity—according to the one correct text—the Bible—according to the one correct literal/metaphorical interpretation. And for that answer, I guess you just have to take your pick here among Catholic, Mormon, Jehovah's Witness, Episcopalian, Methodist, Seventh-day Adventist, Baptist, Southern Baptist, Lutheran, Eastern Orthodox Catholicism, Presbyterian, Church of Christ, Pentecostal, Mennonite, Assembly of God, and hundreds of other Christian denominations and subgroups.

Moreover, there are differing versions of the Bible and other supplemental texts that many of these religions use as their "true" interpretations and translations. For example, Jehovah's Witnesses have their own New World Translation, and Catholics have the Douay Bible, which includes some texts (whole books or portions of books) that are considered doubted or even heretical by Protestants. The Mormon Church uses the King James Bible, but only "insofar as it is correctly translated," and supplements it with other texts, including the Book of Mormon—the most widely known—and *The Pearl of Great Price* and *Doctrine & Covenants*, the latter of which includes the doctrine that men can take on multiple wives—at least until the US Supreme Court ruled otherwise. The Seventh-day Adventist Church apparently has its own version of the Bible and other books that it uses as definitive non-biblical sources of guidance such as cofounder Ellen G. White's *The Desire of Ages.* Adventists may not consider White's works to be scriptural or infallible (as the Mormon Church does with respect to certain Joseph Smith and Brigham Young writings), but White is still considered to be a prophet. Some denominations may designate a preferred version of the Bible to be used across the denomination or may allow each parish or congregation to decide instead of commissioning their own "official" translations.

Despite all of these differences, God must think that we Americans and other Christian based nations are quite special and much more deserving than all of the other human beings born in different places, times, or cultural circumstances (or even on other planets as similar beings, if such beings exist), for had we been born where Christianity is not the dominant religion, then, according to some fundamentalists, we likely would have been involved in a wholly misguided spiritual endeavor. In fact, that is the reason why fundamentalists tend to have so many missionaries who are always going on foreign missions—to convert all of the various mistaken infidels throughout the world to their respective Christian religions and to thus save all of these lost souls from Hell and their incorrect understandings of God.

In any event, it is a bit troubling to think that whatever religion we may happen to be in this life is mostly just a function of whatever religion our parents happen to be. For example, would my concept of God be Allah and Mohamed had I been born in Afghanistan, Buddha had I been born in China, Gaea, the Earth goddess, who mated with her son, Uranus, the Sky God, to produce the remaining Titans, who were first ruled by Cronus, who was then overthrown by Zeus, had I been born in ancient Greece, Thor had I been born a Viking, the Great Spirit and Mother Earth had I been born a Navajo Indian, or various Hindu gods had I been born in India? Is our concept of the authentic revelation of God all really just a matter of arbitrary geographical borders, historical development, and cultural randomness? Shouldn't God completely transcend such societal flukes and the capricious happenstance of indiscriminately delineated borders? Nevertheless, I still really want to believe in God; but I do not want to delude myself just because it feels more comfortable to believe in the version of God that I, personally, was exposed to while growing up as a Catholic in Pueblo, Colorado, near the end of the 20th century.

Chapter Four

Why a Law Professor Is Writing a Book about Religion, and Why There Aren't Any Footnote References or Supporting Authority in This Book

As a law professor, it was very difficult for me to write this book and simultaneously resist the constant temptation to use scholarly authorities as references to support my arguments and observations. Because I am not presenting this book as any kind of an academic research work, or even as any kind of polemic, however, I have resisted that temptation. This non-use of scholarly references represents a significant departure from my other legal writings, but so be it; this is a wholly different endeavor. This book will either stand or fall on the compelling power of the ideas presented, or on the lack thereof, irrespective of any proper footnoting.[1]

I must admit that it has been very difficult for me to read the text of Genesis literally, as though I am reading a newspaper. There is one fantastic story or account of a historical event after another, each of them often utterly implausible, farfetched, and requiring a complete suspension of scientific reality, along with an unconditional acceptance of epic, bizarre, supernatural miracles. Some accounts in the text are inconsistent, incompatible, or contradictory. Still others

---

[1] As a result, this one footnote constitutes the first, *and the last*, footnote of this book. I have provided this one footnote because I need to recognize that many of the issues posed herein, perhaps even most of them, are concerns that I have heard about or read about at some point. Accordingly, many of the concerns I raise in the book are some intricate combination of my own thoughts and the thoughts of others that I have encountered over the course of my life. In fact, because many of the ideas I set forth in this book are not solely my original thoughts, I violate my own rule about not using a citation so I can make this one rather large reference here. I now cite every person with whom I have ever had a theological or scientific discussion, as well as every book, article, interview, or documentary that I have ever read or seen considering these subjects. I understand that this is a woefully "lazy" and certainly overly generalized citation, but it is still a very necessary acknowledgment for me to make. If I had seriously attempted to properly footnote this book, however, the book would consist mostly of numerous long footnotes that would soon overwhelm the text and quickly bore the reader. The result is that all of these sources throughout my life (both too numerous to mention and, frankly, too difficult to specifically remember) form a significant part of my psyche. As such, they are all partially responsible for the questions that occurred to me as I wrote this book. I am therefore indebted to all of these sources, not only in the writing of this book but also throughout my life for awakening the latent curiosity in me to ponder many of the issues set forth herein.

either do not make sense on their own terms or seem more poetic and metaphorical than they do factual and plausible.

Despite these flaws, there are also some very powerful lessons, great principles, beautiful passages, and profound thoughts throughout the Bible, to be sure, but these aspects about the Bible only lead me to ask if amazing poetry and spiritual depth, as much as I love poetry and appreciate spiritual depth, necessarily qualify as objective, literal, scientific truth from God. In the pages that follow, then, I recount my attempts to read and interpret the text as literally as I possibly can, reminiscent of Isaac Asimov, the famous atheistic Jewish author of science-fiction novels and scientific essays, who undertook a similar endeavor covering the entire Bible, as well as countless others to one degree or another. I take this mission very seriously. In doing so, I ponder the text and its many implications, problems, and possibilities as literally as I can. I do not claim to put the Bible on trial, nor will I attempt to do anything nearly so controversial or adversarial. Neither do I present any earth-shattering evidence. In fact, I do not present any evidence at all. I simply ask what I hope are intriguing questions.

Although I am not an atheist, the reader may think that I must be one because I have chosen to pose the questions I do in a way that can be skeptical, cynical, and even sarcastically disrespectful of religion. My questions (and answers or observations) are not necessarily intended as such, but they are admittedly challenging questions. In Parts Two and Three, I heavily scrutinize the text of Genesis, but this is a necessary function of taking that text literally. In fact, in a way, I am actually respecting the text of the Bible by holding it to such a high standard. I do not think God would really mind that I would ask such questions about what the Bible literally says, especially if He is the kind of God I think He is. It seems to me that God would be exceedingly open-minded and would not be afraid of such questions. After all, the truth, if it is The Truth, should be able to withstand some simple questioning.

See Isaiah 45:11: "Thus saith the LORD...Ask me of things...concerning the work of my hands command ye me." Because of passages such as this, I do not think that God would be defensive or possess a very human-like, easily bruised, and moody ego. Instead, I think God would be like a very patient parent who, without too much difficulty, could tolerate a few interesting and probing questions posed by an inquisitive child just using the mind that he has been given—God might even consider such questioning to be "cute," relatively speaking. We are, after all, God's children, made in His image, right? I just don't think God would get so mad if we were to ask Him a tough question, unless He is a very touchy God who easily loses His temper.

My questions, their possible answers, and the corresponding implications about the text of the Bible are what Parts Two and Three of this book is all about. Moreover, II Timothy 3:15–16 states, "[15] And that from a child thou hast known the holy scriptures, which are able to make thee wise unto salvation through faith which is in Christ Jesus. [16] All scripture is given by inspiration of God, and is profitable for doctrine, for reproof, for correction, for instruction in righteousness," and so if that is true, then there should be no problem in just asking questions.

Chapter Five

But Am I Advocating Atheism by "Attacking" Genesis in This Book?

I am not "attacking" Genesis in this book. It is not that simple. In fact, in Part Four of the book, I explain why, after all I say in Part One, and especially in Parts Two and Three, about the literal implausibility of most of the Book of Genesis, after all I say that questions the existence of the God of the Bible, and even after all I say that agrees with almost all of the arguments provided by atheists, I still believe in God. But how is that even possible? What can I say? It is complicated, to say the least. Keep reading.

I tend to frustrate both the believers I know (because I sound so much like an atheist) and nonbelievers I know (because I still have this admittedly "irrational" belief in God). It is as though I completely agree with the rationale of one side of the debate (atheists) yet still agree with the ultimate conclusion of the other side (believers), although I intellectually reject the "logic" of most of the arguments set forth by believers. It is the ultimate paradox for me. How can I reconcile my faith in light of science and reason? Many people cannot do so, and so they are atheists or agnostics. Like them, I cannot reconcile reason and faith, yet I still believe, even though I cannot rationally articulate why.

I certainly understand that science and a literal interpretation of the Bible often cannot be reconciled, and I can see why atheists might not be able to understand or even respect my belief in God. Still, I am bothered by the inflexible dogma that seems to be present on either side of the debate—believers being certain that God exists and atheists being certain that He does not—while neither side has definitive proof of its central claim (and perhaps proof will never be had). I admit that I believe in God without knowing for sure. This may be because I find it a bit narrow-minded and arrogant for anyone to profess unflinching certainty about any belief, or nonbelief, system.

I realize that I might just be deluding myself by believing in God. I admit the very real possibility that my faith may just be the result of a strong psychological need to believe in something to avoid the colossal fear that there really is: (1) not a God out there watching over me inside this huge, unknown universe; (2) that in the end good will not necessarily triumph over evil; and, (3) that I will not get to live forever. I also realize that maybe I just cannot handle the bewildering responsibility of having to look elsewhere, outside of or beyond the concept of God, to discover the ultimate meaning and purpose of my life and all other life in the universe.

Perhaps the most difficult thing for me to accept if there were no God and afterlife is the cold, hard reality that once I die, I would never see my wife, children, family, or friends ever again. Likewise, I would never get to see my grandparents or other loved ones who have already passed away. That ultimate finality of my existence and of everyone I know might simply be too much for me to take emotionally and psychologically. How utterly tragic if that anticlimactic eventuality is what ends up being our unceremonious demise! I realize, however, that this "tragedy" does not mean that God therefore must exist. Perhaps that is the real reason (and even the cowardly reason) why I believe in God: the simple yet profound fear that this relatively short life may be all there is.

Chapter Six

I Am Not a Traditional Believer, Either

Assuming for a moment that the Bible, God, Heaven, and Hell all actually exist, I wonder what Heaven would be like (assuming that is where I would be going) if, after Judgment Day, someone I knew and loved in life was not there upon my arrival. That is, what if someone I knew and loved in life were sent to Hell instead? As I would be rejoicing in Heaven after I died, presumably seeing many of my loved ones and old friends—as well as many new friends, I suppose—wouldn't I at that very same moment also be plagued by the horrible feeling that certain people I knew and loved in life did not make it and consequently would be tortured in Hell forever?

If Hell literally exists, how could I still enjoy the wonderful paradise of Heaven, knowing that a loved one was burning in Hell at that very moment and would continue to suffer that terrible fate forever? Even if my personal circle of family and friends all made it to Heaven, could we fully partake in the joy of Heaven if we knew that right then, billions of our fellow humans from throughout time were suffering in Hell and would do so forever? Or would God simply wipe away our memories so we would not be bothered by such concerns? How convenient—perhaps a little too convenient, constituting what seems like a very un-Godlike and callous disregard for our fellow human beings, God's creation.

If the Bible instructs that we are to love our neighbors as ourselves ("Thou shalt love thy neighbour as thyself," Galatians 5:14), wouldn't it be better for all of humankind if there were no afterlife—"no hell below us, above us only sky" (thank you, John Lennon)? If so, billions of souls would be spared from the eternal torture of Hell, and considering that we would want to be spared that fate ourselves, the Bible requires that we should want just as badly for our neighbors to be spared as well. Like Jesus, who taught us all about sacrificing to save humanity from Hell, perhaps those bound for Heaven should be willing to sacrifice Heaven so that millions of others would not have to burn in Hell forever. Ask yourself if you would be willing to make that sacrifice—would you be willing to give up Heaven to save others from Hell? Stated differently, wouldn't it be the height of selfishness for me to enjoy Heaven forever while knowing that, for me to enjoy that glorious afterlife, billions of my fellow human beings would have to burn in Hell forever? Put differently, for me to enjoy Heaven, there also would have to be a Hell in which others would have to burn. Would I be so indifferent to their plight that I would rationalize to myself, "Don't worry about them, they are in Hell because they all *deserve* to be there"?

Assuming I could still enjoy Heaven even with the full knowledge that billions of my fellow human beings were simultaneously burning in Hell, would God approve of my indifference? If the horrible fate of other humans would not bother me in the least, *would God be proud of me*? Would God really want for me to show no concern for others because they made a very bad decision in life by either not believing or by betting on the wrong religion? At best, such feelings on God's part would be heavy-handed, and at worst, just plain cruel. Think about it: Does the punishment of eternal damnation really fit the crime after, for example, five trillion years of constant, never-ending burning in Hell? Is such torture really justified, even when there would be no end in sight? Remember, eternity is for an awfully *long* time. Even the Geneva Convention outlaws torture in war as inhumane; it is not only illegal but immoral. By damning a human being to burn for eternity, wouldn't God be sinking *below* that basic standard of morality in war that we humans have set for ourselves here on Earth? People could still be punished without having to be tortured. For example, why not just say that nonbelievers would not get to live forever in Heaven as their punishment? Why the additional, inhumane torture of burning in Hell forever?

The concept of a literal Hell would, by all accounts—even according to the most vehement antiterrorist activists, such as those who advocate waterboarding—qualify as illegal torture. At the very least, punishment in such a Hell would qualify as cruel and unusual punishment, violating of the 8th Amendment to the US Constitution. For example, the thought of a government detective or an army officer putting a blowtorch into the face of a convicted criminal or terrorist—not just for a few moments or a few days or even a few years, but literally *forever* (if a doctor could keep the person alive forever to suffer the nonstop pain of constant burning)—would be the height of cruel suffering and gruesome torment, which no legitimate government would allow. It would simply be considered too barbaric and inhumane, a fate worse than death. Yet God apparently fully justifies this punishment as completely legitimate and deserving, if we take Hell literally. It is quite the severe punishment for the mere thought crime of not believing in an unseen God, or even worse, for just backing the wrong religious horse in a kind of religious sweepstakes of who is right and wrong and therefore of who gets to go to Heaven and who must burn in Hell forever.

Then again, if Heaven and Hell do not actually exist—so we simply die, cease to be, and that is it—this is a very difficult fate to accept. The thought of possibly never seeing anyone I ever loved or knew in life is an overwhelmingly distressing thought. Moreover, to attempt to make sense of why we are all here and what possible purpose there is to our being here is utterly mind-boggling without having some kind of spiritual explanation for our existence and for the non-finality of our death. Life as we know it would seem absurd without some sort of explanation. I will concede here, however, that even if our very temporary existence is all we have, it is not necessarily meaningless, because any experience of reality we may have might be intrinsically valuable, even if all that we believe is that there is nothing to life but the moment we are experiencing here and now.

But even assuming that our very temporary lives would be absurd without a God, such absurdity would prove nothing about the necessary existence of God as described in the Bible or in other texts or religions. For example, is a dog's life, with no promise of an afterlife, necessarily absurd (unless all dogs go to heaven and there are going to be animals in Heaven)? If there is no "dog heaven," why is any dog here on Earth? For that matter, why is a worm or a fly here? Does the absurdity of their existence for only a brief moment in time, with no afterlife for them, necessarily prove that there must be a dog heaven, a fly heaven, and a worm heaven—and some god who must have created them all? And why stop there? Is there a tree heaven or a bacteria heaven? Do plants or bacteria sin or not sin? Do they get to go to Heaven? Why or why not, if they are also life-forms? Could they also make it to "human heaven," which I guess would then just be Heaven?

Even assuming that certain sentimental and even fearful psychological needs may be the real, subconscious reason why I believe in God, I still believe. I believe for what are inexplicable, maybe even indefensible, but still very real reasons to me. For one, I believe that God has to be greater than the draconian, unrealistic, and even cruel God portrayed in parts of the Bible and that maybe someday, it will all be explained in a way that I cannot now even fathom. Faith is hope, a hope for something better than a tyrannical God who gets torturously cruel if you do not believe in Him. So my faith is mostly a hope for something better, deeper, and greater.

I admit that it is very difficult if not impossible for me to accept the biblical God as true, especially when I really think about Him deeply and try to interpret the biblical stories literally. If God gave me a mind and if He created the concept of logic so we might correctly use our minds, then to believe in Him, must I reject the very science, reason, and logic that He created? Does God require me to ignore scientific evidence so I can demonstrate a necessary self-denial of my thoughts and thereby demonstrate my unwavering loyalty to Him? Must we reject science and logic to accept God? If so, doesn't it seem just a little unfair for God to expect us to reject science and reason to escape Hell? Or is that somehow the entire mysterious point of everything? But does saying the words "the entire *mysterious* point" end up being meaningless, but just in a poetically cute way? Is it wrong for me to expect God to be fair according to my concept of fairness? Does God define fair in a way that I just do not understand? If so, then would it be fair for Him to judge me on things that I do not understand or cannot fully comprehend? Isn't that a bit like locking the church doors and then judging those people who are locked out for not being present in church?

Chapter Seven

Believing in God's Existence, while Doubting Men's Abilities

Notwithstanding all of the problems with the Bible, it remains an important resource and religious icon for me; still, I have very mixed reactions to it. There are many wonderful aspects of and valuable life lessons in the Bible; however, there are also many things that I have an awfully hard time believing as the literal truth, and many things that seem as though they would be far beneath a supreme being who created the universe. There are also many serious failings in human speech, communication, language translations, and textual interpretations, and these failings often result in hopeless ambiguity, inconsistency, variance, deviation, and contradiction in the version (or versions) of the Bible we know today.

Thus, I am not necessarily skeptical of God; but I am rather skeptical of human beings claiming to have certainty about whom or what God is or is not. Often, such certainty is based on ambiguous ancient texts as interpreted by various people in very dogmatic and doctrinaire ways that frequently contradict and undercut one another. One does not eliminate all of this confusion and uncertainty among and between the various texts and the various personal interpretations of those texts by merely proclaiming, "I am right, and everyone else who disagrees with me is wrong! Just read the Bible!"

My doubt is compounded when people profess that only what they believe is the authoritative, objective truth about God and the universe rather than having the courage to admit that, whatever may constitute their faith, it is nothing more than their subjective opinion about God and the universe, which they merely *assume*, for whatever reason or combination of reasons, to be true. I doubt the ability of human beings to impeccably decipher a stringent religious code, contained in what is sometimes literal and sometimes metaphorical language, by which we must order our lives or face unimaginable pain and torment as punishment for any doubt, misunderstanding, or noncompliance.

Chapter Eight

What If We Are Not as Important, Nor as Smart, as We Think We Are?

The issues I've previously mentioned remind me of a time when I was walking in a field and came upon a few bees that I stopped to look at. It was a sunny day, and because bees are aware of at least some of their surroundings (such as flowers), I wondered if any bee had ever thought about the sun—what it might be and why it might be there. If a bee could ponder such a thing, what amazing story might that bee have about the sun? Perhaps it would be that the sun is a huge beehive of super bees, or maybe that the sun is the eye of a great Queen Bee protector. If bees were to consider the sun to be the eye of a great Queen Bee protector, what if one little scientist-like bee noticed that sometimes the sun is there but other times it is not? And then what if that curious bee asked all of the other bees why their great Queen Bee protector is never there to protect them *at night*, perhaps even theorizing that the great Queen Bee protector is really not even a bee because it only has one giant bright eye instead of two eyes with thousands of lenses?

This is, of course, a rather farfetched scenario, to be sure. Still, consider how the other bees might react to that one bee's particular question about the sun (or the eye of the great Queen Bee protector). Would the other bees say that the curious heretic bee was clearly wrong because he could not explain for sure what the sun is if it is *not* the great Queen Bee protector that all of the other bees believe it to be? Would another beehive a few miles away have an entirely different story as to what the sun is, such that all of the bees in that particular beehive would generally believe in a very different story about what the sun is?

This thought experiment about beehives and what bees might think about the sun is not so farfetched, at least not for us, because historically, there have been many human cultures in which such a simple discussion about the sun versus a sun god may have and probably did take place. Consider all of the mythologies that have sun gods with different names and somewhat different characteristics—Horus, Apollo, Surya Dev, Hiruko, and countless others. Also, consider that the choice of December 25 as Jesus's birthday is likely related to pagan sun practice because it is close to the day when the sun wins over darkness and days become longer—analogized to spiritual light and truth winning over darkness. Light overcoming darkness is an interesting metaphor for Jesus, and it also possibly provided a nice harmony for the ancient Romans to accept Christianity without having to abandon their pagan beliefs wholesale.

I wonder if we humans are a bit like these hypothetical believer and atheist bees. Think of early human cultures, all of whom would have been wrong about and probably would have had no idea about what the sun really is or how our solar system actually operates. They might not have been much further beyond our hypothetical bees that might believe that the sun is just some giant personification of the believer, such as a great Queen Bee protector of bees, or a hive of super bees, or even that the sun was created by a great wind god, who then created bees and then everything else. Just like bees, which probably cannot fully conceptualize the way our solar system functions or, for that matter, quantum mechanics, calculus, or electricity (at least I don't think they can), perhaps we humans are also far, far away from fully understanding the true nature our universe and the complex spiritual and scientific aspects of it.

Human religious experts all seem to have their own wildly different views about the nature of God, but if I dare to doubt any one of those human experts' personal versions of the God they say exists, or the manner in which they interpret their Bibles, I am the one who is called a heretic, nonbeliever, atheist, or some other dirty word. Or, at best, I am pitied as some unfortunate dupe who has been fooled by Satan, that evil fallen angel who is now trying to recruit my soul for an eternity to be spent in Hell (perhaps in the same way the Catholic Church originally thought Galileo, Kepler, and Copernicus were duped with Satanic and deceitful astronomy as revealed by newly invented telescopes). And even though I claim that I believe in God, such experts still doubt my claims, because if I did actually believe in God, I would agree with them and their perspectives about God.

Because I question any dogma, I also question the other experts on the universe—scientists. Although I respect scientists, they really don't have a definitive, final answer about our universe or ultimate origin, either. Just like the little skeptical bee that would question whether the sun can be the eye of some great Queen Bee protector but still could not definitely explain what the sun truly is or how the solar system actually works, neither can our science currently explain *everything* about the universe. For example, even though Albert Einstein developed the theory of relativity that explains the cosmos, we have yet to come up with a unified theory that can reconcile quantum mechanics, which explains how the world works at the subatomic level. Why does the size of objects make things behave so differently when they are still part of the same universe? And of course, our science cannot definitively rule out the existence of God.

A critically important difference exists between science and religion, however: At least science can explain *some* things about our universe—and do so with actual proof and evidence. And at least with science, there is a perpetual quest for more knowledge based on evidence, rather than continuous professions of truth based only on intuition or scant assumptions that are deemed to be true based on religious faith with no definitive evidence or testing. Unlike religion, science does not need to rely on supernatural "miraculous" pious explanations to supply those critical missing elements.

Some religious believers critique science for being inconsistent and always *changing*. It is not that science is inconsistent or always changing, however; instead, what science discovers is continuously *expanding*. For example, science at one time said that there was only one planet but later determined that there were at least three planets in our solar system, and over time, as astronomers discovered even more planets, we eventually got up to nine. Recently, however, that number has been decreased by one planet, as Pluto has been downgraded to a giant ice ball, a non-planet. So the question is: What will science say about the number of planets in our solar system in the future, and if that number changes once again, how can we *ever* rely on science for answers when science is constantly changing? In other words, don't the latest new exciting scientific discoveries actually harm, rather than help, the overall credibility of science?

The short answer is no. Science will explain whatever truth is discovered about our solar system, or any other subject, based on the available observable evidence that we are able to competently analyze—so it is not that our solar system keeps changing the number of planets it has (although that might be conceivably possible). What has changed over time is only what we have been able to *discover* about the number of planets that are in our solar system based on the available evidence, our better observations, and our better-informed analysis. From this perspective, science is not inconsistent simply because we frequently make scientific discoveries. We therefore should acknowledge that continually being able to add to our overall knowledge base is a valuable and good thing, not a suspect and bad thing. Also, note that not only scientific discovery changes and develops in this way, but that religious thinking also changes and develops over time. For example, the God of Abraham described early on in the Bible is quite different from the God described by John, the author of the last book of the Bible, Revelation. God was described in Genesis (according to the King James Version) simply as three men standing outside of Abraham's tent—see Genesis 18:1–3:

> [1] And the LORD appeared unto him in the plains of Mamre: and he sat in the tent door in the heat of the day;
> [2] And he lift up his eyes and looked, and, lo, three men stood by him: and when he saw them, he ran to meet them from the tent door, and bowed himself toward the ground,
> [3] And said, My Lord, [referring to the three men, the holy trinity, standing outside the tent] if now I have found favour in thy sight, pass not away, I pray thee, from thy servant.

From that simple view of God by Abraham in Genesis, John, by the end of the Bible in Revelation, used the metaphor of God having seven horns and seven eyes as seven spirits gone out into the world. See Revelation 5:6:

> [6] And I beheld, and, lo, in the midst of the throne and of the four beasts, and in the midst of the elders, stood a Lamb as it had been slain [Jesus, the slain savior, referred to here as "the Lamb"] having seven horns and seven eyes, which are the seven Spirits of God sent forth into all the earth.

So, to progress, be it through religion or science, we must change. We cannot change, however, unless we are willing to ask meaningful questions about what we may know and what we may believe. And we are sure to have many more questions ahead of us because neither science nor religion has the ultimate, indisputable, and provable answer about God and His existence and the complete explanation of the universe.

Perhaps that is why we humans should exhibit a little more humility when discussing our professed knowledge of God as well as the nature of God—much like bees probably should exhibit some humility if they ever pontificate regarding the nature of the sun. For example, it is annoying to me that certain fundamentalist believers (not all, but some) paint God as an angry, judgmental, legalistic tyrant with an impossible—and sometimes contradictory—list of "dos and don'ts" and who is bent on punishing us unless we submit to some rigid religious construct as conceptualized by them. It seems like that is a gross oversimplification of what should be an extraordinarily grandiose thing, the most awe-inspiring thing possible: the God of our universe. But it looks as if they reduce the immensity of God down to a retrofitted Christmas carol:

> You better watch out.
> You better not cry.
> Better not pout.
> I'm telling you why.
> [God, your judge,] is coming to [earth].
> He's making a list
> And checking it twice;
> Gonna find out who's naughty and nice.
> [God, your judge,] is coming to [earth].
> He sees you when you're sleeping.
> He knows when you're awake.
> He knows if you've been bad or good,
> So be good, for goodness' sake!
> O! You better watch out...

Is the God of our universe really that simple? Are we? Actually, the view of God as a stern, holy dictator who is making a list and checking it twice seems to be more blasphemous than does asking the kinds of questions I set forth in this book. Although I may be asking very challenging questions, I simultaneously have exceedingly high expectations of God and what must be His colossal magnificence and nuanced complexity, as well as of how He might actually write something in a specific text for all of humanity to refer to throughout time if He were to actually write that text Himself. In the same way, it is just as annoying when certain atheists portray God in this imbalanced, dictatorial way. I understand, however, that they do not believe in *any* god and so when they do this, they are really just attacking a simplistic construct of a supposed god. I remain decidedly skeptical, however, about anyone, on any side of the debate, who professes to absolutely know the truth about either the existence or the nonexistence of God.

Chapter Nine

God, Science, Logic & Evidence

If there is a God, it does not seem like He would just leave us all hanging here with no written guidance or clear and exclusive communication of any kind. Even my sons' video games come with very thorough and detailed instructions. The problem, however, is that I am not so sure which way that cuts. Does it mean that we should believe that God must have written the Bible because God would not just abandon us, without any text upon which to base our beliefs, without any official instructions from Him, so the Bible must be true? Or does it suggest that, because any written message from God has been or always will be filtered through essentially flawed human perception and therefore misconceived to some extent, in the end nothing, is definitively and clearly from God? Moreover, because a true God would not have just forsaken us and simply left us with numerous competing, unclear, and misconceived understandings of His true nature, then that resulting lack of clarity as to which is the one true definitive written work of God must mean that God does not exist at all.

In other words, wouldn't God have only one "official" book? Imagine a video game that had more than 3,000 sets of different, and in places, contradictory, instructions? Imagine further that over time, all these different sets of instructions had been posted on the Internet by various alleged expert game users, with none of the instructions clearly being the true *official* set of instructions but all *claiming* to be the one true set of official instructions. Would a loving God wanting us to know Him really allow us to be confused this way with so many competing sets of instructions? Perhaps leaving us guessing—with seemingly endless spiritual options, including atheism—is exactly the point, however; maybe God wants to see how we will react in this most grand experiment called life. If so, is it up to each of us to create our own religion, just for ourselves and for anyone else who might be willing to follow? In a way, like it or not, that is exactly what historically seems to have happened here on Earth with religion.

First, based on the huge preliminary assumption that a god of some type must exist, personal religious ideas and interpretations of God were developed. Some of these faded away while others gained acceptance. Then people began to follow others' ideas of God. As a result, leaders emerged as prophets who may have had special access to God, or to critical spiritual information, or to both. They wrote some of this information down or interpreted the information that had already been written, often claiming that what was written was not written by any human but actually by God.

Next, often, a larger movement would stem from the interpretation of those writings and gain momentum over time. Then, before we knew it, an "official" religion was born, or at least some subsection or offshoot of an existing official religion. The glaring question is, How much of that whole developmental process, if any, was actually directed solely by God, and how much of that process was just an elaborate function of assorted social-psychological movements of various peoples who decided to believe certain religious constructs of either their own or someone else's making?

If the preceding summary can serve as a brief history of religious phenomena on Earth, which among the vast number of religions is ultimately the right one, if any? Indeed, aren't we all just the blind leading the blind, with the various leaders claiming that only they can actually see? I do not claim to have any special knowledge; neither have I been given any prophetic revelation or arrived at any ultimate conclusion about God and the universe. I do have one modest but rather skeptical observation about all of these great questions, however, and it is simply this: *I don't know for sure, and I don't think anyone else does either.*

That does not mean that it is not worthwhile to keep asking such questions and searching for answers, however. I believe we should search for answers but that when we do, we should do so without considering science, logic, and evidence as the enemies of God. I do not think that true faith in God means that we must stubbornly stick our collective head into the sand when it comes to science, logic, and evidence, or that we should do the equivalent of excommunicating a modern-day Kepler or Galileo simply because we do not like what his or her scientific findings seem to suggest about a traditional, literal interpretation of an ancient text. This method of questioning and searching without ruling out science and logic is a way to derive viable spirituality from the universe as an alternative to a fixed, static religion based on a literal, and often scientifically implausible, understanding of God's alleged written message to humankind. This alternative is a relationship based on trust and on the goodness of God, but one first must have the courage to question and then to trust in this relationship. I therefore challenge every reader to at least consider thinking about this book in that way.

If there is a God, it seems like He necessarily would expect a far more rational response and a much more intellectually mature approach from His followers than simply the denial of science and evidence (like those who deny that the Holocaust happened and seriously posit that six million Jews did not actually die before and during World War II and that it was all a big lie made up by manipulative Jews and others for political purposes—not to mention the flat-earthers, or those who claim the photos of astronauts on the moon were faked). If we are required to deny science and evidence to believe in God, what would that requirement say about God? Perhaps, more precisely, what would that requirement say about the legitimacy of someone's concept of God? Quite to the contrary of what deniers seem to believe, science, logic, and observable evidence should be consistent with God and should only be considered to be the enemies of God if one's ultimate conclusion about God is going to be that God must be an unscientific and illogical myth—something that I clearly do not want to believe is the case—and fundamentalists, I would assume, should not want to believe that either. So my spiritual quest—and the one I encourage everyone to embark on—is to conceive of a God that is not at odds with the very science that He is alleged to have created.

Chapter Ten

God Is on My Side (Of Human Beehives)

It is interesting that we humans often form into political or other social groups and attempt to enlist the concepts of God and religion to be "on our side" to suit our own political agendas, as if our personal agendas were somehow also part of God's agenda. The hypocrisy of the Crusades and the Spanish Inquisition immediately come to mind. Even more poignant in modern times would be that everyone from the extreme Christian Right; to the Taliban and Al Qaeda; to Gandhi, Martin Luther King Jr., and liberation theology priests, have appealed to religion in a way that largely has supported their own political ideologies. Occasionally, it can appear as though political, economic, or social ideology ends up being the true God for some, which is conveniently supported by their selective and self-serving interpretations of the religious texts and doctrines to which they appeal. For example, according to folklore, during the Civil War, a woman once told Abraham Lincoln that she hoped God was "on our side," to which President Lincoln is said to have replied, "I should rather hope, madam, that we are on God's side." In either event, notice how a religious assertion often all comes down to a subjective interpretation by individuals justifying some desirable political result. It makes one wonder if conservative "white" churches are praying to the same god as radical "black" churches?

Not surprisingly, there are also those people who blame most, if not all, of the world's political problems on religious dogma and religious intolerance. Although that may be a valid critique in many instances (the Crusades, 9/11, the Spanish conquest of the Americas, and so on), religion cannot be solely responsible for all of the evil in the world. For example, personal religious beliefs did not seem to figure prominently in motivating the likes of Stalin or Pol Pot, or the Rwandan genocide in Darfur, although those atrocities were not specifically carried out in the name of atheism, either. Whether Hitler was an atheist or a Catholic, he carried out the genocide of Jews, which was religious persecution, even if not specifically carried out in the name of Catholicism or atheism. Still, one should not ignore some of the good that has come from, or at least overlaps with, traditional religious values.

Nevertheless, perhaps one of the longest running and most vexing political disputes in the world—the struggle in the Middle East between Jews and Muslims—has religious beliefs at its core, as do so many of the world's conflicts both now and throughout history. Suffice it to say that believers and nonbelievers alike have done plenty of both good and evil throughout history and thus, religion and atheism are both historically mixed bags of good and evil—but again, although there have been atheists who are evil and kill, they do not appear to have done so in the name of atheism, whereas many religious persecutors in history have done evil and have killed in the name of their religions or have used religion to justify their violent or oppressive actions against others. These are fascinating issues, and everyone seems to have a religious opinion, often informed by political ideology.

Chapter Eleven

The Limits of Literal Interpretation

Even assuming that the interpretation problems that arose as the text of the Bible was translated from one language to another and handed down through the centuries can somehow be surmounted does not address an even larger problem. Even a text written in only one language, and fairly recently (within 250 years), such as the US Constitution, can still pose a huge vexing intellectual challenge in trying to figure out the one and only, correct interpretation of that text. The assertion that interpretation is simply a matter of reading the "plain meaning" of the text, as if that is all that is necessary to solve interpretation problems, is reminiscent of the claim of those who read the text of the US Constitution and claim that they are not *subjectively* interpreting that text with their own values and personal ideology. Instead, they believe that all they are doing is reading the text literally and objectively and that the truth of the unambiguous text is revealed simply in consultation of the dictionary definitions of the words used.

Those who believe that they can literally interpret a text as complex and multilayered as the US Constitution think that they are doing nothing more than, as in math, merely plugging numbers into neutral legal equations and obtaining "fair" answers to legal disputes. They appear to truly believe that their interpretation is devoid of any personal ideology and political or economic influence. I admit that sometimes it can be that simple; if we could never interpret our laws in a literally meaningful way, then we would never have any settled, agreed upon, and predictable laws, and obviously, we do. The interpretation of our written laws is not always that easy, however, and that it is why there can be so much disagreement as to what the law means and how it should be applied, even among United States Supreme Court Justices. In fact, a famous Supreme Court Justice, Benjamin Cardozo, once said that although "we may try to see things as objectively as we please...we can never see them with any eyes except our own." That is the essence of the problem—the text still must be filtered through the intellectual perception of the person who is interpreting that text and applying it to new and ever-changing circumstances.

When the US Constitution—or any written law, for that matter—is interpreted, all judges claim that they are interpreting it objectively according to the literal meaning of the text, or at least that they are attempting to do so. Certainly, none claim to be interpreting the law incorrectly, in bad faith, or according to their own personal whims contrary to the "plain meaning" of the text. If they are all interpreting the law objectively and according to one true and strict literal interpretation of the text, however, why do they fundamentally disagree so much of the time as to what the text means? Shouldn't they all be coming to the *exact* same conclusions *every* single time about what the text means, if it is simply a matter of interpreting the text literally according to the plain meaning? Why is there any disagreement at all between those who claim to be interpreting and applying the text *literally*? That is the crux of the problem.

WHO AM I TO QUESTION A LITERAL INTEPRETATION OF THE BIBLE?

It is revealing, for example, that in 2008, of the seventy-four cases decided by the US Supreme Court, twenty-three (nearly one-third) were decided by a 5-4 split, largely along left-right ideological lines. Why can the best legal minds in the country not always agree on what the text of the Constitution or statutes mean? Very simply, it is because reasonable people can, and often do, differ on such matters. This obvious fact was what drove this nation's founders to create the United States Supreme Court with nine justices instead of just one sole interpreter. They had discovered from bitter experience that an unchecked individual appointed as an infallible interpreter and enforcer of the law—like a king—was not necessarily infallible or just. It therefore would be overly simplistic to assume that some unaffected decider could tell us "objectively" what the Constitution really means.

The Founding Fathers realized then, when they wrote our Constitution, that neither written law nor human expression is simple arithmetic. They knew that reasonable people can and do differ as to the meaning of a text, even when, unlike the Bible, there is but one official version of that text, written in only one language, and with no comparable loss in translation issues over thousands of years to worry about as with the Bible. In such a world, we all could agree with a Constitutional interpreter on what the Constitution means, because all that would be necessary is for that person to interpret the text literally and impartially. Reasonable people would not and could not differ…ever. Taking this premise to its logical extreme, if reasonable people could not differ, then we would not need judges to interpret the Constitution at all, because it would be obvious to everyone what our statutes and our Constitution mean according to what the text literally says. As a result, all judges, and the Supreme Court itself, would be rendered unnecessary and superfluous.

The concern about not being able to always interpret the Constitution literally is also present, perhaps to an even larger extent, with not being able to always interpret the much more poetic and metaphorical Bible literally. I cannot imagine the added and compounded difficulty with interpreting the US Constitution if we could not even agree on which text version of many possibilities was *the* correct version and which translation or translations of that version from language to language would be *the* correct version of the Constitution that should be used for the interpretation. Even when we have amendments to the Constitution, at least we can all agree on what the text states in one language, even if we cannot always agree on what it means. In short, imagine the added difficulty and personal subjectivity in interpretation if we had several competing versions of the Constitution from which to choose.

This, of course, leads one to ask why there are so many diverse religions, gods, doctrines, teachings, and beliefs in the world if there is but one true God and only one true and correct belief system. Even when people are of the same religion, however, say, Christianity, there are still monumental differences in how the leaders of the various religious subdivisions interpret their own particular doctrines and the texts of their Bibles.

Fundamentalist literalists often will cite II Peter 1:20: "no prophecy of the scripture is of any *private interpretation*" [emphasis added], and argue that all of these different interpretations are a direct function of people simply engaging in their own subjective, private interpretations instead of the correct, literal interpretation of God's Word (and not limiting it to just prophecies), but the problem is that all religious leaders profess to be the only ones actually using the correct interpretation, while they accuse anyone who disagrees with their interpretations as engaging in forbidden private interpretation. But who is utilizing the legitimate interpretation of the Bible, who is utilizing the illegitimate interpretation, and, most troubling, how are we supposed to know the difference?

The point is that *all* interpretation is "private" interpretation because each one of us must decide for ourselves exactly how we are going to interpret the Bible or whom among the many interpreters we are going to follow. It was somewhat simpler when there were only the original Hebrew and Greek manuscripts and the Latin Vulgate that no one but priests could read and interpret, but it began to get complicated when the Catholic Church "allowed" the scriptures to get out of their control, coupled with the invention of the printing press, and it was even further exacerbated when these "unauthorized" translations in the language of the common people started to get printed.

Chapter Twelve

A Personal Experience with Interpretive Challenges

How does some poor soul who may be unsure about all of the various biblical interpretations go about figuring out which is the correct religious horse to bet on in an effort to avoid eternal damnation? For example, Baptists believe that a sinner is saved (gets to go to Heaven) by grace—an undeserved gift from God—which requires repentance and then acceptance of the Son of God, Jesus, as one's personal savior. They also believe that one can be saved without being physically baptized in water as an adult because water-immersion baptism is merely a public profession of faith, a "work," but not a requirement for salvation. The Church of Christ, in contrast, teaches that one must be physically baptized in a water-immersion ceremony, among other things, as a requirement of salvation.

This irreconcilable dispute actually became a huge issue for me during my teenage years. As a sixteen-year-old boy who had already accepted Jesus as my personal savior in a Baptist church, I believed that I had been saved and as such would go to Heaven when I died; however, I was later told by a Church of Christ deacon that I was going to Hell if I did not get baptized with the "correct understanding" of what baptism meant. Shocked and dismayed, I demanded proof of his claim, so he got out his King James Bible and read to me Acts 2:38, which provides that one must repent *and* be baptized to be saved, or, in the exact words of the verse, "and ye shall receive the gift of the Holy Ghost." For The Church of Christ, baptism is a necessary part of salvation, not merely a public profession of faith.

As you might imagine, I became a little more than concerned. *But wait*, I thought, *I was baptized as a baby when I grew up as a Catholic.* Problem solved. You see, Catholics believe that one should be baptized as an infant, as I was, or as soon as they become Catholic. The problem, however, was that merely sprinkling water on the forehead of a baby, although an acceptable form of baptism for the Catholic Church, is not acceptable to the Church of Christ. The Church of Christ requires a complete water-immersion ceremony as an adult, accompanied simultaneously by a full understanding of the significance of that act, for someone to be correctly baptized and therefore to be truly saved. As a result, I assume they must believe that few or no Catholic Christians are going to Heaven. Anyway, in response to this dilemma, I thought, *I know, I'll just get rebaptized, and then that way, I can cover all my bases, no matter who is technically right or wrong about the baptism issue.*

Unfortunately, solving my baptism dilemma would not be that easy. My Baptist youth minister told me that if I got rebaptized to "really" be saved, I would not be acknowledging that my salvation was by grace rather than by personal acts (other than by my repentance and acceptance of Jesus as my savior). According to this youth minister, baptism is, and can only be, a public profession of faith, not a necessary step to salvation. In other words, if I got rebaptized, I would be trying to *work* my way to Heaven instead of just accepting salvation as the gift that it is. As a result, I would not really be saved because, according to Baptists, no one can work their way to Heaven. Instead, salvation is a gift of God that we cannot earn but can receive only by grace. (Ephesians 2:8: "For by grace are ye saved through faith; and that not of yourselves: it is the gift of God.") Complicating the matter even further was the idea that one could not "work one's way to heaven," although works can apparently still be circumstantial evidence of faith:

> [14] What doth it profit, my brethren, though a man say he hath faith, and have not works? Can faith save him?...
> [17] Even so faith, if it hath not works, is dead, being alone.
> [18] Yea, a man may say, Thou hast faith, and I have works: shew me thy faith without thy works, and I will shew thee my faith by my works....
> [20] But wilt thou know, O vain man, that faith without works is dead?...
> [26] For as the body without the spirit is dead, so faith without works is dead also. (James 2:14, 17–18, 20, 26)

I became quite distraught by this literal, "damned if you do, damned if you don't" Catch-22 dilemma of faith versus works. This can be very disconcerting for an impressionable young person who is desperately trying to get baptized correctly and ultimately be saved but is not exactly sure precisely *how* one is supposed to be baptized, or even *if* one must be baptized, to be saved. If I got rebaptized, would I be "un-saving" myself—literally going from the proverbial frying pan into the fire (of Hell)?

I finally decided that because Jesus saved one of the thieves on the cross with whom He was crucified, and obviously that crucified thief never got a full water-immersion baptism just before he died but still got to go to Heaven, I similarly did not need to get rebaptized "correctly" to go to Heaven. That worked for me (at least for the sixteen-year-old me) because I had found an example from the text in which someone got saved and still got to go to Heaven without being baptized in a full water-immersion baptism (a legal precedent of sorts).

This little interpretation drama got me thinking, however. How fair is it if someone were sent to Hell just because he or she guessed incorrectly and got the whole baptism works-versus-grace thing wrong? After all, the Church of Christ deacon told me in response to the unbaptized-thief-on-the-cross-who-got-to-go-to-Heaven-anyway argument that the baptism requirement for salvation did not become effective until *after* Jesus died. Jesus was *still alive* when He told the thief on the cross that the thief would be in Paradise with Him forever as a result of the thief having confessed his sins to Jesus, so although the thief on the cross did not need to be baptized to be saved, I did. I needed to be baptized because, for me, Jesus had long since died, so the rules of salvation were different for me than they were for the thief on the cross because baptism symbolically represents Jesus's *death* (the water-dunking) and then His rising from the dead on the third day (the arising out of the water). Because Jesus had not yet died and arisen, the need for baptism had not been necessary for the thief on the cross. But then I thought, *Well then why did Jesus get baptized, and why did John the Baptist go around baptizing people before Jesus ever died?* Didn't that render the timing argument wrong? By the way, these are pretty sophisticated legal interpretation arguments being made here, so in retrospect, this Church of Christ deacon and my Baptist youth minster also would have been very crafty and resourceful lawyers—maybe they had missed their calling, or maybe they hadn't.

In response to this argument from me, the Baptist youth minister said that baptism as defined in Acts 2:38 is baptism "of the Holy Spirit," not a water-dunking baptism. So the Baptists say one need not be baptized to be saved. I always thought it was kind of weird that Baptists call themselves Baptists yet do not require baptism as a part of their salvation. Logically, it seems like Church of Christ members should be the ones who call themselves Baptists if baptism is such a necessary tenet for one's salvation.

So what did I do to ensure my spot in Heaven? Of course, I never fully resolved this interpretation dispute. I just started asking more hypothetical questions, such as, What if a person who was not saved was stranded on a desert island, found a Bible, and then wanted to get saved, but there was no one there to baptize him or her? Would that person die and go to Hell, or could God still save him? The Church of Christ gave me an answer: God would not put a person who would be saved in that situation to begin with, because God already knows who will accept Him and who won't. To this, I asked, "Well then, why are we even here? If God already knows that, what's the point?" In other words, why must we go through life if God already knows who will be saved and who won't be, and such already has been predetermined in a Calvinistic way?

Still, the arguments of both the Baptists and the Church of Christ had some merit, or at least I could see some logic in each interpretation, but the most troubling thing for me was that I saw people of good faith and intelligence on both sides who were really trying to understand the text but in so doing reached diametrically opposed, mutually exclusive (yet still plausible) conclusions. Somehow, it didn't seem right that one group was going to Hell while the other was going to Heaven, depending on what side of the argument they fell on. Moreover, they would not know for sure one way or another until they died and found out by God's judgment, to either their joy or their utter horror. It did not seem fair. It just did not seem like the supreme being of the universe would be as picky, technical, formulistic, and fastidious as that.

When I asked about the fairness issue, the answer, once again, depended on whom I asked. Some said, "God knows your heart," so I would still be saved no matter what side I took because I was trying, in good faith, to be saved; others said, "The way to the Lord is very narrow," so I had better get the technicality right if I was not too keen on spending eternity in Hell. Perhaps this interesting interpretation dispute is one of the reasons why I was eventually drawn to law school. I thought that perhaps in law school, the expert law professors would teach me exactly how to interpret such contradictory inferences, maybe by using some special secret legal techniques to solve such interpretive conundrums. Oh, if it were only that easy! My law school professor colleagues and I still laugh at that one.

Nonetheless, law school was helpful insofar as I learned how to consider and analyze arguments and to conduct statutory interpretation, even though my dad now says that law school just confused me even more with "moral relativism" and the ability and the need to see all sides of an argument. Have I become so enraptured with the ability to see all sides of an argument that I have now forever lost the ability to make a substantive decision about right and wrong ever again? Imagine that: Open-minded reason and the ability to see things from many perspectives as a liability. I just can't get a break.

Chapter Thirteen

Belief without Proof?

Consider the biblical story of Thomas, who was a disciple of Jesus who refused to believe that Jesus had arisen from the dead after Jesus had been crucified because it didn't make logical sense to him that a dead person could be alive again. Doubting Thomas just could not accept the fact of the dead coming back to life on faith alone. Thomas had to see with his own eyes that Jesus had arisen and was alive before he would believe that Jesus had been resurrected from the dead. When Thomas finally did see the risen Jesus and examined His hands and His side with the puncture wounds from the crucifixion nails and the crucifixion spear, he finally believed that Jesus was the risen savior, but in response to Thomas, "Jesus saith unto him, Thomas, because thou hast seen me, thou hast believed: blessed are they that have not seen, and yet have believed" (John 20:29).

The story of Thomas makes me think that, despite everything, my unorthodox faith is actually a very strong faith because although I do not see—in the sense of logically and scientifically understanding most of the literal accounts of Biblical stories—I still believe in God. In fact, that belief is truly a faith that is sight unseen. The reality is that it requires a great deal of faith for someone like me to believe, especially when I do not see in the metaphorical sense yet still believe. Although my faith is not based on reason, that non-rationally based belief is true faith: "[5] Trust in the LORD with all thine heart; and lean not unto thine own understanding. [6] In all thy ways acknowledge him, and he shall direct thy paths. [7] Be not wise in thine own eyes: fear the LORD, and depart from evil" (Proverbs 3:5–7). My challenge to any faith, therefore, would be a challenge only to a professed faith based on alleged appeals to science and/or logic as "proof" of one's faith.

Perhaps it is much easier to believe when one can see how the Bible all somehow makes logical, literal, and consistent sense. If this is the case, then maybe what I have written about in this book is really about an even greater faith than that of a traditional believer. Why? Because I believe with nothing to support that belief in terms of science, logic, or evidence; it is 100% pure faith. It might be much easier for me to believe if I were convinced there is some actual, tangible, and rational proof that God exists. In short, the more "proof" there is, the less need there is for faith. This paradox of faith and rationality is what Part Four of the book is about.

If I am open-minded, though, then I also need to be mindful of the fact that maybe my faith is just a manifestation of my own grand delusion, because I choose to believe despite the fact that science, logic, reason, and evidence all seem to strongly indicate otherwise. I would, of course, criticize any of my first-year law students who came to a conclusion completely unsupported by any evidence or logical analysis; yet here I am, perhaps hypocritically so, still wanting and trying to believe in something that admittedly cannot be established with reason or scientific proof. It is as though I am hypocritically telling my students, "Do as I say, not as I do!" And so, back to square one: Is there a God who requires faith without rationality as a condition of that faith, or is such faith merely a rationalization for a superstitious belief that lacks any logical proof?

Chapter Fourteen

For the Reader before Beginning Part Two

If you are a believer, this book may test your faith by causing you to doubt the literal interpretation of the Bible to which you subscribe, whatever that might be, or even to question your faith in God. In contrast, perhaps this book will serve only to strengthen your existing faith and solidify your walk with God. If you are an atheist, this book may give you pause to possibly reconsider God's existence and the true meaning of faith. In contrast, all that this book may do is convince you that I simply do not have the courage to join you in your rational, even brave, lack of faith. For me, however, such a complete lack of faith, in and of itself, also represents a problematic leap of faith, similar to—although of a very different kind—the leap of faith required of those who believe in God.

Whatever the outcome of your reading of this book, it is my hope that you will at least be challenged to reconsider and think more deeply about your faith, or lack thereof. It is my further hope that you will do so rationally and fearlessly as you try to determine what, if anything, biblical scriptures can and should mean for you.

My ultimate goal is for all of us as a species to be able to look as deeply inward as we do outward for answers about God's existence and the meaning of life in our universe. In doing so, it might be wise for us to heed the words of one of America's most thoughtful founders and most talented and intellectual former presidents, as well as the principal writer of the Declaration of Independence, Thomas Jefferson. On the issue of faith in God, Jefferson advised us:

> Question with boldness even the existence of a God; because, if
> there be one, he must more approve of the homage of reason,
> than that of blind-folded fear.

> -   Letter to Peter Carr,
>   August 10, 1787

But if that is true, perhaps we should not have faith without reason and proof to back it up. So now what? How can I possibly justify my admittedly "irrational" faith if we are not to ignore the requirement of reason in our quest to find God?

*   *   *

WHO AM I TO QUESTION A LITERAL INTEPRETATION OF THE BIBLE?

Although the questions and observations contained in this book concern only the first eleven chapters of the book of Genesis, I often will refer to other parts of the Bible throughout to make a point. Many of my questions are rhetorical in nature and therefore are not really meant to be answered. Instead, they are posed simply to demonstrate a logical or scientific impossibility or problematic inconsistency in the text. I think these issues are so important to highlight because there exists a false sense of security in simply assuming that all of the answers to life's mysteries are contained in some book interpreted by self-proclaimed objective interpreters. In addition to my questions, I often offer substantial commentary and thought experiments to the same effect. Other questions, however, are more genuine theological questions that are actually intended to elicit sincere and authentic theological as well as scientific answers.

I spend a great deal of time and effort, perhaps even too much time and effort, on Part Two, which is exclusively on the very first verse of the first chapter of Genesis involving creation. I do this because that one verse on creation is so very important and encompasses so much. There are a total of fifty chapters of Genesis, so this book easily could have become a multivolume treatise if I were to spend that much time dissecting each and every verse of Genesis; even then, there still would be much more to cover and to consider. After I analyze the first verse, however, I cover the rest of the text of the first eleven chapters of Genesis in a bit less detail.

I decided to use the King James Version of the Bible as the text because many Christian fundamentalists, who argue that a literal interpretation of the Bible is possible, use the King James Version. The Early Modern English used in that particular translation (originally published in the year 1611, although the version now commonly in use is the 1769 Baskerville Birmingham revision) made it difficult to understand (whereas the Middle and certainly the Old English is now almost impossible to understand, given the evolution of the language). However, the language translation concerns are just one of many problems with assuming that a literal interpretation of the Bible is possible. As I read, I found myself asking hundreds of nagging little (and big) questions about the text, so I decided to write down those questions, as well as my reactions to those questions and how I think they should or could be answered, to see whether I could come to any meaningful conclusions.

In any event, please enjoy this literal, and I hope very challenging, exploration of the text of the first eleven chapters of the book of Genesis. As you ponder the questions and issues posed in this book, try to keep a working, open mind if you can and, even more importantly, if you dare.

PART TWO

GENESIS 1:1
"IN THE BEGINNING..."
THE FLAWED FOUNDATION

Chapter Fifteen

Is This Really All There Was to Our Entire Universe When God Created It?

Genesis 1

[1] In the beginning God created the heaven and the earth.

If we unleash our perspective from the binds of unquestioning faith, we can read these first words and naturally wonder: Did the writer of this verse have any awareness at all of the true nature of our vastly immense universe? It appears as though the writer considered only that which he could literally see at the time, which would have been just the visible sky directly above him and the tangible ground directly beneath him.

Of everything that composes our immeasurable universe, however—potentially an infinite number of planets, solar systems, star systems, quasars, galaxies, clusters of galaxies, gamma rays, and black holes, as well as magnetism, gravity, dark matter, and dark energy (many aspects of which only generations to come will fully discover)—only the sky immediately above us (the heaven), and the ground immediately beneath us (the earth), were mentioned as the beginning of *all* creation. To set up only the earth and the sky above it as the sole focal point of the universe, wholly independent of everything else making up the universe, suggests that the writer was completely unaware of the colossal complexity and the majestic grandeur of the universe. Moses is usually credited with writing the first five books of the Bible around 1450–1410 BC, but Moses was no scientist, as his entire concept of the universe was only the earth and the sky above it.

Based on this literal interpretation of Genesis, the Judeo-Christian world believed for many centuries that a flat Earth was at the center of a small universe. This belief was so central to a religious foundation that the Catholic Church either excommunicated or threatened to excommunicate famous astronomers such as Copernicus and Galileo because they dared to assert that the earth was not at the center of the universe. The work of Copernicus, Kepler, and Galileo eventually showed unequivocally that the earth actually revolves around the Sun, as do all of the planets in our solar system, not that the sun moves across the sky every day over a flat static Earth. Unfortunately, this simple scientific truth was deemed to be anti-biblical heresy, much as many aspects of basic geology, paleontology, and evolutionary biology are considered by some people today.

"In the beginning God created the heaven and the earth" as a statement means that the ground and the sky were created but that the earth was not revolving around the sun, or anything else for that matter. There was no sun around which to revolve, because the sun and the stars were not created, according to Genesis 1:14–19, until the fourth day of creation. Moses must have been asserting that God created the earth and the sky above it so that Earth was suspended or resting on something about which we are not told in the text. At this point, Earth was not rotating or revolving, nor was it a part of any solar system, because in the beginning, there was no solar system, only the heaven and the earth, presented as stagnant and alone in the universe.

By stating that God created the earth and the sky/heaven first and then, at some point, everything else in the universe (even though most of that remainder of creation is never specifically mentioned nor fully explained anywhere in the Bible), Moses obviously started and finished with the only two elements in the cosmos that he could see with his naked eye and comprehend with his limited knowledge. It is hard to blame him for his limited knowledge, however, given that he was writing the Bible thousands of years ago, before telescopes and sufficiently developed science existed to reveal the true and more complete nature of our universe and of Earth's relatively miniscule place in it.

Moses's very limited and rudimentary view of the universe reminds me of the brilliant and insightful old Gary Larson *Far Side* cartoon "Carl Sagan as a Kid":

Carl Sagan as a kid

Gary Larson's "Carl Sagan as a Kid" depicts Carl Sagan (the late famous astronomer) as a young boy gazing up at the stars one night and exclaiming, "Just look at all those stars… there must be HUNDREDS of 'em!" instead of his now famous mantra when referring to the vast nature of our galaxy (let alone the entire universe): Billions and billions of stars. The point is that Moses was much like a metaphorically young Carl Sagan, just trying to make sense of and understand the universe, or Creation, with what very limited astronomical knowledge and cosmological awareness he had at the time.

We, of course, still have very much to learn about the full and true scientific nature of the universe, which we may never fully be able to grasp; however, science has brought us much further along than Moses ever did when he wrote Genesis 1:1. Moses might have at the time believed that God was speaking to him, but either Moses was incorrect about what he thought God was telling him or, for whatever reason, he was unable to understand much of what God was attempting to transmit to him.

Chapter Sixteen

Assuming That God *Eventually* Created the Remainder of the Universe, Why Was That Creation Never Explained in Detail in Genesis?

Even if God did not wish to tell the entire detailed explanation of the creation of our universe, why not mention at least some of the more rudimentary elements? For example, why is there no mention that planets and asteroids in our solar system revolve around the sun and that moons revolve around the planets? Why nothing on how the tilt of the Earth on its axis, coupled with its yearly revolution around the sun, is what causes our four yearly seasons (when one is not near the equator)? Why no explanation that our days and nights are a function of a *spherical* Earth rotating on its axis about every twenty-four hours instead of a flat Earth that has a sun supposedly moving across the sky in a rising and setting pattern every day? As a quick thought experiment, just pick up any elementary school science book explaining basic astronomy, and then compare its contents to what we are told in Genesis about the universe! The name of the television quiz show—*Are You Smarter Than a 5th Grader?*—takes on a whole new meaning in this regard.

Not only are so many basic facts about our universe not mentioned in Genesis or anywhere else in the Bible, but much of the contents of the Bible suggest that these facts were just not known by any of its human authors. These significant omissions of information about our universe, ironically limiting the information provided to just what humanity knew about the universe over 3,500 years ago, are quite alarming omissions if the Bible is supposed to be interpreted literally as God's direct words to us. If the writings of the Bible were in fact limited to the human knowledge in the era in which they were written, this suggests that such writings probably were more humanly inspired than divinely so.

If God created all the wonderment that is our universe and the beautiful setting of our Earth, perched just far enough away from a star like our sun so that life as we know it in its multitude of forms would flourish here, and if God wrote the story of the creation through a group of men so we might be informed and guided by the Bible, then why would God omit the bulk of the most important and critical information about the universe? Why would God simplify it down so much (Earth and sky/heaven) that it would actually be a misleading description about the universe and the world? Would that constitute "*deceptive* intelligent design" by God?

Would God actually write in mistakes on purpose? For example, in Joshua 10:12-14, there is an account of how God helped Joshua wage war (it is interesting that God is often portrayed as taking sides in very violent armed conflicts, and He will even rain down "great stones from heaven" to kill the enemies of Israel, see Joshua 10:11). During the battle, Joshua prayed to God asking Him to "make the sun stand still" until Israel could prevail over its enemy in the battle.

> [12] Then spake Joshua to the Lord in the day when the Lord delivered up the Amorites before the children of Israel, and he said in the sight of Israel, Sun, stand thou still upon Gibeon; and thou, Moon, in the valley of Ajolan. (Joshua 10:12)

It is interesting that Joshua would talk directly to the "Sun" and to the "Moon" almost as if they are real entities that have personalities. Notice that the names of the sun and moon are capitalized here like proper names, but later they are not capitalized when they are not being addressed directly. Instead of God just stopping these inanimate celestial objects in their tracks, God seems to have told them to stop their movement across the sky and they appear to obey His command.

> [13] And the sun stood still, and the moon stayed, until the people had avenged themselves upon their enemies. Is not this written in the book of Jasher [although "Jasher" is not any official book of the Bible]? So the sun stood still in the midst of the heaven, and hasted not to go down about a whole day. [14] And there was no day like that before it or after it, that the Lord harkened unto the voice of a man: for the Lord fought for Israel. Joshua (10:13-14)

The text says that God made the sun and the moon stop moving for almost a whole day—but it really must have been that God stopped the earth from spinning for almost a day, although it actually does not say that as the writer obviously did not know that the earth spins on its axis and thus only makes it *appear* that the sun moves across the sky and that the moon moves during the night. These passages are written in such a way that it is clear that the writer is completely unaware that the earth revolves around the sun, or that the moon revolves around the earth, and that their daily "movement" in the sky is just an illusion caused by the earth spinning on its axis.

If the earth actually had stopped spinning, there would have been huge cataclysmic effects on the earth as its inertia first would have come to a screeching halt, and then later would have had to speed up again to its regular rotation speed. But even putting aside those earth-shattering practical issues, because God can do anything, the text still says that the sun and the moon stopped their *movement* across the sky. Why would God, who knows all things, incorrectly communicate the idea that the sun actually moves across the sky every day (revolves around the earth) when it does not do so? Although the moon revolves around the earth, the sun does not, and it is only Earth's spinning that provides the illusion of these bodies moving every day and every night. This is a huge astronomical error written here, if we interpret these words literally.

Chapter Seventeen

Did God Create a Flat Earth?

Consider another specific, obvious example of an astronomical error and omission in the Bible—the geometrical shape of the earth. For centuries, Bible-believing Christians incorrectly thought that the earth was flat. As we shall see, in various places, the Bible suggests that the earth is flat. Did God really intend that? Again, is the Bible limited to the incomplete human understanding at the time when it was originally written? If so, can it be regarded as only divinely inspired or influenced, rather than as the exact, true Word of God? Or did God purposefully not reveal the complete truth about the universe to Moses and the other writers in order to test our faith in the written word of the Bible so that when we would learn more about the universe and how scientific knowledge is often not consistent with the Bible, we could still "pass the test" if we just maintained faith in the Bible's deficient and often blatantly incorrect explanations?

Should Christians therefore not regard the Bible as the *complete* revealed word of God because when Moses was writing the Book of Genesis, he either did not have or was not given full information? It might be that Moses simply got much of what he was receiving wrong. In contrast, maybe Moses could not understand what God was telling him, so he did not record it all correctly or completely when he relayed the information God gave to him in writing Genesis.

But it all seems rather farfetched to argue that whenever a literal explanation in Genesis is either lacking or dubious, it is done so on purpose by God just to test our faith, as if there were a biblical disclaimer that read, "What this book says is true, unless it is wrong, in which case it is only wrong *on purpose* to test your faith. At other times, it is not really wrong, however, but just seems wrong or lacking, for now, but such mysteries will all be explained later when we get to Heaven." Doesn't "the Bible may be wrong here, but if so, it is on purpose just to test your faith" smack of a very weak rationalization?

Even if the Bible were not to explain every detail of the story of creation, why not explain even just a few key facts in Genesis (like the earth is a sphere that revolves around the sun)? At least that would have avoided the seriously mistaken belief that the earth is flat and static instead of being part of a solar system of planets revolving around the sun. Such a simple explanation about the earth, not to mention how our solar system works, if it had been provided in the Bible at that early point in history, would have supported at least an inference that the Bible might be the inerrant divine Word of God.

Aristotle and Eratosthenes (Greek philosophers and scientists from 250 BC) appear to be the first ones to at least suggest scientifically that the earth is a sphere. Their work was all done BC (before Christ), pre-New Testament. This is significant because in the New Testament Gospels of Matthew and Luke, written around 100 AD and thousands of years after Genesis, the Bible incorrectly suggests that the earth is flat. In Matthew 4:1–11 and Luke 4:1–13, the Bible recounts how Satan tempted Jesus by taking Him up to a high mountain to show Jesus "all of the kingdoms of the world" that could be His if Jesus were simply to bow down to Satan: "**[5]** And the devil, taking him up into an high mountain, shewed unto him all the kingdoms of the world in a moment of time.**[6]** And the devil said unto him, All this power will I give thee, and the glory of them: for that is delivered unto me; and to whomsoever I will I give it. **[7]** If thou therefore wilt worship me, all shall be thine" (Luke 4:5–7).

Of course, no matter how high that mountain was, it would have been impossible to see all of the kingdoms in the world because Earth is a sphere. Stated differently, if the earth is a sphere, seeing the entire surface of Earth from one vantage point simply cannot physically be done. Additionally, there were kingdoms in China, Africa, Europe, and Central America at the time, but Matthew and Luke seem to be unaware of these other countries or the other continents of the world, because they do not refer to them.

Consider the following diagram:

Sittin' on Top of the World

Being Able to See It All if It Were Flat

Being Able to See Only Half, at Most, if It Were a Sphere

The biblical passages in Matthew and Luke make sense only if you incorrectly assume that the world is flat. Notwithstanding the fact that the earth is not flat and therefore these accounts in Matthew and Luke are monumental biblical errors, why would Jesus, the Son of God who *is* God, even need to be taken to the top of a very high mountain to see all of the kingdoms of the world in the first place? Certainly, if Jesus truly is God, then He already would have been fully aware of all of these kingdoms of the world.

It also does not follow that Satan was more in control of all of the world's kingdoms than God was, with the result that Satan had the power to grant wishes to God (Jesus) if God would just bow down to him. If Jesus really had wanted to, couldn't He have just taken control of all of these kingdoms anyway without having to bow down to Satan? Was Satan more powerful than God in this regard—with the power to grant (or deny) God's wishes? Does God play a sort of game with Satan, granting Satan the power to take his best shot at Jesus or us (as God seemed to do with Job, allowing Satan to heap any and all misfortunes on Job just to see if he could take it)? If Satan was "testing" Jesus with "temptations," how could an infallible God, Jesus, possibly fail, unless Jesus was more human than He was God? If it is a sin to lust in one's heart and thus commit adultery (Matthew 5:28: "whosoever looketh on a woman to lust after her hath committed adultery with her already in his heart"), did Jesus commit any sin simply by virtue of being tempted by Satan? When I am tempted, do I get to blame that evil sinful thought all on Satan who is tempting me by planting evil/sinful thoughts in my mind, or do I have to take at least some responsibility for even thinking about and considering committing that evil sin—like a thought crime?

In addition to the premise that the earth is flat, Matthew and Luke lead us to the belief that the world is much smaller than it actually is, given the assumption that the top of a high mountain could facilitate a clear view of all the kingdoms on Earth. But maybe Jesus enjoyed Godly, super eyesight that could bend light to see around to the other side of the world. Or maybe Jesus had x-ray vision that could see right through the earth; however, if that were the case, why was there any need to take Jesus to a high mountain to see kingdoms that He already had the ability to see—not to mention the fact that Jesus already was fully aware of these kingdoms and therefore already would have known all about them and everyone in them?

Assuming, however, that this trip to a high mountain happened and "all of the kingdoms" were really just the kingdoms that somehow could be seen in a certain area of the earth near the Middle East, to what high mountain on Earth were the biblical writers referring? Mt. Everest (in Nepal), the highest mountain on Earth, is extremely difficult for human beings to climb, not only because of its steep, icy terrain but also because of the deadly storm conditions that swirl by the mountain nearly continually. In addition, most people cannot function or even survive in the thin air at such altitudes, as oxygen levels deplete more and more as one approaches the 29,029-foot peak. But if Satan and Jesus could easily reach the top of Mt. Everest because of their special powers and overcome all of the aforementioned obstacles, they would arrive at a place where their view of "all the kingdoms" would be blocked, as a clear view for miles is unlikely from a place that is above the clouds in almost constant precipitation. These problems would arise with almost every other very high mountain around the earth, and lower mountains require us to ask how limited the area to be seen must have been in the minds of the writers.

The flawed assumption of being able to view all of the kingdoms of the world reinforces the naive belief held by the biblical authors that the world was flat and very small and therefore endured the sunlight of day or the darkness of night *all at the same time*—the text says "shewed unto him all of the kingdoms of the world *in a moment of time.*" (Emphasis added). The writers did not even realize that there are relative time zones because of the spherical shape of the earth so that noon in Jerusalem might be 5:00 a.m. in Mexico City and 7:00 p.m. in Japan (depending on daylight savings times). If there were any such awareness by the writers that it is always both day and night somewhere in the world, wouldn't there have been some reference to being able to view only the *half* of the kingdoms that were lit by the sun at any one particular time or to somehow being able to also view the half that was under the cover of night at a time when there were typically no bright city lights illuminating any kingdom (unless there just happened to be a bright full moon out lighting up the other half of the earth at that time)? Recall that there was no electricity and there were no kerosene lamps more than 2,000 years ago. Would the kingdoms that would have been seen at night have been seen because of their campfires or, again, because of the special eyesight of Jesus, which also could light up the dark? This brings us back to the question of why Jesus would climb a high mountain for a view He could have had without needing a mountaintop vantage point anyway or, more fundamentally, how Jesus could view the entire surface of the earth at once, even from the vantage point of a high mountaintop, when from the orbit of the space station, even the astronauts cannot see the other side of the spherical earth.

Perhaps these literal questions are inapplicable here because these accounts in Matthew and Luke are just *metaphors* about God's resistance of Satan's temptation and therefore are not intended to be taken as a literal description of an actual event. If that is the case, however, we then move away from *literal* interpretation into the wholly different world of personal, metaphorical, or private interpretation—and who is to say which biblical stories are to be taken literally, and which are mere parables and metaphors that are *not* to be taken literally? Not that it would be wrong to take any or all of the stories metaphorically only, but this move away from strict literalism represents a huge departure from those who argue for the literal interpretation of *everything* in the Bible.

Changing from the literal to the metaphorical is a very convenient "out" whenever the literal interpretation is problematic. If we step into the realm of personal interpretation and out of the world of the literal approach, then the Bible could send a very different message to each of the billions of people on the planet. And then how would we know which religious leader or which church was interpreting the Bible correctly so we could decide whom to turn to when seeking guidance in our worship? If the writers intended this story to be taken literally, then we are left with an implausible, illogical fallacy because the earth is not flat and there is no mountain or other location on Earth from which one can see all of the kingdoms of the world.

Another biblical reference makes the same mistake about the earth being flat and very small. In Daniel 4:10–11, a king reportedly saw a tree of great height at the center of the Earth: "and the height thereof reached unto heaven, *and the sight thereof to the end of all earth*" (emphasis added). One object on Earth being visible from everywhere on Earth reinforces the fact that the biblical authors, be they men or God, adhered to the incorrect assumption that the world was flat. Instead of a very tall mountain from which Jesus could view the entire world, this verse tells us that all humans in the world, none likely to have superhuman eyesight or special powers, allegedly could see this one tall tree *from any point on Earth*. Again, if this is just hyperbole or metaphor, how are we supposed to know when to interpret the Bible literally and when to interpret it metaphorically? Although this tree was a vision in a dream of Nebuchadnezzar, and so perhaps only metaphorical, the assumption about a flat earth is inherent in the description that such a tree, if it were tall enough, of course could be seen from every point on Earth. So, if the assumption is still literal, then it is an example of a passage in which the writer did not divine God's message correctly, or at all, or filled in incorrect information that God had not intended for him to relate. In any event, it is a clear mistake existing in an allegedly perfect, inerrant book. Did God write that mistake? If not, then a human must have.

When I told my father (who, you may recall from the introduction, is a fundamentalist pastor who promotes an absolutely literal interpretation of the Bible) about these problematic biblical verses and their mistaken flat-earth implications, interestingly, he was not bothered by them. He said, "Yes, I have heard about this 'flat-earth' charge before, only in a different context. Recall that when Jesus returns after the Rapture—in which all the saved Christians are to be taken up in the air to Heaven just before the world ends in Armageddon—the Bible, in Revelation, says, 'Every eye shall see the return of Jesus.' Of course, the only way everyone on Earth all would be able to see Jesus's return is if the earth were flat." That was a very astute observation by my dad, because it is true that the only way everyone on a spherical Earth could simultaneously see Jesus's return in the sky is if the earth were flat, which we know is not the case. I was impressed that my dad had thought of and was acknowledging this point; my dad had an explanation for this, however. He said, "Every eye still shall literally see Jesus's triumphant return, despite the earth being round, because when Jesus returns, it will be covered on live television, by stations like CNN! So the Bible accurately predicted television some 2,000 years ago! This proves the existence of God and that the Bible is accurate to each word!" I had to concede that his explanation made sense—or at least arguably *could* make sense—as every eye could literally see Jesus's return on TV and God knew live television would one day be invented. In other words, the Bible is not wrong, *and* it even predicted the invention of television over 2,000 years ago—impressive.

"OK, Dad," I said, "let's assume Jesus's return will be covered on live TV or on the Internet so that 'every eye shall see' His return simultaneously. Were there television sets and the Internet 2,000 years ago? If so, did Satan take Jesus up to a very high mountain just to get good reception on a television set [or a Wi-Fi computer] with a live feed from the other side of the world? You have simply answered your own question about how every eye shall see Jesus's return in modern times [predicted in Revelation], but you have completely ignored my original question about Jesus being able to see every kingdom of the world from a tall mountain over 2,000 years ago [in Matthew and Luke] as well as the question regarding how every human could see a tall tree from everywhere in the world thousands of years ago [in Daniel]."

In response, my dad simply said, "In the end times, son, wise men will become fools." OK, but this response can actually cut both ways. For example, if I make a bad/illogical argument against a literalist believer, then it is just a bad/illogical argument and I would lose on that point. If I make a good/logical argument against a literalist believer, however, then somehow, I am really just a latter-day fool engaging in foolishness, assuming that we are now living in the end times, and so I would still lose on that point. Imagine that, no matter what, I lose. How does one possibly argue with that kind of "heads I win, tails you lose"—"I am right and you are wrong, and even when you are right, you are still wrong"—mentality?

I guess my dad was really saying, without intending to do so, that it is fine to use logic to argue in support of the Bible but that if the argument ends up being inadequate in comparison to a scientific counterargument that defeats it, it is best to say, "In the end times, wise men will become fools." In this way, a bad or illogical argument in support of the Bible can still and always be considered correct. It appears that literalist believers need to be careful here, however; if they use the "wise men will become fools" response, then whenever they actually have a logical argument, it will backfire on them, as they are then themselves the wise men who will become fools—unless, of course, this observation about wise men becoming fools is something that never can apply to them, only to others. This must be what they think, even if they are not willing to admit it.

I was talking to my older brother, Ken, about this flat-earth implication in the books of Matthew, Luke, and Daniel. Like my dad, my brother is extremely knowledgeable about the Bible as well as various other related subjects. I was excited to share with him this biblical error that I had stumbled upon, irrespective of my dad's TV-in-modern-times explanation, but my brother had a unique yet equally problematic response. He explained that in the book of Isaiah, another Old Testament book, the writer suggests that the earth is round by referring to it as a circle: "It is he that sitteth upon the *circle of the earth*, and the inhabitants thereof are as grasshoppers; that stretcheth out the heavens as a curtain..." (Isaiah 40:22; emphasis added). So if it says "circle," then it is close enough to mean "round," or a "sphere."

A circle, however is still two-dimensional (like a flat, circular disc), whereas a sphere is three-dimensional (like a round basketball); therefore, the word circle is not a correct description of the earth's round shape. The earth is *not* a flat circle, like a disc; instead, it is a three-dimensional, round sphere. What if the writers in this passage were to have referred to the earth as a square or triangle (flat, two-dimensional shapes) instead of as a cube or pyramid (their related three-dimensional objects)? Wouldn't the earth still be flat, even though its perimeter would now be in the shape of a square or triangle instead of a circle? If one were to go to a high mountaintop (like Jesus and Satan apparently did), one would perceive the horizon as it falls off on all sides. As such, one would see a flat earth that appears to be circular in shape, because one can see only as far as one can see from one spot, and if one looks all around, that person's depth perception would show something like the radius of a circle, with that person in the center, and thus the earth would appear to be a flat circular disc. Consider the following diagram.

As Far as the Eye Can See

Looking all *around,* where the line of vision length is equidistant in all directions

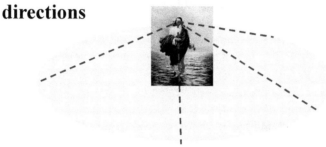

Although there apparently is no word for sphere in the original Hebrew language, if God truly is all powerful and He wrote the Bible, then perhaps He should have made sure there was a word for sphere in Hebrew. If that is what He meant to communicate, and God is infallible and the Bible is His inerrant word, why would such a simple linguistic obstacle get in God's way? After all, if God can create the universe and everything in it, He certainly could have correctly described the shape of the earth by making sure that there was a word in Hebrew that correctly described its shape. There is no disrespect intended here; I am just taking the exact language of the Bible—which asserts that the earth is a circle instead of a sphere—very seriously and very literally and interpreting it accordingly.

So, my brother brought to my attention this reference to the "circle" shape of the earth, which is a little closer to the actual shape of the earth. My brother, by the way, is not your typical biblical scholar, at least not on the surface. As I alluded to earlier, he rides a Harley, has many tattoos, is a child of the '60s, and is very much a free spirit. Like Jesus, he is a talented carpenter who cares a lot about other people. Notwithstanding the surface differences with my conservative preacher father, my father and my free-spirited brother are alike in many ways and agree on many subjects, yet a milieu of theological and other disagreements keeps them apart to this day. One thing is certain, however: They are both extremely knowledgeable about the Bible and, along with my older sister, Viki, are much smarter than I am, and in many different ways.

In any event, when my brother saw that I was about to concede the point that in Isaiah, the Bible at least *implies* that the earth is of roundish shape (a circle), he proceeded to inform me, just for fun, "You know, Isaiah may suggest that the earth is a sphere, if you interpret 'circle' to mean 'sphere,' but you should also know that in the Book of Job, the Bible definitely acknowledges the existence of, get this...unicorns."

"Unicorns!" I exclaimed. "You mean, like, a horse with a single, twisty, cone-like horn growing out of its forehead unicorn? You mean bedtime-story, fairytale unicorns?"

"Yeah. Interesting, huh?"

According to Isaiah, the earth is a circle (which is at least close to a sphere, so the Bible *almost* gets it right in at least one part), but according to Job, unicorns used to live on the circle Earth: "Will the unicorn be willing to serve thee, or abide by thy crib? Canst thou bind the unicorn with his band in the furrow?" (Job 39:9–10). If this is literally true, then there must be fossils of unicorns somewhere on Earth…but none have been found. Perhaps unicorn fossils are the Bible's own version of a missing link. Of course, creationists make much of the fact that there are alleged missing links in the fossil record that prove evolution is wrong in general. Evolutionary biologists actually claim, however, that there are thousands of examples of missing links in the fossil record supporting evolution; it is just that not *every single conceivable* missing link was necessarily fossilized and has been discovered so far. There will be more on this later, but the juxtaposition of the circle of the Earth (if "circle" is interpreted as round) as stated in the Bible, along with the reference to the apparent existence of unicorns (unless it was a reference to a mythical animal), is just fascinating. It is like having a scientist explain quantum mechanics at least partially correctly but then having that same scientist warn us about dangerous thunderbolts hurled by Zeus. Why would God allow such a big mistake in the Bible, not only about the shape of the earth but also about the existence of unicorns? Is it really just a way to test our faith?

Maybe the reference to a unicorn is really just a goat or a rhinoceros reference that somehow got translated incorrectly in the Bible, but a strict literal interpretation would not allow for such corrective "Monday-morning quarterbacking" to explain away the existence of unicorns. Why would an infallible God allow such a mistranslation of His Word? If it is just a mistranslation, then what other similar translation mistakes are in the Bible? If the passage in Job is just a reference to a mythical unicorn, then where does the passage in Job, or a passage anywhere in the Bible, literally say that, where would that it-is-just-a-mythical-unicorn interpretation be coming from?

Despite the incredulous unicorn reference in Job, it is still impressive that the Bible, in Isaiah, almost got the round shape of the earth right that long ago. Did the Bible as a whole, however, really almost get this shape-of-the-earth issue right? If the Bible implies in Isaiah that the earth is round (a circle), or even if Isaiah had gotten it exactly right by stating that the earth is the shape of a sphere but then later—in Daniel, as well as in Matthew and Luke—implied that the earth is flat, then, at best, the Bible is contradictory and inconsistent. It is wrong to say that the earth is *both* spherical and flat. It is either one or the other, but it cannot be both. (It can be a circle and still be flat, however.) So, which is it—spherical or flat? More importantly, why is there any inconsistency in the Bible if an inerrant God wrote every literal word? A person is not right about an assertion just because that person makes two conflicting assertions and it just so happens that *one* of those assertions turns out to be correct.

For example, suppose a grade-school student took a science test that asked whether gravity exists. If that student were to answer, "Yes, large masses produce a force called gravity, which attracts other objects to the mass," but went on to say afterward, "There is no such thing as the force of gravity; it is only God's love that keeps us all from floating away," should that student receive full credit on the exam for the one correct answer about gravity, or would the teacher need to be worried the student was merely covering all bases because the student apparently doesn't know for sure how, whether, or why gravity exists? For our purposes, if God wrote the Bible, why would He contradict Himself in it? Why would God not speak with certainty and specificity about things like the shape of the planet he created but instead allow a contradiction or inconsistency to exist, if He is in fact in control of all things? Another possibility is that God did not write or divinely inspire the Bible and that it was written merely by fallible men. If so, perhaps God could still be God without necessarily being the one who wrote every word of the Bible.

Where does this leave us? If we go back to the text of Genesis 1:1, the creation of only the earth and the heaven, could it be that the only reason that "the heaven" and "the earth" are mentioned is simply because they were the only two things in the universe visible to the naked eye of a person writing at that time? Surely, God, as the creator of everything, would have been aware of His own creation and would have been able to correctly and consistently describe not only the correct shape of the earth but also the many biblically ignored elements and characteristics of our universe.

Chapter Eighteen

But the Bible Is Not a Science Textbook

I understand that the Bible is not supposed to be a literal book of science. I also realize that the Bible is, at its core, religious literature that may have been given to us from God to provide us with rules and suggestions for life as well as spiritual guidance and a plan for salvation after death. But I am not the one who is saying that all of the claims about the earth and the universe and that everything else in Genesis can and should be taken literally as though they appear in a science book—fundamentalist believers are the ones saying that! In accordance with the literalists' views, when the text of Genesis makes certain audacious scientific claims about the creation of the universe, that text ought to be able to withstand some equally bold scientific and logical scrutiny. A literalist believer should not be allowed to put forth self-assured claims contained in Genesis as indisputable fact and then be allowed to run behind the protection of arguments such as "You have to spiritually understand that the Bible is not some science book" or "You don't understand because God has not opened your spiritual eyes; instead, Satan has fooled you with fallible science and questionable human logic" when confronted by logic that contradicts the literal claims from Genesis that they put forth. The Bible either is or isn't literally true. If religious believers are going to claim that it is literally true, they should stick to that by tolerating and responding to arguments against a literal interpretation with logical examples and interpretations of the words in the text.

My overall point is that the absence of a coherent, complete, and consistent explanation of our solar system, much less of the entire universe, suggests that not God but merely an ancient writer with a very limited knowledge of the universe was the one who wrote this first verse of Genesis. This passage does not seem to be the infallible work of the God who created the cosmos. Failing to mention the rest of the universe and the significant elements in it is a curious deletion for a book that is claimed to have been written or divinely inspired by God. This is especially true for a book that is noted for alleged detailed prophecies, the fulfillment of which is posited as "proof" that the Bible could only have been divinely inspired by God rather than written by mere mortals who would have been unable to accurately predict future discoveries and specific future events.

Some creationists, on the other hand, might admit that Genesis 1:1 does not explain the universe in scientific detail. They might go on to argue, however, that neither does the verse explain any of the most immediately obvious characteristics of the earth in any detail, such as the existence of rocks, dirt, lava, exotic plants, dinosaurs, etc., and that this omission obviously does not mean that such things do not or did not exist. In fact, we know they do or did exist. The difference is that the Bible acknowledges the existence of many of these elements of the earth at some point in later chapters and books. Moreover, it is important to note that the earthly elements that are eventually mentioned in the Bible are all things that still would have been *visible to the naked eye* of an ancient religious human writer.

So, although the Bible may mention things such as water, rocks, and mountains, it completely fails to account for *microscopic* elements on earth such as bacteria, viruses, atoms, molecules, cells, subatomic particles, and the like. Such microscopic elements definitely are a part of the earth, too, but obviously were not visible to the naked eye of the ancient writer. Once again, this kind of omission supports the notion that the writer never mentioned such things because the writer was simply unaware of them, even though the omniscient Creator of everything speaking through him certainly would have been.

Although the catchall phrase "every thing that creepeth upon the earth" is used later in Genesis (1:25), it does not specifically refer to microbiology as we know it but instead seems to refer to the huge number of insects, worms, spiders, and countless varieties of bugs that would have been easily observable without modern technology. It is obvious that the author of Genesis had neither a telescope to view distant galaxies nor a microscope to view microscopic elements and therefore could go no further in his explanation of the earth, so the question remains, Why would the true God of the universe, if He really wrote or inspired this verse, have been so limited in explaining His glorious creation? Why would God be able to include only that which could be seen from the earth by the naked eye of an ancient non-scientist? Again, perhaps it is because ancient human beings, rather than God, actually wrote the Bible. In short, maybe Moses really was like the Gary Larson *Far Side* cartoon of "Carl Sagan as a Kid"—not advanced enough to correctly and fully describe the true nature of the night sky he gazed upon.

With that in mind, imagine that you were given Moses's job of putting pen to paper (or ink to parchment or chisel to tablet) to transcribe the book of Genesis. Because God would be the one writing the substance of the book through you and because God cannot lie, you would be made aware of God's perfect knowledge about the universe. Thus, if you were given Moses's job, you would have been privy to the ultimate truth about the universe as known by God, *not* merely what the ancients thought about the nature of the universe thousands of years ago. For example, if you were aware of our solar system, of all of the stars and galaxies, of black holes, that the earth is a sphere, that Earth rotates on its axis, and that Earth revolves around the sun, ask yourself how you would have written these creation passages and described the universe and the earth in Genesis.

Do you think you would have written about it the exact way Moses did? Would you leave out much of what you would be aware of about the universe and the true nature of the cosmos as related to you by God Himself? Would you ignore that which you currently know about the universe even just from high school science? When one does this thought experiment, one often realizes that it does not seem like someone with complete and perfect knowledge about the universe—to the same extent God Himself would know about it—would describe the universe as it is described in Genesis.

Perhaps God had a very good reason for omitting a lot of this scientific information. People with little or no formal education and almost no understanding of science at the time would not have been able to understand these cosmological explanations even if God had tried to explain them. Although God does not lie, He could have left out information without being deceitful if He believed such information would leave the reader so confused or astonished that he or she simply could not make use of what God shared. As a result, perhaps God gave the most basic explanation of creation as possible so we would not get confused, especially if the details of how the universe was created are not relatively important or central to the overall spiritual concerns of the information He was imparting.

Consequently, maybe God wrote through the limited faculties of an uneducated author and did so for the least knowledgeable of God's present and past biblical audience. For example, maybe Satan took Jesus into space and around the globe to view all the kingdoms of the world but when God tried to explain this to the writers of the Gospels, they had so little understanding of space that they wrote simply "a high mountain" because they did not and could not understand it the way God may have explained it to them. So maybe the question for the thought experiment is not so much what you would have written were you Moses, but what you would have said to Moses, were you God.

In that sense, this explanation that God had to dumb everything down for us is plausible, although it also is a convenient rationalization for the Bible not being correct or complete beyond what human writers knew and could understand at the time of writing. Part of good writing and good communication is making the complex accessible and understandable to one's audience without simultaneously engaging in oversimplification and superficiality. I do not believe these high standards and expectations would be too high for God as a good writer and as a good communicator; after all, He is God! I therefore have some difficulty accepting such an explanation for Genesis because it reminds me a little too much of Jack Nicholson in the movie *A Few Good Men*, when he said, "You want to know the truth? *You can't handle the truth!*"

As we read later passages in Genesis, come back to this thought experiment and ask whether someone with even modern scientific knowledge (forget God's perfect knowledge) about the universe would write Genesis this way and describe the universe and the earth in the manner used in the first verses of Genesis. What does Genesis's simplistic account of our planet and our universe say about who must have really written the book of Genesis if a reasonably informed tenth-grade science student could write a far more complete and correct description of the universe, galaxies, black holes, gravity, comets, electricity, our solar system, magnetism, Earth, the moon, and our seasons than God Himself supposedly wrote in Genesis?

Chapter Nineteen

Why Were the Earth and Sky Created First, and Then the Rest of the Universe?

Why was the relatively *tiny step* of creating just the earth, in what would be a very distant and isolated part of the universe, taken first, only for our solar system, the Milky Way, and all of the other countless galaxies to be created later? Why wouldn't God instead create the universe all at once, especially if the universe is an example of His splendid, grand design? Recall that the sun and all of the stars were not created until the fourth day, in what seems to have been just a simple little afterthought explaining the existence of the nighttime lights Moses saw when he looked up: "[God] made the stars also" (Genesis 1:16).

Why would God be able to create the entire universe (if that is what "the heaven" means) in just one day but then need five more days to create other, much smaller and relatively insignificant, things associated with just the earth, such as an entire day for plants, or an entire day for animals, all of which are extremely small in comparison to the other things He supposedly created (unless He were also creating all plants and animals on countless other planets in the universe capable of supporting life, about which we are not specifically told)? Most exemplary of my point is the fact that on the fourth day, God managed to create sextillions of stars (and perhaps more), all of the planets, and all of galaxies of the universe and did all that in the same amount of time—one day—as it took Him to create just the earth and its atmosphere.

For that matter, why did it take God six days, as opposed to only one day, to create everything? Was it just too big of a job for God to complete in one day? Is that really the position of creationists who believe in an all-powerful God who can do anything? Consider the possibility that we have a God who can do anything but is limited to one major project at a time. There will be more on this later, but the idea is reminiscent of the old teaser challenging God's power: "Can God create a rock so heavy that even He can't lift it?" In this context, "Can God have a creation project so big that even He cannot complete it in just one day?"

Chapter Twenty

Why Create Such a Vast and Complex Universe if That Vast, Complex Universe Ends up Serving No Religious or Other Apparent Purpose?

It would appear from the Bible that with respect to the universe, God is mostly concerned with what is happening with humans on Earth. Almost all of the text in the Bible addresses human affairs on Earth and mostly ignores our vast physical universe other than Heaven and Hell, wherever they might be. If all that is necessary in God's plan is for humankind to be tested during our lifetimes on Earth, with the earth being the critical venue of everything, why did God bother to create anything much beyond the earth in terms of outer space and other galaxies? Everything else in our universe seems to form a colossal theological wasteland that is void of life and God's spiritual concern. Although Heaven is God's concern, the entire universe is not Heaven. For example, I would not be considered in Heaven simply because I was traveling in a spaceship to another galaxy where Heaven physically exists.

So, if the rest of the universe, beyond our sun and the earth, is theologically unimportant, and serves no apparent spiritual purpose, why did God bother to create such a huge and vast wasteland (or "waste-universe") that serves no purpose? Why waste an entire universe on nothing of any import (except for what happens on the earth)? Whatever purpose our universe might have outside of our life on the planet Earth and limited exploration of our own tiny galaxy, Moses seemed to be completely unaware of it when he wrote the text of Genesis.

Is the reference to the term "the heaven" just a reference to the sky above us, or does it also include the entire universe? The term "Heaven" in the Bible must at least include the space and atmosphere directly above the earth; if it did not, the Bible would fail to account for the obvious visible space immediately above the earth, the clouds, the blue sky, and the air that we breathe in our atmosphere. This much seems clear. Interestingly, in the Spanish language, the terms for "sky" and "Heaven" are the same, *El Cielo*. In English, however, the term "Heaven" is different from and encompasses more than does the term "sky." Moreover, the term "Heaven" obviously cannot logically imply the creation of the entire universe as we know it, because there were no light-producing objects at the point when God created "the heaven." That is, stars had yet to be created when Heaven was made; the sun and the other stars, the only light sources in the universe, were not created until the fourth day!

When God created "the heaven and the earth" on the first day, there were therefore no stars yet because stars obviously emit light energy. This means that the universe with all of its countless stars and galaxies did not yet exist either, unless all of the stars were created but somehow not yet "turned on" by God. It would defy logic, however, if a star, made entirely of burning gases that by definition produce heat and light energy, could exist if God had not created light yet, unless light already existed (Genesis 1:3 says, "Let there be light") and God was just letting already-existing light "be" at this later time somehow. But if so, then when, specifically, did light get created? How could light even exist if there were no sun and stars at that point, unless, for some strange reason—perhaps just to trick us to test our faith—God created light paths coming from stars that did not yet exist?

Once God created all of the stars, why are stars still being created, even today? Stars do not reproduce like animals or plants, but they do form, die, and reform. This all shows that the writer thought that the stars were created (past tense) at one time and then remained static throughout their existence. The writer did not realize that stars are continuously dying, and being created in an ever-expanding universe.

But again, is it possible for a star to even be a star if there is no such thing as light? It is true that black holes emit no light to the rest of the universe, but they still have light "in" them; it is just that the gravity is so intense in the black hole that not even light can escape it. Maybe in the beginning, the entire universe was a black hole, but then God expanded it to allow ("let there be") light—but there were still no stars yet in the universe, so where would that light have possibly come from? And if a black hole was the first thing that God actually created, why doesn't the Bible say so?

Based on these questions, the term "the heaven" appears to refer to only the sky above us and not to the rest of the universe as we know it. Because, according to Genesis, there was no light when "the heaven" was created and because the universe obviously contains light energy, given the trillions (perhaps more?) of stars that exist, the creation of "the heaven" must have been the creation of the earth's atmosphere, excluding the star-riddled universe. Accordingly, there is no explanation of the rest of the entire universe simply by the use of the term "the heaven." This suggests that the writer ignored the rest of the universe because the writer was completely unaware that the rest of the universe even existed and consequently did not, and could not, include any rational, coherent, and complete explanation of it.

In contrast, perhaps when God said, "Let there be light," after creating just the physical space of the universe with no stars in it, He was creating our sun as a special star and then He created all of the other sextillions of stars on the fourth day (after He had created land and water on the second day and plants on the third day). The sun is not simply light and nothing else, however. Although the sun may *produce* light, the sun itself is much more than that. What if, instead, the Bible said, "Let there be warmth"? Would that have been a correct description of the creation of the sun, or would it be just a description of one of the byproducts of the sun? Perhaps the description of the sun should have been something like "Let there be fusion of various gases that can produce sufficient light and heat energy to make life as you will come to know it possible and sustainable on Earth." At least that would have been a more complete, and arguably better, description of the sun. In any event, light is merely a byproduct of the sun but is not the sun itself. "Let there be light" referring to the creation of the sun requires our assumption about what God must have meant, but not what the Bible literally says, especially if the sun was not created until the fourth day with the moon and the stars, according to Genesis.

Chapter Twenty-One

How Could There Even Be the Concept of a Day if There Were No Sun Yet?

We are told that the heaven and the earth were created on the first *day* ("in the beginning"), but how could there have been a day if the sun had not yet been created? A day occurs only because the earth is a sphere that rotates on its axis approximately every twenty-four hours as it orbits the sun and receives daylight for a specific period. Maybe the term "day" in the Bible is referring to something different than the day (or night) as we know it. Or perhaps a day in the Bible is more than twenty-four hours. Or perhaps a day really should be thought of as only twelve hours, and a night should also be thought of as twelve hours—although such an even split between day and night would happen only twice a year (fall and spring equinoxes), and even then only at the equator. Otherwise, depending on the season and the location on the earth, day and night would be of various periods that would always add up to approximately 24 hours, with days being much longer in the summer and much shorter in the winter. But still, how can there be a day if there is no sun?

Whenever a day became a possible thing (I guess it would really have to be on the fourth day, when the sun was created, if we interpret "day" literally), the Bible contains some conflicting notions about how long a day is, or it at least distinguishes how long a day is for a human compared to how long a day is for God. In the New Testament, II Peter 3:8 suggests that a day for God is equal to 1,000 years for us: "But, beloved, be not ignorant of this one thing, that one day is with the Lord as a thousand years, and a thousand years as one day." But when is "day" supposed to be interpreted as 1,000 years and when is it just twenty-four hours (or twelve hours)? For example, in the New Testament, Jesus was crucified and then arose three days later—so was it three twenty-four–hour days later, or was it 3,000 of our years later? If a day is 1,000 years, then Jesus would not rise for almost another 1,000 years. This leaves Easter, arguably the most important religious holiday in the Christian faith because it is the celebration of Jesus's resurrection, a celebration of an event that would not yet have happened.

Some Christians interpret the seven days of creation as really 7,000 years of creation, making the earth at least 13,000 years old (7,000 years to create plus 6,000 years of biblical Earth history), which is at least closer to the 4.5 billion years old that scientists think the earth is, or to the 13.7 billion years old they think the universe is. Asserting that the seven days of creation actually took 7,000 years is a bit of a problem when asserting a strict literal interpretation, however. How are we supposed to know when to interpret a day as a God day—1,000 years to us—and when to interpret a day as a human day—twenty-four or twelve hours to us? Whether a day equals approximately 12 hours, 24 hours, or 1,000 years, from where does one claiming to be strictly interpreting this text get that extra information to make sense of the text? Perhaps we are supposed to just interpret the text so it makes sense logically, but if an interpretation would cause a logical impossibility, would that mean that it must be the wrong interpretation, or would it still be correct because with God, despite any logical impossibility, "all things are possible," as we are told in Matthew 19:26: "But Jesus...said unto them, With men this is impossible; but with God all things are possible"?

So if sometimes a day equals 1,000 years, if one interprets it this way when reading Genesis, did it take God seven God days (7,000 years) to create the universe? If so, that would mean that God created all of the plants and vegetation on Earth on the third day (from years 2,000 to 3,000) but did not create the sun until the fourth day (years 3,000 to 4,000, when God also created the moon and the stars). So, did some plants exist on Earth for 1,000 years without the sun, surviving on some other source of energy, and then later evolve the ability to photosynthesize sunlight? Or, as discussed before, did Moses not realize that the sun is a star and thus referred to the sun as "light," in which case the sun was created on the first day before the plants were? And when God rested on the seventh day, did He really rest and do nothing for 1,000 years? Along the same lines, after Noah built his ark, did it rain for forty days and forty nights, or did it rain for 40,000 years? If I definitively choose any of these interpretations, would I be engaging in a legitimate literal interpretation of the Bible or in my own illegitimate private interpretation?

Chapter Twenty-Two

Is Heaven a Physical Place, or Is It a Spiritual or Conceptual Place?

There is one more aspect of the term "the heaven" I want to explore. "The heaven" includes not only the sky but also apparently refers to the place where God and the angels reside—we should not ignore the angels. It is unclear, however, if Heaven is supposed to be a physical place where God actually resides, where, for example, we conceivably could travel in a spaceship if God would allow the spaceship to enter, or whether Heaven is just a spiritual place where God conceptually resides, where we could *not* physically travel in a spaceship, even if God would allow us to enter, because it would exist in a completely different dimension.

The issue can be a little unclear because Heaven can be referred to in many ways. II Corinthians 12:2–4 says, "[2] I knew a man in Christ... [3] [who] was caught up to the third heaven... [4] [and]...he was caught up into Paradise." So there is not just Heaven but possibly a first, and a second Heaven, and then a "third" Heaven, which seems to be different than Paradise. Are these places what is meant by the plural "heavens," or are these terms synonymous with one another? Whatever they may be, are they *physical* places or *spiritual* places? While we are at it, the Gospels also refer to "the Kingdom of Heaven" (Matthew 3:2; 4:17; 5:3, 19–20) and the "Kingdom of God" (Mark 1:15; Luke 6:20, 22)—are they the same or different?

Either way, it seems to diminish God to think of Him as residing someplace the same way I might reside in a house at a specific street address in my neighborhood. Is God really just living in a specific location in the universe, maybe sitting on a throne on a specific planet? The Bible implies in many references that Heaven is a physical place where God and the angels actually reside, where Jesus is seated at the right hand of God. (See Mark 19:19: "So then after the Lord [Jesus] had spoken unto them, he [Jesus] was received up into heaven, and sat on the right hand of God.") If God is omnipresent, existing everywhere simultaneously, however, how can He ever be in just one specific place? Perhaps the Holy Trinity explains it: God the Father and God the Son, Jesus, are physically in Heaven while God the Holy Spirit is the only part of God that is actually omnipresent.

If it is just God the Father and God the Son who reside in a certain location called Heaven, are they really two distinct Gods with two distinct bodies, or are they the same God with two or three different alter egos? Does God essentially have a three-way split personality, or is He three separate Gods "unified" into one overall God? This concept of "The Holy Trinity" is important if we are to read the Bible literally and think seriously about what it must mean. This leads to the question, What else is there in Heaven? Is Heaven made up of just clouds, or are there structures, buildings, and houses or other living quarters there? If there are structures, does God live in at least three separate structures, one for each part of the Trinity, or is there just one structure where all three Gods live together as one God, sharing the same space? If they live in one structure, do they each have their own rooms? Jesus told His disciples:

> [1] Let not your heart be troubled: ye believe in God, believe also in me.
> [2] In my Father's house are many mansions: if it were not so, I would have told you. I go to prepare a place for you.
> [3] And if I go and prepare a place for you, I will come again, and receive you unto myself; that where I am, there ye may be also. (John 14:1–3)

It can be very revealing to think about these things in such a literal way because you see how difficult it is to not only figure out the important details but to also make the whole thing make logical sense, if that is even possible.

Speaking of Heaven, what will people actually do in Heaven? We may "be" with God, but be there doing what? Will there be any kind of work or any specific delegated duties and responsibilities? Many have wondered whether it would be incredibly boring in Heaven. What would we, or could we, do there? Am I being disrespectful even for just wondering?

What if someone wanted to do something that was not allowed in Heaven? Would anyone in Heaven even want to do something that is not allowed? Is it possible for someone in Heaven to sin? But how could that be, if sinning is not allowed once a saved human is in Heaven? If sinning is not allowed but someone elects to sin anyway, would that person then be sent to Hell? Or once a person has made it into Heaven, is that person in forever, regardless of any "sinning" or insubordination that may occur in the future so that once a person is in Heaven, that person can never be kicked out? If this is a non-issue because there is no sinning in Heaven at all, would it be because people who enter Heaven also then cease to have free will?

In contrast, if we have free will in Heaven but still elect *not* to sin, would it be only because we would have then become Godlike and simply would not choose to sin at all, like Jesus? In Heaven, do we therefore graduate, in a sense, and become equal to Jesus, who was perfect and never sinned? If we are not on the same level of goodness as Jesus in Heaven, yet there is no sinning in Heaven, then would it mean that we no longer have free will in Heaven to ever commit a sin? If God gave us free will on Earth so we ultimately could *choose* good over evil instead of being programmed like robots incapable of sin, then why would God turn us all into such automatons incapable of sin, with no free will, for eternity once we get into Heaven?

If we do become perfect with no sin, then it is very unfortunate for the history of all humanity on Earth that God did not make us this way to begin with, because there never would have been any sinning at all, with *not even an option* for us ever to have engaged in sin, and therefore, there would have been no need for anyone to ever go to Hell. All it would have taken was for

God to not allow the option of evil to enter His universe, as is apparently the case in Heaven (unless sinning is somehow still allowed in Heaven, even though Satan originally got kicked out for sinning). Finally, perhaps the free will to choose good over evil on Earth would be a more authentic choice for us if there were not such a horrible threat: the disincentive of burning in Hell for eternity if one fails to choose God. This leads one to ask whether there might be some who believe in God only because they are "scared straight"—that is, they believe only because they are afraid of Hell and want to hedge their bets with a "free pass" in the event the Bible as literally written is true.

Once we get into Heaven, will we be on par with God, on par only with the angels, or neither? It seems logical to assume that God would be at the top of the hierarchy in Heaven, but if angels serve God, would angels also serve humans who make it to Heaven? Or are humans in Heaven co-servers of God with angels? If not, would people then be below angels and serve angels as well as God? Could we enhance our status while in Heaven, or is our status based solely on how good we were while on Earth? Would we be compensated for our jobs and responsibilities in Heaven? If not, and everything is free in Heaven, do right-wing Christians think Heaven is a communist dictatorship where we all share and no one is greedy and we all work for the communistic good of everyone else? But if there is no work or toil in Heaven—it is Heaven, after all—what would we do all day, all eternity, when we are there? Would we just sort of hang around for all eternity and think deep thoughts and feel deep feelings like glorified monks? I don't know. Do you? Does anyone? Can anyone know such things?

Chapter Twenty-Three

But Why Even Assume That There Had to Be a Beginning?

An even bigger issue raised by the first verse of the Bible is the assumption that the earth and the rest of the universe had to have some grandiose, instantaneous moment in time when it all began ("In the beginning...") such that nothing could have been in existence before that majestic beginning moment. Even if God created everything as explained in the Big Bang theory or created everything in some master stroke that we cannot now imagine, the assumption is that there still had to be some sort of an ultimate beginning moment when everything, including life, and perhaps including time itself, must have begun.

A glaring question that logically should be asked regarding the "beginning of everything" idea, however, is, What was God doing *before* the grand act of creation, *before* this assumed beginning took place? Was He just frozen in time because time had not yet been created? The problem with the assumption that there had to have been an ultimate beginning moment is that no matter when any such beginning moment took place, in that moment just before it all began, there must have been something *already in existence* to make it all begin. If there was a Creator, then we can just keep reducing the time backward and asking, "Well, then who created that Creator?" and then, "Who created *that* Creator?" and so on. If one really thinks about it, however, one might find that a true beginning of time might be a logical impossibility—just like the end of time might be a logical impossibility if time goes on into infinity—but if infinity goes through time forever, should it not go on forever in *both* directions?

How can time be infinite in one direction (forward into the future with no end) and not also be infinite in the other direction (backward into the past with no beginning)? Even more profoundly, if everything must have a beginning, as creationists seem to assert about the universe, then when and how did God get His beginning? If God's existence is not infinitely backward in time, then what could have possibly been in existence *before* God existed? How is it logically possible that God Himself did not have a creator if *everything* must have a beginning in order to exist? How could God create Himself? Wouldn't that completely defy logic? In short, why do creation literalists assume that there necessarily was a beginning of everything? Indeed, maybe there is no need to determine when life began, because life, in some form or other, may always have been in existence somehow, somewhere, in the universe from the infinite past.

Chapter Twenty-Four

Did Everything Except God Have a Beginning?

Creationists offer a huge exception when it comes to God. They state that God has "always been." (Revelation 1:8: "I am Alpha and Omega, the beginning and the ending, saith the Lord, which is, and which was, and which is to come.") The alpha and the omega are the first and last letters of the Greek alphabet—a *metaphor* used to show God's timelessness; however, even the most technical literalist would not argue that God is *literally* the first and last letters of the Greek alphabet! If the answer to our puzzle is that God has just "always been," that nothing created Him and He never had a beginning, then creationists do not actually believe that there really was not a specific instantaneous moment in time when *everything*, including time and life itself, began, because God Himself would have already been in existence. If we accept that proposition—that God had no beginning—then why can't we accept that the universe, like God, may also have always existed in infinite time backward forever without the need for an instantaneous moment in time when the entire reality encompassing the universe, including life, was created? The major point here is that if God exists without having first been created, then other things can also exist without having been first created—our universe, and even time and life itself, for example. Thus, the mere existence of the universe, or the existence of anything, does not necessarily mean that it had to have been created, and created by a God that we personally know. Big Bang proponents, however, really have the same dilemma, which I will discuss later.

Some creationists argue that although God has always existed, He exists more as a spirit concept or an idea than as a tangible, real entity with a physical body. Perhaps God is becoming conscious of Himself through our physical existence, such that the more we consciously realize God, the more self-aware God becomes. Maybe there is something to this nonentity concept of God. Perhaps God always has existed as an idea and, as such, needed no beginning, whereas a physical object, like a universe and everything in it, including life, still had to have been created at some point in order to *tangibly* exist. But if God is merely a spirit concept and not a real, tangible entity, then, in a certain sense, God does not really exist, at least not as a physical entity. Put more clearly, God exists, but only to the extent that any other purely mental concept or idea exists—God would exist more in the minds of those who acknowledge His spirit concept as a thought or idea than in those who don't. For example, beauty may exist as a *concept* outside of human existence, but it would not exist as a separate *entity* that can do things such as think, be self-aware, or create a universe with life in it.

Thus, although nonentity concepts such as justice, or fairness, can exist independently of human existence, they are nothing more than concepts that are clearly not self-aware entities. If God is not a self-aware entity but rather just a concept, then the theological tables are turned such that God did not create us but perhaps we created God as a construct of our own imagination. In this way, God being a mere concept does not bode all that well for the creationists' account of how God exists and created everything else. It is really very simple: Only real things are real, and imaginary things are not. As such, an imaginary thing, by definition, exists only in our imaginations, as a concept, and therefore, imaginary concepts as beings are not real, precisely because they are imaginary. At most, they are mental concepts that are not self-aware entities. In short, the concept of joy may exist, even independently from human existence, but it is not a self-aware, cognizant entity that can create a universe full of life.

Consider that sometimes young children have imaginary friends. Eventually, those children realize that their imaginary friends are not real, even if the children's psyches would like for their imaginary friends to be real. These imaginary friends are not real, at least not as tangible, self-aware entities, during the time the child allows them to exist in their minds as concepts, thoughts, or ideas. Accordingly, it really does not help to think of God as a mere concept or spirit idea instead of as a tangible, self-aware entity because if that is all He is, He could never "do" anything like create the universe. Also, God as a mere concept does not help to show that God did not need to have a creator in order to presently exist. If God is not a real entity that exists beyond an idea, then He is not real as a self-aware entity and therefore exists solely in our minds. If He is real and is an entity that can actually do things, however, then *when* was He created? Don't we need to know how He *started* as a self-aware entity that turned around and created everything else in the universe *if* we assume there must have been a beginning?

Let us assume that God is a self-aware, tangible entity that exists beyond a concept, thought, or idea and has so existed, since forever. Even if God were just spirit energy, or some kind of force, He would still be very real and tangible, like light, heat, or gravity are still very real and tangible forces, even though they lack physical bodies like people and are not physical objects (although light does contain photon particles and heat is fast-moving molecules). The key question is this: If God has existed since forever, then why can't the universe, like God, also be without a beginning? If God had no beginning, why can't the universe also have had no beginning and thus confound the assumption that the universe *necessarily* must have had a creator in order to exist?

Perhaps the universe and time always have existed in an infinite cycle of contraction and expansion and will continue to always exist in some such form, no matter how drastically it might change throughout time. Scientists today might be hopelessly distracted by trying to figure out the ultimate beginning of the universe while the reality might be that it never really had a beginning. It may be false dilemma in that scientists are simply failing to see the possibility that the universe, like God, might never have had an ultimate beginning.

If there was a beginning, however, and if absolutely nothing was happening before time began, then how could anything have ever started time? It is truly an epic, cosmic chicken-and-the-egg type of question. For something to happen, time must already be in existence, because the word "happen" refers to an occurrence taking place at a specific instance *in time*—so can time ever really start and thus change the status quo from nothing into something, if time needs to already be in existence for any change in the status quo to occur via a sequential measurement of time? In this sense, time would have to be infinite backward, because wherever the starting point would be, no matter how far back it may go, time already would have needed to have been in existence at that point for there to be any *change* in the status quo. The status quo would have had to have changed from existence *without* time to existence *with* time.

Chapter Twenty-Five

Science Also Assumes That There Was an Ultimate Beginning

I have often wondered why scientists, like creationists, assume that there must have been some kind of absolute, ultimate beginning. Most scientists believe the universe is at least 13.7 billion years old, based on the radioactive decay from when the Big Bang occurred, but *why* have they been trying to discover an alternative beginning theory of the universe to rival the biblical account of creation? It might be because the universe is expanding and has been doing so for billions of years. Because the universe is expanding, scientists assume it must have started expanding at some particular point in the past after a big explosion or big expansion, which is just assumed to be the creation of everything. This is where we get the Big Bang theory.

It is interesting, however, that the expansion of the universe is apparently speeding up, not slowing down. This speeding up runs counter to the idea that the universe originally blew up or expanded in the Big Bang; if the universe began this way, it should now be slowing down because of gravity and slowing inertia, not speeding up. This is true unless there is some reason, other than or in addition to the original inertia from the Big Bang, why the expansion is speeding up. For example, dark energy may be expanding the universe from within. Although dark matter may also be what is still holding the universe together (because there is not enough recognizable matter alone to create enough gravity to hold it all together); we just do not know.

We do know, however, that the universe is currently expanding. In the 20th century, renowned astronomer Professor Edwin Hubble discovered this phenomenon by analyzing the color of the light waves being emitted from all of the galaxies in the universe. If light is coming from a galaxy that is moving *toward* us, that light has a blue wave in it. If the light is from a galaxy that is moving *away* from us, it has a red wave in it. The interesting thing is that all of the galaxies in our universe have red waves, called "red shift," meaning that they are all moving away from us and from each other!

This blue wave-red wave phenomenon is similar to the Doppler Effect with respect to sound. Imagine hearing a car, while you are standing still, coming toward you, then going by you, and then speeding away from you. As the car comes near, it is "pushing" the sound waves, making them shorter and thus producing a higher pitch because the sound waves are getting bunched up, but as the car goes by and then moves away from you, the sound waves become longer (they are "pulled" or "stretched"), which produces a lower-pitched sound: A car going by sounds like "vaaaaaaaaroooooom." Similarly, when looking at galaxies, instead of seeing blue light waves, we see only red light waves. The red shift we see thus suggests that we are all, in a sense, driving away from one another in the universe—and the further away a galaxy is from us, the faster the movement away from us appears to be. It is also possible that the space between galaxies is still expanding, which would make galaxies that are further away seem to be moving away faster than closer galaxies,

How can all galaxies simultaneously be moving away from one another if we all started in the Big Bang—shouldn't there at least be some stars and galaxies that are moving toward us, or at least with us? If all galaxies are moving away from us, could it be that we are at the center of the universe, as the epicenter of the Big Bang? Probably not; it helps to think of the Big Bang like a bicycle wheel. Let's say the hub of the wheel is the Big Bang and the spokes are the trajectories of various galaxies and other objects that are spreading out from the position of the original Big Bang. The spokes are getting farther apart as we progress from the hub of the wheel to the rim. Thus, two galaxies traveling at exactly the same speed from the hub will always be at exactly the same distance from the hub (traveling, for example, on adjacent "spokes") even as they move away and apart from each other.

Also, as galaxies move farther away from the epicenter of the Big Bang, they speed up, so the galaxies in front of us are moving away from us faster than we are moving, and the galaxies behind us are not moving as fast as we are (so we are also moving away from them faster than they are moving toward us). In addition, all other galaxies are moving away from us in various directions (thus all displaying the red-shift light waves that we see throughout the universe). It may also be that galaxies are speeding up as they all move away from each other because there is not enough gravity in the universe to hold everything together and so it becomes easier to move faster as the gravitational pull of all of the matter in the universe weakens. At some point, maybe there will not be enough matter, and therefore not enough gravity, to hold it all together, and as a result, the entire universe will rip apart. We do not know yet. Again, maybe the mysterious dark energy and dark matter are holding the entire universe together—or they could be what will eventually help to tear it apart.

For whatever reason, all galaxies in the universe appear to be moving away from one another, as evidenced by the red-shift light waves (with notable exceptions, such as the Galaxy "Andromeda," which may collide with our Milky Way Galaxy in 3-5 billion years). Before these findings about the red shift were confirmed, the Big Bang theory had caused a raging debate between Big Bang theorists (who believe in a grand explosion or immediate expansion of dense matter and energy to begin the universe) and Steady State theorists (who believed the universe has always existed in the state in which it currently is) in physics during the early part of the 20th century. The Big Bang theory eventually won out as the prevailing theory because scientists found a cosmic "smoking gun" of sorts—the residual heat and energy flowing in the universe from the Big Bang—plus the fact that the universe is definitely expanding. The fact that almost all galaxies are moving away from one another suggests that in the beginning, they were created by a giant explosion, so the Steady State theory fell into disfavor because the universe is obviously not in any kind of steady state but rather is dynamic and constantly changing and, as we now know, continually expanding from what apparently was a huge explosion.

Perhaps the mistake of the Steady State theory was not the basic notion that there was never an ultimate beginning to the universe. Instead, however, maybe the mistake was simply in assuming that the universe always has been in a calm, static, unchanging, steady state. Assuming there was a Big Bang, that giant explosion does not necessarily prove that the Big Bang was the beginning of everything, even time, space and the universe. Instead, perhaps the universe has been *perpetually* expanding and contracting since infinity into the past and will keep doing so into infinity in the future. Perhaps the extremely violent contraction and the Big Bang explosion completely wiped out all trace evidence of any previous universe(s). Maybe there has been more than one Big Bang, and perhaps there now is no proof of anything before that Big Bang other than our completely reconstituted, "new" and current universe, which has wholly new laws of physics that completely confound the physics of pre-Big Bang universes (and future post-Big Bang universes).

As a result, consider that the current expansion of the universe might be, cosmologically speaking, a recent phenomenon. Perhaps we have been having big bangs throughout time in an infinite cycle of contraction and expansion. If this is true, maybe the current expanding universe at some point will stop its expansion and start contracting. In this case, the universe might eventually violently converge on itself only to blow up once again in another big bang—reconstituting everything as we know it and recognize it—and keep on doing so in an infinite cycle of expansion and contraction.

In contrast, perhaps the expansion will be infinite. The expansion could be speeding up, not slowing down, but a new universe may begin when our current universe is eventually ripped apart. Either way, perhaps our universe is part of an infinite cycle of new universes created within old ones. We, of course, cannot say for sure one way or the other, but the question remains: Why must there necessarily be an ultimate beginning of everything and, for that matter, an ultimate end of everything? In short, is it possible that the Big Bang was the beginning only of our *current* universe and that we cannot detect earlier possible universes because no detectable evidence of them remains?

It appears that scientists, atheists, and creationists alike all seem to think or believe that there is never going to be an end of time or an ultimate end of everything. Maybe our sun will eventually supernova and destroy the earth, but it will not destroy the entire universe or time itself. Even if all of the energy in the universe eventually burns out, so that the universe comes to a very cold, still "end," the matter and time making up the universe might still remain in some form, until another universe is "created" or a parallel universe starts all over (again). Indeed, maybe there have always been perpetually newly created universes for infinity into the past and they will exist in some form through infinity into the future.

We seem to be able to somehow grasp that there may not be an end to everything, but that there may be no beginning to everything is a much more difficult idea to fully conceptualize. This no-beginning concept appears to be very difficult for us to grasp when we are surrounded by beginnings for everything that we know and understand. Somehow, grasping the idea of infinity and the concept of no end of time appears much easier for us to comprehend and readily accept because we are, at least, already here. We can imagine that it can just continue like so forever, but grasping that it has always been seems to boggle the mind. This difficulty may be psychological to some degree; our evolutionary tendencies may prefer beginnings, as they represent birth, resurrection, and passing our genes, whereas endings represent death, destruction, and the loss of the ability to pass our genes. Could it be that we see an ultimate beginning as positive but an ultimate end as negative and we therefore cannot abide the idea of an ultimate end? We know we had an ultimate beginning at birth (unless we believe in preexistence), but we don't want to face the fact that we have an ultimate end (and perhaps that is why we created the concepts of Heaven and everlasting life). Hence, many religions have us survive in some afterlife after physical death; perhaps far fewer religions contemplate a personal existence prior to physical birth (our beginning).

The transition from nothing to something and then from something back to nothing is not only difficult to fully comprehend, but makes one wonder if such transitions are even possible. In other words, although we know that there is now definitely something—because we are here and we are now experiencing the reality that is our universe—is the complete state of nothingness, either before or after the something that we know, even possible? Can something exist after nothing, and can nothing exist after something?

According to the first law of thermodynamics, it is impossible to either create or destroy energy; all that can be done is to *change* energy's form. If all energy can do is change, not be created or destroyed, however, how can these transitions involving the wholesale creation and then eventual destruction of all energy everywhere be possible? This law, of course, applies in a "closed" system, and the universe may be an "open" system—although if the universe is not infinite, then perhaps it might be "closed." If the universe is a closed system, or even if it just behaves like a closed system, then this first law of thermodynamics would mean that these transitions would be impossible.

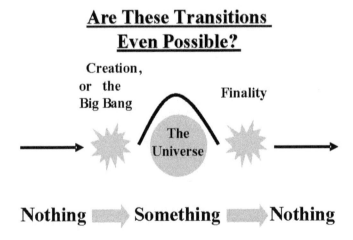

Are These Transitions Even Possible?

Although it seems like the universe should not all just end at some point in the distant future, the second law of thermodynamics posits that entropy (or, loosely, disorder) is forever increasing and thus, the universe is "winding down." Creationists often use this argument to attack the theory of evolution, saying that things are not getting better (evolving) but they are instead getting worse (devolving). Although taken to its logical extreme, everlasting life into infinity would be impossible if devolving entropy is the inescapable scientific death sentence of our universe, perhaps when this winding-down period gets to a certain critical point, it implodes and the whole big bang process starts all over again. Maybe the universe is "alive" as a huge entity, so even if it "dies" (runs out of energy) another life form universe will just take its place.

In terms of an ultimate beginning, however—in which the state of nothingness would have existed—how could there have ever been no mass or no matter whatsoever and then, all of a sudden, there was mass and matter—something literally out of nothing (*ex nihilo*)? It is not simply that mass and matter were very dense (referred to as "singularity") and then exploded or expanded very quickly in the Big Bang but that they didn't exist at all. Where, then, did that dense mass and matter come from to then be expanded by energy, which supposedly cannot be created or destroyed but only changed? According to the All about Science Web site (http://www.allaboutscience.org/first-law-of-thermodynamics-faq.htm):

> In its simplest form, the First Law of Thermodynamics states that neither matter nor energy can be created or destroyed. The amount of energy in the universe is constant—energy can be changed, moved, controlled, stored, or dissipated. However, this energy cannot be created from nothing or reduced to nothing. Every natural process transforms energy and moves energy, but cannot create or eliminate it. This principle forms a foundation for many of the physical sciences.
>
> The First Law of Thermodynamics is one of the absolute physical laws of the universe. Everything in the entire universe is affected by this law, as much as time or gravity. There are three Laws of Thermodynamics. The Second Law (Increased Entropy) and the Third Law (Zero Entropy at Zero Kelvin) are dependent on the First Law and each other. Together, these laws form part of the baseline for all modern science. No exceptions or contradictions to these laws have ever been observed.
>
> Energy that enters a system must either be stored there or leave. A system cannot output more energy than it contains without an external source of more energy. This energy can be in work, heat, potential, or kinetic form. On a small scale, this can be explained this way: "Change in internal energy equals the difference of heat transfer into the system and the work done by the system." On a large scale, this Law is still observable. Oceans and planets and solar systems all operate under the control of the First Law of Thermodynamics.

So perhaps there was no beginning in the sense of one ultimate, absolute beginning. Even if we assume singularity and then the Big Bang was the ultimate beginning of our *current* universe based on the fact that our universe appears to be continually expanding, that may not necessarily lead to the conclusion that we can measure when time began. That we can measure the movement of a comet as it approaches or moves away from the sun, for example, does not necessarily mean that the comet has *always* been moving in that particular direction and at that speed and rate acceleration since the beginning of time. It would be incorrect to think that the comet has always been speeding toward the sun since the beginning of time just because we can now measure its *current* movement toward the sun, even if it is currently speeding up, not slowing down, and has been doing so since "the beginning." If we could stick around long enough, the comet might eventually reverse course and then speed away from the sun and the entire solar system on its continual, infinite trajectory. Although a comet may be a bad example, as it often has a localized periodic course (similar to the earth's course around the sun) whereby from our point of view the comet continues along a period path (e.g., Haley's comet, which revisits us every seventy-odd years) but travels with us in a galaxy that is constantly moving away from the center of the Big Bang at the same rate that we are, the overall point about a perpetual cycle is what is important. We should not assume that movement or expansion in a certain direction unavoidably means that there was nothingness beforehand as that trajectory necessarily measures time, or at least "the beginning" of time.

So, perhaps the Big Bang created *this* universe but not a universe that may have existed before our current universe and that was itself created in a similar or even a completely different manner than was our current universe. Thus, although the Big Bang may have been a significant start of something *different*—the universe as we now know it and are experiencing it—it might not have been the *absolute* beginning of everything, because perhaps there was something here before (another universe of some sort) that we cannot now conceptualize, measure, or detect in any way. That we cannot now detect it does not necessarily mean it never could have existed.

Returning to the comet example, it would be a mistake for us to assume that the comet has *always* been moving along the same path toward (or away from) the sun in only one direction, the direction in which it is currently travelling, since the beginning of time simply because that is all we can currently measure. The problem is that we do not know how many times the comet has revolved around our solar system. Such is the case with any cycle; no matter how long it may take, it can continually repeat into perpetuity. Thus, although the universe's current expansion is all in one direction and is even speeding up, and this is the entirety of what we can measure at present, we do not know if that expansion might just continue forever or one day start on some kind of return cycle of contraction in which everything in the universe becomes a dense microscopic speck and then spectacularly expands again in yet another big bang. There is no physical proof of such a cyclical expansion and contraction at this time, and I suppose there *could never* be proof if the previous universe is completely destroyed with no trace evidence and everything begins anew with a big bang. Accordingly, perhaps the only logical "proof" of previous universes back through infinite time is simply the fact that time, by definition, could not have "begun" in a truly ultimate sense, considering that things like matter and energy cannot be created from nothing—so perhaps the imagined state of complete nothingness is really impossible in light of the fact that there is now something.

Based on the scientific premises just discussed, time is likely infinite in both directions—both past and future, forever—and perhaps is infinite in terms of physical space too. If we live in a house in a city in a state in a province in a country on the earth in our solar system in the Milky Way in our universe, and so on, why should that expansive progression of physical space stop there, with that last category called the universe (can there even be a "last category")? In fact, maybe it is even incorrect to say we live in "the universe" (singular), because maybe there are an infinite number of universes such that we actually are inside of some grandiose multiverse consisting of an infinite number of universes. This all leads to the possibility that both space and time are infinite in all temporal and physical directions so that there never was a complete state of nothingness out of which God created something, or out of which the universe somehow created itself. Instead, maybe there always has been something and there always will be something, and that something is a multiverse made up of an infinite number of universes such as ours.

Some current scientific thinking posits that there was a beginning to the universe but that literally nothing caused that beginning, because it occurred spontaneously. Such spontaneous creation is said to occur at the level of subatomic quantum mechanics. In a book entitled *The Grand Design*, Stephen Hawking and coauthor Leonard Mlodinow suggest that new theories make the concept of a creator redundant: "Because there is a law such as gravity, the universe can and will create itself from nothing. Spontaneous creation is the reason there is something rather than nothing, why the universe exists, why we exist. It is not necessary to invoke God to light the blue touch paper and set the universe going."

Perhaps the assumption that there must have been a cause of creation can be discounted because the beginning of the universe could have just appeared naturally, without a specific cause. As stated above, there are examples of randomly occurring elements in quantum mechanics, but note that although those elements may appear on the scene spontaneously, the scene itself is *already in existence*. If something changes to a new form, that change does not necessarily mean it has been created from nothing. To the extent that the great scientist Stephen Hawking posits this theory, it is quite presumptuous of me to challenge his scientific thinking in this regard. Still, I guess if there are no sacred cows for me regarding religious theology in this book, then I should also question the current scientific thinking about the assumption that there must have been some ultimate beginning of everything. Of course, perhaps, even probably, I am wrong in all areas, but it is more interesting to at least venture toward challenging some conventional thinking, be it religious or scientific thought/belief, than it is just to accept things idly.

Chapter Twenty-Six

Challenging Both Religion and Science with This Infinite-Time, No-Beginning Idea

The notion of infinite time—there was never any beginning at all—is contrary to Genesis 1:1 because the Bible starts out by assuming that there was, in fact, a beginning, (at least for everything except God Himself). Infinite time is not a foreign concept in the Bible, however. In fact, infinite time is a concept taught in the Bible. The concept of infinity with no beginning is difficult to comprehend when one thinks deeply about it, yet creationists seem to casually attribute an infinite, no-beginning-and-no-end concept to God with little intellectual, metaphysical, or existential difficulty or fanfare.

Believers also assert that they will spend eternity in Heaven. They believe that they will have life everlasting into the future without end (and they believe the same holds true for poor "unsaved" nonbelievers who are to be tormented in Hell forever, without end). If there is life everlasting forward into infinity as the Bible teaches, however, then we should ask why infinite time could not also extend *backward* in time such that there really is no beginning of time, just like there is no end of time. If we can live forever in Heaven, how can creationists claim that there is no possible way the universe also could have existed since forever?

One can analogize a timeline of the entire universe and God with a simple number line in math. If there is no such thing as the last number because one can always just *add* another number to that current number all the way to infinity, then there also should be no such thing as the first number, either, because one can always just *subtract* a number from that current number all the way to infinity. Even if one argues that 0 is the first number, the designation of zero as the beginning becomes meaningless once we acknowledge that numbers go on into infinity along an infinite number line in both directions—both positive and negative.

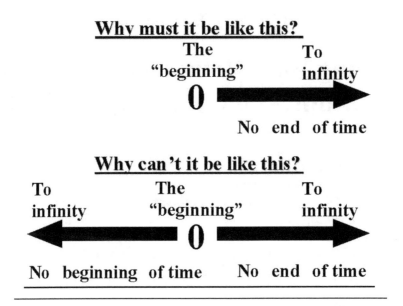

Indeed, there can even be an infinite number of number lines going in an infinite number of positive and negative directions (and maybe even in three dimensions, not just in the linear two-dimensional timelines, forward and backward), but some might argue that if time is actually infinite from the past, then it would be impossible for us to be here now (unless we are created to experience time in a linear fashion), even though time itself is non-linear and indeed is infinite in any direction.

The idea is that if time is infinite backward, we could never be at the point at which we are now, because if time goes back infinitely, then time literally could have never gotten here—to where we are now—and thus we could not, and could never, be here. But that there is never a beginning or an ending of time does not mean that we can *never be anywhere* at all along that infinite timeline—because we can be where we are right now, both coming from infinity and continuing into infinity. In short, we have to be *somewhere* in time—somewhere on the infinite timeline—or at least be experiencing ourselves as being somewhere in time. That a timeline is infinite backward does not mean that one cannot move at some point, somewhere, along that infinite timeline.

Stated differently, the number 0 is just a positional idea for the person who is doing the counting. Zero is an arbitrary number that is nothing more than the designation point of a particular position along an infinitely expanding timeline in both directions. No matter where one may be on the timeline, one will always be just as far away from the beginning as from the end because with infinity there really is no beginning and no ending.

This simple observation that perhaps there never was a creation is a direct challenge to the argument used by creationists when they attempt to prove how there must have been a creator because "the creation itself proves the existence of a creator." Actually, the existence of the universe does not *necessarily* prove a creator. Why? Because just like God's very existence does not *necessarily* prove that God must have had a creator (and creationists acknowledge that God did not have a creator), the universe's existence also does not *necessarily* prove that the universe had a creator, either; instead, both God *and the universe* (both current and past) could have always been in existence since forever.

Chapter Twenty-Seven

Do the Order and Majesty of the Universe Prove That It Must Have Been Designed by a Creator?

The notion of intelligent design is the creationists' attempt at a scientific argument to support creationism. The intelligent-design argument is based on the assumption that a higher order of being such as humans cannot simply appear but instead must have had a creator or an intelligent designer. This is also the creationists' argument against the theory of evolution. Evolution, however, does not purport, and never has purported, to be a theory about how the universe *began*; rather, it is a theory limited to how already existing life-forms on Earth can adapt, change, mutate, survive, and successfully reproduce through natural selection and other processes over vast periods of time.

Intelligent-design theorists argue that life-forms had to have had a creator, as only a creator can make things appear from nothing. If God exists but did not Himself have a creator, however, then His existence *without a creator* violates intelligent-design theory because, according to this theory, nothing in the universe, especially something fairly complex, can exist without an intelligent designer. It is therefore not necessarily self-evident solely from the existence of the universe that there must have been a creator of that universe, because if everything must have a creator, then so must God, which leads to the question: Who created God, the supposed creator of everything else? Isn't God's self-evident complexity proof that a creator must have intelligently designed Him; for God could not have just appeared out of nothing as some random accident, right?

The idea of infinite time backward, coupled with God's existence, though He lacks a creator, poses a huge logical problem for intelligent design as a legitimate explanation of how the universe began. This notion that God did not have a creator (a position firmly held by creationists) undercuts the whole notion of intelligent design as a *scientific* theory of how the universe necessarily must have begun. Intelligent design is actually an outgrowth of creation science, which courts of law already have determined was merely religion masquerading as science and therefore could not be taught in public schools as an alternative scientific theory. When courts struck down creation science some years ago, members of the group changed the name from "creation science" to "intelligent design theory." They then attempted to get their theory taught in public schools as science. The courts, however, were wise to the attempted substitution and resurrection and once again struck down intelligent design in the *Dover* case. (See *Tammy Kitzmiller v. Dover Area School District*, 400 F. Supp. 2d 707 (M.D. Pa. 2007), holding that intelligent design is not a scientific theory but merely a religious belief attempting to pass itself off as science.) The claim "God exists without being created Himself is just a religious mystery" is not a scientific argument, nor is it even a supportable rhetorical assertion.

Although redundant, it is worth restating in summary so we see what this argument looks like in its final form: If we accept God as a reality, then God is a very high form of complex being, certainly a higher form than, say, an amoeba. To use intelligent design terminology, God is "irreducibly complex." If even an amoeba had to have a creator/designer to exist as a complex organism life form, however, then certainly, God also had to have a creator/designer. God could not have just evolved out of nothing by accident (in fact, "accidental evolution" is a major argument used by creationists against atheists and evolutionists). If God did not have a creator, however, the whole theory of intelligent design falls under the weight of its own logic that says *everything* must have had a beginning and must have been intelligently designed, because God Himself exists without ever having been created and intelligently designed by some other earlier God. The essence of the debate is actually quite simple: Who or what intelligently designed God? If creationists assert that God has always been and therefore did not need a creator, that acknowledgment at least opens up the possibility that things, especially irreducibly complex things, do not necessarily need to have a creator in order to exist! The logical conundrum becomes impossible for creationists to escape, because to argue that nothing can exist without a creator means that God himself had to have some other creator or else God could not now exist—something that creationists obviously do not support.

If it is at least possible that the universe has always existed (or universes have always existed in some form or another), our current universe did not need to be created, and neither did life, which undercuts the intelligent-design theory that everything needed to be intelligently designed in the beginning in order to exist. God did not (and logically could not) create Himself ("In the beginning God [who obviously was *already alive and in existence*] created the heaven and the earth"). Besides, a creator who also creates Himself is a logical impossibility—if God were not yet in existence, how could He create or do anything before He ever was?

Even if a person subscribes to intelligent-design theory despite these logical concerns (perhaps rationalizing the lack of logic as merely "our puny minds cannot understand the complexity of God"), that person still must decide exactly *which* intelligent designer, out of the many possible candidates, he or she believes in, and why. This issue is not an officially recognized part of intelligent-design theory but is a logical extension and assumption made by the proponents of intelligent design. Would the creator be the Judeo-Christian God, or would it be Uranus or Thor or the Great Spirit of the Native Americans, or would it be a master race of space aliens who view us as nothing more than an experiment in their cosmic Petri dish? It is a little easier to understand this damaging critique of who created the creator when one assumes the creator is someone or something *different* from their own concept of the creator. As a result, there is also great disagreement as to *who* the intelligent designer, if there is one, would be, with absolutely no proof or reason as to whom or what it is. Creationists quickly become full-fledged "atheists" once it is assumed that the intelligent designer need not necessarily be the God of the Bible but could be some other intelligent designer. Intelligent-design theory as a scientific theory, of course, should not fall completely flat on its face just because one assumes that the intelligent designer is someone or something *other* than the biblical God, just as a mathematical or scientific formula should not succeed or fail as a logical principle based merely on the differing numerical data plugged into it.

It is beyond the scope of this book to recount all of the hundreds and even thousands of religions throughout the world and throughout history, each with its own creation stories and myths, but a quick sampling follows. Some Chinese believed there was chaos (whose name was Hun dun and who was zapped with lightning bolts for seven days), and from there, life was created. The Greeks believed that at first there was Mother Earth (called Gaea) and Father Heaven (called Uranus) and from them came a one-eyed Cyclops, powerful giants called Titans, the gods who lived on Mount Olympus, and, after some warfare, regular human beings. The Egyptians thought the world began as an ocean called Nun and that a sky goddess then pulled a mountain out of the ocean and the earth began. Hindus believed there was a dome-shaped Earth supported by six elephants that were standing on giant tortoises that were resting on a snake. Like the God of the Bible, who created a man out of dust and then pulled out one of his ribs and created a woman, none of these creators were ever themselves created but just sort of always were and then they started doing various things that led us to the present. For a list of and explanation of more than 3,000 worldwide gods and creation myth stories, see http://www.godchecker.com/.

Chapter Twenty-Eight

Even if There Were a Beginning, What Was God Doing before That Beginning Took Place?

Even if we accept the God exception as truth—that everything except God Himself had to have a creator and that only the God of the Bible was the intelligent designer—that still does not answer one other fundamental question. Consider the following thought experiment: Assume that God has existed forever but the universe has not. That proposition leads one to ask, What was God doing for all of this infinite time in the past *before* He created everything? Did He simply do nothing for eternity, literally forever? Are we to believe that God did nothing and there was no creation—no universe, stars, Heaven, or Earth, absolutely nothing—and God simply remained completely idle for trillions and trillions of years, and even more, for eternity, into the past? God simply did nothing in a void of nothingness forever until the recent past few thousand years?

Even if this is what took place before our universe began—an absolute void of nothingness for trillions and trillions of years (and then some)—how could God have been so frozen in time, and why would God suddenly (and logically somehow) unfreeze Himself in time? How is it rationally possible to create everything out of the total nothingness that had been void forever until approximately 6,000 years ago? The age of the earth is 6,000 years, give or take a few thousand years, according to the literal interpretations of the Bible and the Young Earth creationists. How did God first get into that frozen state inside of a universe that did not yet exist because nothing existed at that point? How or why would God do absolutely nothing, frozen in a void of total nothingness forever into the past, maybe just thinking deep thoughts?

Given that most believers assert that God is a conscious being, wouldn't He absolutely have been bored out of His Mind? Wouldn't God have simply gone mad with nothing to occupy his consciousness for eternity? If God has the power to see all of us at once and hear every one of our prayers and basically govern and run this planet and our species, what did God do to occupy such complex and powerful faculties all that eternal time in the past? Most importantly, why in the world would God have done nothing for so long? Why would He have done nothing, frozen in a void forever, but then suddenly, just over 6,000 years ago, somehow awaken to action and then create the entire universe?

Chapter Twenty-Nine

Is Our Universe Really Only 6,000 Years Old?

According to literal genealogy lines in the Bible, some of which are whole chapters in Genesis—in which each father begets a son, and that son begets another son, and so on, as each such generation is traced back—the Earth literally is only about 6,000 years old, or perhaps as old as 10,000 years, depending on how the generational counting is done. As a result, some literalist creationists believe that fossils that have been on Earth, according to scientists, for millions of years, are actually not millions of years old, and the universe with stars that appear to have been in existence for billions of years was created only 6,000 or so years ago.

How is that even possible, given that there are stars that are billions of light-years away from Earth and yet we can still see the light from them here on Earth? If the universe were really only 6,000 years old, we would not see the light from any stars more than 6,000 light-years away because the light coming from them could not yet have arrived here! In other words (according to science as we now know it), light cannot travel faster than the speed of light, so any light that we can see from a star that is more than 6,000 light-years away (and there are trillions of them that are billions of light-years away) suggests that the universe has been here for much longer than 6,000 years. In short, because we can see light that must be billions of years old, the universe must have been in existence for at least all of those billions of years.

This is a difficult argument to address if you are a Young Earth creationist who believes literally what the Bible implies regarding the universe being only 6,000 years old. But "with God, all things are possible," so the creationists could find a way out of this scientific dilemma with just this phrase. Maybe God sped up the light from these stars by using "warp speed," like on *Star Trek* or *Star Wars*, so that the light from a star a billion light-years away could still get here in less than 6,000 years! Or when God created the stars, maybe He created them with "mature" starlight, that is, with starlight that was *already in existence* and fully on its way to Earth and beyond, like creating an already flowing river instead of a water source that begins flowing and then eventually becomes a river in time. Presumably, however, there would also be some "immature" light from "new" stars arriving here from those stars that we cannot see at present.

Let us assume that God created all of the sextillions of stars and then simply warp-sped the light coming from them. This otherwise would be impossible because light cannot travel faster than light, but let's assume it is possible that light can travel faster than light if God says so. That is the thing with religious explanations—they can always allow God to violate His own laws of physics whenever necessary because, well, God is God and miracles are miracles. If one must artificially manipulate evidence and stand science on its head to make a metaphorical story plausible, however, one is not really "doing" science. Many scientists do, however, suggest that the speed of the expansion of the universe at the moment of the Big Bang was perhaps faster than light and anything else we know, while others suggest that nothing can move faster than light. Still, if the universe expanded so fast, perhaps time stood still while it expanded (if that is even possible and if it even makes sense, like time theoretically stands still at the "event horizon" near the edge of a black hole). Also, maybe we will find that some particles (like neutrinos) can travel faster than light as we learn more from supercolliders.

Another theory, however, could possibly reconcile the light from distant stars reaching Earth though the earth may be only 6,000 years old: Even if light cannot travel faster than light, we do not need for it to do so if we assume, because of the red-shift light waves we see being emitted from all galaxies and stars, that the universe is expanding as scientists assert. If we make the assumption that the space in the universe is itself expanding, then we need to take into account how space-time might be spreading, or stretching out, the universe (which perhaps could "speed up" the light traveling through that expanding space). It might be that by the time the light reaches us from a distant star, that star would be much farther away from us than when that light originally left because space-time had expanded during the light's journey. In short, by the time the light gets here from the star, that star now might really be much farther away.

For example, assume I am driving a car from New York to Los Angeles (which is about 3,000 miles away when I would first start in New York) but that the land between New York and Los Angeles is expanding along the way, so when I finally arrive in Los Angeles, New York is 10,000 miles away from Los Angeles—even though I would not have driven a full 10,000 miles to get there. Scientists think the universe is about 13.7 billion years old, but they also think that the universe stretches across at least 92 billion light-years of distance; this could only work out if the space in the universe has been expanding during the 13.7 billion years. If so, then the universe could have expanded such that light from a star that is *now* a billion light-years away may not have actually travelled all of the billion light-years of distance to get here.

The problem is that the land between New York and Los Angeles (or the universe) could not expand faster than I could drive the car (or that light could travel through the universe), or else I would never get to my destination—it would be as though I were trying to walk down an escalator that was moving up faster than I was moving down and thus I could never reach the bottom of the escalator. If there are stars billions of light-years away, it therefore cannot be that the light from them has been travelling to get here for only 6,000 years and the universe has expanded during those 6,000 years a distance of billions and billions of light-years. If that light had been travelling for only 6,000 years, but the universe had expanded by billions and billions of light-years of distance, that light could never have gotten here in the first place—at least not within 6,000 years—because that light's destination, Earth, would have been in space that had been expanding away from it much too fast. But, theoretically, we cannot add speeds to the speed of light.

Still, it is critical to understand that if the universe (space-time) is expanding, it is expanding in *all* directions, such that I would have to chase the destination point that is simultaneously racing away from me as a result of expansion even as the point from which I left is also expanding away from me. The universe would have had to expand billions of times faster than light can travel, and then mostly expand behind the light, not in front of it, for this theory to work!

But perhaps the light from such distant stars got to Earth in fewer than 6,000 years through a wormhole. A wormhole is a theoretical shortcut in both space and time. Imagine that the universe is a flat piece of paper with point A on one end and point B on the opposite end. Assume also that the entire length of the paper must be travelled to get from point A to point B. If the paper could somehow be bent or folded over so that points A and B are physically much closer to one another, and if a little tunnel in space (outside of the "universe" that is just the paper itself) could be made that would allow travel from point A to point B, that little tunnel (that is not part of the paper, the regular universe) would be like a wormhole in space-time where travel would be much shorter than going along the entire length of the paper to get from Point A to Point B in regular space time.

Not only could great distances be covered through such a theoretical shortcut, the wormhole, but time travel could also be possible if the paper represents not only physical space but also time. Of course, notice that the wormhole exists in a physical space "outside" of the paper itself, so to traverse through the wormhole, physical space that is not a part of our universe would have to be accessed (because the space making up the little tunnel shortcut is not within the piece of paper itself—our physical universe). In the larger argument of light being faster than light because it could have gone through a wormhole, even if the wormhole could have been accessed and traversed, the entire universe could not be a wormhole for all light in the universe from all stars to pass through in all directions.

One can imagine, though, that light was stretched because space-time itself was stretched. God somehow could have sped up the light from stars or expanded space-time so that we can now see the light from stars billions of light-years away simply as a way to trick us into thinking that the universe must be billions of years old. So maybe God did all of this on purpose because He simply wants to see if we will *still* believe what the Bible implies about the earth being only around 6,000 years old.

That is always a convenient argument, though. Any evidence suggesting that the biblical explanation about the universe is not true or is incomplete can be explained away by saying that such contrary evidence was actually put there by God *on purpose* to test our faith in the literal word of the Bible. It seems counterintuitive, however, to think that God, compassionate, loving, and honest as He is, would purposefully attempt to deceive us in that manner, saying "Thou shalt not lie, but sometimes I might need to lie just to trick you in order to test your faith." This is especially disturbing when there might be incredibly disastrous consequences, like burning in Hell forever, for a human being who falls for the trick simply because that person made a rational decision based on the available evidence and information about the universe (light from stars being billions of light-years away must mean that the universe is billions of years old if we can now see that light). Not only that, but according to the Bible, God cannot lie: "[I]t [is] impossible for God to lie" (Hebrews 6:18).

Chapter Thirty

Watch out for Tricky Tests

Before dismissing the fact that God might be tricking us or misleading us to test our faith, consider the story of Abraham and Isaac in Genesis, Chapter 22. Although Abraham dearly loved his son, Isaac, God commanded Abraham to sacrifice Isaac to the Lord—to kill him with a knife on an altar in a real ritualistic human sacrifice! Perhaps the most shocking thing about this is that Abraham agreed to do it. Moreover, Abraham's willingness to kill his own son was actually seen as a good thing. Accordingly, as a great act of faith and loyalty to God, Abraham was willing to kill his own son (not exactly a good example of family values, by the way), but just as Abraham was about to kill his son, an angel interceded and stopped him, apparently saying the biblical equivalent of "Never mind!" The demand for Abraham to kill his own son had all been just an elaborate test of Abraham's faith in God—and God was *pleased* with Abraham's willingness to *kill* his own *son*. Because Abraham showed himself willing to perform the murder, having Abraham actually go through with the killing was apparently not necessary for God at that point. One would think that Isaac probably breathed a great sigh of relief, too, once he learned that this whole death scenario did not have to be played out just to make a point to God!

If these events truly happened, shouldn't the lesson of the story be very different? Instead of passing God's test, Abraham's willingness to kill his own son as a sacrifice to God really meant that Abraham failed God's test because Abraham obviously did not know God and His character of goodness very well. Abraham was much too quick to believe that God could be as cruel and unjust as to actually demand the killing of an innocent boy by his father as a mere gesture of loyalty to God. Why would Abraham believe that God could ask such a thing in the first place? Why didn't Abraham think that this request must have been some kind of trick from Satan because the true God of Abraham would never engage in the barbaric practice of the human sacrifice of an innocent child just to prove someone's obedience? Satisfying such a demand by killing any innocent person would be an immature "what have you done for me lately?" kind of serious sin.

The interesting question is whether God committed a sin when He asked Abraham to do this. What would God think of me if I required that my son kill his pet rabbit just to prove that he loves me more than he loves his rabbit? Wouldn't that be a sin—a serious moral, ethical, and spiritual wrong—even if I stopped him just before he would kill his rabbit, satisfied that my son really must love me? What kind of psychological aftermath must Abraham have faced, knowing that he had almost killed his own son, not to mention the damage he had done to Isaac's mental health, just to make a point of his loyalty? How did this episode affect Isaac's relationship with his father, or does that not matter?

Was it not a failure of Abraham's faith because he did not stop and think for a moment, *Would God really ask me to violate one of the Ten Commandments?* [The commandments were still to be written at this point, but we assume that murder was a sin even though God had not yet officially said it was.] *Would God really ask me to murder my own son in a child sacrifice just to please His very demanding ego?* It seems like Abraham, quite wrongly, completely underestimated God by assuming that God would *actually* let him commit a cold-blooded murder-sacrifice of his own son, for whatever reason.

Of course, on another level, the story of Abraham and Isaac reads like ironic foreshadowing, given God the Father's willingness to sacrifice His own Son, Jesus Christ, thousands of years later to die on the cross for the world. God allowed Jesus's crucifixion for the sins of all of humanity, assuming that the wrongful death of an innocent somehow equals the forgiveness of sins for all of the guilty people in the world. Still, God's gesture was not stopped short. Instead, He actually went through with the sacrifice of His own Son. And Jesus was as innocent, even more innocent, than Isaac was, yet God the Father put Him to death for the sins of undeserving others. Also, Isaac and Jesus were both products of miraculous births: Isaac to an old and barren woman, Jesus to a virgin. Thus, Isaac can be seen as an archetype of Jesus and thus a necessary (not cruel) story for God to give a clue about the ultimate sacrifice (Jesus) who was to come later.

The sacrifice of Jesus, however, was different from what Isaac's sacrifice would have been in at least a couple of significant respects. First, Jesus rose on the third day and has been with God the Father, reigning in Heaven ever since. Would Isaac have been so lucky had he been sacrificed? Second, God the Father never really sacrificed someone else, because God the Father and Jesus are one and the same and God cannot actually die—whereas Isaac, if he had been killed by Abraham, would *not* have been resurrected on the third day to be with Abraham forever. Instead, Isaac would have died and would have remained dead. Still, perhaps this episode with Abraham and Isaac was just a foreshadowing of God's great love for us that He would actually sacrifice His own innocent Son, Jesus Christ, even for those three days.

There still remains a bit of a troubling, law-related issue—how Jesus's crucifixion somehow pays the penalty for all of the sins of humanity (or perhaps just for the sins of those who accept and are saved, because the rest of humanity that is not saved must still suffer in Hell and thereby serve out their own sentences). In law, if a criminal is charged and then convicted of, say, armed robbery and sentenced to ten years in prison, the legal system demands that the criminal *her- or himself* serve the time and suffer the punishment. If the criminal's father or mother, for example, offered to serve the ten years in place of the robber, the legal system would not engage in a simple substitution of bodies. Why? That would be seen as neither legal nor, more importantly, fair. It is not just that ten years of prison time must be served to the state by someone, anyone at all; instead, for the punishment and the sentence of the criminal to be meaningful, it has to be served by the guilty defendant himself, instead of just some proxy.

The punishment must be served by the actual perpetrator of the crime because it would serve no rational purpose to put the criminal's parent, or anyone else who was innocent, in prison for ten years to serve out the sentence. Two of the main reasons why we punish criminals are to deter them from committing another crime in the future, and to remove their liberty as an act of retribution against them, but these reasons are really not served by a substitution of parties. We accept this method of specific punishment of the wrongdoer (not just some proxy) as justice. So why are we so accepting of Jesus being punished for what we have done wrong, especially when He never sinned himself? Such a substitution, in which an innocent person trades places and takes the rap for some guilty person, would be, at best, the result of a very underdeveloped system of justice.

Even if this innocent-for-guilty substitution of persons were somehow deemed appropriate for serving a criminal sentence; that punishment at least would have to be for the same duration of time and involve the same amount of suffering. For example, if the innocent parent of the criminal were going to take the rap for his or her son and such surrogacy were fair, wouldn't that parent have to serve at least the equivalent sentence of ten years in prison and not just a few days under house arrest? To extrapolate, if every unsaved human being bound for Hell must suffer the torture of burning in Hell *forever*, which is a sentence of infinite duration in eternal pain, that is a much harsher sentence, at least in terms of time, than what Jesus had to endure for just three days (unless we weigh time differently for the suffering of an innocent deity than for the suffering of a guilty human being because perhaps even a microsecond of Jesus's suffering may equate to the suffering of all mankind in Hell for all of eternity). Although Jesus's suffering was great during that time and His crucifixion and everything leading up to it was horrible, the actual crucifixion of Jesus did not last more than a few hours and He was dead for less than three days before His glorious resurrection soon allowed Him to be back reigning in glory with His Father in Heaven. Remember that unsaved humans must go to Hell forever. These are two very different sentences if Jesus is supposed to have really taken the *entire* rap for us.

This does not necessarily present a contradiction, nor does it represent a denial of an immensely selfless act of love by God for humanity; it is just a surprising concept of justice to substitute one innocent, divine person, Jesus, as a proxy for the guilt of literally billions of humans throughout time, and then to substitute a sentence of a matter of a few hours on the cross and three days of death (even if they were spent in Hell) by Jesus for an infinite duration of suffering by humans (burning in Hell forever).

Pontius Pilate, the earthly judge of Jesus, allowed Jesus to be crucified even though he found no fault in Jesus. Given the relatively undeveloped concepts of crime and punishment at the time, however, Pilate had to let some guilty person go free in exchange to make Jesus's sentence seem fair, and that person was Barabbas. It is revealing that the act of substituting the innocent for the guilty, just as long as somebody, anybody, served the sentence, was considered a just result in the criminal jurisprudence of those ancient times. Although such interchangeability of persons and the swapping of their sentences of punishments was seen as legitimate in those times, it would not be anywhere near a legitimate administration of justice in a modern context.

Notice that much of what is written in the Bible is suspiciously reminiscent and reflective of the prevailing beliefs of people at the time it was written rather than what we might think God actually would believe beyond such historical conventions and trends. For example, as we discussed earlier, the conception of the universe is reflective of what was known at the time. This seems to indicate that the Bible was written by humans, not by God, and the same argument can be made here. The fact that God had a very similar sense of justice as the judges and people living at the time the Bible was written would seem to indicate that the writers of the Bible were people who projected their conceptions of right and wrong onto God. This contrasts with a Bible written by a God who might have described concepts more befitting a God who held ethical and moral beliefs independent of, divergent from, and, most importantly, superior to those of the people living at the time.

Going back to whether Abraham passed the test of faith that God had laid out before him, consider what Abraham would have done, or should have done, if God had instead demanded that Abraham *rape* his own son. Would Abraham still have been willing to do so because his faith in God was so strong, or would Abraham have said, "Wait a minute, is God really telling me to rape my own son just to prove a point about my loyalty to God?" Why would a demand allegedly by God for Abraham to rape his own son be so suspect when God demanding that Abraham kill his own son would not be?

It is true that animal sacrifice was a part of the culture and part of remission of sins and rape was not. Although ritualistic sex, as well as the sacrifice of virgins, is part of some religious traditions, there does not appear to be any such analogue for rape as proof of loyalty or remission of sin in the Judeo-Christian tradition. Murdering a human being is not just like the sacrificing of an animal in this religious tradition, however; and even if it were, how could rape somehow be a worse sin than a murder? In short, would we still revere Abraham had he actually been willing to rape his own son for God? If not, given the fact that God would never really ask someone to do such an immoral act (to rape one's own son on an altar to God), why should we revere the fact that Abraham was willing to murder his own son on an altar for God? Why should we believe that God would actually ask someone to perform such an immoral act in either case?

Lest we forget, however, God is God, and therefore He is able to do whatever He wants to do in this universe that is all His, including even tempting us with actual scientific evidence about the universe that might logically lead us to believe in the wrong thing if our faith in the Bible is not strong enough. But that is the troubling thing about religious faith: one can always play, or at least attempt to play, a pious supernatural trump card to account for any inconsistencies, improbabilities, or impossibilities in the Bible. If those problems do not make sense or cannot be logically or scientifically explained, one can always just say that the problem is there as a way to test our faith. This way, it still can make sense to a believer given that special caveat.

It is like a math problem involving undeniable logic but that can still be denied. For example, in math, 5 is less than 10 and 10 is less than 15. If, however, the Bible were to say that although 5 is less than 10, 10 is *more* than 15, a literalist believer in the infallibility of the Bible would simply believe that 15 must really be less than 10, despite the logic of math. Such a believer probably would assert something like the following: "God's math is more complex than our human math, so who are we to question God's math? After all, God created math!" And to explain why God would assert in the Bible that 10 is more than 15, such a believer might argue, "When we get to Heaven, God will explain why 10 is actually more than 15 in a way that our puny human brains now simply cannot understand at this point in time. Remember, God not only created math, He also created the mathematicians!" Such a believer might also reason that before scientists discovered calculus or black holes, calculus and black holes existed and consequently, God already knew what science had yet to figure out, and therefore mathematicians have just not yet figured out why, mathematically, 10 is really more than 15. Conversely, we might hear the rationalization that "God said 10 is more than 15 in the Bible, on purpose, just to test our faith and to see if we will trust Him no matter what, and so, like Abraham, we ought to, on faith alone, believe that 10 is more than 15 and accept it. Ours is not to question God but only to obey Him."

If the Bible asserted that 2 + 2 = 4, however, a literalist believer would quickly change gears and probably say, "You see how science and logic actually prove how the Bible is literally true and support the Lord's assertions? Praise God! The truth is right there, plain for all to see." In this last instance, God would not be testing our faith with a questionable assertion, although He might test our faith with questionable assertions in other contexts. In short, if the Bible asserts something like intelligent design, then so be it, but if so, we move away from a strict literal interpretation when we allow for *deceptive* intelligent design just to test our faith, given the Bible says God cannot lie. If we admit that God sometimes deceives us in the Bible just to test us, then we necessarily admit that the Bible sometimes is literally not true, so when the Bible says God cannot lie [Titus 1:2: "In hope of eternal life, which God, that *cannot lie* promised before the world began" (emphasis added)], does that statement, in essence, really mean that although God cannot lie, He can mislead us if He has a good reason to do so, such as testing our faith and testing our unquestioning commitment to His Word?

Chapter Thirty-One

More Tricky Tests

Of course, God's asking Abraham to kill his son just to test his faith and not really meaning that Abraham should have actually gone through with it, does not even begin to address why God has allowed such things as the fossil record here on Earth, evidence of an Ice Age as recent as 10,000 years ago, or the existence of dinosaurs hundreds of millions of years ago. Indeed, if dinosaurs actually roamed the earth with humans, why is there no discussion of dinosaurs in the Bible (as actual dinosaurs, not just leviathans, as leviathans are not dinosaurs)? Although the Bible does mention creatures such as leviathans, which some have equated to dinosaurs, such creatures are more likely to be a reference to some sort of monster as mythical as Job's unicorns (unless unicorns really existed, "for the Bible tells me so"). Why are there no accounts of people being killed by dinosaurs? Why no mention of the mass extinctions of dinosaurs that would have had to have taken place in the past 6,000 years? Why hasn't there been any newer and better technology that can date fossils and rocks to demonstrate scientifically that there is nothing in existence on Earth that is more than 6,000 years old? Is there really a huge conspiracy among all current scientists in the world to lie and make us all think that there was a completely fictitious Earth in existence here long before 6,000 years ago?

For hundreds of years now, modern geologists, anthropologists, and paleontologists have been finding prehistoric fossils by doing elaborate and painstaking digs at various sites throughout the world. As organisms die, their bodies are slowly covered by dust and earth, and if certain conditions and circumstances are met, they can become fossilized. Most organisms simply disintegrate after they die, or become oil (fossil fuel), however, so not every organism that has ever lived is now a recognizable fossil. Fossils are quite rare, relatively speaking, so it is fortunate to find any of them.

It is logical that older organisms would be buried more deeply than more recent organisms. A quick summary of evolutionary forms is thus: invertebrates, vertebrates, fish, amphibians, reptiles, birds, mammals, and, finally, primates. Unless all scientists who have ever conducted digs are lying, the fossil record fully supports this general order. At the lowest levels, they find noncomplex invertebrates and vertebrates; then slightly more complex forms such as dinosaurs, amphibians, reptiles, and birds; then even more complex mammals of all kinds; then primates; and, finally, modern humans. If all of these life-forms lived on Earth at the exact same time (within the past 6,000 years or so), we would find fossil remains of all life-forms buried indiscriminately together, all at the *same* depths, but that is just not the case. That is significant evidence. The only way out of this one is to argue that the creatures in the fossil record all *did* exist at the same time and we do have a young Earth but that because of Noah's worldwide flood, all the remains of the killed creatures settled into layers in the earth not by time period but by weight! Of course, there are remains of small dinosaurs at lower levels, and underneath them all are smaller, wormlike creatures that were not heavier than dinosaurs.

It is also revealing to consider that the DNA of all living things in the world is strongly related. Moreover, vast arrays of animals on Earth are related tetrapods. This means that many classes and types of animals all have four legs—two front legs (arms) and two hind legs, with one bone in each of the upper arms and thighs and two bones in both the lower forearms and the lower legs. Each tetrapod also has knees and elbows connected to feet and hands through wrists and ankles, with a pelvis for the back legs and a rib cage to protect vital organs, such as a heart to circulate blood, two lungs to breath air, and a digestive system for the food that is eaten through a mouth, as well as kidneys, livers, skin, a spine and nervous system connected through a neck to a brain in a head, with a face that has two eyes, two ears, two nostrils, and a mouth. This is true for all mammals, dinosaurs, and reptiles, and even snakes, birds, and fish have evidence of a similar tetrapod structure, as shown by the bones in their wings and fins. All DNA is related in a very general sense, but, admittedly, some structures are more related than others, as we are closer to mammal tetrapods than to, say, jellyfish or plants.

Reinforcing the notion that the older fossils are buried more deeply than newer fossils is the fact that the older fossils are also dated to be older—much older, tens and hundreds of millions of years older—than the fossil remains of more complex organisms buried not as deeply. These fossils are all dated by their levels of radioactive decay (a scientific process metaphorically similar to checking the grains of sand that have fallen through an hourglass). In fact, the atomic bomb is possible based on the reliability of this phenomenon of atomic decay. Various forms of scientific dating all show that dinosaur fossils are hundreds of millions of years old, historic human (*Homo sapiens sapiens*) skeletons are dated to be only hundreds of thousands of years old, and primates and hominids are only a few million years old. And finally, contrary to creationist assertions, there are transitional fossils, including fossils of extinct nonhuman but non-modern ape hominids, like Neanderthals.

Think what the existence of this undeniable fossil record really means. One would have to believe that all scientists and researchers are lying in a huge conspiracy, where they otherwise could be easily exposed. They all would have to be lying about at least two significant topics: (1) that dinosaur bones and human bones and fossils of all types are actually found together at the same depths and (2) that all age-dating devices used by scientists and researchers are either designed to lie or seem to always malfunction so as to incorrectly date dinosaur bones as hundreds of millions of years old while human bones are always dated to be hundreds of millions of years younger. Why would all scientists lie in such a massive conspiracy that would be so easy to expose, especially when exposure of false or incorrect findings about the world in which we live is exactly what science is all about?

Moreover, where are all of the many teams of scientists who would and could present credible scientific evidence that the world is really just 6,000 years old, who are actually scientists and not just creationists posing as scientists? What is so hard to believe is that virtually every current bona fide scientist of the world (in many related fields, such as geology, paleontology, anthropology, astrophysics, astronomy, and more) is really just an atheist liar who puts forth all of her or his scientific papers, studies, evidence, and theories just to trick us into believing that there was a fictitious ancient world here. In light of this implausibility, it becomes very hard to believe that, in reality, such an ancient world did not exist just because the Bible says—or because the Bible really only *implies* and through various genealogies from Adam to Jesus and never *literally* asserts—that God did not create the earth and the universe until about 6,000 years ago. Ironically, it is the group of religious thinkers who require the Bible to be taken literally who have developed a theory of creation dependent entirely on an inference (rather than explicit assertion) from the text.

Remember, this same mentality—that all scientists must be evil liars because they make claims that contradict the Bible—is exactly the one that some people and the Church had about Copernicus, Kepler, and Galileo just a few hundred years ago when they stated the blasphemous heresy that the earth revolves around the sun instead of the other way around and that the earth is not at the center of the universe. What would we think, then, of believers today who argue that all telescopes are faulty devices because the sun really revolves around a flat earth located at the center of the universe the way God made it, and these so-called scientists are all just a bunch of atheist liars? We would think that such believers were ignorant as well as wrong—because, after all, they were (and are).

It is amazing that some literalist believers continue to think of science as a fraudulent attempt, motivated by Satan, to deceive us all about the earth and the universe. Remember that the paramount goal of science is not to perpetrate frauds but is exactly the opposite. Science is the attempt to expose mistaken beliefs using available empirical evidence, logical analysis, and scientific plausibility. Examples of such evidence include measurements and observations from space showing that the earth is not flat and that it, along with the other planets, revolves around the sun, or the fact that mental illnesses and other diseases often have chemical, viral, or psychological causes we can monitor, measure, and record via neurological activity or chemical analysis rather than being functions of demonic possession. Why has not a *single* scientist exposed the allegedly fraudulent conspiracy designed to make us think the earth is much older than 6,000 years—if the earth truly is only 6,000 years old—and gone on to win a Nobel Prize for making such a fantastic scientific breakthrough?

There is a creation museum where these types of "scientific" claims are actually made. From Wikipedia (http://en.wikipedia.org/wiki/Creation_Museum) is the following description of the museum and its controversy:

> The **Creation Museum** is an American museum located near Petersburg, Kentucky that presents an account of the origins of the universe, life, mankind, and man's early history according to a literal reading of the Book of Genesis.

> The museum has been heavily criticized by the scientific and academic communities as promoting "fallacy over fact" and attempting to advance the tenets of a particular religion while rejecting scientific knowledge. Its exhibits reject universal common descent, along with most other scientific findings regarding evolution, and assert that the Earth and all of its life forms were created 6,000 years ago over a six-day period. In contrast to the overwhelming scientific consensus, exhibits promote young Earth creationist claims, including the idea that humans and dinosaurs once coexisted, and that dinosaurs were on Noah's Ark. The scientific consensus is that the Earth is approximately 4.5 billion years old, and that the dinosaurs became extinct 65.5 million years before human beings arose. The museum has generated criticism by the scientific community, several groups of educators, Christian groups opposed to young Earth creationism, and in the general press.

Apparently, the 1960s television cartoon *The Flintstones* was correct in its assumption that modern humans and dinosaurs actually lived together on Earth at the same time—but still, even if creation is only 6,000 years old, the question remains, What was God doing in all of the time before He allegedly created everything? Perhaps during the infinite time that was pre-creation, God was busy creating other universes and has been doing so forever. There is no mention of this in the Bible, however. That, of course, does not necessarily mean that God did not do so, but if He did, there does not appear to be any explicit textual support of such other creation endeavors beyond our world. If God has done this before, however, how many times has Jesus had to be incarnated into some alien body and suffer the equivalent of being crucified for the sins of those alien beings that have existed before us (assuming they too had chosen to eat some form of forbidden fruit). Still, how could that have ever happened if nothing were created before the "beginning"? Was God forever idle with no universe to exist in, no Heaven to live in, and no other beings to communicate with, until the creation of our universe? It strains credibility to think God did absolutely nothing in a void for forever. And if He did do something else, then why is there no explanation of that something else in the Bible? Even if we are not told specifically what he did in that time, how could God have been doing anything if there was no universe within which to do it?

If God resides in Heaven but Heaven was not created until "the beginning," some 6,000 years ago, where did God live *before* Heaven was created? If God has always existed there, why hasn't Heaven always existed too? Why did God deny Himself a Universe and a wonderful place to live for all of eternity in the past and then, just 6,000 years ago, suddenly decide to create Heaven and the rest of the universe? Also, how is it possible that Jesus has always been in existence (because God has always existed)? Would Jesus still be Jesus with a human body in a void universe that did not yet exist, and would He yet somehow have half of the DNA of the Virgin Mary (who did not yet exist herself, nor did her DNA, because nothing had yet been created)? For example, how could I be me if all or even just half of the DNA defining me did not exist? Perhaps Jesus has existed as a spiritual being forever but only received His DNA when He was incarnated as a human being.

Chapter Thirty-Two

Creation and Big Bang Similarities

Scientists should not get a free pass any more than literalist believers should. The issue about what was happening before the universe was created is just as vexing an issue for Big Bang theorists as it is for creationists. If there was a beginning and that beginning was the Big Bang, then the same question applies—what was happening where the universe now exists *before* the Big Bang took place? How was it possible for there to have been complete nothingness and then for both time and space to spontaneously come into being? If there really was just a void of nothingness right before the Big Bang occurred, how could there have been anything inside of that nothing (no matter how small or dense) to expand in the Big Bang and start the universe from nothing? How did the energy responsible for the Big Bang come into being if there was absolutely nothing in existence beforehand? Whatever started that process leads one to ask, "If *something* started the Big Bang process, what was that something that was already in existence when there was supposed to be complete nothingness beforehand?"

Perhaps there was something that was very tiny and dense before the Big Bang, but we have no knowledge of it because the event horizon we call the Big Bang erased, in a sense, all record of what happened before. Thus, life before the Big Bang is not only unknown but is perhaps unknowable. Science should not be faulted for not yet having all the answers—or for not ever being able to answer certain questions. Instead, perhaps science should embrace the inability to define a true beginning of any kind. It's better to be honest and say, "We just don't know, but we're still searching," than it is to say, "I know how the universe began: either (1) God created it because it is all written here in the Bible; or (2) "It somehow created itself in a spontaneous explosion/expansion." The third possibility is that maybe the universe wasn't created in any ultimate sense, because maybe there was something here even before the Big Bang, and there has always been "something." The burden of proof is on anyone asserting there was nothing before there was something.

Scientists say that time itself did not exist so nothing could have been happening before time itself began—but *how* did time start, and how can time as it now exists ever stop? A critical step in the analysis is missing here because one can always ask the same cause-and-effect, reductionist question, which is: What was transpiring the very nanosecond *just* before it all began? Whatever the effect was, there had to have been a cause and something to cause that cause. So what *caused* the Big Bang; what was happening in that space *just* before the very moment the Big Bang took place? Scientists ultimately come up short here in much the same way creationists do, although at least creationists posit some kind of cause, albeit a completely supernatural, nonscientific cause consisting of a deity who created everything except Himself. Scientists, in contrast, just say there was no cause and the Big Bang spontaneously happened.

Flaws in creationism aside, it defies logic that space and time did not exist, and then for no apparent reason whatsoever spontaneously just began. How could this happen? Even if time completely has stopped inside of something like a black hole, *how and when* did that black hole originally become a black hole? Where did the mass and energy that make up a black hole come from, and how did it get into its present state of being?

Here is another conundrum that science does not seem to be able to provide a satisfying response to: That we can measure the universe's expansion does not necessarily mean that the universe is expanding, if we assume that the space in the universe is infinite. If the universe is not infinitely big, presumably, there must be some sort of boundary that constitutes the edge of the universe. If so, what is behind or beyond that boundary? Parallel universes? If so, where are they, and what is behind *them*? If the universe is very big, but still finite, yet is still expanding, how can the universe expand into space that does not already exist? What is now in the space that the universe is yet to expand into—and what is behind that? Is the universe still being created right now in the sense that it is still expanding? Scientists have provided no evidence that says this is not possible, but this does not prove that the universe necessarily had a beginning. Maybe the universe has *always* been expanding, forever. Can we say that the beginning of the universe is therefore still occurring because the universe is still expanding? In short, is the Big Bang *still occurring*?

If the universe is infinite, perhaps it is not really expanding, at least in an infinite sense. Returning to the number-line metaphor, suppose that I am at the number 2 and then I slowly count along the number line up to the number 100 and I also count the other way, down to –75. I clearly would have measurably moved along the number line, or expanded my position from 2 to 100, and from 2 to –75, from a finite point of view, but when I get to 100 or to –75, I would be no closer to either infinity or "negative" infinity than when I was at 2, because infinity means literally no end. So, although there may be measurable expansion from 2 to 100 and from 2 to –75 in my finite context, that expansion is ultimately meaningless in infinite terms. I cannot add to or subtract from in a meaningful way that which is already infinite: Infinity + 1? If I could, infinity would not really be infinity, or perhaps there are different kinds of infinities. What this means is that just because the universe is measurably expanding, it did not necessarily have to have a beginning, even though one may begin the counting at a certain number on the metaphorical number line. Maybe we just think that the universe is expanding because we can measure perceptible movement, but that movement is just a movement phenomenon along an already infinite number line that already exists forever.

Chapter Thirty-Three

When Did the Angels and Lucifer Enter the Scene?

Another curious omission in Genesis 1:1 is of the creation of various inhabitants of Heaven. Did God create all of the angels in the first verse of the Bible when He created Heaven, or was just Heaven itself—just the physical, tangible, location or place—created at that point, and then all of the angels were created later? If all angels exist in Heaven but there was no Heaven until God created it, then all of the angels did not exist until they all were created as a part of Heaven—unless they, like God, always have existed and were part of the void where God allegedly existed before the beginning of the universe. The question this gets at is why, if angels are mentioned throughout the Bible, the creation of angels is not mentioned in Genesis's creation story. If angels were created when Heaven was, it is interesting to note that they all quite literally would have been in the dark in Heaven because light had yet to be created. We shall return to the issue of angels in general, but first, let us consider angels behaving badly.

When and how did the head evil angel, Lucifer, become Satan, or the Devil? That is, how do we account for Lucifer, the most important angel gone bad in the Bible, who eventually became Satan? When did Lucifer lead a failed rebellion in Heaven? And how soon after that did he get kicked out of Heaven? Is he even in Hell right now, or will that come later? At what point did he become Satan? Did evil already exist in the universe, or was Satan the one who created evil? How could a mere angel create anything? If Satan did not create evil, then God Himself must have created evil, because God created the universe and everything in it. Even if God merely created the option for others to commit evil, He still created that option. If God had never created that option, evil never could have been introduced into the universe by Satan, or by anyone else.

Because Genesis 1:1 is silent on when and how the inhabitants of Heaven got created and how and when the angel Lucifer became the Devil, I asked my dad for a literal biblical explanation. Quoting several Bible verses (that did not seem all that literal to me), my dad basically gave me the following fundamentalist Christian view of what happened: Soon after Heaven was created, Hell was created, because Lucifer had only a matter of a few days to rebel and to become Satan in time to tempt Eve as a serpent in the Garden of Eden. The timing is critical here because Lucifer turning into Satan and being sent to Hell and becoming the evil tempter of humankind all had to take place almost immediately after the first day of the six-day creation. Consider all that needed to happen very quickly: Lucifer and all of the angels had to be created, exist in Heaven, and then have Lucifer lead a failed rebellion of one-third of the angels. After all of that took place, Lucifer would have had to have become Satan. Then, Satan would be banished from Heaven (perhaps to Hell at that point or later) with his rebellious angels (who became demons).

All of that significant activity would have had to occur first in order to set up the ultimate struggle on Earth between God and Satan that started soon after the six days of creation.

Of course, this all assumes Satan is the serpent referred to in the Garden of Eden. That is the common view, but the temptation story in Genesis never mentions Satan or Lucifer by name as such. If we take all in the Bible literally, why make this grievous omission? If the serpent was only symbolically or metaphorically Satan, then we have the same problem as discussed earlier: When should the Bible be taken literally and when is it metaphor? Of course, if this serpent was not Satan, who was he? Why was he able to talk to humans, and why did he seem to know all about good and evil and the Tree of Knowledge of Good and Evil? Revelation 20:2 says, "And he laid hold on the dragon, that old serpent, which is the Devil, and Satan, and bound him a thousand years," but that was written thousands of years after Genesis was written. As an aside, it is interesting that many religions around the world have a snake or serpent or even a dragon as some sort of symbolic deity of some kind.

Assuming, however, that the serpent was Satan, in the temptation story, Satan would have had to have been incarnated and sent to Earth as a talking serpent who would tempt Eve to eat the forbidden fruit. As we shall see, she and Adam ate the fruit of the Tree of Knowledge of Good and Evil, disobeying God, apparently just after she was created from Adam's rib. Of course, God did not want them to eat that forbidden fruit. So, Lucifer first disobeyed God in Heaven, and then convinced Eve to eat the forbidden fruit, and Eve then convinced Adam to also eat the forbidden fruit.

Incredibly, all of this tumultuous activity would have had to have taken place in a matter of just a few days if we take the Bible literally (unless we assume different celestial and terrestrial time because a day to the Lord is as a thousand years and a thousand years is as one day—or even Einstein's allegories about time when travelling at or near the speed of light or near huge gravitational fields). Again, just think about all the monumental events that must have taken place before Lucifer appeared on the scene as a talking snake in the Garden of Eden. How Satan and the other rebellious angels learned so much about creation and the universe and then almost immediately—indeed, within just a few days—rebelled against God and presumably got sent to Hell is a mystery. It is also unclear why Satan, since the beginning, has so often gotten to visit the Earth and tempt humans and cause all kinds of mischief if he is supposed to be receiving punishment in Hell, or elsewhere. Why does he get a work release or furlough of sorts from Hell? Is he simultaneously suffering in Hell while getting to cause trouble by tempting people here on Earth? Will he be sent to Hell only after Judgment Day (after the end of the world)? According to Revelation 20:10, "And the devil that deceived them was cast into the lake of fire and brimstone, where the beast and the false prophet are, and shall be tormented day and night for ever and ever." Why is Satan even allowed to visit the earth if humans have long since had the knowledge of good and evil, as we are now born into Original Sin, such that we are quite capable of choosing evil all on our own? Do we really need that evil genius Satan, to help us concoct sinful things to do on Earth? Can Satan really talk to and tempt billions of people simultaneously in an omniscient, omnipresent way similar to how God can answer prayers?

Chapter Thirty-Four

Other "Christian" Views about Satan (and Race)

Of course, some Christians from various sects have *extremely different views* of how everything all began in Heaven. For example, the Mormons (Church of the Latter-Day Saints) believe that it all began when a spirit child was born to unknown gods in the universe. The spirit child was named Elohim and eventually was elevated to godhood (notice that there is not a beginning here in the sense of something appearing out of nothing; instead, the story just seems to pick up already in progress with these unknown gods/creators/parents of Elohim with no apparent explanation of where they came from). Elohim, who is God, the Heavenly Father, lived with many goddess wives on a special planet (without any apparent explanation of where all of these goddess wives came from). Elohim and all of his wives produced billions and billions of spirit children—including all of those who would later be sent to Earth (all of humankind throughout time) to be born into physical, mortal bodies on Earth, starting first with Adam and Eve. Every time a child is born on Earth, it is to provide a mortal physical body for yet another one of these original spirit children lying in wait to enter the earth and live as a human.

Before the first spirit children would be put into physical bodies here on Earth, however, there was a big conference, a great council meeting in Heaven, to determine how to deal with all of the spirit children once they came to the newly created Earth. Elohim's two eldest sons were Jesus and Lucifer (notice that Lucifer is not just an angel here but, according to the Mormons, is actually a fellow, righteous Son of God, along with Jesus, and essentially equal to Jesus at that time—this is a very big and controversial difference). Jesus, and *His brother*, Lucifer, then came up with competing visionary plans as to how to deal with the spirit children once the spirit children were actually on Earth with physical mortal bodies. Lucifer's plan was that all of the spirit children would become like gods and therefore would do no evil on Earth, meaning that none of them would ever be condemned to Hell (in fact, there was no Hell). The result of Lucifer's plan was that Lucifer would effectively become the savior of all humankind because no one would ever need to be sent to a place called Hell.

Opposing Lucifer's plan was Jesus's plan, which provided that humankind would instead be required to choose between good and evil. Jesus's plan was of free agency for all humans. Jesus would become the savior of the world, but only for those who actually chose Him as their savior. Interestingly, notice that under Lucifer's plan, no human would have ever ended up in Hell because they would not have known, and therefore could not have done, any evil while on Earth but under Jesus's plan, humans would know and be required to choose between good and evil (having free agency). Consequently, all of those people who would not choose Jesus would end up suffering forever in Hell. After much campaigning, one would assume, Jesus's plan was finally approved through a vote (apparently, there is a democracy in Heaven), so Jesus would become the savior of the world for all of those who would choose Him instead of choosing evil.

Because Lucifer's competing plan was not chosen, he became enraged and convinced one-third of the spirits to rebel with him against Elohim (God) and Jesus. Because of this sinful rebellion, Lucifer became Satan, his followers became demons, and they were all denied physical bodies and were destined for Hell; they could never become human and ultimately make it back to Heaven. During this epic struggle in Heaven between the forces of Jesus and those of Satan, the spirit children who fought with Jesus against Satan's rebellion would become physical humans born into Mormon families on Earth that had fair skin (European descent?), while those who remained neutral in the great battle would be cursed with dark skin on Earth (African descent?), and as a further result of their neutrality, those cursed with dark skin could never enter the Kingdom of Heaven.

Many Mormons also believe that dark skin is a curse from God for actions of certain humans done on Earth. Adam's son, Cain, who killed his brother, Abel, was the first to be cursed in this way. In the Book of Mormon, God also cursed a group of New World inhabitants with dark skin called Lamenites. See 2 Nephi 5:21. This is interesting because many, if not all, biblical figures probably were not white, Anglo-Saxon, or Germanic Aryans but were instead "dark people," because people from the Middle East are dark (or at least not white): Arabs, Persians, Palestinians, Israelis, North Africans, etc. I fear that acknowledging that most biblical figures were not Anglo-Saxons may be fighting words for some who would consider it to be utter blasphemy to think of Jesus, for example, as anything but a "pure" white person with blue eyes and light brown hair.

Of course, I do not know what race Jesus was/is, and I am not sure if anyone really does; however, given when and where Jesus was born into the world, and comparing those around Him at the same time and place, it would appear highly unlikely that He was an Anglo-Saxon or any kind of European Aryan with blue eyes and light brown hair as depicted in paintings by European artists in the Middle Ages. If it is highly unlikely that Jesus was some type of white Northern European, why would God curse Himself, at least to some extent, with dark skin, or even semi-dark skin, if dark skin is supposed to be a curse?

I do not think Jesus's race should matter at all to us, but Mormons are the ones who suggested that dark skin was a religious curse. I certainly did not (especially being a "dark-skinned" Latino, myself). In fairness, however, this issue of dark skin as a curse changed for the Mormons in 1978—some fourteen years after the Civil Rights Act of 1964 and twenty-four years after the famed Supreme Court *Brown v. Board of Education* school-desegregation case of 1954—when Mormon church leaders had a special revelation from God that dark-skinned people should no longer be considered to have been cursed and can now enter the Kingdom of Heaven and the priesthood. So Heaven literally became desegregated. Thus, it is important to give credit when credit is due. Whether it was actually caused by God or just unrelenting political pressure here on Earth, the Mormons rejected this overt form of doctrinal racism against people with dark skin. It is still unclear, however, whether Mormons as well as other fundamentalist Christians still believe that Jesus was/is white.

Again, Jesus's race probably should not matter to any Christians, be they white or non-white ("dark-skinned"); however, I wonder how it would be received by some if a group of, say, Chinese people began to suggest that Jesus was neither a dark Middle Eastern person, nor a white Northern European, but instead was Chinese, like them. If so, although it still should not matter, I guess I again would point out that Jesus being Chinese would probably be very unlikely, given where and when He was born into the world. I would refer to the same evidence of the type of people born in the Middle East more than 2,000 years ago and make the same observation that Jesus probably was not Chinese or, for that matter, Spanish, Australian, Brazilian, or French, *merci beau coups!*

This race issue reminds me of a classic *All in the Family* episode. *All in the Family* was a groundbreaking television comedy in the 1970s featuring a lovable bigot named Archie Bunker (played by the actor Carroll O'Connor). Archie's racism and discriminatory beliefs were a staple of the show. *All in the Family* covered many political issues and current events of the era using witty satire and biting sarcasm.

In one particular episode, Archie got locked in a cellar for several hours. He could not escape. There also happened to be many bottles of wine in this cellar, so, being bored and melancholy about his predicament, Archie began to drink. As he got more and more inebriated, the show became funnier and funnier; a classic one-man show in front of a live audience. At a certain point in this episode, Archie began to pray aloud, asking for God's intervention to get out of the cellar. Archie began to think that he might die locked in this cellar, and so, in addition to drinking, he began negotiating with God and asking for a miracle. Right at that moment, Archie heard a noise as it appeared that the cellar door was being rattled and might be flung open. Excited that God had come to rescue him, Archie was beside himself, saying, "Here I am, Lord," for he was about to lay his eyes on his rescuer, God Himself! As the cellar door was opened so Archie was about to see God, to Archie's complete surprise and utter horror, a black man (a mere passerby) opens the door and frees Archie. As Archie stood there completely dumbfounded, confronted with this most ironic development, given his racist beliefs and the fact that God apparently was black, all Archie could say was a very heartfelt, "Forgive me, Lord… the Jeffersons [the black family living next door] was right!"

This episode makes me wonder if certain Christians would still even be Christians if irrefutable evidence was discovered proving that Jesus was/is actually black, or an Eskimo, or something other than white. Would their racism outweigh their love of Jesus so they would believe in Jesus, but only if Jesus were the "right" race? Even if Jesus was/is white, how could any

Christian be racist against what would be some of God's other children, or I suppose from their point of view, some of God's other, inferior children?

Continuing from when Mormons believe Satan fell from Heaven and up through the time Mormonism was created, the spirit children are believed to have first come to the earth through Adam and Eve. Later, more than 2,000 years ago, Elohim Himself visited Earth and had sex with, up until then, the Virgin Mary to give His spiritual son Jesus a physical body on Earth—so God had physical sex, not just symbolic or spiritual sex, with the Virgin Mary (who after that was no longer a virgin). Jesus then had at least three wives while on Earth—Mary, Martha, and Mary Magdalene—and they had many children, of whom Joseph Smith, the modern founder of Mormonism, claimed to be a direct descendant. Jesus taught and preached and then later was crucified and was resurrected.

After Jesus was resurrected, He returned to Earth, but this time, He came to the Americas (but apparently only to what is now the United States, not to Central or South America or even to Canada) to preach to the Indians (native North Americans), who were considered to be a lost tribe of Israel, although it is not clear how this lost tribe of Israelites ever got here, especially when modern DNA analysis does not support that Native Americans are of Middle Eastern or Palestinian descent, but does support the fact that Native Americans are of Asian descent and therefore probably crossed over the Bering Strait (when it was not covered by water) from Asia to Alaska and down through North America. Apparently, there were also white people in the Americas at that time (no explanation as to how they got there), and Jesus established His church here in the Americas as He had in the Middle East, but by 421 AD, the dark-skinned Indians had killed all of the white people. The culture and religious knowledge of those white people was not lost, however, because they had written extensively about their civilization on golden plates that were hidden before the people died off in ancient America.

Approximately 1,400 years later, in the mid-1800s, Joseph Smith, the founder of the modern Mormon Church (the Church of Jesus Christ of Latter-Day Saints) claimed to have found these golden plates near his home in upstate New York; with them, he organized the modern Mormon Church, with much of its vast teachings contained in these golden plates. The golden plates were translated by Joseph Smith (apparently, they were not written in English), who also found a pair of magic/miraculous glasses with which to read the golden plates and interpret them into what is now the Book of Mormon. Smith is claimed to have been a prophet because by then all other Christian religions had become an abomination but he got the Christian church back on track the way God, Elohim, wanted. Mormon believers follow elaborate codes and ceremonies for themselves and the dead (many wear special white underwear for reasons about which I am not sure), and they are saved by Jesus Christ. Also, those who are sealed in the eternal religious marriage ceremony eventually expect to become polygamous gods (at least the men) who will reign forever in Heaven, the celestial kingdom, on a planet with huge families, so saved Mormon men on Earth can become Gods after they die.

There is yet another division in Christianity, between more fundamentalist Mormons, who believe that polygamy (in this case, when a man is married to many wives simultaneously) was, and still is, God's will for us here on Earth, and more mainstream Mormons, who now believe that polygamy on Earth is *not* God's will and who accept the fact that polygamy is illegal under our laws. If polygamy is now also immoral and is even a sin, according to the more mainstream Mormons, then it makes one wonder why it was *ever* allowed by the Mormon Church, why it was ever practiced, and why it apparently will be practiced again, in Heaven. Why would God allow, and even promote, anything that is/was a sin and that is even now considered to be illegal? Was Jesus sinning when He, according to Mormons, had three wives? I wonder what Mormon presidential candidate Mitt Romney thinks about all of this and if Fox News will make a huge issue about these beliefs the way it did about the statements of Barack Obama's former pastor, Reverend Wright, during the 2008 presidential campaign. In America, religion should not disqualify anyone from being president—JFK's Catholicism should have put that issue to bed—but I wonder if Romney's Mormonism will be held against him by Christian fundamentalist Republicans.

There is, of course, far more to Mormon doctrine and Mormon religious history than my overly generalized account, and admittedly, I probably have not done Mormonism justice, as there are certain to be Mormons who would disagree with some of what I have recounted here (again, I wonder what Mitt Romney, specifically, would agree and disagree with here). Still, this basic description of at least some basic Mormon teachings is accurate enough to serve the very simple and limited purpose of showing how there are extremely different accounts among various Christians about the historical events in Heaven leading to how Lucifer became Satan and to the beginnings of humankind on Earth—the creation story—as well as about various significant religious events in human history. Why would fundamentalist Christians reject these teachings and claim there is no scientific or historical basis for them, yet still argue that there is scientific and historical basis for their own particular fundamentalist Protestant beliefs?

It is interesting that some Christian fundamentalists strictly following Genesis and other portions of the Bible—for example, television host Mike Huckabee, Facebook politician Sarah Palin, Texas Governor Rick Perry, and Congresswoman Michelle Bachman—would greatly differ theologically with these Mormon teachings as well as with various aspects of the Book of Mormon and would challenge whether the Book of Mormon is the revealed Word of God. Politically, however, they still might fully support presidential candidate Mitt Romney or conservative talk-show host and Internet blogger Glenn Beck, who are Mormons, without holding against them their divergent religious Mormon beliefs, especially that Jesus had three wives and that Satan was also the Son of God and brother of Jesus. These are very significant theological differences. Imagine if President Barack Obama believed those things; what might they have to say about him and his unorthodox beliefs when many people still don't even trust his Hawaiian birth certificate? Moreover, despite the great theological differences Christian fundamentalist have with Mormons, many such politically conservative Christian fundamentalists often vehemently oppose President Obama, who is a Christian with more traditional beliefs (I don't think, for example, that Obama believes Satan was ever the Son of God and the brother of Jesus at one time or that Jesus really was a polygamist with three wives).

Perhaps that is why conservative Mormons and conservative fundamentalist Christians can together attack President Obama's form of Christianity and why they do not seem to have much of a problem with allowing the president to be defined as a non-American, Kenyan-born, "self-proclaimed" Christian who is really either a Muslim or at least a Muslim sympathizer, and who is out to destroy traditional American values. They also focus on what Reverend Wright, the pastor of a church that President Obama once attended, preached in various sermons, rather than on what the Bible says or on what President Obama himself actually has said about religious issues. This narrative allows them to think of President Obama as a religious outsider, and it allows the conservative Christian fundamentalists and the conservative Mormons, despite their deep theological differences with one another, to be political allies without attacking each other's particular forms of Christianity like they do to President Obama. These various religious-theological and political-social divides and alliances are fascinating to observe, no matter what religious and/or political side one is on.

Whatever the true story of how Lucifer fell from Heaven and eventually into Hell, whether Mormon or fundamentalist Christian, it has always made me wonder why there was never another rebellion by these already rebellious demons against Satan himself. If they would revolt against God, their own creator, just days after God created them, why do they now remain so loyal to Satan, their failed rebel leader, after all these millennia? Why don't these former angels, turned rebel demons, view Satan as a wholly incompetent rebel leader who disastrously led them to Hell in an ill-conceived, poorly planned, unwinnable, failed coup in Heaven? What was Satan thinking, and why are these otherwise very rebellious demons still so loyal to Satan even up to this day?

What about demons that now may regret their decision to follow Satan but are still doomed to Hell? Are they to be punished in Hell forever even if they now genuinely want to say to God that they are truly sorry and wish to be forgiven? Why is there no redemption for truly sorry demons/former angels? Does God discriminate against angels who have sinned and now want forgiveness, but not against humans who have sinned and now want forgiveness? Is that fair? Does God have to be fair? Is it a sin to be unfair? Does God's status as the Creator of everything mean that He gets to discriminate between humans and angels because He created, and therefore legally "owns," us all and thus is above owing fairness to any of us? Is it as simple as angels obviously *knowing* for sure that God exists, so it does not require any faith on their part to believe that God exists, whereas humans do not know for sure if God exists (at least not modern humans, who do not have audible conversations with God like humans in the Bible often reportedly had) and therefore can be saved from Hell if we have faith that God does exist and we accept Jesus as our savior—but fallen angels cannot? Speaking of angels and their status, what about an even more rudimentary issue about their physicality? (See the next chapter.)

Chapter Thirty-Five

Do Angels Have Wings, and, if So, Why Would They Need Them?

In the Bible, angels sometimes appear in physical form in front of people (so apparently, they have, or can have, tangible physical, visible, incarnate bodies). Sometimes, they can even pose to humans as other human beings (Hebrews 13:2: "Be not forgetful to entertain strangers; for thereby some have entertained angels unawares"). Angels are also often invisible to humans (e.g., if I turn around quickly, I cannot see my guardian angel), however, and they presumably live somewhere in Heaven, and so maybe they are just spirits of some kind, so it is unclear whether they have physical, visible bodies and to what extent their bodies are similar to or different from our own. Note, for example, that Jacob allegedly physically wrestled with an angel (Genesis 22:24–30):

> **[24]** And Jacob was left alone; and there wrestled a man with him until the breaking of the day.
> **[25]** And when he saw that he prevailed not against him, he touched the hollow of his thigh; and the hollow of Jacob's thigh was out of joint, as he wrestled with him.
> **[26]** And he said, Let me go, for the day breaketh. And he said, I will not let thee go, except thou bless me.
> **[27]** And he said unto him, What is thy name? And he said, Jacob.
> **[28]** And he said, Thy name shall be called no more Jacob, but Israel: for as a prince hast thou power with God and with men, and hast prevailed.
> **[29]** And Jacob asked him, and said, Tell me, I pray thee, thy name. And he said, Wherefore is it that thou dost ask after my name? And he blessed him there.
> **[30]** And Jacob called the name of the place Peniel: for I have seen God face to face, and my life is preserved.

Although the text says Jacob wrestled with a man, or even perhaps with God Himself because Jacob saw "the face of God," many simply have interpreted Jacob's encounter here to be with an angel. This leads one to ask (if it really was an angel, and certainly if it was God Himself), Why didn't the angel (or God) easily prevail over Jacob, a mere mortal, in this supposed all-night wrestling stalemate?

This angelic wrestling match brings up even more puzzling issues about angels, however. Let's go back to the idea that Heaven was created before light was created. Did angels need light to see in Heaven before light was created? Do angels have eyes, like our eyes, which operate as light receptors transmitting images through optic nerves to brains and allowing them to see, or are angels just spirits without physical bodies and thus do not need light to see? None of this is explained. If angels have physical bodies, many logical questions about the nature of their bodies follow. Do angels have internal organs? Do they have hair, and if so, does their hair grow? Do they have fingernails, and if so, do those grow? Do angels eat? Do they go to the bathroom? If so, are there sewers in Heaven, and if so, where does the sewage go? Can angels lift weights to get stronger? Are any of them overweight? Do they get tired if they run? Do they run? Do they breathe oxygen? Do they get sick? Do they drink water? Do they age? Do they bleed? I assume the answer is no to all of these questions, yet angels seem to have physical bodies, at least sometimes.

Also, angels apparently look very much like humans, only they have wings—so were angels created in God's image, like us, or do their wings alone sufficiently disqualify them? Are there male and female angels? If so, does that mean angels have male and female genitalia? Are there baby angels born in Heaven that grow into adult angels? If not, and if there is no reproduction, is there sex in Heaven, or no sex, because no one has any genitals for sex?

Let's just focus on just one of these questions about angels' physicality: Why do they have wings? Do they need their wings to fly? Note that gravity would not need to be defied by angels using wings if they are in the weightlessness of outer space or in Heaven, unless there is gravity and some type of atmosphere in Heaven that allows them to propel themselves with their wings. So do the laws of physics apply in Heaven? If there is gravity in Heaven, does that mean that there is some large mass, such as a planet, as the "ground" in Heaven, to generate a meaningful gravitational force?

How big would angels' wings have to be to generate enough lift to fly a 150- or 250-pound humanlike body around? What would the musculature have to be like where their wings would attach on their backs? I wonder if it would even be possible, from an aerodynamic point of view, for an angel (a human body with wings) to be able to fly. That is to say, would it be aerodynamically possible for an angel to fly, or would it be a miracle that an angel could fly, despite any dubious aerodynamics of such flight?

Even if angels use their wings just to propel themselves somehow through vacuous space, why don't their wings, and their bodies, and their robes for that matter, burn up from the friction upon their entry into Earth's atmosphere? Even in the Superman comic books, the writers provide an explanation as to how Superman could fly (but notice that in the comic books, he did not need wings to fly). Anyway, although Superman did not burn up on entry into Earth's atmosphere because of his dense body molecules, which were invulnerable in our world, he was still in need of a cape and clothing made of a special invulnerable material that would not burn up on entry into Earth's atmosphere (got to give the comic book writers some credit for at least thinking about this realistic scientific concern, which is a function of the fact that at least they were aware, unlike Moses, of this issue).

Now just go with me here for a minute, as my purpose is to take everything 100% literally—just as fundamentalists tell us we can, and should. Such a cape and clothing would need to be made out of the same kind of material used in the protective tiles on the space shuttle that allow it to reenter the atmosphere without burning up from the friction of the atmosphere. So do angels have robes that can withstand Earth's atmosphere upon reentry? If so, who makes their robes (by the way, why wouldn't angels be naked, especially if they have no genitals and therefore nothing to cover up, or at least no shame, like Adam and Eve were originally naked in the Garden of Eden without shame because of their purity before they sinned against God)? Of course, maybe the possibility of angels' robes burning up on reentry into Earth's atmosphere is a nonissue because angels know that they need to sufficiently slow down as they enter the Earth's atmosphere—important safety tip. But suppose an angel forgot to slow down, flew in too fast, and then was burned upon reentry. Would that angel die? If angels die, do they go back to Heaven after they die? If so, do they get new angel bodies, as well as being told to sufficiently slow down when flying into Earth's atmosphere? Even if they don't die, would their robes and hair burn up on reentry, or are their clothing and hair also made of an invulnerable material like that of the space shuttle tiles?

I realize that all of these questions and observations about angels are very sarcastic and might even be offensive, but I ask them to make a very serious point if we are to take the Bible literally. If the answer is that angels can fly but are *not* subject to the laws of physics, biology, aerodynamics, or space travel, then we are being asked to believe in a supernatural miracle in which angel bodies are not subject to the physical laws of the universe (and thus, the earth) the same way that you and I are subject to those same laws.

Chapter Thirty-Six

Angels' Wings and Santa Claus's Sleigh

Consider what an unacceptable answer it would be to explain other alleged supernatural phenomena that seem difficult, if not impossible, to believe by using the same logic used to explain angels' wings. For example, for many Christmas seasons, my young son Julian, and his younger brother, Johnston, believed that during the night of Christmas Eve, Santa Claus would come down our chimney and leave toys for them that were made by elves. Our boys believed that Santa had carried those toys in a magical bag containing a toy or two (or more), for every boy and girl in the world. Santa would fly in his magical sleigh from the North Pole, pulled by flying reindeer from house to house throughout the world in just one night—breaking supersonic travel speed records, not needing protective gear or oxygen, and not needing heat-protection tiles on his sleigh. Obviously, science does not support such a story. To believe that story, one must suspend belief in science and accept a supernatural, nonscientific, logistically impossible explanation of events.

As our sons grew older, my wife and I even took the Santa Claus story a little further. On Christmas Eve, we would leave carrots and lettuce by the fireplace for Santa's obviously tired and cold flying reindeer. Later, my wife and I would sneak downstairs in the middle of the night, distribute the presents allegedly from Santa under the tree, and even nibble a little bit on the carrots and lettuce that had been left for the reindeer. The next morning, our sons would be in complete shock to see all of the Christmas presents that Santa had apparently brought for them during the night. Moreover, their eyes would light up as they saw the additional proof of Santa's visit: partially nibbled carrots and lettuce that the flying reindeer supposedly had eaten the night before. At that point, the boys never questioned why the reindeer would not eat *all* of the carrots and lettuce, nor did they ask why (or how) these gangly reindeer could also fit with Santa down the narrow chimney just to nibble a little bit on some carrots and lettuce and then leave.

I was fully aware that one of the Ten Commandments is "thou shalt not lie" (or "bear false witness"), so I had some trouble rationalizing the fraudulent scheme that we were perpetrating on our sons, but I began thinking about whether I must also take that commandment entirely *literally*, without exception. If we are to take it literally, then I began to wonder whether it would be a sin for an undercover officer to lie about being a DEA agent during a staged drug deal so that he could then arrest the criminal drug dealers. Similarly, was it a sin for the Gentile family who hid Anne Frank's Jewish family from the Nazis during WWII because they told a lie to the Nazi officers when asked whether they were harboring any Jews? Surely these types of lies must be reasonable exceptions to the literal commandment not to lie, but to read in such exceptions requires one to interpret and apply the application of the commandment in light of the situation. Wouldn't that be an example of improper private interpretation or, to put it in legal terms, improper judicial activism of someone not just interpreting the commandment but going further by making up exceptions and thereby going beyond what the text of the commandment actually says?

Literalists therefore might say that one cannot read in such exceptions because the text of the commandment contains no explicit exceptions. Reading in exceptions that are not contained in the explicit text, however, would be a personal interpretation rather than a literal application of the text. Others, however, might allow the reading in of such reasonable exceptions as part of the commandment because fighting crime and saving lives of innocents is important and, at a minimum, not antithetical to God's will—or, because the commandment says, "Do not bear false witness," maybe that only means that you cannot lie under oath in court as a witness, but perhaps it is allowable in other circumstances? What about "thou shalt not kill"? Are there no similar exceptions, such as in self-defense, or in war, or must we always be pacifistic conscientious objectors in every situation? There is no "kill or be killed" justification (or "murder or be murdered") if *all* killing is a sin according to the literal text of the commandment?

In the same way that such exceptions might exist despite the literal text, I guess I, less profoundly, found a reasonable exception to the "thou shalt not lie" commandment in creating a special childhood memory of Christmas for our young sons. Still, I felt a little guilty for essentially tricking them, and even for planting and then manipulating evidence, to convince them of what was clearly an elaborate scheme and outright falsehood, even though it made for a nice story. So, I thought about it, felt guilty for a moment or two, and then proceeded to rationalize it all as harmless. Why spoil the innocence of children with the boring truth? Why spoil the joy of the Christmas story and our Christmas traditions with a cynical scientific and logical explanation detailing the obvious implausibility of the story, making the whole beautiful symbolic myth celebrating gift-giving at Christmas fall flat on its face? They would eventually figure it all out on their own someday anyway, and someday soon, so we thought, why not?

Trusting us, as well as having the story reinforced by the strong traditions of our culture and by the media, our sons fully believed in Santa Claus and his flying reindeer. One year, we added to the story by leaving a note from one of the reindeer, thanking our family for the carrots and lettuce—but a note written by reindeer? It didn't matter. There was no protestation such as "Hey, wait a minute, c'mon, although reindeer may be able to fly, they can't really hold pens in their hooves and write us notes in English, can they?!"

But as our older son, Julian grew from five to eight years old and we kept repeating this elaborate fraudulent ritual every December 24 and 25, he, like all children, eventually began to ask some rather probing questions. "How can Santa carry gifts for everyone in the whole world in just one bag?" he asked.

"Why, it's a Christmas miracle, son!" I proudly proclaimed.

"How can reindeer fly?"

Maybe I could finesse that one a little—at least he was still willing to believe that reindeer could fly—but I had to decide if I was going to try to come up with some kind of scientific explanation of how it could be possible for reindeer to fly or if I would just rely on "Christmas magic" and Julian's trusting innocence.

Then his question morphed into "How can reindeer fly when they don't even have wings?" I had to come up with something. Would I make up some kind of scientifically plausible argument, or would I just rely on the supernatural "Christmas magic" rationale?

"Son, I am not an expert on flying, but think about how nice Santa's gift-giving is for all the good little boys and girls everywhere in the world on Christmas morning. That's what's important." I was using some creative misdirection (I used to be a lawyer, after all), not really answering his question, and even simultaneously making him feel a little guilty for even asking such a skeptical, doubting question about the mystery of how Santa shares his goodness with all of us.

"But how can Santa travel around the world and drop off all of the toys in just one night?"

This was not good! If he had been more of a math nerd at that point, he would have calculated that Santa could spend only a fraction of a nanosecond in each household if he were to actually drop off hundreds of millions of presents throughout the world (but I suppose not in the Muslim, Jewish, Buddhist, or otherwise non-Christian world) in roughly twenty-four hours. I decided to trot out again, "Why, it's a Christmas miracle, son!"

"Can Santa's sleigh really go that fast, faster than a jet engine?"

Ouch! Well, like many typical youngsters, he went through a pesky rocket-and-airplane stage.

"His sleigh must go that fast, son. If it didn't, well, then you wouldn't have all of these nice gifts that Santa brought to you, now would you?" Yes, I used the undeniable existence of the gifts themselves as solid proof that Santa must have been the one to bring them, because "The gifts could not just have appeared out of nowhere, now could they?" Nice. Consider the logic of the argument: If the presents are there, it must be because Santa brought them—what other explanation could there be? The gifts certainly could not have somehow just appeared out of nowhere by random chance, all neatly wrapped up and intelligently designed for my son to enjoy, like the creation itself proving the creator!

I of course acknowledge that this is not really a completely fair analogy because we obviously know for sure that Santa did not deliver the presents under our tree, as my wife and I actually put the presents under the tree. Thus, there is definitive scientific proof that Santa did not bring the presents to my son, while there is no such definitive scientific proof that God did not create the universe. As *far as my son was concerned*, however, how the gifts got under the tree was still an open question. My son chose to believe the supernatural explanation that it was Santa Claus because he had been told by us and by our culture that Santa delivered the gifts to him as part of the Christmas story and because he had yet to discover and apply any contrary plausible scientific explanation regarding the gifts. At that point, he *personally* had no proof that Santa did not exist.

Just like my son did not know at the time that there was a non-supernatural scientific explanation as to how the gifts got there (my wife and I) and therefore believed the supernatural, nonscientific explanation (Santa Claus), so too might we humans be too young in our development to fully understand the scientific, non-supernatural reason behind how our universe (the metaphorical Christmas gifts) came into existence. In fairness, however, that argument can also cut the other way. Perhaps our spiritual progress is not developed enough to understand how God might have used science to create the universe, in light of our current superficial understanding of science and our lack of ability to understand God. Thus, it is unclear whether we have to grow up *scientifically* or grow up *spiritually* to understand. Fair enough.

We still need to be careful, however, about simply equating supernatural, nonscientific explanations with natural, scientific explanations as if they are complete logical equivalents, simply because we do not know for sure how the universe came to be. Neither side can definitively say for sure how the universe came to be, but that does not necessarily mean that we have two equal explanations. This is true because not all hypotheses are created equal. Although it is true that there are more-plausible, scientific, and natural-based theories on the one hand, and less-plausible, nonscientific, and supernatural-based theories on the other, it is not intellectually honest simply to treat them as if they are *equally* plausible competing explanations. Why? We'll examine this in the next chapter.

Chapter Thirty-Seven

Pick a Theory... Any Theory

To answer the question posed at the end of the previous chapter, let's take an even easier example to make a point about the inequality of two such competing "theories." Assume that there is a carpeted one-room house located on an uninhabited island, with a vase resting on its side on the floor of the house. There is nothing else in the house except a note about why the vase is on its side. There is only one window in the house, and it is open.

Assume we have no definitive scientific proof for why the vase is lying on its side in the room (that is, no authentic, non-photo shopped videotape that recorded exactly how the vase came to be in its current position) but that two groups of people develop competing theories about how and why the vase is lying on its side in the room. Assume the first group offers a scientifically possible, non-supernatural explanation. They theorize that an unidentified animal of some type on the island came through the open window of the room, placed the vase on its side, and then left, given what appear to be some kind of animal tracks left by the vase. It is only a theory as to what happened; thus, it may be right or wrong, but at least it is based on a plausible assessment of the available evidence and on the fact that some types of animals on the island might be able to do this. At least it doesn't rely on any nonscientific, supernatural events to explain it. Assume the other group, in contrast, offers a completely different explanation based on the note left on the floor (which said, "An angel of the Lord flew through the window, put the vase on its side, and then left").

It would be true that we would have two competing theories at this point and that neither would be definitive, but can we really say that we would have two *equal* theories requiring an *equal amount of faith*? No. They are *not* equal theories, because the first theory is at least a plausible scientific theory based on observable evidence of the dexterity of some animals and requires no secondary leap of faith into the supernatural. I easily could see someone such as an FBI agent, using logic and deduction, pose a credible theory, consistent with plausible science and the available evidence, that some kind of animal came through the window and somehow placed the vase on its side.

In contrast, the plausibility of the angel-of-the-Lord theory relies on an entirely unscientific, supernatural scenario not normally observable in the real world. Therefore, I could *not* see the FBI agent posing a credible evidence-based theory that an angel of the Lord flew through the window and put the vase on its side as alleged in the note. True, there is the note on the floor that says an angel did it, but that is mere hearsay. What if the note said that a fairy did it or a ghost did it, or King Kong and Godzilla did it, or the flying spaghetti monster did it? Such a note would not constitute a plausible scientific, non-supernatural theory explaining what happened.

Instead, it would be an unsubstantiated supernatural assertion. Moreover, a devout believer in the explanation that an angel of the Lord placed the vase on its side would immediately become a full-fledged nonbeliever in the note if the note alleged that a magic fairy or a wicked witch, instead of an angel of the Lord, placed the vase on its side. Accordingly, the second theory relies completely on the supernatural.

The logical-deduction explanation is based on scientific plausibility and on the available evidence in the natural world. A theory that some type of animal came through the window and somehow put the vase on its side, coupled with the apparent tracks left behind, does not have to rely on a supernatural, nonscientific belief as part of its explanation. The angel theory, however, requires an additional belief in the supernatural. Maybe both theories are wrong, because, after all, perhaps it was just the wind blowing through the window that caused the vase to be on its side, or maybe an animal simply knocked the vase over as it passed by, instead of stopping and placing it on its side, or perhaps the vase has *always* been lying on its side so that any theory as to how it go to its side would be wrong. Indeed, maybe the original human owner of the abandoned house simply left the vase on its side there—but notice that, unlike the angel theory, none of these other plausible evidence-based scientific theories requires an extra leap into the supernatural involving deities or ghosts as part or all of the explanation.

Whatever the actual reason for the vase's position might be—which we may never, at this point, be able to prove or disprove—at least one of the competing theories is a much more realistic, and scientifically plausible, explanation than the other. Admittedly, the theory that some type of animal came through the window and placed the vase on its side, if it is ultimately accepted as the truth, requires a certain degree of faith, no question about that. But it does not *also* require, in addition to a certain amount of faith in the explanation itself, the acceptance of a nonscientific, supernatural belief in a god of some sort as a part of the theory. This is the critical distinction. The theory that an angel flew through the window and placed the vase on its side requires not only a certain degree of faith in what happened but also requires *an additional* kind *of faith* in how it possibly could have happened. It requires faith in a *supernatural being* beyond what we know scientifically and in reality. Pure faith in the supernatural is required to make up for the missing natural evidence in the angel theory.

Believers might argue that if the note also had great advice for living and contained predictions about future events, many of which may even have come true, that would be sufficient confirming "scientific" proof that the note was reliable. Nostradamus, the famed oracle from the Middle Ages, is also said to have made uncanny predictions, many of which have come true, but that does not prove he was writing for God or was divinely inspired as he wrote and that 100% of what he said is scientifically provable and correct. So, even if it were the case that the Bible contained various fulfilled prophesies, it would not change the fact that the angel theory at its core would be based on implausible supernatural, unscientific explanations that go beyond the natural world.

Although our limited understanding of science and our limited ability to perceive the available evidence make a complete comprehension of the cosmos down to the last detail impossible, all we really have in the pursuit of objective knowledge is science and the logical consideration of the available evidence. It would therefore be silly to argue that because it is impossible to obtain perfect knowledge using science, reason, and evidence, we therefore should not even try and our attempts at understanding the cosmos should be satisfactorily left to purely subjective beliefs and supernatural stories because, well, nobody can really know anything for sure. It is therefore incorrect to argue that all guesses, no matter what their bases, supernatural or scientific, are created equal and that all scientific impossibilities can thus be ignored.

The thing about science is that it takes the available, observable evidence, into consideration, searches for more evidence, and then tries to come up with a plausible explanation based on physical laws and natural phenomena. For example, if the window were too small for an animal to fit through, the theory that an animal came through the window would be less likely, notwithstanding the apparent tracks. Also, science is always considering new physical discoveries in the natural world and attempting to apply them; so, for example, if there were monkey DNA evidence on the vase and some monkey tracks in the room, that evidence would be supportive of the theory that an animal (a monkey) came through the window and somehow placed the vase on its side. Still, that evidence would not prove anything for sure because we would not know how, why, or when that DNA evidence and the tracks got there or how the supposed monkey got into the room and put the vase on its side, but the point is that the scientific method continually searches the best available evidence and attempts to come up with a plausible, logical, scientifically based, provable solution. That is its strength, not its weakness. That is how we actually learn about the world in which we live and discover why things are the way they are.

The thing about religious faith is that it is not really searching for a scientifically plausible knowledge-based solution given the available evidence. Instead, it *already* has its conclusion/belief and explanation—such as an angel of the Lord placing the vase on its side—such that any contrary evidence is considered to be something that is either misunderstood or evil. Meanwhile, the unscientific, supernatural, otherwise implausible aspect of the religious explanation is simply accepted as the truth because faith trumps all. Thus, science is considered correct, but only if and when it confirms the preexisting conclusion that an angel of the Lord laid the vase on its side. If science does not support that preexisting, supernatural conclusion, that science is rejected as heresy or even as an evil deception—just ask Galileo, Kepler, and Copernicus. In such a religious construct, science is reduced to a mere guess that is considered to be no better than any other guess, even a guess based on a nonscientific, religious, supernatural story.

The most problematic aspect in this simple example is that if scientists cannot offer a *definitive* answer for how the vase got on its side, even though there are sound, real-world, evidence-based, scientifically plausible theories such as that an animal somehow did it or even that the wind blew it over (neither of which have to rely on the supernatural), those theories are simply rejected because they are considered no better than the supernatural story that an angel of the Lord put the vase on its side, as set forth in the sacred note that at some point had been left behind. Even more disturbing, the vase being on its side would be considered by some to be legitimate evidence that an angel must have placed it on its side, according to the sacred note— but, interestingly, creationists would argue that the vase being on its side is *not* evidence that a *fairy* or *space aliens* laid it on its side, if some similar unsubstantiated note were to have made that assertion. The lack of any proof that an angel laid the vase on its side is simply filled in with the need for faith in what had been written about the vase's position in the sacred note.

I realize that this example is, of course, not exactly applicable because an animal placing a vase on its side is quite different from a spontaneous big bang and then evolution occurring over millions and even billions of years, and therefore they are not the same as a specific, one-time event like an animal placing a vase on its side. Still, this metaphor is helpful to make the general point about theories based on *non-supernatural explanations* and theories based on *supernatural explanations*, and how one should not simply equate them as alternately valid theories.

This example also underscores the important point about the word "theory" and how creationists often consider that term to be synonymous with a speculative guess that does not have to be supported by scientific evidence and observable facts in nature. As a result, something like the theory of evolution is considered by creationists to be no more legitimate an explanation than the creation story about plants, animals, and humans in Genesis, because both of these "theories" are mere guesses attempting to explain humankind's early history and we can therefore make a choice between equal theories and legitimately choose to believe one just as easily as the other.

In science, however, the term "theory" is actually much more involved and amounts to more than just a mere speculative guess. In science, there is actually a hierarchy of terms. Listed from their least important to their most important, there are observations, then facts, then hypotheses, then laws, and then theories. People often turn this order of importance upside down, however, and believe a theory is considered to be a mere guess at the lowest level that, if tested, can go on to become a hypothesis, and if that hypothesis is confirmed by experiments, it can then "graduate" into a law supported by facts. This reverse hierarchy is a common, and even understandable, but still incorrect, conceptualization about the meaning of those rudimentary but very important scientific terms.

Actually, in science, at the most basic, unremarkable level are *observations* (in our example, it would be that the vase is currently resting on its side). A scientist merely records what she perceives to be true based on what she observes in front of her. Next, those observations, if confirmed by other scientists, become *facts*, or *confirmed observations* (independent teams of scientists could confirm that the vase is, in fact, resting on its side and is not, for example, just a mirage). At that point, a scientist might form a *hypothesis* about *why* the vase is lying on its side.

To truly become a law, however, the hypothesis must be repeatedly testable by scientific experiment. For example, when Sir Isaac Newton observed that an apple falls to the ground, he formulated a hypothesis that gravity was pulling the apple to the ground because the Earth's mass created a powerful gravitational force. His hypothesis could be tested repeatedly, and because the experiments with apples and other objects always falling to the ground confirmed his hypothesis, his hypothesis became a *law*—the law of gravity. The law was further confirmed when we sent astronauts into Earth's orbit in space and they became weightless when they were far enough away from the mass of the Earth to create only a faint gravitational pull. The law of gravity was predictive; apples don't fall in space. Some scientists, however, actually refer to it as the theory of gravity.

Scientific laws are confirmed explanations of phenomena. In our example, there could be no law, explaining how the vase got on its side because how the vase got on its side is **not** testable by repeated experiments. The vase being on its side is a specific historical happening, and there is no way to test any explanation for it unless we had a time machine or a reliable recording of how the vase got on its side, which we assume does not exist. In other words, we cannot prove the hypothesis through repeated testing, given that the vase being on its side has already happened and we can't test an explanation to any definite conclusion. But we can formulate theories based on nature, science, logic and observations that do not have to rely on supernatural explanations. Consequently, some people would mistake a rational scientific theory for a mere guess because it can never graduate to be a testable hypothesis that, if confirmed, could become a scientific law. Accordingly, some mistakenly assume that one guess (theory) about what must have happened in the past is just as valid as any other guess (theory) about what must have happened because they are both just guesses, after all, and nobody really "knows" for sure.

A scientific theory is much more than just a speculative guess, however. A theory is a scientific explanation of complex phenomena based on a series of observable facts, available evidence, and rational, scientifically based logic that does not and cannot rely on supernatural events that are not observable in the known world, such as magic or superstition. Going back to our simple example, the "theory" that an animal put the vase on its side would be a scientific theory, because it would be based on the available evidence (apparent tracks, as well as circumstances allowing an animal to enter the room) and would be a rational, scientifically based explanation for how this particular vase got on its side (animals exist and can physically move objects), and other scientists could be engaged in a vigorous academic pursuit to try to disprove the theory if they could.

In contrast, the "theory" based on the sacred note that an angel of Lord flew through the window and put the vase on its side would not qualify as a scientific theory because it is an explanation that relies on unscientific, supernatural, unobservable phenomena not of the natural world. It is, by definition, not rationally based on reality but is instead just a personal religious belief. There is no room for such supernatural or superstitious or magical explanations in a rational scientific theory based on the available observable evidence in the natural world, however; therefore, to assert things like voodoo, black magic, or a witch's curse as explanation for someone's apparent bad luck does not qualify as a legitimate scientific theory—unless it involves something like a psychological self-fulfilling prophecy in which the victim unwittingly created his own bad luck simply because he believed so strongly in the alleged superstitious causes (similar to a placebo effect in the practice of medicine, in which people take a non-potent pill but found that taking the pill somehow made them feel better, thereby proving that the "cure" can be a psychologically-based cure).

If there were no meaningful difference between theories based in science and logic and theories based in religion and the supernatural, then Santa Claus delivering presents last Christmas Eve to one's house would be just as valid a theory about how those presents got under the tree as would the explanation that a human being (probably a parent of young children) secretly put them there. There would be no testable hypothesis about what specifically happened in that particular household last Christmas Eve because, assuming no recording, that all witnesses are now dead, and that we cannot go back in time to see who or what actually put these particular presents under this particular tree in this particular household last year, we cannot say for sure how those particular gifts got there. Instead, it would be a mystery for which all we have to work with would be trace evidence and logic, but it would be silly to suggest that we would have two equally competing theories for how the gifts got there—either Santa brought them or a human being put them there—because either one of these explanations is just as valid as the other, given the fact that they are both just guesses, just speculation and conjecture, neither of which can be proved or disproved definitively, at least in that particular household. ("Maybe Santa did not visit your household, but I believe he visited mine, and you can't prove that he was not here in spirit.")

A videotape of what actually happened would be nice, but where do we get a videotape of how the universe began, if it ever began, or of how and when the earth was created? Still, it is interesting to think about how when we on Earth can observe a distant star blow up in a supernova, we are actually witnessing something that happened millions of years ago, depending on the distance of the star from Earth (assuming God did not just speed up that light). The light from a star that is millions of light-years away obviously takes millions of years to get here (even if the universe is expanding), so we are quite literally witnessing ancient history millions of years old when we observe that star. If we were advanced enough, perhaps we could invent a super-focusing telescope that could allow us to see the light from a planet in that star system. And what if we could focus that light enough to see what was happening on the surface of that planet millions of years ago? If there were such a planet three million light-years away that has advanced aliens with such a super telescope, then conceivably, right now, they could be viewing light from the Earth that would reveal what was actually happening on the surface of the earth some three million years ago (assuming the earth existed and was reflecting light that long ago).

Just like a video camera now captures escaping light and records an event, perhaps a super camera millions of light-years away could capture and record escaping light from the earth from millions of years ago, assuming that that ancient light would not be so dispersed, reflected, or rerouted that it would be impossible to reconstruct. But even then, maybe that light somehow could be reconstructed enough to reveal what was happening. In short, is there, right now, light somewhere far, far away in the universe that is still traveling after reflecting off of a dinosaur roaming the earth millions of years ago?

Wouldn't it be amazing if that light could be captured and recorded as real evidence of Earth's history? Maybe a videotape of past events might still be possible someday. Indeed, what if the universe is not infinite but is shaped like a sphere, like the earth is a sphere, so that if one travelled in a certain direction in space long enough, one could actually arrive back at the place in the universe right where one started (like a baseball [light photon] thrown in one direction on Earth that, if thrown hard enough and fast enough, could travel around the earth and back to the place from which it was originally thrown a few weeks before)? If the universe is a sphere, could light reflected from Earth millions or even billions of years ago be making a huge universal round trip and, as a result, possibly pass by us once again so we perhaps could capture that ancient light and see the actual past of the earth transpire right before our modern eyes? Until such time as a super-advanced camera is invented and we could somehow see what it recorded it from our past (because perhaps our own ancient light would pass by us again on a universal round trip), however, we only have unconfirmed theories as our explanations.

Going back to the example of the gifts under the tree, the two explanations for how the gifts got there would not be equivalent unconfirmed guesses; instead, one explanation would be a scientific theory (parents), whereas the other would be a holiday belief (Santa). Again, I acknowledge that this simple example is not exactly equivalent to Science versus Genesis because we have actually witnessed humans putting gifts under trees and we can actually disprove Santa Claus, although we cannot disprove God; however, the point is not lost. For example, we have witnessed evolution in the world already in terms of adaptations and mutating viruses, and it is easy to extrapolate from there that such small adaptation and mutation over millions and billions of years' time logically could account for organisms evolving. Also, the fossil record, as well as the dating of the fossils, generally supports the theory of evolution. Although there is much debate and controversy about evolution, the bottom line is that there is nearly 100% agreement among scientists that the theory of evolution is true. Most importantly, that a human put a gift under a tree would be a theory about the past that does not need to rely on supernatural explanations unsupported by observable facts in nature, like Santa Claus bringing the gifts, because the theory that it was probably a human being that left the gifts under the tree would be a plausible and logical explanation not having to rely on supernatural implausibility or magic of any kind.

Going back to the vase lying on its side, perhaps most telling, religiously speaking, is to consider what should happen to a person, after that person dies, who in life decided to believe the FBI theory that an animal, instead of an angel of the Lord, probably placed the vase on its side. Would a just and fair God say that the punishment for guessing that the FBI theory sounded more plausible (and therefore more likely to be true) than the angel-of-the-Lord story should be that the person must burn in Hell forever for not guessing correctly? Should that be the cost for not believing the more farfetched supernatural explanation and instead believing the more rational explanation?

Whether the person was good or bad in life would not matter because all people are considered sinners bound for Hell unless they get saved by believing in God and accepting Jesus as their savior. In short, if God gave us the ability to reason, why would He punish us for simply using that God-given reason in a logical way?

I recently found on the Internet the following diagram that adequately captures the overall point that I am making here about two theories not just being two equal guesses.

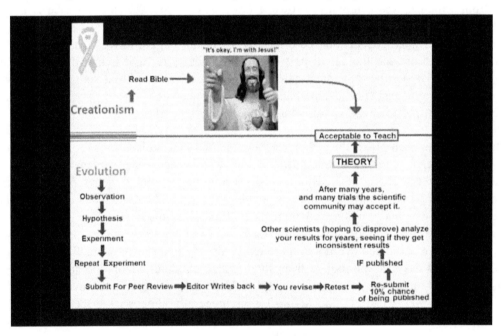

There is an interesting legal civil procedure (which happens to be the name of one of the courses I teach in law school about how to file and conduct proper lawsuits) comparison here. In our court system, we have trials in which juries consider conflicting factual evidence. The jury for a trial deliberates and then makes its best guess as to which evidence is credible and which is not. Ultimately, the jury makes a finding of fact, called a *verdict,* which we consider to be the truth about what happened in the case (for example, the defendant negligently ran a red light). In criminal cases, there is something called jury nullification, allowing jurors to make irrational decisions if they do not agree with the law. In civil cases, however, jurors must be able to base their verdict on available produced evidence in order to make a rational determination about what happened. The jury's verdict cannot simply be a wild guess or a guess based solely on personal feelings. Instead, the verdict must be an educated, or rational, guess based on evidence produced at trial.

If a civil jury cannot base its verdict on rational proof and instead bases the verdict on pure conjecture or whim—for example, the plaintiff alleges that the defendant put an evil curse on him and is thus causing him injury and so the plaintiff is entitled to money damages from the defendant—that case would have to be dismissed, based on a *lack of sufficient evidence* that would allow a jury to make a *rational* finding that the defendant put an evil curse on the plaintiff and that money damages should be awarded to the plaintiff for the wrong committed by the defendant. In state courts, this is called a directed verdict (the judge directs the verdict in the only rational way possible), and in federal court, this is a Rule 50(a) dismissal pursuant to a judgment as a matter of law for the defendant because there would be no rationally based evidence upon which a jury could make a finding for the plaintiff that the defendant's evil curse is the actual cause of the plaintiff's money damages. In the same way, we should make findings about the universe and its history based on rational proof. Supernatural explanations may be fine for religious faith, but they do not suffice as proof in a rational context such as in a court of law, or in a scientific experiment.

Chapter Thirty-Eight

The Christmas/Santa Claus Theory Again

Perhaps supporting the notion that there is an extremely important difference between a scientific theory and a religious theory and that they are not both equally valid "guesses," our son Julian's skeptical, logical, and doubting questions about the Santa Claus myth kept coming up as he got older. It was not that he was being skeptical for the sake of being skeptical. It was just that the Santa Claus story began to lack plausibility for him as he grew older.

One day he asked, "How can Santa even fit down our chimney when he is so fat?"

Now that was just funny. "Um ... it's a Christmas miracle?"

My stock answer, as any parent who celebrates the Santa Claus story knows, eventually became an unsatisfactory and even a pathetic explanation of events. Not surprisingly, eventually, the Tooth Fairy, the Easter Bunny, and the Boogie Man all would suffer a similar fate. The stories could not withstand scrutiny. It was a bittersweet process for me, watching our son grow and develop. Understandably, I was a bit sad that my son's Santa Claus bubble was being burst by the harsh realities of science and logic and that his youthful innocence of being so amazed by Santa was fast becoming an early childhood memory for him. A big part of me also was actually quite proud of him, however; I am his parent, after all. Our young son was developing the intellectual ability to question assumptions and to successfully put two and two together. My unsatisfactory and unscientific answers that Santa's sleigh was magical, that his reindeer were special, and that Santa had Christmas spirit that allowed him to carry millions of gifts and to move so fast that he could deliver those millions of gifts in just one night were all met with my son's disapproval and disbelief. Finally, he would have no more of "Why, it's a Christmas miracle, son!" That explanation for him grew tiresome and unacceptable, and even insulting, to his maturing intelligence.

"Papa, if Santa really brings all of the gifts to everyone," he asked, "why do you receive gifts from other people, and why does Grammy give me gifts? And why are there sometimes gifts under the tree even way before Santa ever comes on Christmas Eve?"

He was getting better at his critique. Another course I teach in law school is called Evidence, which one can think of as the law of the trial: determining which offered testimony and exhibits are admissible, or not, as evidence. My students take the class integrated with Trial Advocacy and have a mock trial at the end of the semester. I am always amazed at how well the law students are able to conduct devastating cross-examinations during their mock trials by the time the term ends. It is remarkable to watch their professional development. With our son, I found myself being similarly impressed with how, in his own seven-year-old-boy way, he was developing the ability to conduct at least a very rudimentary but nevertheless very effective cross-examination of me and my assertions about Santa Claus.

After it became clear that I could no longer hold him at bay, I had to admit to Julian that the Santa Claus story was not true, but at the risk of perpetuating the hypocrisy, we told him not to tell and spoil it for his little brother, Johnston! Julian quickly agreed, and now that he was in on the Santa Claus ruse too, he enthusiastically became a part of our fraudulent Christmas story on Johnston for years. Of course, as he grew older and wiser, our younger logical and discerning son, Johnston, also soon began to ask all of the same questions that his older brother previously had asked. Johnston, however, pretended to accept my "why, it's a Christmas miracle, son" explanation of events for a little while longer, at least for our sakes—but Johnston is just that way; in fact, that is one of the many beautiful things about him—he sensed that my wife and I really wanted to continue with the Christmas story every year, so he played along. It was very clear that Johnston no longer actually believed in Santa Claus or the Tooth Fairy, but, in an interesting twist, I guess he just didn't want to burst *our* bubble by leaving behind our Christmas-morning rituals and relegating them to the dustbins of early childhood memories. Our Santa Claus story represented the youth of our two boys, and as the youngest, Johnston sensed that my wife and I were not quite ready to let go of the story and the youth it represented. I guess it became a little blurry for us, too, at that point, as we realized that the Santa Claus story was no longer just for Johnston but had really become more for his parents.

Our boys were growing up. That's life, a bittersweet reality. In any event, I now often smile wistfully as I think about our great memories of our Christmas mornings, and I know that we will always cherish them in our hearts—although I am convinced that Johnston will always believe in the Tooth Fairy as long as he has teeth to lose that he can exchange for money, especially in light of his recent explanation to us of how the Tooth Fairy needed to start taking inflation into account so that the money left under his pillow is increased to "keep up with the times." He had seen an X-ray of his teeth when we were at the dentist one day and saw that his wisdom teeth would need to be pulled in the future, exchanged by the Tooth Fairy, and added to his college fund.

Chapter Thirty-Nine

Santa Claus and the Separation of Church and State: A War on Christmas or a War on the 1st Amendment?

The celebration of Christmas with our boys brought up a very important point about religion and separation-of-church-and state issues. One past Christmas season, the boys talked to us about how they got to celebrate Christmas at their Catholic schools and how a priest even gave a mass; but before, when they went to public schools, there had been no similar official Christmas masses or prayers. They asked why that was the case and if it meant that their public schools had been against Christmas. We told them no, that in our country, under our Constitution, people get to celebrate Christmas, or whatever other religious holiday or religious ceremony or idea they want, in their own homes, their houses of worship, and/or their private institutions—such as private Catholic schools. In fact, the 1st Amendment to the US Constitution protects our religious freedoms from intrusion by the government (the Free Exercise Clause), but the 1st Amendment also means that the government—through a state-run, public institution, like a public school—cannot do anything to establish any one religion over any other religion or non-religion (the Establishment Clause). This public-private distinction is called "the separation of church and state."

Certain Christian fundamentalists disagree with this "alleged" separation of church and state because the 1st Amendment does not use those words—and they are right about that—those were the words of Thomas Jefferson written in a letter describing the 1st Amendment. The words "separation of church and state" never appear anywhere in the Constitution. Also, these fundamentalists argue that we live in a democracy, in which the majority rules and a majority of people in the US are Christians and the majority of Americans have always been some type of Christian, so therefore it is anti-democratic to prohibit the religion of the majority to be heard and seen in various public contexts. They further argue that because our whole system of government rests on the consent of the governed, symbols and practices of the Christian majority should not be prohibited in government institutions such as public schools and government buildings. We the people (the governed) should not have to bend to the will of the government, but instead, the government should have to bend to the will of the people, and the majority of the people in the US are Christians. It is just that simple.

These arguments would be correct if the founders of our country had thought that the free exercise and the non-establishment of religion should *not* be a matter of constitutional rights but instead should be subject merely to a simple vote in which the majority rules. That is clearly not the case, however. Instead, the free exercise and the non-establishment of religion are protected constitutional rights and have been found to be so according to several US Supreme Court decisions. They are rights that are protected even from the will of the majority. That is what makes the Bill of Rights a true bill of rights: They are rights that are not subject to mere voting. Indeed, our constitutional rights are beyond voting, unless the Constitution itself is amended with supermajorities in both houses of Congress and then ratified by the states. Think what would happen if, for instance, our rights of freedom of speech were put to a simple vote—the popular political majority could always just vote down any unpopular political minority and could even vote to keep that minority from being able to voice its political opinions in the town square. We probably all would agree that such a denial of free speech, even if voted on by a clear majority, would nonetheless be unconstitutional and un-American.

Many conservative Christian fundamentalists often contend, however, that the government is not allowing Christians to freely exercise their religion when the government (through the courts) prohibits activities such as prayer in schools. This reminds me of the old joke that there is now and always will be prayer in schools as long as there are tough final exams! Christian fundamentalists argue that *official* public school prayer is not the establishment of religion but is merely the promotion or allowance of the religious faith of the majority inside of a democracy. They further argue that there has been a loss of societal values and a growth of general immorality in our country that directly coincides with the government prohibiting official prayer in public schools. Interestingly, however, it is amazing how those same Christian fundamentalists immediately become champions of the separation of church and state if we are talking about Islam or any other religion besides Christianity being established, promoted, or allowed by our government in official public contexts.

For example, conservative Christian fundamentalists appear to staunchly oppose the Taliban or Al-Qaeda running a radical Islamic theocratic government in Afghanistan, Iraq, Egypt, or Iran under Islamic or Sharia law instead of establishing a more secular and free democracy where Christians would be free to practice Christianity, even though they would be in the political minority. Also, closer to home, if Muslims one day were to become a political majority in this country, or even just in a US city, and they voted to pass an ordinance that required scriptures from the Qur'an to be enshrined in city government buildings or Islamic prayers to be said over loudspeakers before public high school football games, then these same Christian fundamentalists would be the first to seek the protection of the Establishment Clause under the 1st Amendment so they would not have to view scriptures from the Qur'an in their public buildings or listen to Islamic prayers before their public high school football games. The argument that the city government would not be establishing the religion of Islam by taking these actions but merely promoting or simply allowing the religion of the Islamic democratic majority to be freely exercised would probably fall on very deaf ears. Christian fundamentalists probably would challenge these Islamic-related city ordinances as unconstitutional, despite the fact that in our democratic system, the "majority rules."

Of course, these Christian fundamentalists would be entirely correct to appeal to the 1st Amendment's separation of church and state in such circumstances because public Islamic prayers being said at state-run institutions like public high schools and the enshrinement of scriptures from the Qur'an in city buildings would be stark examples of the government being used improperly to establish, promote, or allow one religion over another, but that really just proves the very general point that we all need to be consistent here, no matter our religion. Can it be that when it would be Christian scriptures and Christian prayers in public places, they should be allowed because that would not be establishing a religion but would just be that the "majority rules" and the Free Exercise Clause would protect those Christian-related laws from government prohibition but that when it would be Islamic scriptures and Islamic prayers in public places, they should be prohibited because that would be establishing a religion, in violation of the Establishment Clause and those laws should not be allowed under the Free Exercise Clause because the "majority rules" idea must sometimes give way to constitutional principles? That kind of double-standard hypocrisy cannot be what the 1st Amendment really stands for. That would be like saying, "The Free Exercise Clause means that *only my Christian religion* is a proper religion for government promotion, but not your religion; while the Establishment Clause means that *your Islamic religion* is an improper religion for government promotion, but not mine."

The thing about a constitutional principle, or *any* principle for that matter, is that it must be applied *consistently*, no matter what side of the issue one is on. As such, the 1st Amendment is *not* a simple "might makes right" or "majority makes right" kind of proposition such that, depending on who is in the majority, one religion gets superior billing by the government over other religions (or over non-religion) in the public square. And this religion–non-religion neutrality does not mean that the government necessarily must be supporting atheism. That was never the point of or the intention behind the 1st Amendment. Instead, the government is simply putting *all* religiously based issues into a *private* sphere such that individuals can practice their religions free from government interference (the Free Exercise Clause), without the government officially taking any sides with respect to any religion in the *public* sphere (the Establishment Clause).

It therefore is a mistake to think that the principle of the separation of church and state means that the government unfairly suppresses our right to practice our own religions. It does not. It is just that in a pluralistic, diverse democracy, the government should not be used or captured by any one particular religion to *officially* promote or establish that religion in any public institutions. Of course, privately, people may worship however and whenever they please, without government interference, as long as they generally do so without violating any laws in the process.

Just as the government should not intrude into the sphere of churches, synagogues, and mosques (the Free Exercise Clause), neither should churches, synagogues, and mosques intrude into the sphere of the government (the Establishment Clause). It does not matter who is in the political majority or the political minority, because constitutional rights are protected, even from the democratic will of the majority (unless the Constitution is amended by political supermajorities). Remember that our constitutional rights also protect us from the potential tyranny of the majority, so the government is not the enemy here—in fact, we are the government, because in a democracy, we the people are the government, but the government is subject to the rights and protections of citizens as set forth in the Constitution. Of course, we can always amend our Constitution to provide that the 1st Amendment does not apply to the establishment of the Christian religion and can, as a result, become a theocratic, Christian-based nation instead of a constitutional, democratic republic with no official religion. The Constitution has never yet been amended in that particular way, however.

Thus, with all of this in mind, my wife, our boys, and I get to fully enjoy celebrating Christmas together, both religiously and traditionally, in whatever manner we see fit. We get to include false stories about Santa, we get to engage in gift-giving (which, among other things, is a great help to our economy), and we get to put Christmas trees (adopting what was originally a European non-Christian pagan tradition) as well as other various decorations in our living rooms. And amid all of this, we can even include a nativity scene depicting the birth of Jesus ("the reason for the season"). We appreciate the fact that we live in a country that allows us to do so in our own home, in our own church, and in our kids' private Catholic schools, all without any interference from the government, provided that we do not violate any existing laws in the process. But we also appreciate the fact that the government is not allowed to publicly advocate any one religion over any other religion, or non-religion, even if the one being advocated is my religion (because one day, it might be someone else's religion). Instead, the Constitution leaves religion (and to some extent religious holidays) completely up to each citizen individually to practice our own religions for ourselves, according to our own consciences and our own spiritual choices, whatever they might be, without the interference or promotion of the government one way or another. In short, there is no war on Christmas by liberals, as many conservatives charge. To the contrary, I submit that if any war is actually going on, it might better be thought of as a war on the 1st Amendment by certain Christian conservatives.

Indeed, the freedom to exercise one's own religion, along with the freedom from having the government establish any particular religion, is a freedom often cited as why people long ago decided to come to this country, even before it was a country. Those reasons were to escape the religious persecution of state-run religious theocracies in Europe, as well as to be able to freely practice religion without any governmental interference and without the government being able to establish or promote any particular religion. Accordingly, this is why the founders of our country put these important concerns and concepts into the 1st Amendment of the US Constitution. When we adhere to those principles, the 1st Amendment separation of church and state is one of the many things that make this country a great country. One should also note that the Bible seems to recognize the profound wisdom of the concept of the separation of church and state when Jesus commands us to "render to Caesar the things that are Caesar's, and to God the things that are God's" (Mark 12:17).

In fact, when we look at the life of Jesus, we see that Jesus always appealed to people's *individual* hearts and minds about all religious and spiritual matters. In doing so, He did not seek to pass public civil laws establishing or promoting various Christian religious doctrines, teachings, and practices, for He clearly did not try to use the law or politics to promote or politically establish His own religion or His own religious message as an official public act. He did not use the government to try to force the acceptance, or even the recognition, of religion. Instead, He mostly *personally* ministered to people, heart to heart, as private individuals, not as potential voting blocks. Jesus did not find it necessary or, apparently, wise to minister through official government channels and public, government-run institutions. Perhaps this separation that Jesus exhibited during His life on Earth is still a good example to follow even today, not only for Christians but for all Americans.

My older son, Julian, has always enjoyed Christmas, and although he understands the separation of church and state, he also is a very strong believer in the literalism of the Bible (I guess this stuff just skips generations, or God has a really ironic sense of humor by sandwiching me in between two literalists—my dad and my eldest son). Anyway, Julian began to question me about what the wholly fictitious Santa fairytale had to do with the reality of why we celebrate Christmas—the birth of Jesus Christ. He came to view the Christmas story as antithetical to Christianity and to Jesus's birth. Instead of a church-versus-state issue, he had a Santa-versus-Jesus issue. Julian was troubled that the farfetched Santa myth had nothing to do with the reality of the Virgin Mary's miraculous conception of Jesus by receiving the seed of the Holy Spirit of God and then giving birth on the night a bright star was shining in the east in celebration so that the three wise men from the east could come bearing gifts… Hmm. On the one hand, the Santa story is definitely false because it is scientifically impossible, but on the other hand, certain stories in the Bible that are scientifically impossible are nevertheless to be taken literally as entirely true.

Be that as it may, I tried to answer Julian's concerns. Why do we have this silly Santa Claus *fairytale* that hides the *true* story of the young Virgin Mary who was told by an angel that she would be impregnated by the seed of the Holy Spirit and then give birth, as a virgin, to the Son of God, who would be unjustly crucified and therefore atone for all of the world's sinners so they can go to Heaven when they die instead of burning in Hell for eternity? …Wow. Which of these two stories is actually the more unscientific and logically implausible? There was just no escaping it: The Santa story and many Biblical stories, as *literal* renditions of events, require a huge amount of pure logic-suspending faith in *supernatural, scientifically impossible miracles*. By the way, many other religions and societies claim the virgin birth of religious/political icons, such as Jesus, Perseus, Buddha, Attis, Huitzilopochtli, Genghis Khan, Krishna, Horus, Mercury, to name just a few.

My point is *not* that God and the angels do not exist simply because they are somehow equivalent to a nonexistent Santa Claus and his implausible flying reindeer. Instead, my point is this: If we take the Bible *literally*, then we are often required to suspend science and logic to use the exact same kind of supernatural, miraculous assumptions to explain away inconsistencies and scientific impossibilities. The Santa Claus story may be a myth and the biblical rendition of supernatural miracles may be true, but in *both instances*, we still must suspend science, logic, and reality in the same way to accept the literal supernatural explanations of what would otherwise be implausible and unscientific events. It takes the same amount of faith in the supernatural to believe either story. Still, we can disprove Santa, but we cannot disprove, or prove, God.

So helper elves are fairytales but celestial angels are real? We know elves are not real because we can go to the North Pole and not find any elves or any conditions that would support humanlike elf life in a workshop. If elves are not considered real because we cannot see them, why are angels real when we cannot see them or visit the place where they live, either? Assuming angles are real, just unseen, however, let's explore some further issues regarding angels in the next chapter.

Chapter Forty

Are There Slaves in Heaven?

God's creation of the angels seems to undercut the entire notion that God is all-powerful, because it shows that He apparently needs the help of angels to carry out His plan(s). If God can listen to the prayers of billions of people simultaneously and then answer them all (as well as create the universe)—truly super Godlike feats—why would He need any assistance from angels? Wouldn't He have everything pretty much covered and under control all on His own? If God really has it all under control, angels would have no purpose, because God is truly all-powerful (omnipotent) and all-knowing (omniscient).

Even if God does not need the angels, perhaps angels still have desirable purposes. Maybe the purposes of angels are to protect people on Earth, to deliver God's messages to people, to help humans in various ways, and to assist God in general as celestial servants. But can't God protect people directly, deliver His own messages (like He allegedly did to Adam, Moses, and others), and generally help all of humanity in various ways, all on His own? Why would an omniscient and omnipotent God be in any need of help from angels to run the world, Heaven, and the universe? God seems a little too humanlike if He actually needs the assistance of others to administer all of creation. Is it possible that God can actually get tired of running the universe? After all, He apparently needed to rest on the seventh day after creating the universe. Is the occasional humanlike need for rest the reason God created angels in the first place—to do the more mundane celestial tasks in the universe that He apparently is either too tired or too bored to do Himself and therefore delegates to His subordinate helpers?

If so, it would be rather disturbing that God would create angels for this exploitative purpose. If God needs or wants assistance from angels, is it right—indeed, is it the act of a moral God—to create a permanent class of servants, or celestial slaves, who must carry out all of His wishes? If these slave-angels fail to do what God says, apparently, they get sent to Hell as evil demons in the service of the evil and rebellious Satan. It would appear that God created angels as celestial servants who must obey Him, or else!

Either involuntary servitude is wrong or it is not. It cannot be wrong for humankind to enslave others but OK for God to do so. Is God above His own law? Perhaps having angels as slaves is not a contradiction, because slavery appears to be acknowledged, even allowed, throughout the Bible. For example, slaves (bondmen) are considered the property of their owners (Leviticus 25:45: "and they shall be your possession"), but why would God allow some of His children to enslave and own other of His children? Why would God approve of such immorality?

> **[44]** Both thy bondmen, and thy bondmaids, which thou shalt have, shall be of the heathen that are round about you; of them shall ye buy bondmen and bondmaids.
> **[45]** Moreover of the children of the strangers that do sojourn among you, of them shall ye buy, and of their families that are with you, which they begat in your land: and they shall be your possession.
> **[46]** And ye shall take them as an inheritance for your children after you, to inherit them for a possession; they shall be your bondmen for ever: but over your brethren the children of Israel, ye shall not rule one over another with rigour. (Leviticus 25:44–46)

So the Bible approves of owning slaves, as long as they are "heathens," or the children of heathens (or strangers or foreigners). Notice, however, that there seems to be a different standard for owning Hebrew slaves (Exodus 21:2–4):

> **[2]** If thou buy an Hebrew servant, six years he shall serve: and in the seventh he shall go out free for nothing.
> **[3]** If he came in by himself, he shall go out by himself: if he were married, then his wife shall go out with him.
> **[4]** If his master have given him a wife, and she have born him sons or daughters; the wife and her children shall be her master's, and he shall go out by himself.

How fair is that? Does the Bible not only approve of slavery and of owning people but then also discriminate on the basis of race, ethnicity, and religion, by setting forth a different standard when it comes to owning Hebrew slaves, as opposed to all other slaves? This is *not* just work for hire. How is it that the master can keep the wife and children of even a Hebrew slave? If God approves of slavery and of owning people and their children and even has different standards involving racial and ethnic discrimination between slaves, then could gender discrimination be far behind (as God apparently also approves of sex slavery, if He was the one who wrote these verses in the Bible)? Does it seem like God would actually write verses in the Bible explaining how one should go about selling one's own daughter into slavery? If not written by God, perhaps the following verses were simply written by a man who lived in the Middle East some 3,500 years ago as he discussed what were acceptable cultural norms at the time.

> **[7]** And if a man sell his daughter to be a maidservant, she shall not go out as the menservants do.
> **[8]** If she please not her master, who hath betrothed her to himself, then shall he let her be redeemed: to sell her unto a strange nation he shall have no power, seeing he hath dealt deceitfully with her.
> **[9]** And if he have betrothed her unto his son, he shall deal with her after the manner of daughters.

[10] If he take him another wife; her food, her raiment, and her duty of marriage, shall he not diminish.

[11] And if he do not these three unto her, then shall she go out free without money. (Exodus 21:7–11)

This appears to refer to sex slavery, or at least to some form of prostitution, or perhaps polygamy (but not adultery?), because the maidservant, whom the master has betrothed to himself, is supposed to please her male master. If her master takes another wife—thereby equating the sex slave-maidservant with a wife—the Bible provides instructions, but logically, it would matter only if the maidservant were having a sexual relationship with the slave owner who bought her. Would God really approve of a father selling his own daughter to another man as a maidservant to please the male buyer in a wifely manner?

Along these same lines, is God compassionate because, although He may approve of a slave owner *physically beating* his slaves, at least God seems to *limit the severity* of those beatings? There were also such statutes in the Old South, where a master was allowed to beat a slave, but just not so severely as to cause permanent damage. It reminds me of a more modern legal context in which it is perfectly legal for a human to own a dog and even to physically discipline (beat) that dog, but if that physical discipline (beating) is too severe so that it crosses over into animal cruelty, it becomes illegal. We are once again led to the fundamental question: Why can humans own other humans as slaves in the Bible, and why can slave owners beat their slaves with a rod, provided that beating is not severe? Ask yourself who must have written the following biblical passage:

[20] And if a man smite his servant, or his maid, with a rod, and he die under his hand; he shall be surely punished.

[21] Notwithstanding, if he continue a day or two, he shall not be punished: for he is his money.(Exodus 21:20–21)

So as long as one does not beat his slave to death with a rod, that beating is OK and the slave owner should not be punished? Did God actually say that? If so, are we to believe that God approves of this referenced slavery, of beating slaves, of fathers selling their daughters, and that God even regulates (although not very much) the institution of slavery in these various ways? If not, is that an admission that God did not write the Bible, or at the very least that God did not write these particular verses of the Bible?

Either God approves of the immoral institution of slavery or God is not the author of the Bible—or at least not of these particular slavery-related verses (and other similar verses throughout the Bible that seemingly acknowledge and condone slavery as a commonly practiced institution with no clear disapproval as there is unequivocal condemnation for failing to keep the Sabbath holy or for using the Lord's name in vain). One would think that slavery would be strongly prohibited rather than tolerated and even approved by God. To the extent there might be contrary verses condemning the institution of slavery, then, *at best*, the Bible would be inconsistent and contradictory on the issue of slavery.

Assuming that slavery is allowed or approved of by the Bible, given these verses, an interesting dilemma is raised for Christian fundamentalists who quote the US Constitution to which we have a patriotic, as well as a legal and even moral, duty to follow. It is a dilemma because the 13th Amendment to the US Constitution makes slavery (involuntary servitude) unconstitutional. Consequently, should Christians follow the Bible or the US Constitution? Should Christian fundamentalists at the time slavery was about to be abolished have been against the abolition of slavery because abolishing slavery was contrary to biblical teachings approving of slavery? Or should patriotic Christians have supported the abolition of slavery because emancipating slaves in America upheld our statement in the Declaration of Independence that all men are created equal? Of course, perhaps when it said, "all *men* are created equal," the Declaration really meant only rich, landowning white men are created equal and specifically did not include any women, and certainly not any racial or ethnic minority. After all, Jefferson Davis, the leader of the Confederate South at the time, said the following about slavery being the will of God:

> [Slavery] was established by decree of Almighty God.... [I]t is sanctioned in the Bible, in both Testaments, from Genesis to Revelation....[I]t has existed in all ages, has been found among the people of the highest civilization, and in nations of the highest proficiency in the arts.

A good question to ask might be "What would Jesus do" (or have done) regarding slavery? Would Jesus have been for or against slavery? I do not think anyone would seriously argue that Jesus would be *for* slavery, but if Jesus definitely would be against the immoral institution of slavery and if God truly wrote the Bible, why are there verses in the Bible that seemingly condone, or at least allow, slavery? Even if we do not know for sure what Jesus would do, at least we do know what Abraham Lincoln did—he fully opposed slavery through the Emancipation Proclamation, and he supported the 13th Amendment to the US Constitution, which prohibited slavery once and for all, any contrary biblical verses notwithstanding.

If the Bible allows for slavery as a legitimate institution, then it should not be all that surprising that the writers of the Bible would portray God as having celestial servants called angels. Still, Moses would be told by God that the bondage of the Jews by an Egyptian pharaoh was wrong and that the pharaoh should "let [His] people go." But if it was wrong for the Egyptians to enslave Jews, then was it not just as wrong for God to create a group of celestial slaves called angels? Are certain forms of slavery not immoral? Is it justified because God's angels are willing to be His slaves?

Is slavery any less wrong if the slave is a "willing" or even "happy" slave? In the Confederate South in the US, there are many accounts of certain house slaves that did not join with the North against the South. Some of these "willing" slaves even fought alongside their Confederate masters against the Union Army. Was their slavery any less objectionable because they appeared to be willing slaves on behalf of their masters? Was it possible that the subjugation process of a life of slavery was so complete for some slaves that it also enslaved their minds into thinking that their masters' enslavement of them was something worth fighting for—even against the Union Army forces that sought to liberate them? If so, would that mean that the enslavement of willing (or even "happy") slaves was not immoral based on a theory of the consent and waiver of rights?

What if right now, an angel in Heaven were not to do exactly as God instructed? Presumably, angels still have free will, just as Lucifer and one-third of the original angels had free will when they were originally created in Heaven. If they had had no free will originally in Heaven, Lucifer, turned Satan, never could have rebelled against God. So, assuming the free will of angels in Heaven now, would God punish a disobedient angel to gain compliance? Do angels now tremble in fear that if they do not obey God, they will end up in Hell just like Satan and the former-angel demons? If so, how is it not a form of slavery to be born into celestial servitude forever? (Angels do not die or even get to retire from their life of servitude.) Do angels understand that if they do not serve and do not obey forever, they presumably will receive the ultimate punishment of Hell, forever, for their disobedience? Is that really fair? Is it right?

I am not at all arguing for complete moral equivalency here, but recall that Moses was a rebellious slave against Egypt. Moses was rewarded by God for his leadership of the Hebrew slave rebellion against the immorality of the Egyptian slave masters. Satan, in contrast, ended up in Hell forever for leading one-third of the angels in their rebellion against God, their master, or king, in Heaven. It seems, however, that *all* slavery should be considered immoral and wrong, not just some instances of slavery, as when humans enslave other humans (which is evil, at least in this one instance) or when God enslaves others (because, as God, He "owns" them and therefore can do whatever He wants with His property). Is it a satisfactory answer to this question about God to say that I have no right to ask such questions?

It is true that God loves us and creation but if the Egyptian pharaohs loved their slaves, would that love have justified enslaving them anyway? I don't think so. Just how far do God's property rights over us, the angels, and all of creation extend? Think about how angels must serve God forever with no apparent autonomy or pay for their work and no retirement plan. Why should that not be considered exploitation of angels? Although angels may get to live in Heaven, servitude is servitude. Were slaves in the Old South really not slaves after all because they got "free" room and board, some of them even getting to live in a nice plantation house, as long as they obeyed their masters?

Finally, it is strange that an all-powerful and all-knowing God would even create these particular angels in the first place, when He obviously knew (remember, God has foresight; He knows the future because He is omniscient) that one-third of them and Lucifer would eventually rebel against Him, introduce evil into the universe, tempt billions of humans, and eventually lead many humans into Hell forever? Why was it necessary to give angels free will in Heaven and allow them to choose between good and evil? Is it really a choice to say, "You can either serve God in Heaven or burn in Hell," and therefore it is not slavery if they "chose" to serve in Heaven rather than suffer punishment in Hell forever?

Also, when one-third of the angels rebelled, didn't that prove there was a monumental and catastrophic design flaw in how God engineered/created the basic "software package" of angels, at least when He created the eventually rebellious one-third of the angels? So who is ultimately responsible for how these particular angels were originally wired? (There will be more on this later when we come to Adam and Eve's Original Sin and their alleged free will to choose evil when God was actually the one who created humans and created a universe wherein evil would be a possible option for them to choose.) Finally, why wasn't Lucifer's original sin against God visited on *all* of the angels (like Adam and Eve's Original Sin is visited on *all* of humanity throughout time), instead of just the specific one-third of the angels that decided to rebel with him? Is it because it would be unfair to hold all angels responsible for the sins of only Lucifer and the one-third who followed him? If so, why is it fair to hold all humans responsible for the sins of just Adam and Eve?

Chapter Forty-One

And Now a Word from My Very Disappointed Mother

I must pause at this point in my general discussion of angels to share the fact that my mother really does not like this part of the book very much. She actually has problems with the entire book (except for Part Four, to some extent), but she especially has a big problem with all of my disrespectful, skeptical questions and sarcastic observations, particularly about angels.

My mom can be described as a mystic, astrology-consulting, yet still traditional and very staunch Catholic. She prays the Rosary every morning, like my grandmother did before her. In her house, my mom has seemingly endless statues and knickknacks of Jesus, of Baby Jesus, and of the Virgin Mary (as well as the Latina version, La Virgen de Guadeloupe), not to mention statutes and pictures of various patron saints, such as St. Jude, St. Peter, and St. Paul, as well as religious art that gives her house that special suburban-medieval look. But it doesn't stop there, *no*…idolatry and false Gods be damned!

There are also candles everywhere, in various nooks and crannies, and in all of her numerous little makeshift religious shrines throughout the house. Of course, there are also crosses to be found, crosses with Jesus on the cross, crosses without Jesus, and crosses in the garage—yes, the garage (to bless the car and to keep her safe while driving). But now to the main point: There is also nonstop artwork of… you guessed it, *angels*! There are serious do-not-mess-with-me-or-God angels, harp-playing peaceful angels, little baby cherubs, angels with swords, angels without swords, angels protecting children, angels praying, angles singing, angels rejoicing, and so on. And just to show that she has a sense of humor about it all, she even has a picture of two little devious angels drinking a beer and smoking a cigarette! … I really don't even know what to say about that one.

Now that the imagery is clear, as I said, my mom does not like what I have to say about angels in this book. After going over some early drafts of things I say about the angels one day when I was visiting her, she said to me, as if I were about to be grounded, "Why do you have to pick on angels so much in this book of yours—this book that is not even about the law, Mr. Law Professor? Why don't you leave the angels alone? They never hurt nobody. They're only there to help you, anyway. So enough about angels already, and their wings! …And they're not slaves, either! What the hell's the matter with you?"

That's my mom! To give you more of an idea about her character, when she was 73 years old, she fell down one day and dislocated her shoulder and tore some shoulder tendons. Instead of calling an ambulance, she drove herself to the emergency room, using her good arm and cursing the whole way there because she was mad at herself for falling down. When she got to the hospital, the doctor scolded her for driving herself while she was injured and in so much pain because she could have fainted and possibly gotten into an accident. Her explanation for driving herself was that she "did not want to pay for no damn ambulance that would have taken their sweet time getting to the house anyway." She has insurance and Medicare that would have covered it, but, again, that's my mom.

As she was scolding me for writing all of these various things about angels and for daring to ask such sarcastic questions about their physical bodies and their literal existence, I just dismissed it as her providing a loyal, predictable, religious, Catholic defense of angels. I should have known better. Just when I thought that was the end of it, she delivered the following devastating zinger that made me think twice: "Hey, you had better watch it…. Your guardian angel may not be there when you need him someday, and then what, huh? Then what are you going to do, smartass? Leave the angels alone; I know what I'm tellin' you!"

I didn't dare ask her right then about what *her* guardian angel was doing the day she fell down and dislocated her shoulder, but when I finally did ask her about it, she said her fall was actually "all part of God's plan" because it ended up being a very good lesson for her. So God let her fall, but only to dramatically remind her always to be careful and, as she put it, so she would always "watch what the hell I'm doing!" But if that is true and God wants us, and already teaches us, to be careful, then why do we even have guardian angels? Do they protect us or not? Maybe they just say, "Watch out!" whenever there is danger? If we are protected by angels but we still get hurt sometimes, then we can always just say that our getting hurt was actually all part of God's plan to begin with. Thus, no matter what happens—either God protects us or He lets us get hurt on purpose to teach us a lesson—it is covered, kind of like my dad's "heads I win, tails you lose" argument. My mom's other explanation about what her guardian angel was doing the day she fell down and dislocated her shoulder was "making sure I didn't fall down *even worse* and maybe even kill myself!" How does one even argue with that kind of logic?

"Oh, Mom. You have to understand that I am not intending to disrespect angels. In fact, they seem like very interesting creatures to me—seriously, they do. It's just that, well, some of what they do, and how and why they exist, if you take it all seriously and very literally, it just, you know … seems, a little farfetched, dontcha' think?"

No response. Nothing. She just stared at me with her deafening silence of disapproval. Nothing, not even "in the end times, son, wise men will become fools," like my dad. Nothing. After an awkward pause and a nervous clearing of my throat, I said, "Well, Mom, I suppose I already have made all the necessary points about the angels that I need to make, so you're right, no use in unnecessarily belaboring the issue about the angels any further. I'll just move on to address Verse 2 of the first Chapter of Genesis."

AND NOW A WORD FROM MY VERY DISAPPOINTED MOTHER

"Good."

OK, well at least she spoke, even though it was only a one-word response.

"Plus, you know, Mom, I really need to move a little more quickly through the verses, anyway. I have spent far too much time on just the very first verse of Genesis."

"Yep."

I hope I can have half, just *half,* of this kind of parental guilt-tripping control over my two sons when they are grown men—*allegedly* grown men. Both my mom and my dad are masters at using disapproval and parental disappointment as a very effective argumentative technique, at least against me. But they are also very loving and caring—those evil geniuses!

As I was returning home from this visit with my mom, there was just one last thing that I kept thinking about: What if I actually did have this potentially vengeful guardian angel? Would he really let me get hit, maybe by a truck or something, after I wrote this book, just because I made him angry and he therefore wanted to teach me some kind of lesson for my disrespectful questioning? I hoped I was just being paranoid, but then I thought, *Oh no, sometimes paranoid people may really have something to be paranoid about; indeed, their paranoia might be completely justified! Although they may think that they should not be paranoid, that is exactly why they* should be paranoid, *because they are not prepared for something bad happening to them. So even if I manage to dodge all future oncoming dangerous trucks, a boulder still might fall on me–in my sleep, no less*!

Wait a minute! Really? Seriously? I could not believe that I had been actually entertaining, even for a moment, a concern about some vindictive guardian angel assigned to me that would let me get hit by a truck because I would dare to write such things in a book. Those catechism nuns must have really done a number on my psyche as a child! Still, just in case my guardian angel would do such a thing, I then wondered if I could sue him, or her, for breach of the fiduciary duty owed to me, as my duly appointed guardian angel upon whom I am reasonably relying for my safety, and whether I could even get punitive damages if he, or she, were to *intentionally* allow me to get hit by an out-of-control truck or let me stumble and hit my head. Actually, I think I would have a pretty good case, although serving court papers on a guardian angel, as well as getting personal jurisdiction in state or federal court over that angel, could still be a bit of a problem.

It is funny how the one thing my long since divorced and embattled parents—my dad now a fundamentalist preacher, and my mom a mystic Catholic—who throughout my childhood could never seem to agree on anything now, finally, can agree on at least one thing: Neither one of them likes my book very much. … Great.

I was at least hoping that my very loving and understanding wife, Christine, would be a little more sympathetic regarding what I have written about angels. A few years ago, however, many of my wife's clients began referring to her as an angel because she is so helpful to them with their legal problems. They often said it was as though they were being helped by an angel when my wife represented them. She now has her own very successful law practice, and in honor of those clients, she named her business Angel Law of Sacramento. Needless to say, with a name like Angel Law, she is not exactly thrilled by this portion of my book, either, even though she understands the rhetorical points I am making by asking such questions about angels and their literal existence. Nonetheless, the best I could get out of her about the whole topic was, "You're weird and interesting and that's why I love you." And so, with that ringing endorsement and vote of complete confidence from my life partner, I press on to the second verse of Genesis!

PART THREE

POST-CREATION EARLY HUMAN HISTORY

Chapter Forty-Two

The Rest of the First Day of Creation (of the Earth)

Genesis 1

[2] And the earth was without form, and void; and darkness was upon the face of the deep. And the Spirit of God moved upon the face of the waters.

What does it mean that the "earth was without form, and void"? Literally, that would mean it had no shape and there was nothing on it, and perhaps even that it was hollow. It does not seem to make sense literally. If the earth had no form and was void, how could there already be water on it, "the deep" apparently meaning oceans and seas and lakes? If the earth had no form how was it possible for oceans to exist on a formless void planet? Also, why no mention of the creation of water or the creation of the earth's atmosphere ("let there be water" or "let there be breathable air")? What about letting there be gravity, or letting there be energy, or letting there be magnetism, or letting there be atoms and molecules, or letting there be time—all extremely important ingredients in the universe? Does the writer even understand what gravity or energy or magnetism or time is, and how any of them work, and how they too would have had to have been created? How did all of these fundamental things get here without any explanation in Genesis?

Also, wouldn't the Spirit of God, being omnipresent, *already* be upon the face of the waters? Wouldn't God's Spirit be everywhere simultaneously *already*, instead of moving from place to place, like moving upon the face of the waters? Does "the face of the waters" mean only the surface of the waters? If so, does that mean God's Spirit was not *in* the oceans or *in* the atmosphere? Why this particular description of *where* God's Spirit was if God's Spirit is supposed to be omnipresent, continuously present everywhere?

[3] And God said, Let there be light: and there was light.

Recall that on this first day, there were no sun and no stars yet because they were not created until the fourth day. That means that there were no light-producing objects in the universe at that point, yet on the first day, God said, "Let there be light," and there was light. Somehow, light was created at that point, but from where, and from what, was this alleged light coming? How can there be starlight if there are no stars; sunlight, if there is no sun? Did God somehow create light coming from nonexistent stars? It is as though the writer was so unaware of how the universe works that he did not realize that the light which lights the universe all comes from stars and that our sun is a star. But if there were no stars and there was no sun, there could not have been any light at that point, meaning the verse is logically and literally impossible. If Moses meant the Sun when he said "light," why didn't he write that God said, "Let there be a sun, to give light as well as warmth and energy to the earth"?

Maybe Moses thought that because there is still daylight when it is cloudy out, light somehow can also come from a source other than the sun or the stars. It would have to be some kind of mistaken assumption like this, because there could not have been light in the universe if there were no stars in existence yet to produce and sustain that light in the universe. Did the light come from fire? What would that awfully big fire have burned/consumed? Logically, light would have been impossible at that point unless God just made some other unidentified sustained light source and then apparently destroyed that unexplained, now apparently nonexistent, light source once the sun and the stars, from which essentially all light in the universe now emanates, were created three days later to take over all lighting duties in the universe.

If there somehow was light, then God must have "let there be light" from some completely unknown light source that served its purpose for only three days in the beginning, until the sun and all of the other stars were created on the fourth day. (And, as stated earlier, how can there even be a day, or three days, when there was no sun, which would be needed to even define a day, in the first place?) So at this point, there could be no light as we experience it if there were no light-producing objects in the universe because they had yet to be created. There literally would have had to have been light bulbs, or some such other form of light, in Heaven for this to be true. Perhaps the light referred to here was light coming from God Himself—but if so, why wasn't there *already* light in the universe because God has existed for eternity?

If light is symbolic or represents something else, like lightning or light-producing chemicals such as those produced by fireflies, fine, but then one must concede that the Bible should not be interpreted literally, according to the "plain meaning" of the text. After all, God probably did not light the entire universe for three days using fireflies until sextillions of stars took over, especially because God had created no animals or insects yet (that would not be until the fifth and sixth days—see below).

The need to correct the error, or to interpret the passage in such a way as to mean something not explicitly stated in order to have it make sense, means that one must either concede that the Bible contains an error and therefore cannot be the word of a God that is incapable of mistakes or that the Bible cannot always be interpreted literally and still make logical sense. This is the problem with a literal translation and interpretation of the Bible: One constantly runs into logical or logistical scientific impossibilities. One either has to accept the impossibilities and reject science and logic, or one must supply a nonliteral interpretation of some sort to have the story make logical sense—like God made fireflies or continuous and sustained lightning bolts—instead of the stars and the sun—as the source of light in the universe, at least for the first three days of creation (which may have been for 3,000 years, recall, if a God-day is equal to 1,000 years).

Chapter Forty-Three

Understanding the Point of a Story

The problem regarding the appropriateness of literal interpretation in the telling of stories reminds me of a very valuable lesson that I once learned from a federal judge for whom I worked just after graduating from law school. I clerked for the Honorable John L. Kane Jr. from 1986 to 1987 and then continued working as a lawyer in Denver after my clerkship with him ended. As a new lawyer, I often would visit informally with the judge and ask him for general advice and wise guidance in my practice. One time, I was involved in a negotiation and, being a new lawyer, was a bit insecure, which led to an overcompensation of ego and bravado, to put it mildly. I took an unreasonably intransigent position in a negotiation and would not budge, no matter what. Because my strategy was simply not working, however, I decided that I should ask the judge about it.

As I told the judge about my tough negotiation stance that just was not working, he sat back in his chair, smiled, and said, "So they are not just giving up, huh? Even though you are being so tough on them? Hmm. Do you know the story about the Old North Wind and the Sun, and the contest they once had?"

"You mean the children's story?"

"Yes."

The judge then told me how the Old North Wind was bragging to the Sun one day and claiming that the Wind was a far more powerful element than the Sun. The Wind was boasting how it should be respected much more than the Sun, given the Wind's greater power. The Old North Wind then challenged the Sun to a contest of power. "You see that man down there walking alongside the road, wearing that cloak?"

"Yes," said the Sun.

"Let's see which one of us can make him remove his cloak!"

The Sun agreed to the contest. The Old North Wind went first. He began to blow a very fierce, cold wind down on the man, but as the Wind blew icy cold, it just made the man hold on even more tightly to his cloak, which was his only protection from the powerful gusts of cold wind. No matter how hard the Wind blew, the man held even more tightly to his cloak. Try as he might, the Wind failed to make the man remove his cloak.

It was then the Sun's turn. The Sun began to shine brightly in the sky and spread warmth to all of those below. Soon, birds came out to sing and small children began to play because the weather was so calm and sunny. Within no time, the man walking along the side of the road decided to remove his cloak to enjoy the warm, sunny day.

"You see, Freddy, in your negotiation, try being more like the Sun and less like the Old North Wind. Give your opponents a *good reason* to do just what you want them to do. Work hard to solve the other side's problem, but do so in a way that helps your client, too. That's how lawyers negotiate; they creatively solve problems."

He's a wise old owl, that Judge Kane. I learned a very valuable lesson from him that day, and I saw it clearly through the story of the Old North Wind and the Sun. The reason I bring up the story is to consider whether that story should be interpreted *literally,* as though it actually happened. I learned the lesson of the story. I saw the reason why the judge had told it to me. I saw how I should apply the underlying message to my negotiation and law practice. Nevertheless, should I also have believed that the story was something that *actually happened* and was historically accurate in a very *literal* sense? Wouldn't a literal interpretation of that story be utterly ridiculous? There obviously is no science or logic in the assertion that the wind and the sun are like humans, complete with human personalities and egos, and actually have interesting conversations and can get emotional and compete with one another. Isn't the point of the story simply to teach us a larger lesson about how to deal more successfully with other human beings, so that it would just be silly to interpret the story literally as meaning that the sun and the wind can actually talk and have personalities and egos like those of humans?

Wouldn't I entirely be missing the point of the story if I found myself embroiled in a huge argument over the literal versus the metaphorical meaning of the story? Imagine the absurdity of arguing with scientists and meteorologists about how the sun and the wind can *actually* speak and *really* do have power contests with one another. Imagine my literal-interpretation-bashing questions then: Does the sun actually have a mouth out of which he can speak and a brain that allows him to think? Is the sun a boy or a girl? Is the wind really an egotistical jerk with an inferiority complex? And just who among us has witnessed the sun and the wind actually talking to one another? What language were they speaking, and where and when did they learn it?

Maybe the whole point here is that much of the Bible is more metaphorical and often with many parables but yet still very meaningful for us, than it is some literal, scientific explanation of the universe. And just maybe meteorologists and astronomers who tell us that the wind and the sun are actually not just like human beings that can actually talk but are instead mere natural elements are not the equivalent of atheist liars who hate God and deny His Word. Neither is the story of the Old North Wind and the Sun told just to test our faith to see if we will still believe in the story literally, despite what science tells us about our weather elements and about the true nature of the sun and the wind. Although some biblical stories may be "obvious" parables, while others may seem like they possibly could be based on actual historical events, many stories, especially those containing supernatural "miracles" and scientifically implausible accounts, are not so easy to categorize as either literal stories or symbolic parables.

[4] And God saw the light, that it was good: and God divided the light from the darkness.
[5] And God called the light Day, and the darkness he called Night. And the evening and the morning were the first day.

To say that God "saw the light" and "that it was good" makes it seem as though the light could have been bad or mediocre instead of good, or that God might even occasionally make mistakes and therefore might, like a human being, need a few initial tries before finally getting it right. If God can see the future, though, shouldn't He have already known whether His creation was going to work out the way He had intended and that what He created definitely would be good? If not, He either is fallible (capable of mistakes) or lacks foresight (does not really know how it is all going to turn out).

In terms of dividing the light from the darkness, there is no division of light and dark in the universe; instead, the universe is filled with light waves/light particles emanating from sextillions of stars inside billions of galaxies. There is only darkness (darkness is not a thing in and of itself but is merely the absence of light) when light is blocked or is faint. Similarly, quiet is not really a thing unto itself but merely describes a void situation—the absence of sound waves that produce sound. From the perspective of someone who does not realize that the sun is *always* shining and that the earth spins on its axis every twenty-four hours such that half of the time we are blocked from sunlight by the other side of earth, day and night could appear to be defined simply by "light" and "darkness."

"Darkness" is not "night," however, especially given all of the stars and the moon, off of which light reflects, and "day" is not "light." Instead, day is just when the sun and the direct light from it are visible. Of course, these sorts of distinctions are less meaningful as we move closer to the earth's north or south poles—where it can be light or dark or dusk or dawn for nearly twenty-four hours a day. One would have to be aware that the earth is a sphere spinning on its axis (tilted at 23 degrees) in order to understand why that is the case, as night and day have very different manifestations if one is near a pole rather than the equator.

Even more importantly, night and day cease to have these meanings once we move to other parts of the universe. For example, the Milky Way, our galaxy, is full of billions of stars. More toward the center of the galaxy, there would be no night because the light from the dense surrounding stars would constantly make it day on any spinning planet in the middle of the galaxy—the nighttime stars would be like many daytime suns. Like many galaxies, however, the Milky Way appears to have an immense black hole at its center; therefore, it might not ever be day because a black hole is so dense that not even light can escape to make it day. Presumably, then, it would be night forever in the black hole. If God really created the universe and wrote all about it in the Bible, of course He already would know all of these things and as a result would have been able to write about them much more accurately and completely. A day is an Earth-specific period of twenty-four (or twelve) hours. As such, the concept is unique to us humans and is not a universal concept. Whether it is day or night at any particular point for us is simply a function of where we are located on the earth as it spins on its axis in relation to our sun in our little corner of the universe.

Chapter Forty-Four

Day Two: A Big Ocean in the Sky?

[6] And God said, Let there be a firmament in the midst of the waters, and let it divide the waters from the waters.
[7] And God made the firmament, and divided the waters which were under the firmament from the waters which were above the firmament: and it was so.
[8] And God called the firmament Heaven. And the evening and the morning were the second day.

I had no idea what this text literally meant; however, I did a little research and found that the early Hebrew view of the world was a very mistaken assumption based on the literal interpretation of these verses. Believers used to think that there was a dome of water above the sky (because God divided the waters with the firmament, or Heaven, so that there are waters above the firmament—in the sky, or behind the sky—and waters below the firmament—in the oceans here on Earth). The firmament is Heaven, with waters above it (behind the sky) and below it (in the oceans). In fact, the New American Bible version even translates this verse by actually using the word "dome" to describe the firmament dividing the waters below it on earth, and above it—apparently in space?

So on top of what would be a dome-like structure above the earth would be some water, and then underneath that body of water is the sky, and then the earth below it, and then the waters of the earth. I guess that is what it literally means, waters in Heaven above the firmament and waters below, down on Earth. The early Hebrews apparently also thought that the earth was flat and apparently resting on columns, as though the earth would fall down instead of being a source of gravity itself. Their explanation that the earth was resting on columns simply stops there. As with the beginning-of-time issue, however, the glaring question becomes "Well, what do these Earth-supporting columns rest on? And what's below those support columns, and what's below whatever that is?" Such a question might seem like a trick question for the ancients, however, maybe their explanation as to what was under the columns might simply have been "Don't be silly, it is columns all the way down!"

The early church, interpreting the Bible literally, also incorrectly believed that it rained because the liquid waters above the firmament (above the sky dome) dripped down through the dome onto the earth (Isaiah 55:10: "For as the rain cometh down, and the snow from heaven, and returneth not thither, but watereth the earth, and maketh it bring forth and bud, that it may give seed to the sower, and bread to the eater.") Of course, the reality is not that some huge body of water exists independently as liquid water like an ocean above the sky. I very much believe in

God and His greatness, but it is simply implausible that there is an ocean of water existing above, in Heaven, "behind" the stars. It is not as though the Bible was referring to clouds in the sky, and if it was, it should have said so. Besides, clouds are not always present in the sky. There appears to be no understanding where rain comes from, either, so it seems Moses as the writer here just assumed a water source existed somewhere above, in Heaven, to explain where rain comes from. Even "Carl Sagan as a Kid" may not have made this very bad and false assumption.

Based on these verses, this was the very simplistic, and quite wrong, literal understanding of the earth, how it is situated, and where rain comes from, because there was no awareness of how evaporation, cloud condensation, and precipitation work and how the water cycle operates to give us rain—water in the oceans evaporates to form clouds, clouds condense to form rain, the rainfall comes down to the surface of the earth, that water eventually flows to rivers, rivers flow into the ocean, and then the cycle begins anew, with evaporation of the water eventually forming clouds, occurring all along the way—not to mention the fact that the earth is not flat and is not resting on top of columns that apparently have nothing under them. Finally, there is no magical, mystical body of water above the firmament (Heaven) that produces our rainfall. In fact, if that were the case, that finite water source above the earth in time would run out.

In contrast, it is true that there are abundant supplies of water molecules, H_2O, existing in the universe, in outer space in the form of frozen non-liquid ice crystals. Could it be that those dispersed ice crystals were the waters above the firmament that the verse is referring to? Such would be impressive if it were the case, but this does not seem to be the waters that Moses was referring to if the verse was an attempt at an explanation of how the water cycle here on Earth works to produce rain—with evaporation from oceans, cloud formation, and then rain. Also, the implication of a division of waters from the waters seems to be oceans of *liquid* bodies of water. This is a perfect example of why literal interpretation can yield very different results, because one has to make a judgment as to what a term like "waters" actually means in this context. It also requires a very nonliteral interpretation to have everything somehow make sense contextually as a logically cohesive and coherent explanation.

There is at least some support for the interpretation that there is water above us in Heaven in the very general sense of small, dispersed ice crystals in deep space, but it is incorrect to argue that this is where the rain on Earth comes from. These waters in outer space could get to us (in very small and rare amounts) only if they were contained in a meteorite that hit the earth (unlike rain). If God really wrote the Bible, then, why would He be so mistaken about where rain comes from and how the water on Earth is recycled to form rain? This is basic grade-school Earth science that the Bible is getting wrong. It also strains credulity to assume that the entire second day of all creation was spent creating a firmament that divided waters of oceans on Earth from what has turned out to be a wholly fictitious ocean of water in the sky that allows rain to drip down (apparently whenever God decides to open the faucet) on Earth. How much confidence can we really have in this explanation in which God allegedly spends one-sixth of all creation of the entire universe to create a wholly nonexistent ocean in the sky as an embarrassingly mistaken explanation of how and why it rains—ice crystals in outer space notwithstanding (which, in fairness, was probably not what Moses was referring to)?

Also, recall in Genesis 1:1 when, in the beginning, "the heaven" (and the earth) was created. In light of that, why does God later create this other thing called a firmament—which has a big body of water above it in the sky—and call it Heaven too? Was there another Heaven (firmament) created after the original Heaven? It must be somewhat different, because it is a different word ("firmament" instead of just "Heaven" again). So, apparently, there is the sky immediately above the Earth, then clouds within the upper sky directly above us, then this firmament, Heaven, then above that, a big body of water to drip rain down on us every once in a while (as if it rains everywhere on Earth simultaneously whenever it rains). Next, above that, somehow, must be the other (non-firmament), original Heaven, where God lives, either along with or above all of outer space and the rest of the stars and billions of galaxies (or more) in the universe, the vastness of which the writer seems to be completely unaware.

[9] And God said, Let the waters under the heaven be gathered together unto one place, and let the dry land appear: and it was so.
[10] And God called the dry land Earth; and the gathering together of the waters called He Seas: and God saw that it was good.

Verses 9 and 10 suggest that at first there was only one big land continent and one big ocean where the waters "gathered together unto one place." There is actually some scientific support for this proposition! From the Encyclopedia Britannica online:

> In early geologic time, a "supercontinent" [called "Pangea"]...incorporated almost all of Earth's landmasses and covered nearly one-third of Earth's surface. It was surrounded by a global ocean called Panthalassa. Pangea was fully assembled by the Early Permian Period, some 270 million years ago. It began to break apart about 200 million years ago, during the Early Jurassic Period, eventually forming the modern continents and the Atlantic and Indian Oceans.

Although there is scientific support for this idea of one big continent and one big ocean, note that this support also suggests that this land existed over 270 million years ago, not just 6,000 or so years ago as literalists assert. Apparently, some literalist creationists will simply overlook 270 or so million years when there is at least some scientific support for something written in Genesis. It is interesting how both believers and atheists will use this kind of semi-supportive information. Atheists, who often castigate believers for being unscientific, will argue that this seemingly scientific support for a literal assertion in the Bible (one continent and one ocean) is merely a *coincidence*—and the same regarding water being in outer space to some degree (waters above the firmament in Heaven). Similarly, believers will often say that science is wrong, unbelievable, "full of holes," a belief system in man's own intellect unto itself, heresy, and the like, but then be the first to point to this kind of semi-supportive scientific information, eager to proclaim how "science actually proves the Bible."

Thus, the Bible gets no credit from atheists even if science confirms something at least generally stated in the Bible, but science and logic get no credit from literalists when they seem to directly challenge certain assertions made in the Bible. This selective support seems opportunistic, either way. Apparently, people just believe whatever they want to believe and then use whatever they can to support their belief, and then attack all contrary positions.

As is often true in legal cases, much turns on who has the burden of proof. Whoever has the burden of proof is usually the one with the more difficult argument to make because they must prove their assertions in the first instance. Perhaps that is why agnostics may ultimately win the overall argument, as they assume no burden of proof either way because they believe that we cannot prove either that God exists or that He does not. As a result, there is no meaningful burden of proof to support the assertion "I don't know." Between atheists and believers, however, believers probably have the harder burden of proof to satisfy because they are the ones asserting the existence of God—and an all-powerful, infallible God who can never be wrong in anything ever asserted in the Bible, at that. The Bible must therefore be literally correct 100% of the time. Even just one error would be fatal to the infallibility of God's literal Word. Because no one can generally prove a negative, such as that some god does not exist somewhere, atheists often end up being able to place the burden of proof entirely on believers and thereby manage to escape any burden of proof on themselves—or they may escape only because they end up having what would be an impossible burden of proof, which is to attempt to prove a negative. If God actually exists, however, that burden should not be impossible to prove—*if* there is proof, unless God is purposefully hiding.

Getting back to the alleged one ocean-one continent assertion in the Bible, this account of how the waters subsided and dry land appeared also provides an explanation for land being under water in the beginning of Earth's history and for the water eventually receding into the oceans and the continents appearing. For additional support, some creationists point to the scientific evidence of fossils of seashells being found today on mountaintops, apparently proving that the entire earth was once under water like the Bible says in Genesis. One should be mindful, however, of the fact that at this particular point in the creation story, no creatures, nor any living thing, had been created yet, so that particular fossil evidence of seashells on mountaintops cannot explain this particular account in Genesis because dry land already had appeared *before* any creature was ever created to leave behind a seashell fossil. We are still only on the second day of creation here, with no plants or animals that later could have eventually formed any fossils.

There will be more on this flooded-Earth idea later when we consider Noah's Ark and how polar bears from Antarctica and kangaroos from Australia must have somehow travelled over oceans (either in a vessel or by swimming) to the Middle East to get on the ark in the first place (not to mention the dinosaurs that must have also been on the ark, unless they did not make it and that is why they are now extinct, or maybe God put only infant or baby animals on the ark in an effort to make them fit). All animals would not have fit, no matter what, and the Bible does not make mention of the fact that all were infant or baby animals on the ark. Also, fossils on mountaintops either means the entire earth was flooded at one time after creatures had been created, or that before these mountains were actually mountains, they may have been underwater and only later geological shifts pushing upward created them as mountains out of earth that was once under the oceans. So maybe there was no worldwide flood, and ancient ocean beds only later became mountaintops because of major geological shifts over time creating our mountains.

Also, the issue of all of that flood water receding so dry land could appear leads one to ask, Where did all of that water go? Moreover, if rain comes from a big ocean in the sky behind the stars, does the water on Earth increase every time it rains so that ocean levels are constantly increasing and never decreasing? If the water dried up (evaporated), that would not really help, as it soon would form rain clouds and eventually return as rain to cover the surface of the earth again. Maybe the waters froze at the polar icecaps during the Ice Age so that the ocean levels dropped and dry land appeared, but the Ice Age could not have occurred in just one "day."

All of this seems to be mere "Monday-morning quarterbacking" anyway, in which literalists try to use a scientific explanation—one not at all mentioned in the text of the Bible—to explain away the logical impossibility of what the text actually says given its "plain meaning." These attempts at explanation are actually admissions that the literal text is deficient and/or just plain wrong, especially when creationists use science to confirm literal biblical assertions, such as Pangea containing all modern continents in one large continent surrounded by one big ocean—270 million years ago—even though the earth (and the entire universe) was supposedly created only 6,000 years ago according to literal biblical lineages.

Finally, there is yet another reference that God saw what He had created—here, the earth and seas—and "saw that it was good." Why is there this humanlike self-congratulatory pat on the back by God for doing a good job of creating things in the universe, when there really should be no other option for an infallible Creator who cannot make mistakes and who also supposedly can completely foresee the future? Did God ever accidentally or mistakenly create things that were *not good*? Shouldn't God have complete control over what He creates and whether it meets His specifications, or are His creations more of a risky crapshoot?

Chapter Forty-Five

Day Three: Plants, Trees, and Vegetation on Earth

[11] And God said, Let the earth bring forth grass, the herb yielding seed, and the fruit tree yielding fruit after his kind, whose seed is in itself, upon the earth: and it was so.
[12] And the earth brought forth grass, and herb yielding seed after his kind, and the tree yielding fruit, whose seed was in itself, after his kind: and God saw that it was good.
[13] And the evening and the morning were the third day.

It is worth comparing what and how much was created on each of the six days of creation of the universe. It took an entire day, this third day, one-sixth of all creation, to have land appear and create the plants on Earth (although it says "grass," "herbs," and "fruits," let's assume that also includes all plants, trees, and other vegetation even though it literally does not say that). It took just one day, however, to create the entire universe (if it is considered "the heaven") or just one day to create all of the billions of galaxies of stars (the sun, moon, and stars were all created on day four, with no mention of planetary systems, other moons, black holes, asteroids, etc.). The lack of proportionality reveals that the writer was obviously not aware of much beyond what he could immediately see around him with the naked eye. He obviously believed the universe was much smaller than it actually is.

How did the earth bring forth grass and grow fruit trees in just one day? More problematic is the fact that plants supposedly grew and survived when the sun had not even been created yet. Of course, plants survive and grow by engaging in photosynthesis—the process of taking in sunlight and producing their food and thus growing—which is obviously necessary for plant life, growth, and survival. It would be one thing if God created plants in one day and then the very next day created the sun. Plants obviously do not die immediately once sunlight is removed; if they did, all plants would die every evening. The text says, the earth brought forth grass during the third day, however, which implies that a growth process was taking place, not that God simply placed all the plants in their mature state and then created the sun. So how did that initial growth of all plants take place *without a sun*? Such is impossible. Plants simply have to have the sun to grow, to be "brought forth" by the earth. This also shows the writer probably did not know that the sun is what makes plants grow; instead, the writer probably thought the earth by itself pushes up (brings forth) plants.

Recall, some literalists assert that a day to God in the Bible equals 1,000 years in time for us here on Earth (II Peter 3:8). If that is so, however, plants could not have lived and grown for

1,000 years without the sun, because the sun, recall, was not created until the fourth day (1,000 years later). The only way literalists could attempt to make sense of this is if God waited literally until the very end of day three (the 999th year, 11th month, and 30th day) to create all the plants and vegetation to still technically fall within the third day, and then immediately created the sun at the very beginning of the fourth day (year 0, month 1, day 1 of the next 1,000 years of the fourth God-day). If so, it makes one wonder what God was doing for 999 years, 11 months, and 29 days of the third day before plants were created.

Chapter Forty-Six

Day Four: The Sun, the Moon, and All of the Stars

[14] And God said, Let there be lights in the firmament of the heaven to divide the day from the night; and let them be for signs, and for seasons, and for days, and years:
[15] And let them be for lights in the firmament of the heaven to give light upon the earth: and it was so.

The Bible states that this one planet, Earth, was created three days before our own sun and before every other planet, star, solar system, and galaxy in the universe. Conversely, scientists believe that nebula and stars are the original building blocks of all planets and virtually everything else in the universe. When stars die (burn out or blow up in supernovae), all of their residual elements slowly begin to cling to other elements from other residual stars and, because of gravity, eventually coalesce into planets that then begin to rotate around existing stars (which become their suns) and slowly begin to form solar systems. It therefore seems entirely backward that a planet would be created before any stars.

But with God, all things are possible, so even if all planets are made up of residual stardust elements, it is possible that God simply made an exception in the case of the earth, and created it first, before creating all of the stars that eventually formed all of the other planets in the universe. If the universe was created only 6,000 years ago, however, all of the other planets in the universe have to have been formed within that 6,000-year period. That is obviously too short a time for stars to be created, live out their lives, then supernova and begin to coalesce with other elements from other residual supernova stars to eventually form planets—a process thought to take millions and millions of years in total, unless God made instant planets and stars, because even impossible things are possible with God, and how can one argue with that? Genesis makes no mention of other planets, however, because the writer did not apparently know that other planets existed, or even that Earth itself is just one of several planets revolving around our sun in a solar system, that all light comes from stars, and that our sun is a star inside of a huge galaxy of billions of stars.

Even assuming the earth was created first and then all of the stars were later created to form lights for those on Earth, however, these lights in the sky—the sun, moon, and stars—are *not* the things that divide the day from the night. The only thing that divides the day from the night is the spherical shape of the earth as it rotates on its axis approximately every twenty-four hours so that at any one specific time, half of the earth has direct sunlight and the other half does not. The writer appears to believe that these lights just appear and then disappear every day and every night—as though they come on stage, do their twelve hours of service, and then move off stage for twelve hours of downtime. If one does not know how our solar system works and just looks up at the sky, it appears as though the sun rises and sets every day while we on Earth stand still. This is what the ancient world thought, because people did not realize that the sun and the stars are always there and that the earth spinning on its axis causes the day and night—but again, God would have known that, even though it appears that Moses did not.

These verses also tell us that the stars change position as signs of the year and the seasons and that they even change their positions during the night. Wrong again. It is not the movement of the stars that cause these nightly, seasonal, and yearly shifts; rather, the movement of the earth around the sun creates only the illusion that the stars are moving during our four seasons. And stars seem to move during the night only because the earth is spinning on its axis, producing another illusion of movement of stars. Although stars do move in the very general sense that the universe is expanding, they do not move to signal seasons; instead, the earth spins on its axis every day and night and revolves around the sun once a year so that our perspective of the night sky changes during the night and over the year as we revolve around the sun.

Moses was obviously completely unaware of these astronomical facts, given the way in which he wrote these particular verses in Genesis. The sun, moon, and stars do not divide the day from the night. The stars are also there in the day but are overpowered by the brightness of the sun—they are always there, but the earth spins on its axis, giving us day and night, and revolves around the sun, giving us seasons based on the twenty-three–degree tilt of the earth that causes our northern and southern hemispheres to be either closer or farther away from the sun at different points during the year. This, in turn, makes it colder or warmer in the northern or southern hemispheres of the earth, causing our seasons as well as the illusion of changing star positions in the night sky at various points during the year and during the night.

What purpose are stars used for when Moses writes that stars are to be used "for signs?" Astrologers use the stars as signs to determine what it might mean to us when the stars are in certain positions relative to the earth's rotation around the sun during the year. Astrologers use these star positions to predict events on Earth and even to give general personal advice to people born during certain times of the year, as though the positioning of the stars determines, or at least affects, one's personality during life (e.g., Cancers are moody). Astrologers, looking for some logical scientific support for their bold assertions, claim that the faint gravitational pull of celestial bodies on humans at different points in the year apparently creates certain identifiable personality traits on fetuses in the act of passing through the birth canal on certain arbitrary days grouped generally into the twelve months of the year. Creationist literalists, however, rightly scoff at these pseudoscientific explanations of how astrology can possibly affect a person's personality, but in the very same breath, creationist literalists also often resist scientific, astronomy-based challenges to their particular literal pseudoscientific biblical explanations about the universe. As these creationist literalists criticize astrology for its scientific implausibility, however, perhaps they would be wise to remember that people who live in glass houses should not throw stones. Often, their pseudoscientific supporting arguments for their bold biblical assertions are just as suspect as the arguments of astrologers.

[16] And God made two great lights; the greater light to rule the day, and the lesser light to rule the night: he made the stars also.
[17] And God set them in the firmament of the heaven to give light upon the earth,
[18] And to rule over the day and over the night, and to divide the light from the darkness: and God saw that it was good.
[19] And the evening and the morning were the fourth day.

From the point of view of a nonscientist writing a book thousands of years ago, this description seems plausible to account for the "two great lights" in the sky, one that rules the day, the sun, and one that rules the night, the moon, and "the stars also." This also shows that the sun and the stars definitely were not created on the first day when God supposedly was letting there be light. This is a rather profound contradiction in the Bible.

The sun, of course, actually emits light itself, but the moon does not, so there is yet another error here. The moon is not a light-producing object like the sun and other stars are; instead, the moon simply reflects the light coming from the sun and does so only when the moon is positioned at certain points during the month with respect to the earth such that the moon's reflection can be seen from Earth.

Why is there no explanation of any of this in Genesis? Why wouldn't God inform Moses when Moses transcribed Genesis that the moon was created to *reflect* sunlight during the night (or sometimes at dusk or dawn, and only then, sometimes, depending on the moon's monthly revolution around the earth, creating a full, half, crescent, or new moon)? Obviously, Moses thought that the moon *produced* light, not just *reflected* it, when in reality, the moon, at times, just partially reflects sunlight in its monthly stages.

Moses also seems to think that the moon and stars are simple little lights in the night sky. Recall that the Bible states in Genesis 1:3 that there are waters *above* the firmament and that is apparently how we get rain. Moses did not know any better and thought the universe was just like a big domed planetarium with some lights up on that dome. In fairness to a nonscientist writer thousands of years ago, it certainly does appear that way to the naked eye when one looks up at the sky, and that is exactly how he wrote it. So, the waters in the firmament are apparently behind all of the stars? Moses obviously had no idea how vast the universe is or how incredibly far away the stars actually are such that a big body of water could not possibly exist behind, or above, the stars (the domed planetarium). Because Moses saw the sky as a dome with lights on it, he also did not realize that some of those lights ("stars") were actually close planets, such as Venus and Mars, reflecting light while other lights were stars hundreds, millions, and even billions of light-years away.

Finally, when Moses noted that God "made the stars also," it seems as though the sextillions of stars that actually make up our universe were a mere *afterthought* at the end of a very busy day spent mostly on creating just the sun and the moon. It is as though Moses tacked on "oh yeah, God made the stars also," which seems logical if all God created was a few hundred star "nightlights" that we can see with the naked eye. This suggests that Moses was profoundly unaware that the universe contains sextillions of stars, because from his perspective, the stars seemed to be just a bunch of little twinkling lights on a dome and were there only during the night. We certainly cannot fault the ancients for failing to make these scientific discoveries about our solar system and universe thousands of years ago, when it has taken that long for astronomers to make these discoveries using powerful telescopes. If God really wrote the Bible, however, why would He write it, or allow it to be written, with such monumentally misinformed, basic mistakes in the literal description of the cosmos, celestial bodies, and the nature of the universe?

Chapter Forty-Seven

Day Five (and Part of Day Six): The Animals

[20] And God said, Let the waters bring forth abundantly the moving creature that hath life, and fowl that may fly above the earth in the open firmament of heaven.
[21] And God created great whales, and every living creature that moveth, which the waters brought forth abundantly, after their kind, and every winged fowl after his kind: and God saw that it was good.
[22] And God blessed them, saying, Be fruitful, and multiply, and fill the waters in the seas, and let fowl multiply in the earth.
[23] And the evening and the morning were the fifth day.
[24] And God said, Let the earth bring forth the living creature after his kind, cattle, and creeping thing, and beast of the earth after his kind: and it was so.
[25] And God made the beast of the earth after his kind, and cattle after their kind, and every thing that creepeth upon the earth after his kind: and God saw that it was good.

God makes all of the animals—birds (air), fish (water), and animals (land), as well as all of the insects and bugs (things that "creepeth")—on the fifth and sixth days (fish and fowl at the end of the fifth day, land animals and insects at the beginning of the sixth day). It is interesting that the Bible states that all creatures first came from water—that is, water first brought forth life. The Bible says this, and evolutionists also believe that all life originated in the water. So are creationists and evolutionists actually agreeing here? Not really, not in light of how they disagree on so much that happened afterward, but superficially at least, they both agree that life began in or emerged from the water.

It is interesting that there is no mention of any complex or vast microbiology (such as bacteria or viruses), however, other than "everything that creepeth on the earth," which seems to be referring only to *visible* insects and bugs. There is nothing at all in the text about molecules, atoms, neutrons, electrons, protons, and the like. Again, wouldn't God, as the Creator of everything, know this? If ancient peoples could not understand this micro-science when it was first written in the Bible, why didn't God require them to have faith that such scientific explanations would be true, instead of requiring us now to have faith in the limited, incomplete, and/or scientifically incorrect text as is?

After creating all animals, birds, sea life, and insects, God "saw that it was good." Was it really all that "good," however, in light of what has happened to most of the species that have ever lived on this earth? Over 90% of all creatures that have ever existed on this planet are now *extinct* because these former life-forms eventually were unable to survive in the world that God created for them. Why would God "bless" these creatures and command that they "be fruitful and multiply," only to have over 90% of them die out because they were ill-equipped to survive in the changing and even hostile world that God had created? It was not the fault of these former species that they were not created in a way to survive as species—animals don't sin and therefore suffer the wrath of God, which would be death and perhaps even the extinction of an entire species, do they? Is that the real reason why dinosaurs eventually went extinct—they were sinners, with free will and the knowledge of good and evil?

Why didn't God better equip all of these creatures to survive, each after their own kind? Why didn't God at least make the earth a more hospitable place so certain species would not be wiped off the face of the earth forever? Did God make a mistake with all of these now extinct species, or did God actually intend for all of these special and unique creatures to eventually die out in the ways they did? As they died off, why didn't God create new "replacement" species with better attributes that would allow them to actually survive on this planet? Many literalists would consider it blasphemy to suggest that God might have done exactly this by using evolution to create better-surviving and better-equipped "replacement" animals in place of some of those that were dying out—"survival of the fittest."

Even literalist believers seem to acknowledge that the reason why animals—all living things—are able to reproduce "after their own kind" is the basic DNA package that each species possesses and passes on to its offspring. In fact, creationists often point to this DNA code for every living thing as evidence of an intelligent designer. DNA is seen as God's blueprints for creation, but why is there no specific detailed explanation of DNA as the blueprint of reproduction that is such a splendid showcase of God's elegant design of everything? Moreover, why does human DNA share over 95% (some estimates are as high as 99%) of its blueprint with chimpanzee DNA if humankind is so unique a creature to be the sole species made in God's image? Does that one percentage point difference in DNA mean chimpanzees are not in God's image? Consider the fact also that humans and primates share certain "pseudo genes" as well, meaning that in our DNA and the DNA of all other primates, certain genetic markers in the same chromosomal locations show that some genes have been destroyed and no longer have the abilities to function as protein-coding genes. Why would all primate species—including humans and chimpanzees—have the exact markers of gene failure in our respective DNA by mere chance, unless we had a common ancestor who passed on that same specific genetic marker to both humans and other primates?

In later verses of Genesis, the Bible incredibly states that the physical characteristics of sheep received from their forebears (such as the type and color of their wool) can be "genetically engineered" by having the sheep look at desirable characteristics (certain colors and streaks) while they are in the act of breeding! What kind of God who supposedly has written every literal passage and word of the Bible would write or allow this monumental mistake in genetic DNA blueprinting to make it into an inerrant Bible?

[37] And Jacob took him rods of green poplar, and of the hazel and chesnut tree; and pilled white strakes in them, and made the white appear which was in the rods.

[38] And he set the rods which he had pilled before the flocks in the gutters in the watering troughs when the flocks came to drink, that they should conceive when they came to drink.

[39] And the flocks conceived before the rods, and brought forth cattle ringstraked, speckled, and spotted....

[41] And it came to pass, whensoever the stronger cattle did conceive, that Jacob laid the rods before the eyes of the cattle in the gutters, that they might conceive among the rods.(Genesis 30:37–41)

Of course, the male and female of any species pass DNA to their offspring, and that DNA produces the physical characteristics of that offspring, but the source of those characteristics is biological, not psychological. For example, human parents cannot simply will their offspring to be tall and have musical talent by the mere act of looking at a tall NBA basketball player while he is playing the piano very well as the parents are in the physical act of conceiving their child. Is this account another biblical mistake on purpose by an infallible God simply to test our faith, or was it the mistaken assumption, given a very limited and incorrect understanding of biology and reproductive genetics, of a fallible human being living thousands of years ago who was a writer of the Bible?

By the way, Greek mythology notwithstanding, if a goat and a human have sex, they do not produce a satyr (a goat-man, who can play a pan flute, no less), and if a human has sex with a bull, they do not produce a minotaur (a bull-man). Thankfully, we now have logic, biology, and genetics to help us dispel such scientifically impossible myths, be they from Greek mythology or from the Bible. Regarding the mistake-on-purpose-to-test-our-faith rationalization, consider the following: Did the Greek gods on Mount Olympus have Greek mythology writers simply make up minotaurs and satyrs on purpose just to test the Greeks' faith in Greek mythology, or does that just sound more like an embarrassingly weak rationalization for an obvious mistaken assumption by Greek mythologists about how human and beast reproductive biology supposedly works?

Chapter Forty-Eight

Day Six: Human Beings

[26] And God said, Let us make man in our image, after our likeness: and let them have dominion over the fish of the sea, and over the fowl of the air, and over the cattle, and over all the earth, and over every creeping thing that creepeth upon the earth.
[27] So God created man in his own image, in the image of God created he him; male and female created he them.

God refers to Himself here in the plural, so apparently the Holy Trinity—God the Father, God the Son, and God the Holy Spirit—all created man and woman. It also must mean that the Holy Spirit is not just a spirit but actually has a physical appearance, as do Jesus and God the Father, and their images are all similar enough to serve as a model for the human form, so God made man and woman in God's image (plural) and put man and woman in control over nature and all living things.

It is interesting that man and woman are created as apparent equals here in the first chapter of Genesis but later, in Chapter 2 of Genesis, the creation story unfolds differently. In Chapter 2, Adam is created first, and then Eve is created as a "helpmate" from Adam's rib. One can see why feminists (and anyone else who believes in basic human and gender equality) can accept much more easily the creation of man and woman together, as set forth here in Chapter 1, rather than the woman being created later from the man's rib just so that Adam would not be alone, as though Eve is a lesser, more dependent, mere companion for the more superior focal point of Adam as set forth in Chapter 2. Still, maybe these initial verses here mean that women are supposed to dominate the world and nature *equally* with men.

Chapter Forty-Nine

Be Fruitful and Multiply—By Having Incest?

[28] And God blessed them, and God said unto them, Be fruitful, and multiply, and replenish the earth, and subdue it: and have dominion over the fish of the sea, and over the fowl of the air, and over every living thing that moveth upon the earth.

Adam and Eve were told to have children, which they did. Of course, once they had all of their children, then incest had to have occurred for there to be any more "fruitful multiplying" to populate the earth with additional humans. Logically, the children of Adam and Eve either had to have incest with one another (brother-sister), or Adam and Eve had to have incest with their own children (parent-child) or with their own grandchildren (grandparent-grandchild). Why would God require the sin of incest for the world to be populated after His initial creation of Adam and Eve?

This is a thorny interpretation problem for literalists who believe that sins are sins and that what is a sin has *always* been a sin and does not change because of changing circumstances. In law, original-intent adherents argue that the principles of the Constitution are not supposed to change with changing circumstances. They refer to such illegitimate change as judicial activism, when judges try to *change* the text of the Constitution rather than simply *interpret* the text of the Constitution at the time it was written. Original-intent adherents demand consistency because absolute truth is not supposed to change over time with prevailing political, social, historical, or situational winds. See Malachi 3:6 ("For I am the LORD, I change not.") and Jeremiah 13:23 ("Can the Ethiopian change his skin, or the leopard his spots?").

In fact, one often hears fundamentalists attack situation ethics, in which ethical principles are thought to change according to the situation. They argue instead that true principle requires unwavering consistency because immutable truths are supposed to be more than adaptable, changeable guidelines. So is their principle being applied here in a consistent way regarding whether incest is a sin? If incest is now a sin and sins are not supposed to be ethical musical chairs, shouldn't incest have *always* been a sin?

If incest has always been a sin because "[n]one of you shall approach to any that is near of kin to him, to uncover their nakedness: I am the Lord" (Leviticus 18:6), why would God create humans and put them in a situation requiring them to commit a sin to populate the Earth? This inconsistency has caused many literalists to try to figure out an exception, or an alternate interpretation, that somehow allows incest—at first, as a non-sin that was required by God to populate the Earth—but then later morphs into a sin because having sex with members of one's family is wrong. So, after Adam and Eve and their kin started to sufficiently populate the world, it may have been time to change the rules regarding incest by making it a sin. If so, there still needed to be a good argument to justify the changing principle.

Maybe one could argue that God's standards simply changed as time went on so that what in the beginning was not a sin eventually became a sin. Thus, perhaps incest was not a sin until it was first *acknowledged* as a sin by God according to Mosaic Law. The problem with this argument, however, is that it suggests that we had a virtual ethical free-for-all in terms of all sins in the Garden of Eden and for a while thereafter, until the time when Moses later wrote (or received) the Ten Commandments and Hebrew Law (a little later in the Bible, in the Book of Exodus). This idea is not entirely consistent, however. For example, one of the Ten Commandments, under Mosaic Law, commands, "Thou shalt not kill," so murder became a sin under Mosaic Law, but when Cain slew Abel (as we shall soon see in Genesis 4:8, long before Exodus), that act of killing was considered a sin right when it occurred, even though Moses had not yet written or received the Ten Commandments, which state that murder is a sin. In other words, murder was not originally allowed by God as a non-sin but then only later became a sin under Mosaic Law when God declared it a sin; murder has *always* been a sin because what is wrong is wrong and a sin is a sin. Murder is *inherently* a sin; it is not a sin simply because God *declared* it to be a sin in some codebook. Any codebook of sins should simply codify that which is *already* in existence as a sin, unless what is a sin can change with changing circumstances.

There are two ways to look at why something is considered a sin, however: Either sins are *inherently* wrong and therefore always remain wrong in God's moral universe, or sins are merely random actions, or non-actions, that God must first *identify*, *categorize*, or *declare* as sins, because nothing is inherently wrong in the universe unless and until God says that it is wrong and is therefore a sin (similar to something not being illegal unless and until it has been declared to be illegal). Whether the nature of sin is inherent (it has always been a sin) or declarative (it was not a sin until it was declared by God to be a sin), there should be a *consistent* answer, or else God's principles are not absolute immutable truths. Is evil inherently evil, or does something became evil only when God *declares* it to be evil?

One interesting argument around the problem is to say that Adam and Eve, as newly created people, did not have any genetic disorders at that early stage of human history and so were pure (having no negative recessive genes). As such, even if this brand-new race of people committed incest, it was not a sin because it could not possibly cause any genetic problems at that point and thus, there was no need to declare incest a sin until later generations of "impure" genes would make it necessary to classify incest as a sin. As a result, incest only became problematic later and God therefore decided to make it a sin under Mosaic Law.

That is an interesting interpretation because it means there has to be a health or logistical reason to justify *why* something is a sin, or else there is *no reason* to call it a sin. The thing about that argument is that it can be reversed and used against literalists who argue, for example, that heterosexual fornication (sex before marriage) is a sin. Maybe it used to be a sin, but only because in the past there were no products for birth-control or condoms to help prevent the spread of sexually transmitted diseases. Now that we have birth control and condoms, however, the risks of venereal disease and unplanned pregnancies are largely controllable and mostly preventable, so there really are no longer any serious health-related reasons to consider premarital sex a sin. Perhaps only unprotected premarital sex is now a sin.

Mosaic Law is from Moses (or was received by Moses), but there is no shortage of individuals who also claim to have received special revelations from God as Moses did and who then justify changing things from the past. For example, recall that Mormons used to think that taking more than one wife, polygyny, was not a sin and was not adultery and that dark-skinned people could not enter Heaven. Those rules have since officially changed for them. Also, in the Old Testament, pre-Christian sinners seeking salvation had to engage in animal sacrifices to pay for their sins before Jesus, the lamb of God, died and shed His blood as the ultimate sacrifice for all sinners of the world. So, change is religiously and doctrinally possible.

Literalists, however, would argue that sex before marriage is still a sin, even if the health risks and unplanned pregnancy risks have been eliminated or least greatly reduced in modern times when condoms are used. Also, they would argue that there are moral reasons, above and beyond those associated with mere health concerns, why premarital sex is a sin. Very well, but again, we must remain consistent. Are there no moral reasons that incest is wrong above and beyond possible health and genetic reasons when family members have sex? What if a brother and sister are infertile and thus cannot procreate? Would the incestuous sex between them not be a sin because there obviously would be no risk of pregnancy and thereby no risk of wrongfully mixing impure genes? If procreation of impure genes is the reason that incest is supposed to be a sin in the first place, then incestuous sex between infertile family members would not be a sin, because there would be no genetic health risks—just like when we humans all had pure genes in the beginning.

Often, the problem with trying to interpret away a biblical inconsistency is the law of unforeseen consequences. One may push in one area of it, but then, as when one pushes on a balloon, that action just pushes air into another area and out pops another unforeseen area of concern. This unforeseen consequence problem occurs here when attempting to interpret away the biblical inconsistency by trying to justify incest for early humans but then later recasting incest as a sin. How about another way of approaching the problem? Maybe incest is and always has been a sin but we can interpret the text in such a way as to argue that the incest that would have been allowed and even required by God to populate the earth never even took place.

It at least *appears* as though God required the first humans to commit incest to populate the Earth, and if incest is a sin, that would present an inconsistency error because God would have required humans to sin to do His will—but maybe God did not require incest to populate the world because God created other human beings, unrelated to Adam and Eve, that we just don't know about? Using the possibility of these other unidentified human beings, some literalists attempt to make the problem go away by engaging in some rather nimble and agile interpretation. Their argument is that God originally created *more* human beings than Adam and Eve, even though these mysterious other human beings are not specifically mentioned in Genesis as contemporaries of Adam and Eve. If God *did* create other humans, it means that Cain and Abel were able to marry non-relative females who came from these other unrelated people, so when God created "man," God actually created mankind, and when He created Eve, He actually created womankind. Accordingly, if other genetically unrelated humans were created, Adam and Eve were just one of the many unrelated couples who were created in the beginning. As a result, no incest! And if there is no inconsistency, then there is no problem.

Well isn't that convenient? If God created these other unrelated groups of people in the beginning and only people from unrelated groups got married and had sex, the world could have conceivably (pun intended) been populated with no need for incest. But where is the textual support for that rather accommodating interpretation? It seems awfully expedient to start making up other possibilities to solve the problem. As a further justification, literalists might argue, "Although the Bible doesn't say that God created other unidentified human beings in Genesis, the Bible does not say that God could *not* have created other unidentified human beings in Genesis; therefore, the creation of other unidentified human beings is possible!"

The problem is that this kind of creative argument leads us away from a literal textual interpretation and begins to call for speculation about what the text must have really meant in order to have everything make consistent sense. Perhaps God should have used a word other than "man" for Adam and "woman" for Eve if He actually meant "mankind" and "womankind" in Chapter 1. Indeed, why didn't God use the word "humankind" if that is what He really meant? It is possible that the word "man" can be used to mean either a singular man, like Adam, or the plural, "mankind," of which Adam may have been only the first man created chronologically and several other men and women were created very soon thereafter.

This discussion of the interpretation of the word "man" as either singular or plural reminds me of the mistake that astronaut Neil Armstrong made when he first landed on the moon in 1969. Recall that as he first stepped foot on the moon coming down the ladder of the Apollo spacecraft, he said, "That's one small step for man, one giant leap for mankind." It would have been a really great quote if he had not misspoken. He mistakenly used the term "man" in the plural sense for the small step, and so it did not really make sense to contrast it with the term "mankind," which is man, in the plural sense, making a giant leap.

What Armstrong meant to say was "That's one small step for a man [singular, referring to himself as a human being merely taking a small step down from the Apollo spacecraft], one giant leap for mankind [plural, referring to our species, humankind, courageously venturing to the moon]." Perhaps Neil Armstrong was just a little distracted with being the first human being ever to set foot on the moon in one of the most fantastic milestones in our exploration of space, so I think we can forgive him for that and respect him for being able to say anything at all in such circumstances. So, did God also use the term "man" to sometimes mean the plural, to signify humankind, and then sometimes just to mean the singular Adam? That interpretation, in which God created man in the plural, meaning humankind, a community of unrelated people, would appear to solve the incest problem.

There is some support for this argument, because the text says God created "man and woman," not that God created *a* man and *a* woman. The only problem then is that every other unidentified group of humans had to somehow have the exact same kind of fall into Original Sin in the Garden of Eden that Adam and Eve did. So, did all of these other couples live in the Garden of Eden too, and did every other single wife of every man also get tempted by Satan, the talking serpent, to eat the forbidden fruit, and then did each of the wives tempt their poor husbands, who all decided to eat the forbidden fruit also? They all would have to commit Original Sin in the same exact way and at the exact same time for the history of the world according to the Bible to make sense. According to the story, however, all of humankind had to have descended from Adam, but that could not be true if there were other groups of first humans as suggested here.

Why didn't any of these other wives ever say to Satan, the talking serpent tempting them with the forbidden fruit, "Thanks, but no thanks; I already have a lot of fruit here, no need to disobey God and ruin everything for all humans in the universe forever by introducing sin and evil into the world whereby billions of people, all of my future descendants, will burn in Hell forever. Yeah, so I'm good; not to mention the fact that I do not want to die. Immortality is good, and I do not want for all women forevermore to be punished by having to bear children and have menstrual cycles every month as punishment for my decision to fall for Satan's sly temptation before my husband, who obviously has no mind of his own and eats whatever I tell him to eat." Why no mention of these other humans and their own ill-fated Original Sins?

Either Adam and Eve were the first humans and we all descended from them and are all subject to *their* Original Sin, given what they specifically did in the Garden of Eden, or they were not the only first humans and there were other original unrelated human beings. The Bible cannot have it both ways just to get around the incest problem, however. The story of what happened in the Garden of Eden, and exactly how it all transpired, is, as we shall see, a rather detailed and complex story, with unique circumstances and a series of interconnected choices and reactions that explain the predicament of humankind in the world, the need for God, and, ultimately, the need for a savior. Does it seem plausible and logical that there were other first humans who were not identified in Genesis but all made the exact decisions and had the exact reactions as Adam and Eve in the exact circumstances? That would have to be the case if the Genesis story of Adam and Eve is the true explanation for creation and for why humankind is in the spiritual predicament it is after the original fall and if there were also these other unidentified, co-original human beings. That there were these other unidentified co-original human beings seems to be more of an attempted convenient interpretation to avoid a glaring inconsistency regarding incest than it does a good-faith attempt to interpret the text of Genesis literally.

Even if this opportunistic reading of Genesis allows one to interpret the creation story as creating "humankind" (plural) so that incest by Adam or Eve or by their offspring never had to occur for the earth to be populated, there is still a problem. A later example in the Bible in which God would require incest to repopulate the world involves Noah and his family. If God later destroyed everyone in the world with a great flood because they (except for Noah and his family) were all wicked (see later chapters in Genesis), Noah's family, too, would eventually have to commit incest (between cousins, between cousins and aunts and uncles, between grandparents and grandchildren, etc.) to repopulate the world—and there were no other unrelated human beings that time, as they all had just died in the flood. Moreover, human genes were probably impure by then, so the purity argument in "favor" of incest falls by the wayside too. Thus, incest as a non-sin is something that runs throughout the Bible in various contexts and was not an issue only after the creation of Adam and Eve. In fact, there are additional examples of Bible-approved incest, one of which includes Abraham marrying his half-sister. (Genesis 20:11–12: "[11] And Abraham said, Because I thought, Surely the fear of God is not in this place; and they will slay me for my wife's sake. [12] And yet indeed she is my sister; she is the daughter of my father, but not the daughter of my mother; and she became my wife.")

Chapter Fifty

On Incest and Literal Interpretation: A Letter to My Father

Years ago, my dad and I had a very interesting exchange on the issue of incest and literal interpretation of the Bible. He had quite a different explanation for why Adam and Eve and/or their children never committed incest. After our discussion, I wrote him a letter about our debate. That letter is set forth below in pertinent part because it addresses the overall issue, along with my dad's very interesting response, and it has a general discussion about the much larger problem of attempting a literal interpretation of the Bible that allows for everything to make logical and consistent sense. The letter follows.

A.   *The Problem*

*Dad, my initial query was: when God created Adam and Eve, He necessarily put them in the unavoidable and inescapable position of having to commit incest with their children in order to populate the earth, **or** Adam and Eve's children were forced into the unavoidable and inescapable position of having to commit incest with one or more of their own brothers or sisters in order to populate the earth. Either way, such is a significant theological problem because it either shows that what is considered a sin in one circumstance, can **change** in certain other circumstances, or, if it always has been a sin and remains so today, then God **forced** them to sin in order to populate the world (with no logistical alternative), which is clearly contrary to Biblical doctrine. In either event, this is a very significant inconsistency problem since, according to you, such is untenable because the "Truth" never changes and God's "Word" is infallible. That is the theological aspect of this problem.*

*Below is a diagram which demonstrates that incest, as a matter of simple logic, must have taken place (unless God created other **unrelated** human beings at the same time as Adam and Eve but never bothered to mention it in the Bible; which, I believe, is the only way out of this dilemma, as I explain later, but if so, then it also creates other interpretation problems). The key is to ask who Adam and Eve's **grandchildren's parents** were. They simply must have been either: (1) brother and sister (Cain, Abel, or another brother with one of their own sisters) or (2) parents and child (Adam or Eve with one of their own children). Such sexual relations clearly constitute incest (assuming no allowance for artificial insemination or an immaculate type of conception), as the diagram below demonstrates.*

*One of the males on the left-hand side of the diagram, **above Generation #1,** would have had to have had sex with one of the females on the right-hand side of the diagram, again, **above Generation #1,** in order to produce **any** offspring who could have possibly constituted **GENERATION #1.***

< -------------------MALES----------------------/	\ ------------------------FEMALES---------------->
ADAM	EVE

CAIN	ABEL	BRO 1	BRO 2	SIS 1	SIS 2	SIS 3	SIS 4

GENERATION #1: GRANDSONS OF ADAM AND EVE, AND SONS OF THEIR CHILDREN	GRANDDAUGHTERS OF ADAM AND EVE, AND DAUGHTERS OF THEIR CHILDREN
GENERATION #2: GREAT-GRANDSONS OF ADAM AND EVE, GRANDSONS OF THEIR CHILDREN, AND SONS OF THEIR GRANDCHILDREN	GREAT-GRANDDAUGHTERS OF ADAM AND EVE, GRANDDAUGHTERS OF THEIR CHILDREN, AND DAUGHTERS OF THEIR GRANDCHILDREN
GENERATION #3: GREAT-GREAT-GRANDSONS OF ADAM AND EVE, GREAT-GRANDSONS OF THEIR CHILDREN, GRANDSONS OF THEIR GRANDCHILDREN, AND SONS OF THEIR GREAT-GRANDCHILDREN	GREAT-GREAT-GRANDDAUGHTERS OF ADAM AND EVE, GREAT-GRANDDAUGHTERS OF THEIR CHILDREN, GRANDDAUGHTERS OF THEIR GRANDCHILDREN, DAUGHTERS OF THEIR GREAT-GRANDCHILDREN.

B.   *Your Response*

*You responded by observing that in the Bible, it states that Adam and Eve, along with their offspring, tended to live incredibly long lives by today's standards, **e.g.,** they often lived to be 800, or even more than 900 years old. As a result, you went on to explain, Adam, for example, could have had sex with one of his great-great-great-great-great-great-great-great-great-etc.-granddaughters, perhaps 10 or 15 generations removed, such that, technically, they would not have committed incest because at that point they would have been so far removed from one another in the gene pool.*

*An interesting argument to be sure, and you are probably correct in assuming that it would no longer be incest between Adam and, say, a 15th-generation great-granddaughter (at least at some point, I suppose, it would no longer be incest), but your explanation, unfortunately, ends up being **completely irrelevant** to the incestuous sexual relations that **must have taken place earlier on up the family tree** in order to ultimately produce that far, far, far-removed great-great-great-etc.-granddaughter in the first place about which you speak. Indeed, the critical question is: How did that far-removed great-great-great-etc.-granddaughter get there? And who, **ultimately,** were **her** parents' ancestors?*

*The point is, no matter how far removed these great-great-great-etc.-grandchildren are from Adam, each of their ancestors, inevitably, leads back to a generation that must have had incest at some point in order to produce all of those far-removed descendants to begin with. It is at that critical juncture, **not later on,** where the unavoidable incestuous relations must have taken place.*

*Thus, the time duration between Adam's immediate family and the births of additional sons or grandsons that you point out is **irrelevant.** I keep coming back to it, but who, other than Adam and other members of his **immediate** family, possibly could have had sex **in order to produce the first generation thereafter?** It could not have been anyone but **immediate family members**—which is incest, plain and simple.*

C.   An Explanation

*Perhaps instead of being a "troublemaker," I can offer a possible solution I have heard about. Maybe God created **other** human beings but did not tell us about them. After all, not **every** human being that was ever created is acknowledged and catalogued in the Bible. Also, perhaps God only found it necessary to tell us about Adam and Even because they were the first chronological people ever to **sin** (thus Adam is the first "man" as we know men today: **sinners** in need of salvation).*

*Another way out of this inconsistency problem as to the immutable truth of what is a sin is to interpret "Adam" in the **plural** instead of **singular.** Perhaps when God created "Adam," he was creating the first group of unrelated individuals constituting the first community of man. That is, perhaps he was creating "mankind" instead of just "a man." I think the meaning of "Adam" can be taken as "man" or "mankind."*

D.   The Inescapable Need for Personal Private Interpretation in Order to Get Around This Problem

*Providing our own logic, however, is always an easy "way out" whenever the Bible seems to contain a contradiction, but even by your own standards, such is not a very satisfying solution. The problem, of course, with "filling in the gaps and holes" in the text with our own logic, and private interpretations, and even plausible guesses, is that it simply raises another nagging problem in that it opens up the proverbial "Pandora's box" of private interpretations. Such interpretation, however, inevitably leads to conflict and even mistakes (witness your own attempt to fill in the gaps and holes in the text by providing the explanation about the long lives of Biblical figures, which ended up being an incorrect, and logically contradictory, explanation regarding why incest did not take place). This type of problem, however, appears to be inescapable whenever we try to **interpret** even simple sentences (let alone a series of books like the Bible).*

*For example, recall how I often have pointed out that the First Amendment to the US Constitution states "Congress shall make no law...abridging the freedom of speech." The problem is not with determining what the words are (they come from the text of the Constitution) or what they mean, individually (their individual definitions can be found in the dictionary). Actually, this is a point you often make with respect to the Bible as well (the text is the Bible; the individual word meanings can be located in various dictionaries). Text and definitions are, undoubtedly, absolutely critical to understanding the concept being communicated. But simply **identifying** the text and **defining** the words of the text cannot, by itself, be the end of the inquiry. Indeed, such is really only the **beginning.***

The problem is, although we may know what words are contained in the text of the First Amendment and we may know their specific definitions, we still do not know exactly, in all circumstances, how to apply that text (where that text is simply words strung together in such a way to form a complex concept and guideline to be used in order to govern future conduct in countless new and differing circumstances and situations).

Returning to my example, the First Amendment is a basic principle of conduct by which to order our public/political lives (much like a Biblical principle to order our spiritual lives), but the First Amendment simply does not state in the text, explicitly, how to proceed in every fathomable situation that may confront us. Instead, that task is left to Supreme Court Justices, who must constantly interpret and reinterpret the First Amendment (as a result, they often disagree, and even make mistakes, which often leads to the "Pandora's Box" about which I talked about in our earlier discussions).

Sure, there are "easy cases." I certainly will concede that the words of the text "have to mean something." For example, Congress clearly could not pass a law stating that no one could ever talk or even think about politics at all. The First Amendment gives us enough explicit text to field that one in a simple, straightforward manner upon which every literate and minimally reasonable person would agree; that we cannot run red traffic lights whenever we get the urge is another. So I am not merely saying that we cannot know anything and we can never agree on anything. Clearly we can, and we often do, and we must, in order to avoid utter chaos. Thus, legal and biblical text can often mean something to us in a way that we are actually able, for the most part, to agree upon, without much, or any, dispute.

*But there are "hard cases" as well, and seemingly many more of them, that require our own thoughtful **interpretation** of concepts and general principles that go far beyond merely defining individual words of the text (e.g., regarding the First Amendment: Can someone encourage someone else to actually overthrow the government? Should pornography or hate speech be protected? How far can advertisers go in trumping up their products [can they lie]? What if someone wants to use a loudspeaker at 2:00 a.m. in a neighborhood in order to talk about politics? etc.). The ultimate answers to those questions are **not explicitly** contained in the text or word definitions of the First Amendment.*

*Instead, to answer such questions, we must necessarily **interpret** the __concept__ of the First Amendment, the __underlying principle__ of the First Amendment. This interpretation does not, and cannot, end merely by defining the individual meanings of the terms "Congress," "shall," "make," "no," "law," etc., or by defining their underlying word derivatives at the time they were spoken, written, or translated, or even by defining their component suffixes or prefixes. That kind of definitional inquiry, although it may be important, can really only be the **beginning of trying to understand the text.***

*Interpretation is a **much more involved, difficult, and ambiguous process** than merely defining the meanings of individual words. We necessarily end up having to say to ourselves: "Well it **must** mean this," or "It could not mean this, because it would be inconsistent with that," or "Maybe it can mean this or that in different situations," or "Maybe we just are not supposed to even ask such questions"—which is always an easy way out, I guess.*

If defining word meanings in the text were all there were to it, then anyone could just punch out queries on a super-sophisticated Bible-dictionary computer or Constitution-dictionary computer and have every infallible, correct, and consistent answer to every imaginable issue, question, or controversy in the world. Most importantly, there would be absolutely no need for a Supreme Court to interpret man's law, and there similarly would be no need for spiritual leaders like you to interpret the Bible for a congregation.

I simply do not believe that it is possible for a computer program containing all possible word definitions, no matter how sophisticated, to give us the infallible, correct, and consistent answer to every conceivable spiritual issue just because the program could define the words used in the Bible and translate each definition back to Greek and Hebrew dictionaries. And although you and I have argued about it in the past, I do not believe you ultimately believe that either.

In fact, if you did actually believe that, then like I said, you, as a preacher, would no longer have anything about which to preach on Sundays because you would also have to believe that everyone and anyone in your church could simply read their own Bibles, for themselves, by consulting their own English, Hebrew, and Greek dictionaries, and they all could arrive at exactly the same conclusions as you do, down to the last minute detail. And you as a spiritual leader would soon become obsolete because a computer could easily take your place! Thus, I do not think you actually believe the logical extension of your own argument. We both know you serve a much more important and helpful, critical role as the pastor of your church beyond what an "objective," "literal" super-computer Bible dictionary could provide.

Moreover, this lack of a need for a pastor and spiritual leader would be true not only for the members of your church but for the members of every church anywhere in the world that consider the Bible to be the controlling text as the Word of God and consider the English,

Hebrew, and Greek dictionaries to be infallible and 100% translatable (which itself is probably open to debate).

*Even more noteworthy, many, many sincere, God-fearing people who do believe the Bible is the controlling text, that it is God's infallible Word, and that it was translated without error from the Greek and the Hebrew—people who believe **just like** you about those basic propositions—**still** have profound, deep, and serious disagreements about the most basic Biblical principles. Keep in mind that these are people who all swear they are **strictly** and **literally** interpreting the text of the King James Version of the Bible using Greek and Hebrew dictionaries. This by itself clearly proves my point about the "inescapable" nature of interpretation—if there were no such interpretation, as you maintain, then why is there all the disagreement in the religious world? Surely you do not believe that you are the **only one** out of every religious person in the world throughout history who has ever managed to "get it right."*

*Whether you will acknowledge it or not, I believe it is undeniable that you are **interpreting** the Bible with your own heart and your own mind whenever you preach. You are not merely a court reporter reading back the transcript and word definitions of the text (although that is clearly an important **starting point** of interpretation). You tell the members of the church **how to apply** various Biblical concepts to their **specific** issues raised in their **individual** lives—that is interpretation. It is the need for constant interpretation that makes texts like the Bible and the Constitution "living" documents.*

You are absolutely critical as the spiritual leader of your church, so do not sell yourself short. Clearly, no dictionary or super-sophisticated computer can do anything close to what you do, because you can apply metaphorical biblical concepts and parables to everyday situations that arise with members of your church. But that really makes my point, doesn't it? Indeed, what makes you more valuable than a supercomputer is the fact that you can interpret and apply biblical concepts in all kinds of individualized situations. Your function is much more involved and high-minded than merely being a giver of word definitions, although text and definitions are clearly the logical starting point from which you jump off of into interpretation. I agree that the text is an eminently reasonable (and really the only reasonable) "starting point." I guess we just disagree on the inescapably subjective nature and depth of the "ending point": our own personal interpretation.

*I want to make clear that I do not believe that there is anything "wrong" with your personal interpretation of the text of the Bible, or with what you do as a religious counselor or spiritual advisor, not at all. In fact, I think you are extremely good at it, and the people in your church are clearly aware of that and they rely on you greatly to provide that important service. My point is simply that there is an **inescapable need** for your private interpretation of the text of the Bible. That is why I argue that you should at least acknowledge that private interpretation is what you, and every spiritual leader anywhere, is necessarily doing.*

*However, I can understand your steadfast reluctance to acknowledge the inescapable need for private interpretation because, as we have seen, private interpretation also has its own set of problems. I understand your reluctance to recognize the subjective and personalized nature of interpretation because once you recognize the need for this personal interpretation, then you have to acknowledge the inherent "**subjective**" nature of interpretation and what you consider as objective undeniable doctrine from God.*

*Apparently that is something you find necessary to staunchly resist because you believe that you are being **completely "objective"** whenever you preach. You believe this precisely because you are relying exclusively on **dictionaries** and the **text** of the Bible "and nothing else."*

I think, however, that is simply incorrect. Although I greatly respect your commendable efforts to keep your sermons "100% objective," the inescapable reality is that there is "something else" necessarily going on when you, or any other preacher anywhere, for that matter, gives a sermon: your own private interpretation of biblical principles, guidelines, and laws. This is true no matter how much you make a good-faith attempt to be completely "objective," and, by the way, I think you make a much greater effort to be objective than any other preacher I have ever heard.

*Still, no matter how much you may try, you are required to read the Bible through your own eyes and understand it through your own heart and mind—and so must everyone else. Thus, every time you give a definition but then "explain it further" by saying, "In other words, the Bible means..." you begin to cross over into interpretation. You are no longer just **reporting**, you have begun **"applying"** the concept to a new, individualized, and specific situation— something which makes you better than, and more importantly, **different from,** a word-searchable, concordance Bible-text computer which merely contains objective definitions and cross-references.*

*Accordingly, I do not share your apparent view that interpreting the Bible is a mechanical "science" devoid **of your own mental impressions** and **reasoning powers** that give contextual meaning to the general concepts set forth in the Bible. If it were otherwise, then reasonable people who can simply read would never, and could never, in any circumstance whatsoever, disagree. Indeed, they necessarily would <u>**always**</u> agree, <u>**without exception**</u>, on every last minute theological detail (which we know is hardly the case) because every issue would simply be a matter of looking it up in the dictionary.*

*In sum, when one strings words together in order to communicate general principles and guidelines (which is what a very metaphorical text like the Bible does), the recipient of that communication (the reader) cannot **solely** rely upon the word choice (the text) and their agreed meanings (dictionary definitions) in order to **apply** those concepts to their individual lives. This is true because there is an **infinite** amount of possible situations that come up all of the time that require **interpretation and application of the governing concepts and principles** to unique (and* *modem-day) situations. The text can be read and interpreted to support contradictory positions—it happens all the time, and if it didn't, there would be no need for lawyers or pastors!*

*Such involves a great deal more on the part of the reader of the text than just simply understanding word definitions. Again, there are "easy cases"; however, I refer to the more difficult cases, especially the cases that cause all of the profound theological disagreement due to the inescapable nature of private interpretation. That is where you come in and why you are so valuable to your church as a spiritual leader. However, I do not believe you can accept that important role while also rejecting the notion that there is an inescapable **subjective** element to what you are doing: private interpretation.*

My poor dad! I don't know how he does it; he must have the patience of Job to put up with me. I tell my dad that his strongest argument that there must be a god is that only God could have given my dad a willingness to read this kind of stuff from me over the years and then still tell me that he enjoys talking to me and receiving my diatribe letters. But make no mistake, my dad also enjoys informing me, with a devilish glint in his eye, that I definitely have received my karma in the form of my most literal, Bible-quoting, seventeen-year-old son, Julian—yes, Julian, who, as I write this book, has his own challenging theological points for me, such as "God thinks differently, and higher, than we do, Dad, so why don't you try thinking outside of your little and very limited human logic and science boxes and have enough faith to believe that God is beyond them and that we are not His intellectual or spiritual equals?" Whatever could I have possibly done in life to deserve such a smart-aleck son who seems to fully enjoy giving his poor old dad such a hard time about theological matters? It truly escapes me.

Chapter Fifty-One

"I'm King of the World!"

What should we make of the pronouncement in Genesis 1:28, "Let them [humans] have dominion over the fish of the sea, and over the fowl of the air, and over the cattle, and over all the earth, and over every creeping thing that creepeth on the earth"? The word "dominion" certainly implies having power, or territorial control, over the earth and all of the creatures and things in it, but is that really how we should interpret that verse? Does it mean that we should *exploit* the earth and all of its resources, so that the earth is here to serve all of the material and selfish needs of humans? That is certainly one way to look at it, and many people do see the earth essentially as a vast resource to be used, exploited, and ultimately conquered by humankind. They even justify that view as the will of God—because God gave us the earth for that very purpose—to control it and use it, sort of like Manifest Destiny, in which we had to "win" and conquer the West, taking it away from heathen Indians and using it the way God intended for us to use the land!

Such an adversarial relationship with the earth is only one way to look at the "dominion" over the earth bestowed on us by God, however, because, as Uncle Ben (who was really quoting Thomas Jefferson) said in the Spiderman movies, "With great power comes great responsibility." So what responsibility, if any, do we have to the earth? For example, I also have been given dominion over my children, but should it mean that they are resources for me to exploit for my own personal use? I may have power over my children, but isn't that power exceeded by my responsibility to love and care for them? In a similar way (but only similar, because I realize that trees, water, animals, and the like are not exactly the same as my own human children), perhaps we could interpret the verse to mean that we humans should have a very respectful and loving relationship with God's glorious creation. Perhaps we should try to coexist with nature in harmony rather than to limit ourselves to an adversarial, exploitative relationship with the environment.

The problem is that many people seem to interpret this verse to mean that we should not see ourselves as *part of* the environment but instead as *superior to* the environment, because God's only purpose in creating the earth in the first place was to give us a resource to exploit and a venue to play out humankind's ultimate decision between good and evil. As a result, they believe that we should not see ourselves as living within nature as an integral part of creation but instead should understand that God created nature exclusively for us to conquer, subdue, and control.

Notwithstanding these divergent views, perhaps there is a happy medium between these two extremes, somewhere between living like wild animals with no civilization and just worshiping nature, on the one hand, and living like arrogant Godlike kings who completely exploit nature to fulfill its only true purpose—to be a servant to us for our selfish needs, because we are superior to everything on Earth, except for God Himself—on the other. Neither extreme appears to be all that desirable. Neither view seems like it would fully encompass God's intentions for us and for the earth.

I have often wondered why there is not much more common ground between very liberal "green" environmentalists and very conservative Christian fundamentalists. It seems like they both would have a very strong love and respect for the splendor and grandeur of God's magnificent creation, Earth. Shouldn't humans be able to "use" the earth and its resources but also "replenish" the earth and its resources, in order to *benefit* from God's creation while still being able to *sustain* it into the future? There are many examples of this overlap. For instance, the Conference of Catholic Bishops and some fundamentalist groups have significant concerns for the health of unborn fetuses and are therefore involved in an effort to minimize the current dangerous amounts of mercury that are found in one of every six fetuses. This high level of mercury can be traced to many environmental factors, one of which comes from coal-fired power plants. Pollution emissions from these plants fall back to earth when it rains, resulting in higher levels of mercury that can harm fetuses, as well as fish. It seems clear that there should be a joint concern of religious believers and environmentalists about this kind of problem.

To find this common ground, we should first get beyond the extreme labels and stereotypes that both sides use to categorize and caricature each other. Business and industry are not made up only of greedy corporations who want to pollute and poison the world for profit and selfish gain; instead, they can be very important job creators who push for scientific and technological advancement that can help ease the human condition and materially maximize our time on earth. Similarly, environmentalism is not just some liberal, hippie, tree-hugging worship of nature in place of God, but shows, instead, a healthy love and wise respect for our environment and for God's beautiful creation. Thus, our stewardship as caretakers of the earth should not be reduced to the mere economic exploitation or poisonous pollution of the planet.

A simple metaphor might be helpful here to make the overall point. If God gave me a beautiful house to live in and said, "You have dominion over this house, and everything in it that I have given to you" would that mean I could burn the house down or bulldoze it over and sell it for firewood if I wanted to? Could I really justify doing so because, it is, after all, *my* house and God gave it to *me*, and my ownership therefore means that I can do with my house whatever I please? Or did God give me the house and everything in it so I could live in the house, benefit from it, and fully enjoy it, but in so doing, not destroy it, disrespect it, or trash it? When God gave the house to me, maybe He meant it to be a gift not just for me but also for my children and my future grandchildren, so that I should sustain the house for them too, even though it is only currently *my* house. Moreover, if the house truly is a gift from God, shouldn't I try to do everything to revere and preserve God's gift to me, my children, and my future grandchildren? Wouldn't that kind of reverent care and concern for His gift be the more rationale, more adult, and more spiritual thing to do with His glorious gift—which I did not even deserve in the first place? Such does not mean that we should worship the house—that is, nature itself—as God but that we should respect and sustain the gift that God has created for us. A little bit of Christian humility regarding God's creation gift of the earth to us would be nice.

With this in mind, consider the following excerpt from a letter written in 1852 by a now famous Native American, Chief Seattle (the letter was dictated orally and translated into English). Although it has been suggested that Chief Seattle did not actually write the letter, the letter nonetheless espouses an important worldview, especially one held by many Native Americans, regardless of the true identity of the writer. At the time, the US government was interested in purchasing many tribal lands from Chief Seattle's people for "settlers involved in the burgeoning westward expansion," or the "conquest and genocide of the West," depending on one's ideological perspective. Perhaps both views are true to a certain extent. In any event, Chief Seattle wrote a marvelous, and even prophetic, letter in reply to the government's request to buy their lands:

> The President in Washington sends word that he wishes to buy our land. But how can you buy or sell the sky? The land? The idea is strange to us. If we do not own the freshness of the air and the sparkle of the water, how can you buy them?
>
> Every part of this earth is sacred to my people. Every shining pine needle, every sandy shore, every mist in the dark woods, every meadow, every humming insect. All are holy in the memory and experience of my people.
>
> We know the sap which courses through the trees as we know the blood that courses through our veins. We are part of the earth and it is part of us. The perfumed flowers are our sisters. The bear, the deer, the great eagle, these are our brothers. The rocky crests, the juices in the meadow, the body heat of the pony, and man, all belong to the same family.
>
> The shining water that moves in the streams and rivers is not just water, but the blood of our ancestors. If we sell you our land, you must remember that it is sacred. Each ghostly reflection in the clear waters of the lakes tells of events and memories in the life of my people. The water's murmur is the voice of my father's father.
>
> The rivers are our brothers. They quench our thirst. They carry our canoes and feed our children. So you must give to the rivers the kindness you would give any brother.
>
> If we sell you our land, remember that the air is precious to us, that the air shares its spirit with all the life it supports. The wind that gave our grandfather his first breath also receives his last sigh. The wind also gives our children the spirit of life. So if we sell you our land, you must keep it apart and sacred, as a place where man can go to taste the wind that is

sweetened by the meadow flowers.

Will you teach your children what we have taught our children? That the earth is our mother? What befalls the earth befalls all the sons of the earth.

This we know: the earth does not belong to man, man belongs to the earth. All things are connected like the blood that unites us all. Man did not weave the web of life, he is merely a strand in it. Whatever he does to the web, he does to himself.

One thing we know: our god is also your god. The earth is precious to him and to harm the earth is to heap contempt on its creator.

Your destiny is a mystery to us. What will happen when the buffalo are all slaughtered? The wild horses tamed? What will happen when the secret corners of the forest are heavy with the scent of many men and the view of the ripe hills is blotted by talking wires? Where will the thicket be? Gone! Where will the eagle be? Gone! And what is it to say goodbye to the swift pony and the hunt? The end of living and the beginning of survival.

When the last Red Man has vanished with his wilderness and his memory is only the shadow of a cloud moving across the prairie, will these shores and forests still be here? Will there be any of the spirit of my people left?

We love this earth as a newborn loves its mother's heartbeat. So, if we sell you our land, love it as we have loved it. Care for it as we have cared for it. Hold in your mind the memory of the land as it is when you receive it. Preserve the land for all children and love it, as God loves us all.

As we are part of the land, you too are part of the land. This earth is precious to us. It is also precious to you. One thing we know: there is only one God. No man, be he Red Man or White Man, can be apart. We are brothers after all. [Emphasis added].

This is NOT to say that there has not been a profound benefit to us all brought by modernization, technology, and development, or that the establishment of the United States was a bad thing. That would be far too extreme to suggest, as it is not that simple—all "progress" is not evil—but the opposite extreme conclusion about the lack of value to the Native Americans' former way of life and perspective is also just as extreme and overly simplistic. That is why I am very troubled by the fact that many "Bible-believing" Christian fundamentalist/literalists might read the "Letter from Chief Seattle" and, instead of seeing it as something humble, beautiful, and respectful of God and His creation here on Earth, might mock it as an unenlightened—and even as a savage, pagan, heathen—worship of Mother Earth over Father God. They might also further assail it as "reverse sexism" (instead of "proper" sexism, I guess, in which any female symbolic gender role [Mother Earth] is inherently less valuable than a symbolic male gender role [Father God]). The overall contrary view, however, against the spirit of the "Letter from

Chief Seattle" leaves little or no room for valuing the humility and respect for God and God's creation that is evident throughout the letter.

Again, on a certain level, it is disappointing that there is not more common ground between believing in the God of the Bible and believing in the importance of respecting the earth such that we see ourselves as meek human beings who are merely fortunate temporary inhabitants of the earth. Does God want for me to humbly respect the earth, as being just a small part of it, or does He really want me to exercise an adversarial supremacy, control, and dominion over the earth, which was created solely for our discrete authoritarian human purposes?

For example, should I feel humbled by the grandeur of, say, a majestic mountain created by God, or should I realize that the mountain, with all of its resources, was put there by God only for humans to use and exploit for its "highest and best" capitalistic use? If that mountain was put there for me, then perhaps that so-called majestic mountain, for which I now have so much respect, ought to instead start respecting *me*, and not the other way around! Indeed, forget just the earth—should I go a step further and believe that the entire universe was created, with no life at all possibly existing anywhere else, because the universe and everything, everywhere, is quite literally all about us, all about me, and nothing else?

Such a narcissistic vision of our humanity is not exactly the most humble and unassuming view of our own importance in the universe. Accordingly, it might be that God would take offense at being used this way by some people to justify such human arrogance, in which we value an adversarial relationship with the earth more than a harmonious relationship with it—and with the universe.

As stated by Adlai Stevenson in his final speech before the United Nations in 1965:

> We travel together, passengers on a little space ship, dependent upon its vulnerable reserves of air and soil, committed for our safety to its security and peace, preserved from annihilation only by the care, the work, and, I will say, the love we give our fragile craft.

Chapter Fifty-Two

Are We Supposed to Be Vegetarians?

[29] And God said, Behold, I have given you every herb bearing seed, which is upon the face of all the earth, and every tree, in the which is the fruit of a tree yielding seed; to you it shall be for meat.

[30] And to every beast of the earth, and to every fowl of the air, and to every thing that creepeth upon the earth, wherein there is life, I have given every green herb for meat: and it was so.

[31] And God saw every thing that he had made, and, behold, it was very good. And the evening and the morning were the sixth day.

Just as an aside, there are occasional grammatical errors throughout the Bible—such as in Verse 29, above "… in the which is the…" Such errors are understandable for humans (for example, the errors that are no doubt in this book, try as I have to catch most of them), but not for God, right—if God truly wrote every word of the Bible? If such errors are just in the translation of the Bible, why didn't God ensure the Bible was translated correctly?

The last few verses ([30] – [31]) describing plants and green herbs for "meat"/food seem to suggest that we should all—including all animals, birds, and insects—be vegetarians. From a health point of view for humans, there certainly would be some benefits to that; from a planet sustainability point of view, it also makes sense, not to mention that it shows a healthy respect for God's creation and God's creatures. It is hard to argue, however, that eating meat, or at least eating fish, is a Biblical *sin*, when God miraculously provided loaves *and fishes* to feed a hungry multitude of 5,000 who were listening to Jesus preach (Mark 6:40–44):

> [40] And they sat down in ranks, by hundreds, and by fifties.
> [41] And when he had taken the five loaves and the two fishes, he looked up to heaven, and blessed, and brake the loaves, and gave them to his disciples to set before them; and the two fishes divided he among them all.
> [42] And they did all eat, and were filled.
> [43] And they took up twelve baskets full of the fragments, and of the fishes.
> [44] And they that did eat of the loaves were about five thousand men.

If it were a sin, or even if it were unhealthy, to eat meat (fish), it is doubtful that Jesus would have given the multitude a sinful or unhealthy non-vegetarian thing to consume, such as Twinkies, vodka, cigarettes, or chili-cheese hot dogs (or fish/meat?).

Still, maybe we humans were all intended to be vegetarians, and maybe even all animals were intended to be vegetarians, given the literal interpretation of these verses of Genesis. The reality, however, is that there are carnivorous animals such as sharks and lions that can eat only meat and presumably, if they tried to become vegetarians, they would not be able to even survive. Perhaps the writer simply was not aware of lions in Africa, tigers in India, sharks in the oceans, and the like, although the writer probably would have encountered either wild or perhaps domesticated carnivorous dogs or cats in the Middle East. So, what is the explanation for the existence of carnivorous animals? I can understand humankind having free will to sin, but not so much for animals. Are these carnivorous animals committing sins by "choosing" to eat meat and not following God's will? Many animals are carnivores, or at least some kind of omnivores that sometimes eat meat of some kind.

Also, if we humans are not supposed to eat meat at all, as suggested in Genesis, why does God go to such great lengths later in the Old Testament to define the difference between clean and unclean animals for us to eat? Some animals are kosher to eat, whereas others are not and therefore should not be eaten, but this distinction implies that clean animals should be eaten—so apparently, eating meat is not a sin, and perhaps it is even healthy, at least with respect to "clean" animals. Consider the following:

[3] Thou shalt not eat any abominable thing.
[4] *These are the beasts which ye shall eat*: the ox, the sheep, and the goat,
[5] The hart, and the roebuck, and the fallow deer, and the wild goat, and the pygarg, and the wild ox, and the chamois.
[6] And every beast that parteth the hoof, and cleaveth the cleft into two claws, and cheweth the cud among the beasts, that ye shall eat.
[7] Nevertheless these ye shall not eat of them that chew the cud or of them that divide the cloven hoof; as the camel, and the hare, and the coney: for they chew the cud, but divide not the hoof; therefore they are unclean unto you.
[8] And the swine, because it divideth the hoof, yet cheweth not the cud, it is unclean unto you: ye shall not eat of their flesh, nor touch their dead carcase.
[9] These ye shall eat of all that are in the waters: all that have fins and scales shall ye eat:
[10] And whatsoever hath not fins and scales ye may not eat; it is unclean unto you.
[11] Of all clean birds ye shall eat.
[12] But these are they of which ye shall not eat: the eagle, and the ossifrage, and the ospray'
[13] And the glede, and the kite, and the vulture after his kind,
[14] And every raven after his kind,
[15] And the owl, and the night hawk, and the cuckow, and the hawk after his kind,
[16] The little owl, and the great owl, and the swan,

[17] And the pelican, and the gier eagle, and the cormorant,

[18] And the stork, and the heron after her kind, and the lapwing, and the bat.

[19] And every creeping thing that flieth is unclean to you; they shall not be eaten.

[20] But of all clean fowls ye may eat.

[21] Ye shall not eat of anything that dieth of itself:...(Deuteronomy 14:3–21, emphasis added in Verse [4] where it appears we are even commanded to eat certain types of meat).

[By the way, a bat is *not* a type of bird (see Verse 18), although bats can fly (and thus probably what led to the mistaken classification here). Instead, bats are mammals, not birds, just like whales are mammals, not fish, even though whales swim in the ocean like fish do. God, the Creator, would know all of this, of course, but whoever wrote these verses obviously did not.]

So why does the Bible allow us to eat certain clean animals, and even instruct us how to do so, if, according to Genesis, we are all supposed to be strict vegetarians? Other verses in the Bible have a yet slightly different perspective but again seem to suggest that meat-eating is not a sin. For example, it is hard to argue that it is a sin to eat meat, when certain portions of the animal sacrifice in the Old Testament were actually given to Aaron and his sons (the priests) for their portion (their payment for their services as priests). Because being a priest was a full-time job, this was how they received sustenance. The fat of the animal was "wholly burnt," and considered to be exclusively God's, whereas certain portions of the meat were given to Aaron and his sons, the priests, for their own consumption:

[31] And the priest shall burn the fat upon the alter; [this goes to God himself, they were strictly forbidden to partake of the fat of the animal] but the breast shall be Aaron's and his sons' [for consumption].

[32] And the right shoulder shall ye give unto the priest for an heave offering of the sacrifices of your peace offerings.

[33] He among the sons of Aaron, that offereth the blood of the peace offerings, and the fat, shall have the right shoulder for his part.

[34] For the wave breast and the heave shoulder have I taken of the children of Israel from off the sacrifices of their peace offerings, and have given them unto Aaron the priest and unto his sons by a statute for ever from among the children of Israel. (Leviticus 7:31–34)

To eat meat or not eat meat may be just a quibble, but I bring it up only to point out the raging debates that occur between various sects of Christians claiming to be living literal interpretations of the Bible, in which some insist that God meant for us to be vegetarians and we therefore should not eat meat at all (Seventh-day Adventists, for example). By comparison, many Christian denominations allow meat-eating and do not seem to make an issue of it in any way, and still others (traditional Catholics, for example—and certainly, "Kosher" Jews) declare that only certain kinds of meat should be eaten, and then only on certain days. They all use various verses from the Bible to support their positions, yet they all come up with very different proscriptions based on their "literal" interpretations of the text, upon which they cannot seem to agree. In the New Testament, Peter is told by God that it is perfectly fine to eat *any* kind of meat:

> **[10]** And he [Peter] became very hungry, and would have eaten: but while they made ready, he fell into a trance,
> **[11]** And saw heaven opened, and a certain vessel descending unto him, as it had been a great sheet knit at the four corners, and let down to the earth:
> **[12]** Wherein were all manner of fourfooted beasts of the earth, and wild beasts, and creeping things, and fowls of the air.
> **[13]** And there came a voice to him, Rise, Peter; kill, and eat.
> **[14]** But Peter said, Not so, Lord; for I have never eaten any thing that is common or unclean.
> **[15]** And the voice spake unto him again the second time, What God hath cleansed, that call not thou common. (Acts 10:10–15)

Many believers say grace before they eat a meal because they are thanking God for the food that they are about to eat, which they believe God has provided for them. If the Lord has provided the food, then can it be eaten, or is that food not from God, and therefore would still be unclean and should not be eaten? In my dad's church, they teach that we should be very strict vegetarians because it is healthy and because that is what God intended in the Garden of Eden. Perhaps that is true, but it is hard to argue that being a vegetarian is clearly and literally what the Bible says or teaches in all circumstances, especially when it literally says, "ye *shall* eat…[various clean types of meat]."

Interestingly, also in my dad's church, they do not believe that it is a sin to go to Las Vegas and gamble. My dad says there is nothing in the Bible that says that gambling is a sin. My dad also makes a very good point by noting that purchasing stock on the stock market is also, in a sense, gambling with one's money but no one would argue that trying to make money by trading stock is a sin (to the extent that it is at least done legally). Similarly, buying a house in a depressed housing market, and then selling it when the real estate market goes up, if it goes up, is a form of gambling with one's finances but is not thought of as a sin. I am rather impressed with my dad's reasoning by analogy here—he sounds like a good lawyer making a good argument that it is perfectly fine for his church members to go gamble in Las Vegas—and maybe even to pray for a special blessing or two at the Blackjack table! My brother, however, raises a very interesting point about my dad's theology: It apparently is OK go to a Las Vegas casino and *gamble* but it is not OK to go to a Las Vegas buffet line and *order a steak*—ouch. My brother can focus like a laser.

ARE WE SUPPOSED TO BE VEGETARIANS?

In my dad's defense, he is in his mid-seventies and is in superb health, is in excellent physical shape, looks great for his age, and is fully enjoying life, so whatever he is eating, or not eating, it appears to be working quite well for him. Most importantly, given his healthy lifestyle, it also appears as though he is going to be with us for a long time, and that is something for which we are all very grateful.

In any event, although the Bible may ultimately be unclear on what exactly we are supposed to eat and not eat, or can eat, an even more fundamental question is, Why did God make it so we even have to eat in the first place? Why did God make it so that his creatures—both people and animals—would starve to death if they do not eat? It is not really all that crazy of a question in light of the fact that God created plants that photosynthesize sunlight. Even we humans have invented solar panels that convert the sun's energy into electricity. That is what plants do, in a sense: convert the sun's energy into another usable form; they sort of "eat the sun." It is true that plants also get nutrients, in addition to water, from the ground through their roots, but still, God is a very capable engineer and Creator, so certainly, He could have, if He had wanted to, intelligently designed our bodies to "eat the sun" so starvation would be unknown and humans and animals would not have to kill each other, or even plants, for food.

People photosynthesizing the sun's energy, and therefore not finding it necessary to kill other things and consume them, may seem a bit silly to suggest, but perhaps not so much when one considers the utter tragedy of an innocent baby born in a very poor country who, through no fault of his or her own, starves to death because there is simply not enough food to eat. Currently, a child somewhere in the world dies every ten seconds because of starvation. What is the purpose of that unjust tragedy, which is simply a random result of the child just happening to be born into a poor family at the wrong time? God easily could have avoided such unfair, unnecessary, and cruel outcomes. After all, His Angels do not starve...do they? Either God's angels always have enough to eat or they simply do not need to eat, but either way, there is no starvation among them.

So many similar tragedies in the world that God created, especially those affecting innocent children, such as birth defects and diseases, not to mention violence and abuse against children, hardly seem justified as any kind of righteous punishment for anything an innocent child or even baby may have done as a sinner, but God allows this kind of injustice to take place every day, even when it is not perpetrated by anyone in particular who might suffer punishment in this life or beyond as retribution. Of course, we are in this universe, and that's the way it is here, like it or not, but if Genesis is literally true, then God could have made the universe very different without so many of these seemingly unnecessary and even cruel injustices to children that easily could have been avoided at the initial design stage when God created Paradise on Earth and humans were supposed to live forever in the Garden of Eden. Original Sin makes *all* humans, even innocent children, sinners in need of salvation, and so perhaps that is the justification for tragedies that children must suffer through—but again, it just doesn't seem fair, especially to very young, innocent children, who at least do not start out life knowing and then doing evil.

Chapter Fifty-Three

Day Seven: God Rests
(But Don't Anger Him!)

Genesis 2

[1] Thus the heavens and the earth were finished, and all the host of them.
[2] And on the seventh day God ended his work which he had made; and he rested on the seventh day from all his work which he had made.
[3] And God blessed the seventh day, and sanctified it: because that in it he had rested from all his work which God created and made.
[4] These are the generations of the heavens and of the earth when they were created, in the day that the LORD God made the earth and the heavens,

Human beings get tired and must rest, but is that also true for an all-powerful God? It seems silly to think that God would ever have to rest because He is so tired from all of His work, but that is what it says here. What happens to God's will, and his answering of prayers and the like, on His days off, or even when He is just resting? If God gets tired and must rest sometimes, does God also have to *sleep*, or just rest? How can God ever take any kind of break at all if He is always "on call," being God, 24/7? The reason for raising this issue is not to be disrespectful to God or to His busy schedule but is simply to show how the writer conceptualizes God in very humanistic terms, with understandable and accessible humanistic traits. There is nothing wrong with portraying God in more relatable terms like this; it is just that in doing so, we once again expose some absurdities that result from a very literal interpretation of the text of the Bible. If the purpose of these verses is to instruct humans to rest once a week and to have a special holy day, that is fine, but that easily could have been just a commandment of God (one of the Ten Commandments, in fact) without assuming that God actually had to rest, Himself.

The larger point is that God is probably so much more than, and so much beyond, a superhuman entity with extraordinary powers and superhero abilities as He is sometimes portrayed in the Bible, if one interprets it literally. The problem is that the writers of the Bible often describe God as having very fallible and humanlike emotions such as anger and jealousy. My belief is that God would be far beyond such limited, human shortcomings. For example, sometimes the writers portray God as capable of becoming so angry that he vents His anger on apparently innocent people, such as the innocent children of the original offenders, and it even appears that God can hold a grudge for a very long time (three to four generations): "Thou shalt not bow down thyself to them, nor serve them; for I the Lord thy God am a jealous God, visiting the iniquity of the fathers upon the children unto the third and fourth generation of them that hate me" (Exodus 20:5).

In one instance, Moses proved to be more reasonable than God—how is that possible, and how is that even believable about an all-knowing, infallible God? God got so angry that Moses had to reason with Him to calm Him down…and it worked!

> **[7]** And the lord said unto Moses, Go, get thee down; [from the mountain after receiving the Ten Commandments] for thy people, which thou broughtest out of the land of Egypt, have corrupted themselves:
> **[8]** They have turned aside quickly out of the way which I commanded them: they have made them a molten calf, and have worshipped it.…
> **[10]** Now, therefore let Me alone, that my wrath may wax hot against them and that I may consume them.…
> **[11]** And Moses besought the Lord his God and said, Lord, why doth thy wrath wax hot against thy people."…
> **[14]** And the Lord repented of the evil he thought to do unto his people. (Exodus 32:7–14)

First, God is capable of evil, or at least thinking about doing evil. Next, God was sorry about that evil ("…the Lord repented of the evil he thought to do…"). Does that mean God made a mistake, and He even admits that He makes mistakes, and at times He even repents for His sin? If He does repent, to whom does He repent? Who forgives God, or can only God forgive Himself?

Maybe this whole angry episode exhibited by God was just a test by God of Moses's compassion for his people or was just a way of teaching Moses a powerful and very dramatic lesson. If so, however, we can always say something similar to excuse any of God's behaviors whatsoever, because He is God, and who are we to question when God might just be testing someone or making an important point? That situational explanation, however, is as silly as if I, as a law professor, make an obvious error or a mistake in my legal analysis during class but, instead of admitting the mistake, I seriously assert to my students, "Uh, yeah, I was really just seeing if you guys are paying attention." I suppose it would be funny if I would not be serious, but it would be rather pathetic if I *were* serious. By the way, in this biblical story, Moses ended up getting even madder at his people than God did and ended up throwing the Ten Commandments at them and burning and punishing them, so even if God's earlier repentance for His evil thoughts was just a lesson from God to Moses, it obviously didn't work too well:

> **[19]** And it came to pass, as soon as he [Moses] came nigh unto the camp, that he saw the calf, and the dancing: and Moses' anger waxed hot, and he cast the tables [the Ten Commandments that God had written] out of his hands, and brake them beneath the mount.

[20] And he took the calf which they had made, and burnt it in the fire, and ground it to powder, and strawed it upon the water, and made the children of Israel drink of it. (Exodus. 32:19–20)

Not only that, but the people had to wander in the wilderness for forty years before getting to the Promised Land: "And your children shall wander in the wilderness forty years, and bear your whoredoms, until your carcases be wasted in the wilderness" (Numbers14:33).

God also was sometimes portrayed as someone who became so angry with the indigenous peoples of certain regions that He ordered Moses to become an assassin; these foreign people happened to inhabit a particular piece of land and had their own system of religion. There are many such instances of this occurring in the Old Testament, including this is one: "**[1]** When the Lord thy God shall bring thee into the land…to posses it, and shall cast out many nations before thee…**[2]**…thou shalt smite them and utterly destroy them…nor shew mercy unto them:" (Deuteronomy 7:1–2).

Indeed, when God takes vengeance, watch out: "Samaria shall become desolate; for she hath rebelled against her God: they shall fall by the sword: their infants shall be dashed in pieces, and their women with child shall be ripped up" (Hosea 13:16). For all the Christian talk about how abortion is the killing of innocent life in the womb, God nevertheless seems to sanction cutting open the stomachs of pregnant women and dismembering their fetuses—such may become necessary if He really gets mad at a certain group of people!

Of course, whenever a radical Muslim group like Al-Qaeda advocates such violence in the name of religion and uses a radical form of Islamic Jihad to justify "killing infidels," fundamentalist Christian literalists recognize it as bad and as a religious perversion. If, in the Bible, however, God literally advocates the same sort of thing, well, then it is the righteous wrath of God and therefore is fully justified. Such literal interpretations can be very dangerous in the hands of radicals who can, at times, justify religious violence and/or religious intolerance in the name of the literal interpretation religious texts.

In sum, it seems odd that the writers of the Bible often portray God as a very touchy, moody, easy-to-anger, emotionally unstable, humanlike God, though He should be so above all of that as the true Supreme Being and Creator of the universe. In fact, it seems quite unfair to God to attribute to Him such humanlike failings as jealousy, anger, and impatience. It reminds me of how the writers of Greek mythology portrayed their gods and goddesses on Mount Olympus with very similar immature, emotional, and humanlike frailties. Frankly, God as the Supreme Being of the universe deserves better billing than the portrayal He often gets in the Bible. I "fear" God in the sense that I am in awe of God and His greatness, but that is different from feeling like I ought to walk around on eggshells with Him because I do not want Him to squash me like an ant if he is in a bad mood—that just seems wholly beneath Him.

[5] And every plant of the field before it was in the earth, and every herb of the field before it grew: for the LORD God had not caused it to rain upon the earth, and there was not a man to till the ground.
[6] But there went up a mist from the earth, and watered the whole face of the ground.

At least this is a better explanation as to why it rains—"a mist from the earth," rather than a large ocean in the sky, dripping water down through some imaginary dome described in earlier verses. Also, although plants need water to grow, they do not need a man to "till the ground"— consider any untilled jungle.

Chapter Fifty-Four

The Creation of Humans (Take Two)

[7] And the LORD God formed man of the dust of the ground, and breathed into his nostrils the breath of life; and man became a living soul.
[8] And the LORD God planted a garden eastward in Eden; and there he put the man whom he had formed.

The usage of "man" here is singular, not plural. Although it says "God formed man...and man became a living soul," it then says, "he put *the* man [singular] whom he had formed" in the Garden of Eden. This suggests that God did not create humankind all at once—creating a bunch of other co-original human beings—but instead first created Adam and Eve, such that it was necessary for them and/or their children to commit incest to populate the world, as discussed in detail earlier; however, Moses probably just overlooked this incest issue altogether as he was writing the first few chapters of Genesis. He just didn't think about it. This oversight, in turn, suggests that a human authored this portion of the Bible and engaged in a simple human error/oversight, rather than that an infallible God writing about His creation of the universe, the world, and humankind's origins. That explanation seems much more plausible than taking the text of Genesis literally and assuming that God wrote every word of it for our literal consumption.

[9] And out of the ground made the LORD God to grow every tree that is pleasant to the sight, and good for food; the tree of life also in the midst of the garden, and the tree of knowledge of good and evil.

So did God make *every* tree or only trees pleasant to the sight—pleasant to whose sight? Are there unpleasant, or ugly-to-the-sight, trees? Is *every* tree pleasant to the sight such that this is a compliment to God for making only beautiful, pleasant-looking trees in the world that are also "good for food"? Maybe so in the Garden of Eden, but what about the fact that most trees, as it turns out, are really *not* good for food—unless this passage is referring only to fruit and berry trees? What about bushes, shrubs, vines, cacti, vegetables, grasses, flowers, and the like? Were they in the Garden of Eden, too, or in the rest of the world?

Also, this passage does not explain what the Tree of Life is, but whatever it is, it appears to be a metaphor of some kind requiring private interpretation beyond the literal words used here. Literally, it would appear that if Adam and Eve ate of the Tree of Life, they would have everlasting life—or maybe the Tree of Life is just a metaphor for the Savior, Jesus Christ, who was to come. Perhaps, but if so, where is the textual support for such an interpretation? Our

American founders and patriots in the Revolutionary War against England spoke of the Tree of Liberty, but I am sure it was just a metaphor, as there was no actual tree that, if they ate the fruit of that tree, would make them more inclined to sign the Declaration of Independence and fight in the Revolutionary War.

Similarly, the Tree of Knowledge of Good and Evil is probably also symbolic, unless the fruit from it actually contained poisonous juice that somehow would open the minds of humans to make them aware of evil. Adam and Eve already must have been aware of evil in the very moment they disobeyed God and made the decision to eat the forbidden fruit, however, so the fruit of the tree could not have literally given them the knowledge of evil, because they would have already had to have been evil in the first place (*before* eating the fruit) to even conceptualize the act of disobeying God. Before taking the first bite, they must have *already* known evil. They could not have ever made that fateful decision to eat the forbidden fruit unless they already knew the evil of disobeying God. In criminal law, this is called the *mens rea*—the element of criminal intent—in which, for most crimes, one must first form the intent to commit the crime before actually committing the crime. Thus, the first evil act was actually Adam and Eve's *decision* to eat the fruit (their preliminary mental thought to disobey God) before they ever ate the fruit.

Recall the controversy caused by former president Jimmy Carter when he said that he "lusted in his heart" after the Statue of Liberty. According to the Bible, that would *already* be a sin, even if he did not go on to do the act of adultery—even if there were no *actus reus* in law, or the actual physical acting out of the crime. (See Matthew 5:27–28: "You have heard that it was said by them of old time, You shall not commit adultery: But I say unto you, That whosoever looks on a woman to lust after her hath committed adultery with her already in his heart.") So, where did the evil thought of disobeying God in the Garden of Eden come from before Adam and Eve ever ingested the forbidden fruit? Even if that knowledge came from Satan's temptation, that must mean that Adam and Eve *already knew* what evil was and could understand what it meant, and therefore they really did not need to even eat the forbidden fruit to gain the knowledge of evil— they must have already had such knowledge, for they sinned in their hearts at the moment they made the decision to eat, *before* actually eating it.

Whether the forbidden fruit was symbolic or literal, however, God was still the one who created the tree with the forbidden fruit and the option to eat from it. Indeed, God created the option for both humans and angels (Satan) to disobey Him and thereby introduce evil into the universe, so even though the talking serpent would tempt Eve and Eve would tempt Adam, God is the one who created Adam, Eve, Satan, the tree, the forbidden fruit, the Garden of Eden, the option to do evil, and the entire realm and factual context in which all of this activity transpired, with God's foreknowledge that this was exactly how it would all play out, even before He created any of it.

Chapter Fifty-Five

The Garden of Eden
(And Finding Stuff to Do)

[10] And a river went out of Eden to water the garden; and from thence it was parted, and became into four heads.
[11] The name of the first is Pison: that is it which compasseth the whole land of Havilah, where there is gold;
[12] And the gold of that land is good: there is bdellium and the onyx stone.
[13] And the name of the second river is Gihon: the same is it that compasseth the whole land of Ethiopia.
[14] And the name of the third river is Hiddekel: that is it which goeth toward the east of Assyria. And the fourth river is Euphrates.
[15] And the LORD God took the man, and put him into the Garden of Eden to dress it and to keep it.

We are provided with what appears to be the then location and geographical description of the Garden of Eden. I recognize the names of some rivers and landmarks, but when looking at a map, it is difficult to get a true, specific sense of just where the Garden of Eden exactly was or how big it was. Suffice it to say that it was somewhere in and around Mesopotamia and/or maybe Northeast Africa. Who knows if some of it might now be underneath a sea or an ocean? It is interesting to note that many anthropologists, based on various artifacts, suggest that this very general area is also roughly where recognizable human civilization began—notably the Sumerians and other early civilizations of Mesopotamia, although the first humans and hominids appear to be from fairly nearby Africa, according to anthropologists.

[16] And the LORD God commanded the man, saying, Of every tree of the garden thou mayest freely eat:
[17] But of the tree of the knowledge of good and evil, thou shalt not eat of it: for in the day that thou eatest thereof thou shalt surely die.

Apparently, God used to literally and openly talk very directly to human beings (with a loud, booming voice, one would suppose) just as clearly as in an everyday telephone conversation, so I guess faith in God was not even really necessary or required back then, because it would be so obvious that there was a God—one would know that there was a God and that He did exist for sure because one could actually converse with God just as directly and obviously as one can converse with another human being on the telephone. If I can go to the Grand Canyon and look at it, hike in it, and explore it, no faith is required at all to believe that the Grand Canyon does in fact exist, because I can actually perceive it. True, I would be deciding to "believe" my own eyes and ears, but that is much more tangible and real than faith in an unperceivable mental construct—like an unseen God.

Why wasn't faith in God required back then the way it is now? If God revealed Himself by talking directly to human beings in a loud, audible voice that was unmistakably God, why doesn't God reveal Himself to us now by talking directly to any of us in the same way He used to talk to Adam, Moses, and John? I cannot tell if that "little voice in my head" is really God speaking to me or if it is just a little voice in my head, period. The point is that it is completely up to me psychologically to determine whether God is conversing with me, whether it might be Satan tempting me, or whether there is no one else there and I am just deluding myself about whom I think I may be talking to; apparently, none of that doubt appears to be the case for people in biblical times, who could talk directly with God.

In one of these clear conversations, God threatens Adam with the punishment of death if Adam eats the forbidden fruit, but how could Adam possibly understand the concept of death? Adam was in Paradise, and there was no death, so how could he at that point conceive of what death really meant? Adam was still immortal and without shame in Paradise, and God intended for him to live that way forever, so how could Adam meaningfully comprehend death as a punishment for evil, of which he also had no knowledge or understanding? Recall, Adam supposedly only had knowledge of good at that point, but not the knowledge of both good *and* *evil*. As a result, wouldn't it have been impossible for him to even understand the option to do evil at any time before he ate the forbidden fruit?

In Genesis 2:17, God said, "for in the day that thou eatest thereof [the forbidden fruit] thou shalt surely die." But literally, that was not true; neither Adam nor Eve died on (or "in") the day they ate the fruit like God said they would. In fact, they lived very long lives afterward. There are, of course, other *nonliteral* ways to interpret this statement to not make God mistaken or a liar. For example, on the day that they ate, perhaps God meant that they would *spiritually* die because they no longer would be without sin, or that they would be condemned to death at that point and no longer be immortal, because the wages of sin is death, so they *eventually* would die at some point, just not necessarily that day. That is not what the passage literally says, however; it says that they will die on the day that they eat. If to spiritually die is what God actually meant here, why didn't He just say that? For this verse to have any chance of being a true and accurate statement, it must be interpreted figuratively or metaphorically, *not* literally.

[18] And the LORD God said, It is not good that the man should be alone; I will make him an help meet for him.

There appears to be a translation and even a grammatical error here—"an help meet for him"— what does that mean—a helpmate for him"? Whatever it means, it is contradictory, because in Chapter 1, God created "man and woman" *at the same time*: "So God created man in his own image, in the image of God created he him; male and female created he them" (Genesis 1:27). Here, however, we are told that God first created Adam and then later created Eve: "It is not good that the man should be alone," so God created this helpmate, Eve, for him. Even if this account is just a more detailed version of creation, like a flashback in a novel or movie, it is not logically consistent, because God created man and woman together at the same time in Chapter 1 and first one and then the other (so Adam would not be alone negating the argument that there may have been other mysterious humans at that point) in Chapter 2.

[19] And out of the ground the LORD God formed every beast of the field, and every fowl of the air; and brought them unto Adam to see what he would call them: and whatsoever Adam called every living creature, that was the name thereof.

There is a logistical timing issue here as well. Recall that at this point, all of the animals had *already* been created; they had been created *before* God ever created Adam and Eve. So why was God creating them later (or again), after Adam and Eve, to bring them in front of Adam to be named? The verse implies that Adam was there first, before the animals, but according to Chapter 1 of Genesis, God created the animals first, on the fifth and sixth days, then created Adam and Eve at the end of the sixth day before He rested on the seventh day. As a result, the basic order of events from Chapter 1 is inconsistent with those of Chapter 2.

[20] And Adam gave names to all cattle, and to the fowl of the air, and to every beast of the field; but for Adam there was not found an help meet for him.

Naming every living creature in the world would be quite a daunting task, if not logistically impossible, but perhaps Adam had a lot of time on his hands—he was alone, after all, according to this version in Chapter 2. Still, there are tens or even hundreds of thousands of species and classes of animals and birds to name. Did Adam write all of the names down so he would not lose track of what animals he had named and what names he specifically had given them? Did Adam have pen and paper, and could he write names of the words for each creature that he would make up right on the spot? Did Adam know language well enough to sound out the new words and then write them down, and know how to spell them correctly? How and when would Adam have learned how to write? By the way, who named the fish and insects, and all the various types of trees and flowers—since these naming tasks were not given to Adam—or were those particular names already part of the immediate language vocabulary that God bestowed on Adam and Eve, and on the talking serpent, when God created them (minus the names of all animals—"beasts of the field and fowl of the air"—that Adam would later name)?

Also, similar to what God did for Noah after Noah constructed the Ark, did God have every animal and bird in the world dutifully march by Adam (or appear in front of him)—so he could think of a name and write it down—and then have the animal march back to wherever it came from (kangaroos back to Australia, polar bears back to the Arctic, penguins back to Antarctica, tigers back to Asia, hippos back to Africa, bison back to North America)?

What about dinosaurs? Did Adam name all of the dinosaurs, too, or were they already extinct by then, even though God had just created them? I am really not trying to be sarcastic here, but I am trying to be very literal. If this particular question seems offensively sarcastic, or is taken that way, however, doesn't that really say something more about the person who is offended by this question and the fact that perhaps what is written here in Genesis cannot, or at least should not, be taken so literally? If not, then why should anyone take any offense at all at this question when all I am doing is taking literally that which is written in Genesis?

Chapter Fifty-Six

The Blame Game:
A Woman Causing Trouble

[21] And the LORD God caused a deep sleep to fall upon Adam and he slept: and he took one of his ribs, and closed up the flesh instead thereof;
[22] And the rib, which the LORD God had taken from man, made he a woman, and brought her unto the man.
[23] And Adam said, This is now bone of my bones, and flesh of my flesh: she shall be called Woman, because she was taken out of Man.
[24] Therefore shall a man leave his father and his mother, and shall cleave unto his wife: and they shall be one flesh.
[25] And they were both naked, the man and his wife, and were not ashamed.

Not only is this account of Adam and Eve's creation a contradictory and inconsistent second story of the creation of man and woman, but it also appears to begin laying the groundwork for much of the sexism that runs rampant throughout the Bible. Man is portrayed as the main creation of God while woman is seen merely as a helpmate to the man and is dependent on the man, even to the extent that the woman is merely made from a bone (rib) taken from the man. Also, Adam was the one who got to name Eve as a woman, which is a little condescending, because Adam just got done naming all of the beasts in the field and fowl of the air that God had brought to him to name. Adam is referred to exclusively as a man (not also as a husband), but Eve is not referred to exclusively as a woman; she is also referred to as "his [Adam's] wife."

It would appear that God performed a surgical operation on Adam (complete with putting him under anesthesia) to take out his rib in order to create Eve. Why couldn't an all-powerful God miraculously pull out the rib without having to put Adam under the way a modern surgeon would? For that matter, why would God need a bone from Adam to create Eve, anyway? If God can create the universe from nothing, why does He need to take a bone from an existing man to make a woman—unless it is just a metaphor to symbolize their marriage and ultimate union or connection, which is a very beautiful heterosexual marriage metaphor?

To the extent that pulling Adam's rib out and creating Eve from it is just a metaphor for togetherness and oneness of spirit, why didn't God use a more befitting and symbolically equal, rather than unequal, metaphor, such as creating man and woman out of the same equal pile of stardust to symbolize their equal union and the unity of marriage? The sexist nature of the way it is now written makes one wonder if God really wrote these verses or if Moses had a sexist view that he unwittingly reflected in the way he wrote about God's creation of man (as the first and superior human being) and then woman (as a later, and lesser, human being, whose entire purpose seems to be to help the man, as a mere extension of the man).

Genesis 3

[1] Now the serpent was more subtle than any beast of the field which the LORD God had made. And he said unto the woman, Yea, hath God said, Ye shall not eat of every tree of the garden?

Were there really talking animals back then? If so, and if Satan used a snake to speak to Eve, why didn't God also have to use some type of a talking animal (perhaps a dove) to converse directly with Adam and Eve? Also, instead of a talking serpent, perhaps a snake just happened to be slithering by and what it supposedly said to Eve was really just a figment of Eve's overactive imagination. As the snake came by, was she just wondering why she should not be able to eat the forbidden fruit?

As an aside, if Satan, did actually speak to Eve through this snake, it sure would be nice if Satan had to reveal himself this way every time he tempted us by literally having to use a talking snake. If that were the case, then my general rule of thumb would be that if a talking snake is ever telling me that I should do something, it would be a clear indication that the talking snake is really Satan and I should therefore be careful. It would make it much easier than trying to discern who is actually speaking whenever I hear little voices inside my head: Satan tempting me, God guiding me, or me just having a conversation with myself and/or other imagined entities in my head.

[2] And the woman said unto the serpent, We may eat of the fruit of the trees of the garden:
[3] But of the fruit of the tree which is in the midst of the garden, God hath said, Ye shall not eat of it, neither shall ye touch it, lest ye die.
[4] And the serpent said unto the woman, Ye shall not surely die:
[5] For God doth know that in the day ye eat thereof, then your eyes shall be opened, and ye shall be as gods, knowing good and evil.

As pointed out earlier, Satan did not lie to Eve; instead, he told her exactly what would happen if she ate the forbidden fruit: (1) she would not literally die that day from either touching or eating the fruit, and (2) she would come to know the difference between good and evil—which was reasonable in light of the fact that God Himself named the tree the Tree of Knowledge of Good and Evil. Eve claimed that Satan deceived her or beguiled her, but all he really did was repeat what she had been told by God—and when Satan told Eve that she would not die if she ate, he did not lie; she did not die on the day she ate or touched the fruit, although she would *eventually* die. Maybe God exaggerated to Adam and Eve about surely dying on the day that they touched or ate the forbidden fruit as a very strong warning to keep them away from that fruit? But is it OK for God to lie or exaggerate, even if He does so for our own good, as a warning? Is it OK to lie to our young children about the Boogie Man to get better behavior and obedience out of them?

[6] And when the woman saw that the tree was good for food, and that it was pleasant to the eyes, and a tree to be desired to make one wise, she took of the fruit thereof, and did eat, and gave also unto her husband with her; and he did eat.
[7] And the eyes of them both were opened, and they knew that they were naked; and they sewed fig leaves together, and made themselves aprons.

So like Satan said, Adam and Eve did not die on the day they ate, and they did gain the knowledge of good and evil. And after they ate, they felt ashamed to be naked in front of one another. But why would they feel ashamed to be naked? No one else could see them, because there was literally no one else in the world at that time except the two of them, but they were husband and wife. Was God's image, after which Adam and Eve were created, really something that should be considered shameful by them, because God's image really should be covered up with clothing (although note that Eve remained topless apparently without shame)?

With respect to timing, shouldn't Adam and Eve have been able to see the shameful nakedness of their bodies in the moment just *before* eating the fruit, when they at that point must have already known the evil of deciding to disobey God, rather than after they ate? After Eve ate the forbidden fruit, why did she not immediately warn Adam not to eat because it was evil, or was the knowledge of evil slow to set it (the forbidden fruit had to be digested and enter the blood stream before it would affect the mind)? If the knowledge was not immediate, perhaps this is why sexism has occurred through the ages, because there was an assumption that Eve, the woman, must have realized before Adam that what they were doing was evil, but she did not warn Adam and instead wanted him to join her in her disobedience against God.

Chapter Fifty-Seven

Who Is Responsible for This Evil That Came into the World?

I keep coming back to this issue, but it is very important. Why can evil even exist in a universe created by a non-evil God? If God is only good and He created the universe and everything in it, who or what created evil? Why does evil even exist if God did not create it? Humankind or Satan cannot be the creators of evil, because although they may have *chosen* to do evil, God still was the one who created evil as an option for them to choose. Even if God only created free will or free agency, and not evil itself, that still does not explain how Lucifer-Satan and Adam and Eve obtained the ability to *conceive* of evil using only their original and pure minds, which were completely created and given to them by God *before* any forbidden fruit was ever eaten. What forbidden fruit of the knowledge of good and evil could Lucifer eat in Heaven before he and one-third of the angels became aware of evil and their ability to sin, allowing them to rebel in Heaven against God?

If God cannot sin or be evil, why did God create evil as an option for us to engage in, especially when He knew that billions of people throughout the ages would suffer because of the evil that he allows as an option? It may be true that God Himself does not *do* evil and may not Himself directly be responsible for the evil we choose to do, but just as a programmer of a certain software program is not directly responsible for the choices offered by that software program to an end user, the programmer—as the creator of the software—still controls *all* of the available options that the end user can choose from in that particular program. Indeed, the programmer is responsible for creating the entire "universe" of those computer options. Thus, why would God, as the ultimate "Programmer" of the software program of the entire universe, though He is perfect and without sin, create evil as an option in His program for an end user (Satan or us) to choose? In short, no one could choose to do evil without God first having made doing evil an option in the universe, because nothing could exist if God had not created it.

If we allow that outsiders (humankind or Satan) can hack into the program created by God (which would be the context of this universe) and launch the equivalent of a computer virus (evil), aren't we forgetting that God is supposed to be perfect and omniscient? Why would an all-knowing, all-powerful God allow His program to be hacked into and hijacked by lesser beings unless He purposefully created a defective, vulnerable, unsecured, non-firewalled program? So, who created Satan's ability to conceive of evil? Remember, God created all of the parameters. Why does God, for example, allow evil to be done to the completely innocent? Many fundamentalist Christians believe that human life begins at the moment of conception of the fetus. The issue of when human life, as we know it, actually begins is open to interpretation, but assuming that life begins at conception, as fundamentalist Christians believe, why does God allow people to commit abortions of completely helpless and innocent people—the fetuses (assuming they are equivalent to fully formed human beings so this act would thus be murder) who have never committed sin or even have had the opportunity in the world to commit sin?

My dad and I once discussed this issue; he had an interesting analogy. He stated that although our parents may have created us, they are not the ones who choose evil for us in any way; instead, we choose evil on our own and therefore cannot blame our choices on our parents simply because our presence here is because of them. Similarly, then, we cannot blame God for our evil choices just because He created us and we would not be here if were it not for Him. This argument has some appeal, but only if you assume that parents are creators in the exact sense that God is our Creator as well as the Creator of everything else in the universe. One's parents did not create the entire universe and all of the possible options in it simply by the act of having children, however. In fact, parents really do not create anything; instead, they simply start a process of cell reproduction when a father's sperm and a mother's egg meet, but God is the one who creates the soul of that person who will exist in a physical body in the universe that God has already created. In short, two parents do not create and then program an entire universe and set forth all of the available options in that universe; only God can do that.

This is not to say that we humans should not be held responsible for our evil choices; we should, but perhaps it was evil from the outset for God to create a universe where evil itself was an option to pursue. Also, why should I ever have to suffer the evil choices of other people that I personally had nothing to do with? Why did God create all of us with such a defective design flaw so we not only can choose evil for ourselves but can also choose to do evil to other people? If God is the embodiment of all that is good, how did God Himself ever come to even know what evil is, and how and why did God create a universe that He obviously knew eventually would be full of evil?

It is also interesting that although we are given free will, there is a real issue concerning how free our supposed free will actually is. When God in effect tells us "You humans can either accept me or reject me; it is all a matter of your free will to choose either good or evil," isn't God also saying, "but if you reject me, I will kill you and send you to burn in Hell forever, so you had better make the right choice"? There is a famous line in the Godfather movies that the mafia bosses used to imply that they could always get their way with an offer if they coupled it with violent consequences ("Let's make him an offer he can't refuse.") Having one's thumbs broken, or even getting an ice pick in the ear, pales in comparison to eternal damnation and burning in Hell forever if you do not "choose" correctly.

Finally, I have a minor quibble, but one that makes an important point. Note that animals are life-forms on this Earth, just as we humans are life-forms—so why do animals not have souls, and why are they not judged by God after they die so they go to either Heaven or Hell (or Animal Heaven or Animal Hell)? Most, if not all, Christians believe that animals do not sin and are not even mentally capable of sin. These believers also believe that only humankind has sinned and therefore only humans, and not animals, are suffering from Original Sin and are in need of salvation. In fact, they believe, the reason humans die on Earth and don't get to live in Paradise in the Garden of Eden forever is precisely because we have sinned—"For the wages of sin is death; but the gift of God is eternal life through Jesus Christ our Lord" (Romans 6:23). Therefore, we die because of our sin.

If animals have no sin, though, why must they die like us; and for that matter, why must plants and every other living organism on Earth die? How can death be the wages of sin if animals and plants have no sin? If animals do not sin, why don't they get to live forever in the Garden of Eden as Adam and Eve would have been allowed to had they not sinned? Stated another way, because animals die just like we do but they are *not* guilty of sin like we are, isn't their death very unfair and doesn't it discriminate against animals? If animals do sin, like we sin, but are not judged and condemned to be tormented in Hell forever for their sin as non-believing humans are condemned and tortured forever in Hell, isn't that equally unfair and discriminatory, only this time against humankind? Why would God create humans and animals yet also allow very unfair discrimination to take place that would be either (1) in favor of animals and against humans or (2) in favor of humans and against animals? Doesn't this unequal treatment, to the extent we are all life-forms that either sin or don't sin, seem to be inconsistent?

Recently, I saw a documentary about lions in Africa. One of the most intriguing parts of the documentary was about how young nomadic male lions would invade an existing pride of lions, fight the dominant male, and then kill, indeed murder, the remaining cubs of the lionesses in the pride so those lionesses will come into heat and the invading males can mate with them. The world is a cruel place. Now then, if a selfish and cruel man were to secretly kill the children of a woman just so the woman would then (presumably) desire to have more children and, as a result, the selfish, murdering man could opportunistically have sex with her, that selfish murdering scheme would clearly qualify as an evil sin. So the question is, why do selfish, murdering lions get to do such evil sinning and then die without having to face Hell and eternal damnation for their sins when a human male who would do the very same act must go to Hell and suffer forever for his sins, in the event that he does not ask for forgiveness and accept Jesus Christ as his savior? Have all animals repented and accepted Jesus as their savior?

If we excuse the lion's behavior because we classify such behavior as the mere instinct of an inferior animal, why can't we say the same thing about humankind's sinful (instinctual) acts? Remember that God created both humans and lions and created all of the available options that they may choose to take in the world. Could it really be because the first lion ever created said no when the talking serpent offered him the forbidden fruit from the Tree of Knowledge of Good and Evil and lions therefore have no Original Sin, or any sin at all, because they have no knowledge of evil (even though lions are not vegetarians and would not eat the fruit of a Tree of Knowledge anyway)?

Regarding the lion's behavior, remember that God is the one who created the option for a lion to engage in the evil of killing cubs to have sex with a lioness. Although the lion may not be guilty of sin if the lion has no free will or the mental capacity to make a choice between good and evil, because it is simply a matter of instinct for the lion, God is still the one who created the lion's instinct. God also created the option for a lion to engage in such otherwise sinful, evil behavior in the first place. Why would God give lions the instinct to do such evil things when God created lions and everything in the world in which lions live—their entire context in which to do such evil as a matter of mere instinct?

In contrast, if a lion has free will to choose between good and evil, so that if the lion chooses evil, that would be a sin, then the lion should be held responsible for that choice. In fairness, then, shouldn't that lion be sent to Hell for his sin (unless his sins are forgiven)? Again, consider that a human being making the same choice between good and evil would have to go to Hell to be punished for that evil. Either this is completely unfair against humankind (making God unfair?), or, if the lion doesn't know any better and is acting merely on instinct, it proves that God created the evil option for the lion to take and we simply call it the lion's instinct. Why can't we call our evil choices mere instinct too? The point is that God is actually the Creator of the context and all the possible choices in the universe. If we program a computer or a robot to make choices, then who is ultimately responsible for creating and allowing all of those choices to be made?

Other examples of selfish, evil, behavior in nature exist. For instance, a certain type of wasp will sting an insect victim to paralyze, but not kill, that insect. The wasp keeps that insect alive to lay its eggs, one by one, inside of the paralyzed insect's body. Slowly, those wasp larvae will begin to hatch and then voraciously eat their way through the insides of the still-alive, paralyzed insect victim. The paralyzed host insect lies there helplessly as it is eaten alive from within by larvae. The wasp larvae grow, and then finally emerge from what is left of the eaten host insect, as wasps. Is it not "evil" to do that to another unsuspecting insect life-form? Who or what is responsible for this opportunistic, and even cruel, behavior of wasps? Is it mere instinctual survival, such that a wasp is just "innocently" providing a food source for its eggs? Who created the context in which this all could play out in reality? It was God.

Chapter Fifty-Eight

From Where Did Original Sin Originate, and Is It Fair?

I had another very interesting religiously based exchange with my father a few years ago, mixed in with a contemporary political legal issue. The religious issue was the fairness of Original Sin, because I thought it unfair to punish me, or any human, for Adam and Eve's Original Sin. After all, I did not choose to eat the forbidden fruit; Adam and Eve did. As a result, I asked, Why do all subsequent human beings now have to pay for Adam and Eve's sinful mistake? That substitution and guilt by mere association of being a latter-day human being doesn't seem fair.

Right around the same time, my father and I had a political discussion on the legal issue of affirmative action, in which employers or college or graduate school admission boards take into account the race and/or gender of applicants in an attempt to (1) remedy past discrimination, (2) try to put people into the positions they might have otherwise been in were it not for the original discrimination against them (and their forebears), as well as (3) attempt to value racial, ethnic, and gender "diversity" in their organizations. As a result, there was an interesting juxtaposition because my father and I were on opposite ends of each argument. Although my dad thinks it is fair to apply Adam and Eve's Original Sin to every innocent human being born thereafter, he also thinks it is unfair to discriminate against innocent white victims in college admissions and job applications with affirmative action when they themselves did not own slaves or commit any specific racist acts. For my part, although I think it is fair to have affirmative action plans to address past and current racial wrongs that even might harm innocent white victims, I also think it is unfair that I, as a mere member of the human race, must pay for Adam and Eve's Original Sin. As usual, I wrote a long letter to my dad recounting the exchange; it is reproduced in pertinent part below:

Affirmative Action and Original Sin

    Dad, believe it or not, these two topics on religion and politics are actually related, insofar as when you and I discussed them, I believe a surprising, but very real, inconsistency in your personal and theological sense of justice was exposed.

    *First, with respect to affirmative action, you stated how unfair you thought it was for modern-day white people to have to suffer reverse discrimination for the racism and atrocities of their racist grandfathers ("My great-grandfather may have owned slaves, but I didn't"). You stated how unfair that was because the modern-day individual was not **exclusively** being judged* *based upon his own actions but rather on the additional actions **of his forefathers**—which he "could not have had anything to do with, because he wasn't even born yet!"*

*Curiously however, when I made your same argument in another context regarding Original Sin (how it was unfair that every generation since Adam is plagued with Original Sin such that we are inescapably born into sin and damnation due to the actions of our earliest ancestors, starting with Adam and Eve), you stated, "The Bible says that the sins of the fathers will be visited on the sons." You therefore appear to believe that it is entirely fair and just for modern-day individuals to have to pay for, or at least suffer for, the sins of their forefathers all the way back to Adam and Eve; however, when it comes to affirmative action, you reverse course and maintain that people should be judged only by their **own** actions and not the actions of their forefathers—because only **individual** justice is fair, whereas **group-association** justice is not.*

Clearly, these two points are inconsistent. You either feel that making individuals suffer for the past "sins" (or the racism) of their ancestors is "fair" or that it is "unfair," but it cannot be both at the same time. I suppose that as a pastor, you are not prepared to change your position on Original Sin, so you will have to change your position and agree with me on affirmative action. I am interested to see how you will respond to this obvious inconsistency.

*However, since I am requiring that you be consistent with respect to Original Sin and affirmative action, I guess I too need to be consistent. That is, since I am saying you are inconsistent on two related points, and I happen to disagree with you on **both** of those points, then I too must be just as inconsistent as you are, only on the **opposite sides of the inconsistency,** right? In other words, am I not guilty of the very same inconsistency that I accuse you of, only in reverse?*

That is certainly true to the extent you can just "flip" my own argument against me (which is what I did as I was thinking about this: I asked myself, "Alright then, why is it 'fair' for judges to visit the sins of their fathers on the sons (affirmative action) but 'unfair' for God to do the same thing (Original Sin)?") Note: you can always put this letter down, and just let me argue with myself, which is what you might have planned on doing anyway.

*So I thought: "Just why do I support affirmative action as fair but still maintain that the concept of Original Sin is unfair?" As I stated in the beginning of our discussion, affirmative action is certainly not a **perfect solution** to the modern problems of past racism, and I admit that it does not represent perfect justice, but that is really only because we cannot go back in time in order to address the racism of past slave owners—they are long since gone, but unfortunately, some of the societal effects of their past racism are still present (not to mention that there is current societal racism as well).*

*Moreover, although I really have to concede that affirmative action is unfair at least to a certain degree and in a certain sense, it seems even **more unfair** to me to do nothing about* *modern injustices caused by past racism just because we cannot logistically find the perfect remedy. Recall, I pointed out that in law, there is "the real" (the status quo), "the ideal" (perfect justice), and "the possible" (a reachable goal that is still idealistic, yet realistic as well).*

*Affirmative action, then, is not "the ideal," but at least it is better than "the real" of completely ignoring the remnants of past racism because the worst perpetrators of the racism are now long gone. Instead, it represents "the possible." Moreover, it is not as though racism is completely a thing of the past—freedom is not just the absence of slavery, and equality is not just the absence of segregation. Thus, I am comfortable, although not entirely satisfied, with the need to do "the next best thing" ("the possible"), and that is to at least make **some** attempt to address the unfortunate remnants of past racism through affirmative action (and, again, I do **not** believe racism suddenly **ended** once slaves were set free in 1865; indeed, racism, unfortunately, is alive and well today, despite numerous civil rights victories, which now at least have the government and certain other institutions out of the business of some of the worst forms of overt racial discrimination).*

*The point is, racism still harms modern-day minorities (and not just African-Americans), while "innocent" white victims still benefit to some extent from past slavery, as well as all past racism and discrimination against minorities, insofar as modern-day whites are already, and remain deeply, entrenched as the leaders in almost all benchmarks of progress in American society with respect to such things as income, employment, education, health, political power, etc. I admit that the lead by whites in these areas is not **all** related to racism, of course, as many whites, every day, must overcome their own set of obstacles that have nothing to do with race at all (hard work, sacrifice, the need for intelligence, talent, merit, etc.). Still, at least **some** of benchmarks of progress for some modern-day whites are a function of not being from a traditionally oppressed racial or ethnic group.*

A quick metaphor might help to make my point. If you and I were playing tennis but it was clearly determined that you were "cheating" (the equivalent of racism, slavery, discrimination, oppression, etc.), then it obviously would be unfair for you to keep your ill-gotten lead in our tennis match (you support this insofar as you think it is OK to punish former slave owners—the actual "cheaters" in the tennis match metaphor). But here is where we disagree: I think it also would be unfair even if "substitutes" for your side and for my side continued to play the tennis match in our place, if they did so without evening up, or at least adjusting, the score (the substitutes would be, metaphorically, the descendants of former slaves and slave owners, and people from the same racial groups).

If the illegitimate score were not evened up or at least adjusted in order to take into account the extra points which were obtained through past cheating (racism), then the substitutes (the descendants and group affiliates) would always be subject to the ill-gotten gains of the past cheating. In effect, if the metaphorical score is not evened or adjusted somehow, then the descendants of the cheaters would always be illegitimately ahead of the descendants who suffered the original cheating. This would be true even after the most egregious form of cheating had come to an end (the end of slavery) and the original "players" left the tennis match for good (generations died out and have been since replaced by their descendants).

So if you and I were playing tennis and you were winning 5 games to 2, but we determined that you had engaged in cheating some of the time, then even if you would now agree to stop cheating from here on, in order for it to be truly fair, the score would have to be adjusted (slowly, perhaps over generations in the real-world context). In fairness, I should be entitled to some points, and it would be wrong of you to accuse me of a form of cheating myself (reverse discrimination) just because I was asking for the score to be evened or adjusted as it should be (by adding points to my side to make up for the past cheating/unfair point deficit). This would be true even if "substitutes" (our descendants) had taken our respective places in the tennis match. Moreover, it is incorrect to think that all of the cheating has stopped, as there are still overt and institutional forms of racism alive and well in today's society.

*In short, "innocent white victims" are all not really "victims" of affirmative action; instead, some are merely being put in the situation they likely would have been in from the beginning if there had never been any "cheating" by their ancestors in the first place. Would the later "substitutes" on your side in the metaphorical tennis match be "innocent victims" simply because they were not allowed to keep their ill-gotten lead from the cheating that had occurred? Of course not, so not even addressing **current** racism or **current** manifestations of racism in society (which I believe exist, since racism is still obviously a problem), affirmative action seems to be at the very least a necessary remedy for **past** racism as well, although I agree it is, in a certain sense, not the perfect solution and still can be unfair in certain contexts. The main problem with it is that we now have to **guess** what the new, adjusted score should be, because we do not know for sure how much of the current lead is legitimate and how much is the result of cheating (racism)—much of the disagreement is in this area. I agree that we may not be able to say for sure exactly what the score should be; however, the score should be adjusted, at least to some degree, in order to counteract the past cheating.*

The law is no stranger to handing down such "imperfect remedies." For example, money damages for someone who loses their arm in a car accident caused by a negligent defendant driver is a perfectly acceptable remedy. We do not deny money damages to the victim simply because we cannot come up with the now impossible perfect solution of giving the victim his arm back ("the ideal"); we instead settle for the "next best thing"—money damages based on our best guess of what would be fair—it would represent not the "ideal" but "the possible." Similarly, we do not condemn the injured plaintiff for legitimately trying to obtain redress and compensation for his loss of arm injuries (as a "reverse injury"), so we similarly should not condemn racial minorities for trying to do the same thing ("reverse discrimination").

Another, perhaps even more fitting, example would be damages paid to those of a certain class who are not the original victims of the original harm, paid by some who may not even be the original perpetrators. In law school, I heard about an old case from New York where cab drivers were charging too much money for each tenth of a mile driven charged to victim riders and it would serve as a good example here. Those cab drivers were eventually found guilty of overcharging each rider over a period of time. The remedy (years later) was to force all **current** *cab drivers in the city to give discounts to all* **current** *cab riders as a way to "pay back" damages for the earlier illegitimate overcharging. However, it was impossible to find and pay back every particular tourist and person who had ever taken a cab in New York from years earlier who had been originally overcharged. But it would have been even more unjust to do absolutely nothing about it and let the wrongdoing cabdrivers completely get away with their illegitimate overcharging because the remedy was not perfect. So the imperfect remedy was to allow all future cab riders for a period of time to have a discounted price in order to make up for the ill-gotten profits from the previous illegal overcharges. The best solution, of course, would have been to find, verify, and compensate the actual victim riders who were originally overcharged by the original cab drivers years prior, but such was logistically impossible (how could we possibly find, verify, and compensate every tourist who had ever visited New York years earlier who might have been overcharged in taxicab rides?), so the court did the next best thing—discounted the fares of current riders.*

In any event, that is why, very simply, I support affirmative action. I admit that it is an **imperfect solution** *to a societal problem that may not be perfectly fair in every individual case; but although it may be imperfect, it is much better than simply ignoring the problem all together just because there is not a* **perfect remedy***. It is much better to attempt to "even the score" or at least make the score more reflective of what it should be in order to make the tennis match more fair rather than to let one side benefit from past cheating* **forever** *just because the original perpetrators of the original cheating are now long gone (again, this is not to say that current minorities do not suffer current racism—they/we clearly do—but I am attempting to demonstrate a justification for affirmative action for seemingly "innocent white victims" even when they themselves may have not engaged in the outright racism of slavery and segregation committed by their ancestors). In short, recall the old adage that "perfection should not be the enemy of the good."*

Now then, as I thought about my own inconsistency further, I realized that I was doing a rather curious thing: comparing God to humans, that is, God's law regarding Original Sin with humans' law of attempting to right the past sociological wrong of racism through affirmative action—talk about comparing "apples to oranges." It occurred to me, of course, that God is perfect, unlike humans. Accordingly, God should not be **limited** *in the least to an* **"imperfect solution,"** *as humans often are. I started to realize that my position was not so inconsistent after all, because if humans were "all-knowing" and "all-powerful," we too would not be limited such that we would not have to settle for an "imperfect solution," like affirmative action (recall, affirmative action is imperfect only because we are certainly not God, who can mete out justice to the dead people responsible for the worst racism from the past; the fact of the matter is that we simply cannot go back in time and sue former slave owners in order to make things right; but*

God could, so to speak; plus, only God could know by how much the metaphorical score should be adjusted in every individual context)).

In the cab example, God could figure out all of the cab drivers who actually did and did not overcharge, and He could figure out each and every tourist/cab rider who actually did get overcharged from years earlier, and those who did not, and then appropriately divide and then distribute the damages to each specific deserving victim, and not to allow undeserving current cab riders to take advantage, but humans cannot do so because we are not God. Our records and our evidence are sometimes imperfect, so when they are, we are left with doing the next best thing with whatever we may have. God would know exactly what the metaphorical score in the tennis match should be, whereas the best we can do is merely guess as to what it ought to be (approximately) in light of the past cheating, and that the original individuals involved are now long gone.

*Because humans are **not perfect like God**, and because humans do not have God's unlimited powers, it is not inconsistent for me to simply hold God to a **higher** standard of justice, at least when it comes to a perfect remedy for past wrongs that are not committed by an individual but by his ancestors. God should be capable of a perfectly just solution when it comes to holding individuals responsible for only their **own** injustices, their own sins, and not for those of their forefathers as well (Original Sin), even though fallible human beings, unfortunately, are not always capable, at least **logistically,** of doing the same (affirmative action). So to the extent I am inconsistent, it is only because I do not equate human justice with divine justice. I expect more from God. Accordingly, I do not equate God and humans—do you?*

*In sum, God should have no **practical difficulties** with meting out justice to dead people and meting out perfect justice in every individual situation. Human beings, on the other hand, understandably often fall short of "the ideal" when it comes to perfect justice, especially in the case of affirmative action where it is **logistically impossible** to hand down the perfect remedy. It is not so understandable, however, when God falls short of the ideal; He is God, after all. What is even less understandable is when one allows for a **lower standard of justice** for God but expects a **perfect solution of justice** from human beings. Aren't those expectations entirely backwards?*

*Thus, your position, I am afraid, is still quite inconsistent in that you expect human beings—who are fallible and not capable of perfect solutions to certain logistically problematic sociological problems—to be **completely** fair (when it comes to affirmative action), yet you essentially hold God to a much **lower** standard, since it is apparently OK for God to hold every individual guilty for the sins of their forefathers, and of their forefathers, all the way back to Adam and Eve, over which these latter-day humans had absolutely no control, and nothing to do with (Original Sin).*

*Clearly you do not believe that God should be held to a **lower standard of fairness** than human beings. Thus, I am sure I simply have misunderstood the concept of the "sins of the* *father will be visited on their sons," or perhaps even Original Sin, with respect to how you can conceive of them as perfectly fair, but in the context of affirmative action, as unfair.*

What would be helpful for me, therefore, is if you could set me straight on why it is "fair" that the sins of the fathers can be visited on the sons (Original Sin) but why, simultaneously, it is "unfair" for modern-day whites to have to pay for the racism of their slave-owning ancestors (affirmative action), especially when God is capable of "perfection" and humans, admittedly, are not (which I believe demonstrates why my apparent inconsistency here is not so inconsistent after all, or at least not as inconsistent as yours). I realize that not all whites had slave-owning ancestors, in fact there are probably very few that actually did, but many (and even perhaps most) still have benefited from a system that historically held other groups down and allowed true freedom and justice more often to be obtained by only their dominate class ancestors rather than by others.

I never received an answer from my father to this letter. In fact, I do not really receive any kind of formal direct responses from my dad to any of my letters I write to him about these kinds of issues, but he still does read them (I think; I hope). His non-response might be because my dad is much more comfortable with talking to people than he is with writing to them. Still, I like to write to him about these various issues because that way, I at least can get a word in edgewise—although I have to admit that my dad would beg to differ mightily as to which of us really interrupts the other the most whenever we debate!

My dad came up with a great solution one time as we were arguing in a restaurant: "Only the person holding the salt shaker gets to speak." It was a good idea, and it worked well, as long as my dad got to be the one who was holding the salt shaker. Not surprisingly, we soon began arguing over who was "hording" the salt shaker and filibustering the other side—I, of course, say it was him, but I'll let him write his own book and tell the reader that it was really me. The truth is probably somewhere in the middle (but he still held on to the salt shaker longer than me…at least from my point of view…see how I am?).

Anyway, it is good that we can still laugh about it. Some sons don't really relate to their dads at all. Others relate by talking about such mundane things such as sports, work, or the stock market. I guess my dad and I do it by talking about religion and politics, very intensely, which works, as long as it does not get too personal and remains respectful, which I admit has been a challenge for me over the years. Every once in a while, my dad needs to remind me that one of the Ten Commandments is "Honor thy father and mother." It is a point well-made and well-taken. And it is a good trump-card argument that requires me sometimes to back off whenever the arguing gets a little too intense, but with every passing day, the "honor thy father and mother" argument will help me more and more, as I fully plan to use it on my own two sons someday if they ever decide to get a little too uppity with me. And if they protest, I'll just have to have them take it up with their grandpa!

Chapter Fifty-Nine

A Frank Discussion with Adam and Eve

The exchange with my dad about the legitimacy of Original Sin got me thinking about additional related topics. For example, it made me wonder what I would say to my ultimate grandparents, Adam and Eve, if I ever ran into them in Heaven. Because I like thought experiments, here is what I think I would want to say (although I admit that I would have to tone my statements down some, given the apparent lack of respect I seem to have for my elders):

"Hey! What the hell, you guys? And I mean that quite literally; right now, there are billions of people in Hell because you two screwed it all up in Paradise. In the Garden of Eden, we *all* could have remained immortal, without sin, naked without shame, without hunger, without disease, without death, etc., forever, as God originally intended for humans. He created us, meaning you, at first, but His intent was to create all humans without sin, knowing only good, not evil! Yeah, so, thanks a lot for messing it all up!

"And what about Jesus? If you two would not have completely blown it for everyone, Jesus never would have even had to come down to Earth to be horribly crucified to atone for all of the sins of humanity. Our collective sin was all started by you guys—your Original Sin—and it has been visited on every one of us ever since; so the starting assumption is that everyone is bound for Hell unless they jump through certain hoops! But nooooooooooo...some people just had to eat their little forbidden fruit because they thought it would be cool to have the knowledge of both good and evil, didn't they? What were you thinking? If there was ever a good reason to 'just say no' to something, wasn't that *the* time? I mean, seriously, you literally made it impossible for any human being, ever, to not be a sinner condemned to Hell. Just what do you have to say for yourselves? Did you even think about the consequences?...Don't blame Eve, Adam; that has been a lame excuse for thousands of years now.

"We are, like, so busted now, you guys, and all this pain and suffering, death, and bound-for-Hell stuff, it is totally the ultimate cosmic punishment, the mother of all groundings. I think you need to go and apologize, right now, to every single human descendant of yours who has ever lived throughout time, including all of those who are suffering in Hell right now, and forever, *if* you are even allowed to talk to them from here!...What's that? It's not your fault that they are all in Hell? Well doesn't that just beat all? OK, do I need to remind you that we are in Heaven now? A little humility, responsibility, and concern for others would be nice. Is it even possible for you people to *ever* make a good decision?

"Yeah, I know, who am I to judge you? Good point. Alright, so, all that aside, because we all are God's children...what was it like to be the first and the only two human beings on Earth? What if you had not been attracted to each other? Do you think you still would have decided to get married and have kids? Before you had kids, did you ever get sick of each other, as there was literally no one else to talk to, ever? When Eve got pregnant, did you guys totally freak out, wondering what was going on with her and why little Cain and Abel came out of her when they were born, or did you know that Eve's having to be the one to bear children (and have a menstrual period) was all because she was the one of the two of you who fell for Satan's temptation when he was a talking snake? Did you guys ever miss your childhood? Oh yeah, you never had a childhood, because you started out and were always just adults. And by the way, check it out—you guys really don't have belly buttons, do you? Cool, we've always wondered about that. Hey, Eve, does Adam still think he is superior to you because God made him first and only made you from his rib (assuming Genesis Chapter 2 and not Chapter 1 is the actual creation story), or is there now no sexism, and not even any sex, in Heaven, because we are all now just these sexless, genderless spirits?

"Sorry, but just one last thing—are you guys still married after all this time—I mean still 'happily' married? My wife and I vowed, like most other married couples, to be married 'until death do us part,' but now that we actually have died, we are a little confused about the whole until-death-do-us-part thing, I mean, are we still supposed to stay married forever anyway, or are we now supposed to part, and perhaps even date other people in Heaven? Hey, wait a minute; I would still be pretty jealous if I ever saw my wife, even my now dead wife, with someone else in Heaven. In fact, if she did cheat on me here, would I get mad at her? But maybe now that we are all the same sexless, genderless, non-jealous spirits at this point, there is no longer any marriage, sex, or even dating, right?.."

Well, in reality, if I ever saw Adam and Eve in Heaven, assuming they would still be together, I guess I would not be so sarcastic and irreverent to my very famous great-great-great-great-great-great-great-great-great-great-etc.-grandparents. In a way, it would be like meeting celebrities. I suppose they would deserve some respect as the first human beings, at least when I first would meet them, but I am sure I could not help at least thinking that it seems awfully unfair to heap their Original Sin on me and onto all of humanity. It is one thing to be mature and for me and all of humanity to accept personal responsibility for our own actions, but none of us were even born when all that stuff happened between Adam and Eve and God in the Garden of Eden. Adam and Eve are certainly not responsible for any of my problems, or my sins, so why should I be responsible for theirs just because they happened to live on Earth before I did?

Chapter Sixty

Never Accept Personal Responsibility, and Always Blame Other People When You Can

[8] And they heard the voice of the LORD God walking in the garden in the cool of the day: and Adam and his wife hid themselves from the presence of the LORD God amongst the trees of the garden.
[9] And the LORD God called unto Adam, and said unto him, Where art thou?
[10] And he said, I heard thy voice in the garden, and I was afraid, because I was naked; and I hid myself.
[11] And he said, Who told thee that thou wast naked? Hast thou eaten of the tree, whereof I commanded thee that thou shouldest not eat?

Why would God ever have to ask a question of anyone, about anything? Did God really not know where Adam was? Did He really not know why Adam was ashamed of being naked? In terms of God's questions to Adam, how does an all-knowing God *not* know something? It also seems like the all-knowing God here has to go through the process of trying to put two and two together by slowly figuring out that Adam only realizes he is naked because he now knows about evil, because Adam must have eaten from the Tree of Knowledge of Good and Evil, because Satan must have tempted Eve, and Eve must have tempted Adam. But wouldn't God already be immediately aware of all of this, instead of having to slowly piece it together ("Hey…now wait a minute….Why are you asking me that…could it be? Hey!" God would not really be so slow to figure it all out, would He)?

Maybe God just wanted to see if Adam was going to lie or tell the truth. But wouldn't Adam already know that he could not lie to God and that lying to God would be futile because God obviously already knew the truth, as well as everything else in the universe? Adam is talking to God, after all. It would not make sense for Adam to lie to God, but if it would not make any sense for Adam to try to lie to God who already knows the truth, why would God even go through this unnecessary process of asking questions of Adam if He already knew the answer, and Adam certainly knew that God must have known? Obviously, Moses was not there to witness this alleged conversation between Adam and God. Did God really tell Moses how he ought to quote Adam, and Himself, in this conversation when Moses wrote about it thousands of years later?

[12] *And the man said, The woman whom thou gavest to be with me, she gave me of the tree, and I did eat.*

Again, why would Adam even need to answer and have this whole conversation with God? Wouldn't God already know all of this? Moreover, and my wife loves this part, Adam immediately blames it all on the woman. It is like I always jokingly tell my law students in class—"When representing a client in a lawsuit in the future, never take personal responsibility for anything, *ever*! Instead, always find someone else to blame or sue if you can; however, whenever possible, always take credit for good things that happen, and never share that credit with others, unless to do so would make you look bad—then and only then should you share any credit with anyone." Unfortunately, sometimes, students do not realize that I am joking—but I don't know if that says more about them, or about me.

Adam next provides what is a rather lame excuse: "I know you said we could not eat the forbidden fruit, but Eve gave it to me; what was I supposed to do?" Well, how about trying to take personal responsibility for your actions, Adam, and not just automatically blaming your wife for your failings? By the way, as I am perched upon my high horse here, writing this judgmental diatribe against Adam's sexism against Eve, I think my wife is in the other room just rolling her eyes; but, undeterred, I shall continue.… How about just saying no, Adam, when it came to eating forbidden fruit and not being sexist against your own wife?

[13] *And the LORD God said unto the woman, What is this that thou hast done? And the woman said, The serpent beguiled me, and I did eat.*

God *does* seem to take the bait provided by Adam here, because instead of telling Adam that he should take personal responsibility for his own decision to eat the forbidden fruit and should not just blame Eve, God immediately decides to focus on Eve as to why she gave the forbidden fruit to Adam. Eve begins to realize that it appears as though she is going to have to take the fall for all of this. But maybe she thought, *Wait, Adam just blamed me, and as a result, God focused the blame on me and not on Adam, so why don't I just do the same thing as Adam and find someone else to blame?* And so she does. Eve tells God that it was all Satan's fault; the Devil got her to consider another option—"He beguiled me, what was I supposed to do?" But again, all Satan did was tell Eve what Eve already knew—so how was that "beguiling" her?

Remember that Eve was still completely innocent without even the knowledge of evil before she encountered the serpent, so why didn't God at least warn her that a talking serpent might try to converse with her so she should be leery of him and suspect his motives? We often think that "innocent" children are too trusting of strangers because they do not know any better because all they have known are their loving parents or other trusted adults and have no experience with potentially harmful individuals. We think that children do not realize that they might be at risk, that not everyone has their best interests at heart, and that they should not talk to strangers, who very well might have evil intentions or motives. If we love our children, shouldn't we warn them of such potential dangers out there? Why didn't God, then, at least warn Adam and Eve about that evil talking snake, Satan?

Eve had been exposed only to Adam and God at that point, with no reason to suspect them, or anyone or anything else, in what was quite literally a perfect world, but without any warning, God allowed a very trusting Eve to be approached by an evil talking animal. She was innocent and inexperienced and had no protection because she probably could not imagine that God would even create an evil snake and allow that snake access to her in the Garden of Eden with the sole intention of trying to tempt or trick her to make a horrible decision for herself and for all of humanity for eternity.

[14] And the LORD God said unto the serpent, Because thou hast done this, thou art cursed above all cattle, and above every beast of the field; upon thy belly shalt thou go, and dust shalt thou eat all the days of thy life:

This blaming-other-people technique seems to work pretty well, so God turns His attention to Satan and punishes him for tempting Eve (although tempting people is supposed to be Satan's function in the universe at this point and God was the one who created Satan in the first place, so God is getting mad at Satan for simply doing what he is now supposed to be doing in his tempter-of-humans job in the universe?)—by making snakes have to slither on their bellies, which they now do. God also decrees that snakes will have to eat dust all the days of their life; however, snakes eat other things, so perhaps this is just a metaphor for being on the ground on their bellies and is not a literal pronouncement. This punishment of the serpent also makes one think, *What must a serpent have looked like in the beginning and how did it get around before this particular curse of God was put upon it (did a serpent originally have legs)?* Also, was this talking serpent a python or a garden snake, a rattlesnake or a cobra, a black mamba or a sidewinder, or was it simply some kind of snakelike ancestor from which all of these other types of snakes eventually evolved? If Satan were a particular type of snake, like a rattlesnake, why should all future cobras have to suffer for the sins of a past rattlesnake (if that was Satan's serpent form)? Moreover, why should descendant rattlesnakes suffer for the temptation of Eve done by an ancestor rattlesnake (Original [rattlesnake] Sin), who was really Satan and not a true representative of rattlesnakes in the first place?

So it makes one wonder why snakes, as an entire species, are forevermore cursed by God just because Satan came to Eve *in the form of a snake* (Satan was not actually a snake and certainly did not represent every snake in the world that would ever exist). Shouldn't God have punished Satan for beguiling Eve rather than taking it out on snakes and all of their descendant snakes who were not even born yet? Doesn't it seem beneath God to get angry at the wrong species—a serpent—and have an emotional reaction against an entire species by cursing and punishing this snake and all of its descendants instead of punishing the alleged actual wrongdoer, Satan? But was Satan even the wrongdoer, as it was really just Adam and Eve, or Eve and Adam?

What if Satan took the form of a talking mule to tempt Eve? Would God at least have left poor snakes alone, and would He have instead somehow cursed all mules forevermore—perhaps by giving them even more ridiculous-looking ears so they would listen better? Actually, there is an account in the Bible of a talking mule—this mule belonged to the prophet Balaam, who was sent to put a curse on Israel, but along the way, Balaam's mule saw an angel in the road, and as a result, the mule got scared and refused to journey on any further. Balaam became very angry at the stubbornness of his mule and beat the mule three times, at which point,

> [28] And the Lord opened the mouth of the ass, and she said unto Balaam, What have I done unto thee, that thou hast smitten me these three times?
> [29] And Balaam said unto the ass, Because thou hast mocked me: I would there were a sword in mine hand, for now would I kill thee.
> [30] And the ass said unto Balaam, Am not I thine ass, upon which thou hast ridden ever since I was thine unto this day? was I ever wont to do so unto thee? And he said, Nay.
> [31] Then the Lord opened the eyes of Balaam, and he saw the angel of the Lord standing in the way, and his sword drawn in his hand: and he bowed down his head, and fell flat on his face. (Numbers 22:28–31)

In any event, by cursing snakes as a species for Satan's temptation of Eve, God allowed Satan, the actual wrongdoer/tempter here (if just suggesting possible options is itself evil), to get away with that temptation, instead cursing all snakes, as if it were fair to blame the arbitrary animal form in which Satan came rather than focusing on Satan himself. Perhaps it would be acceptable not to punish Satan for tempting Eve, however, because, after all, Satan's purpose in this world is to tempt people to disobey God. Moreover, Satan was already bound for Hell at that point, destined to burn forever, so how could God have really *added* any more punishment to that?

[15] And I will put enmity between thee and the woman, and between thy seed and her seed; it shall bruise thy head, and thou shalt bruise his heel.

God then comes back to Adam and Eve to punish them and, apparently, all future married male and female couples, by putting enmity between them. Moreover, God sets it up so they can cause each other some literal or at least figurative pain.

[16] Unto the woman he said, I will greatly multiply thy sorrow and thy conception; in sorrow thou shalt bring forth children; and thy desire shall be to thy husband, and he shall rule over thee.

God also especially punishes Eve by making women have the pain and sorrow of childbirth, although birthing a child can also be seen as a beautiful thing, and even an especially important bonding experience between a mother and child that should not necessarily be seen as a bad and sorrowful thing (unless modern medicine and birthing techniques in hospitals were unknown to the writer, whose experience at the time was probably that women had great pain and that many even died during childbirth). Not only that, but what about other mammals, such as horses or dogs, the females of which also have painful live-birthing processes? What did all female mammals do to deserve the pain and sorrow of having to give live birth to their young (assuming birthing is painful for them too)? Did God originally create us to perhaps be able to painlessly lay eggs, or something similar that would not be so traumatic, but when Eve fell for Satan's temptation, thereafter, she and all future women, as well as all other female mammals, must go through a painful live-birthing process as well as have menstrual cycles?

This fateful decision by Eve also seems to be the justification for biblically condoned sexism. Eve sinned (so did Adam, but Eve sinned first, so that is apparently worse), and from then on, men got to treat women as second-class citizens. So, sexism is justified because it is God's will and Eve brought it all on herself (and on all other women thereafter)? It seems awfully harsh that Adam gets to rule over Eve (and all men get to rule over all women) just because Eve ate the forbidden fruit *first* and then Adam ate shortly thereafter.

[17] And unto Adam he said, Because thou hast hearkened unto the voice of thy wife, and hast eaten of the tree, of which I commanded thee, saying, Thou shalt not eat of it: cursed is the ground for thy sake; in sorrow shalt thou eat of it all the days of thy life;
[18] Thorns also and thistles shall it bring forth to thee; and thou shalt eat the herb of the field;
[19] In the sweat of thy face shalt thou eat bread, till thou return unto the ground; for out of it wast thou taken: for dust thou art, and unto dust shalt thou return.

Adam's punishment, and that of all subsequent men, appears to be that he must now work and toil and farm for food and sustenance. No more free food in the nice Garden of Eden; instead, if a man wants food for his family, that man now must plant crops and raise them himself, as well as pull weeds and fight insects, as a farmer. Also, differing sexist gender roles appear to be God's will at this point, assuming that God actually wrote this passage. But most importantly, people now die, and will go to Hell, if they are not saved.

[20] And Adam called his wife's name Eve; because she was the mother of all living.

Recall, Adam named all of the animals and birds and then named Eve. Just another quick note here about some fundamentalist Christians' argument that Adam and Eve and their children never had to commit the sin of incest to populate the world according to God's commandment: Recall that some argue that God created other human beings around the same time that He created Adam and Eve so Adam and Eve were the first but not the only human beings created at that time. With such other unrelated human beings on Earth at the time, Adam and Eve's children would not have had to have incest with their brothers and sisters (and/or with their parents). This argument, however, is completely undercut by this verse stating definitively that Eve "was the mother of all living." She could not be the mother of all living if she were not the mother of these other mysterious unrelated human beings that were supposedly created at around the same time that Adam and Eve were themselves created—there would be *additional* mothers of all living.

[21] Unto Adam also and to his wife did the LORD God make coats of skins, and clothed them.
[22] And the LORD God said, Behold, the man is become as one of us, to know good and evil: and now, lest he put forth his hand, and take also of the tree of life, and eat, and live for ever:
[23] Therefore the LORD God sent him forth from the garden of Eden, to till the ground from whence he was taken.
[24] So he drove out the man; and he placed at the east of the garden of Eden Cherubims, and a flaming sword which turned every way, to keep the way of the tree of life.

At that point, how would Adam and Eve have been able to survive in the real (non-Garden of Eden) world if they did not have the know-how to hunt, raise crops, create shelter, avoid danger in the wild, and so on? All it says is that God gave them their first type of clothing, so they did not even know how to clothe themselves, yet they were supposed to somehow survive in a harsh new environment with no knowledge or experience at all of how to do so. The purpose of life now was to seek salvation—to eat from the Tree of Life (perhaps meaning taking Jesus as one's savior?). In the Garden of Eden, they had no work, no death, no hunger, no thirst, no danger of dying, but then suddenly, they were completely cut off, kicked out, and totally on their own, with no survival training or life-skill know-how whatsoever, in what had become a very hostile and inhospitable environment to them—the real world. They simply would not have been prepared for it because they would not have known how to do anything at all at that point.

Chapter Sixty-One

Welcome to the Real World—
But Now What? From Bad to Worse

Genesis 4

[1] And Adam knew Eve his wife; and she conceived, and bare Cain, and said, I have gotten a man from the LORD.
[2] And she again bare his brother Abel. And Abel was a keeper of sheep, but Cain was a tiller of the ground.

Well, I take back what I said about Adam and Eve not knowing how to do *anything* at first. I guess there was at least one thing they quickly figured out how to do—have sex. So they had two boys, and one grew up to be a sheep herder (Abel) and the other to be a farmer (Cain).

[3] And in process of time it came to pass, that Cain brought of the fruit of the ground an offering unto the LORD.
[4] And Abel, he also brought of the firstlings of his flock and of the fat thereof. And the LORD had respect unto Abel and to his offering:
[5] But unto Cain and to his offering he had not respect. And Cain was very wroth, and his countenance fell.
[6] And the LORD said unto Cain, Why art thou wroth? and why is thy countenance fallen?
[7] If thou doest well, shalt thou not be accepted? and if thou doest not well, sin lieth at the door. And unto thee shall be his desire, and thou shalt rule over him.
[8] And Cain talked with Abel his brother: and it came to pass, when they were in the field, that Cain rose up against Abel his brother, and slew him.

Things are now not going so well. Eating forbidden fruit was one thing, but now murdering a brother in a fit of sibling rivalry? Why did this happen? Abel brought the meat fat of his animals as an offering to God, but Cain merely brought his fruit of the ground for God as an offering. God liked Abel's meat-fat gift but not Cain's fruit gift (which God did not respect). God created both animal fat and fruits, so it is unclear why one necessarily would be a better offering than the other—especially when it does not appear that Cain and Abel were ever even told what would be a proper offering and what would be an improper offering. Besides, what ever happened to the idea that it's not the gift, but the thought that counts? After all, both Cain and Abel were trying to offer to God acceptable gifts of worship that symbolically reflected their life's work on Earth (the animal fat of a herder and the fruit harvest of a farmer). If anything, I would think that animal fat would seem a much more offensive and disrespectful gift than a nice bowl of fresh fruit, but maybe that's just me.

Most disturbing, however, is that once again, God is portrayed as an awfully temperamental, humanlike deity instead of the more loving, rational, and secure Supreme Being of the universe. This rejection by God of Cain's fruit gift later caused Cain to become so jealous that he killed Abel as a result of being "wroth." Could this have been avoided if God had simply decided to accept *both* offerings from Cain and Abel as sufficient symbols of love and devotion, or if He had at least advised Cain beforehand to come up with a better offering than his fruit harvest, so Cain would not feel so rejected and then find it necessary to kill his brother, Abel? Still, Cain made this decision, and it was not all God's fault.

[9] And the LORD said unto Cain, Where is Abel thy brother? And he said, I know not: Am I my brother's keeper?
]10] And he said, What hast thou done? the voice of thy brother's blood crieth unto me from the ground.

Wouldn't God already know that Abel had been killed by Cain? Wouldn't God already know where Abel's body was located? God is asking questions here once again as if He is not all-knowing. Cain answers God's questions with the now infamous rhetorical question, "Am I my brother's keeper?" Of course, if Cain killed his brother, then Cain at least should have known where Abel's body was—so this answer was nonresponsive.

This story, with Cain's brazen "Am I my brother's keeper?" response, represents the larger issue of our own inhumanity, not only in failing to care for the welfare of brothers but also in failing to care for the welfare of fellow humans, as we are all God's children and therefore are all brothers and sisters. It is curious how some believers can read such a passage that seems to be so critical of not caring for the well-being of a brother, of a fellow human being, and then somehow still assail modern welfare programs or healthcare programs as evil socialism, because none of us should have to be the keeper of some "lazy," undeserving brother living off of the state. Perhaps Jesus should not have gone around feeding the hungry, healing the sick, clothing the naked, or giving to the poor, because such socialistic sharing merely served as an incentive for lazy, undeserving people to not work and to fail to pull their own weight?

Although Jesus led an exemplary life, some apparently think that we *as a society* should not follow His example when it comes to caring for the poor and providing for the sick (hence the concern about "socialism"). Instead, maybe we should oppose any such programs put forth by democratically elected representatives as improper government confiscation or our God-given wealth and property. If so, we would then have a good reason for not caring for the poor as a society through our laws and programs. Maybe Jesus was really a capitalist at heart who believed that maximizing profits should be the primary goal of a society and that if we would just focus on that, then money, healthcare, food, and education naturally would all "trickle down" to those in need. In short, we ought not to have government programs for the poor, as we really should not be our brother's keeper, at least in that sense.

Similarly, there are those who also think we should not be tempted by evil socialistic wealth-distribution programs for the poor and the sick and the hungry because the government is the real enemy, trying to take away our freedoms through overregulation and high taxes, which are stolen from the hard-working "makers" and just given over to the lazy "takers" in society. However, those who think that the government engages in evil socialism, also seem to think that corporations and capitalism will save us because only hard-working wealthy people have all of our true and best interests at heart, because God agrees that corporations are good and the government is bad (even though in a constitutional representative democracy such as ours, *we the people* are the government).

If Jesus actually taught that the rich should redistribute some of their wealth to the poor, sick, and hungry, according to some fundamentalists who are also strong pro-capitalists, at that point, there should be a clear separation between church and state here (at least in this particular context of caring for the poor through official laws). Of course, they do not believe so strongly in a separation between Jesus's life example/teachings and our laws/governmental entanglements in other sociocultural contexts such as abortion, same-sex marriage, or prayer in schools, where their religion should be followed not just as a personal matter but also as an official legal and political matter. Perhaps both conservatives and liberals alike need to answer the following question: As a society, should we try to follow *all* of Jesus's teachings or *none* of Jesus's teachings? Or should we follow only the *parts* of Jesus's teachings that we personally like and ideologically agree with?

Chapter Sixty-Two

More Punishment and Divergent Paths

[11] And now art thou cursed from the earth, which hath opened her mouth to receive thy brother's blood from thy hand;
[12] When thou tillest the ground, it shall not henceforth yield unto thee her strength; a fugitive and a vagabond shalt thou be in the earth.
[13] And Cain said unto the LORD, My punishment is greater than I can bear.
[14] Behold, thou hast driven me out this day from the face of the earth; and from thy face shall I be hid; and I shall be a fugitive and a vagabond in the earth; and it shall come to pass, that every one that findeth me shall slay me.
[15] And the LORD said unto him, Therefore whosoever slayeth Cain, vengeance shall be taken on him sevenfold. And the LORD set a mark upon Cain, lest any finding him should kill him.
[16] And Cain went out from the presence of the LORD, and dwelt in the land of Nod, on the east of Eden.

It seems as though this is the very curse God already placed on Adam when God banished Adam and Eve from the Garden of Eden, although Adam had no mark upon him and was not separated to this degree. Cain was further banished to "the Land of Nod, east of Eden" and must till the ground, but recall that God already made it so that Adam would have to till the ground as a punishment. In fact, this is already Cain's occupation—he was a farmer, but he now apparently was not going to be a very successful farmer.

[17] And Cain knew his wife; and she conceived, and bare Enoch: and he builded a city, and called the name of the city, after the name of his son, Enoch.

So Cain was banished "east of Eden in the land of Nod…out from the presence of the Lord" and obviously away from his father and mother, Adam and Eve, as a "fugitive and a vagabond in the earth," yet Cain's "wife" somehow appears out of nowhere. So where did she come from, and who were her parents? Cain "knows" her, meaning he marries her and has sex with someone who must have been his own sister, because the only other people on Earth at the time who possibly could have been her parents were Adam and Eve, Cain's parents.

[18] And unto Enoch was born Irad: and Irad begat Mehujael: and Mehujael begat Methusael: and Methusael begat Lamech.
[19] And Lamech took unto him two wives: the name of the one was Adah, and the name of the other Zillah.

Again, where did these other mysterious wives and people come from so these children could be born (and beget others)? They had to be sisters or daughters somehow, or to come from the same family line in which incest had to have taken place somewhere up that family line. Their origins are mysteriously not explained, nor why taking more than one wife is now perfectly acceptable (perhaps this is why Mormons thought it was okay).

[20] And Adah bare Jabal: he was the father of such as dwell in tents, and of such as have cattle.
[21] And his brother's name was Jubal: he was the father of all such as handle the harp and organ.
[22] And Zillah, she also bare Tubal-cain, an instructer of every artificer in brass and iron: and the sister of Tubal-cain was Naamah.
[23] And Lamech said unto his wives, Adah and Zillah, Hear my voice; ye wives of Lamech, hearken unto my speech: for I have slain a man to my wounding, and a young man to my hurt.
[24] If Cain shall be avenged sevenfold, truly Lamech seventy and sevenfold.
[25] And Adam knew his wife again; and she bare a son, and called his name Seth: For God, said she, hath appointed me another seed instead of Abel, whom Cain slew.
[26] And to Seth, to him also there was born a son; and he called his name Enos: then began men to call upon the name of the LORD.

And so now begins many of the long ancestral lines in the Bible, although this particular line is the line of Cain, which is a different line than the other long ancestral lineages from Adam in various chapters of Genesis, as well as other books of the Bible (see below). Why would God use the Bible to relay to us some of this rather insignificant identifying information of people who are never mentioned again in the Bible? Why does this particular information make it into the Bible supposedly as the direct Word of God?

Genesis 5

[1] This is the book of the generations of Adam. In the day that God created man, in the likeness of God made he him;
[2] Male and female created he them; and blessed them, and called their name Adam, in the day when they were created.
[3] And Adam lived an hundred and thirty years, and begat a son in his own likeness, after his image; and called his name Seth:
[4] And the days of Adam after he had begotten Seth were eight hundred years: and he begat sons and daughters:
[5] And all the days that Adam lived were nine hundred and thirty years: and he died.

Recall that God had originally proclaimed in the Garden of Eden that if Adam (or Eve) ate of the forbidden fruit, "on that day [he should] surely die." Obviously, Adam did *not* die on that day, nor apparently anytime soon thereafter, as we are told that Adam lived to be more than 900 years old. But if we interpret what God had said literally—that "on that day [Adam] shall surely die"— that would make God either a liar or, at best, seriously mistaken. Either God is fallible or the wrong words were used by God, which also makes God fallible *if* God wrote those words and made that original pronouncement about Adam or Eve surely dying on the day that they ate the forbidden fruit. The only other option is to *not* interpret the words of God's pronouncement literally and to interpret those words figuratively instead as meaning Adam and Even eventually would physically die, as all living things do, but that they died spiritually that day when they disobeyed.

[6] And Seth lived an hundred and five years, and begat Enos:
[7] And Seth lived after he begat Enos eight hundred and seven years, and begat sons and daughters:
[8] And all the days of Seth were nine hundred and twelve years: and he died.
[9] And Enos lived ninety years, and begat Cainan:
[10] And Enos lived after he begat Cainan eight hundred and fifteen years, and begat sons and daughters:
[11] And all the days of Enos were nine hundred and five years: and he died.
[12] And Cainan lived seventy years, and begat Mahalaleel:
[13] And Cainan lived after he begat Mahalaleel eight hundred and forty years, and begat sons and daughters:
[14] And all the days of Cainan were nine hundred and ten years: and he died.
[15] And Mahalaleel lived sixty and five years, and begat Jared:
[16] And Mahalaleel lived after he begat Jared eight hundred and thirty years, and begat sons and daughters:
[17] And all the days of Mahalaleel were eight hundred ninety and five years: and he died.
[18] And Jared lived an hundred sixty and two years, and he begat Enoch:
[19] And Jared lived after he begat Enoch eight hundred years, and begat sons and daughters:
[20] And all the days of Jared were nine hundred sixty and two years: and he died.
[21] And Enoch lived sixty and five years, and begat Methuselah:

It is interesting to consider Enoch, who is mentioned here as if a relatively unimportant and insignificant individual in this lineage. When the Dead Sea Scrolls (other original biblical writings, some from the "Gnostic" tradition) were discovered in 1948, however, one of those books was the Book of Enoch. This book was never canonized in the 3rd century or thereafter, so it has been ignored through the centuries by most Christians and has not been considered a legitimate book of the Bible. This book, however, is an ancient writing that easily could have been part of the Bible. Was it divine intervention by God in the 3rd century to have church leaders throw out this type of book, as well as many others, or was that exclusively the decision of church leaders at that time?

The Book of Enoch is a very large ancient text too involved to go into in any detail, so below I provide just a very basic summary and overview about the contents of the book. The first piece of very general information is from Wikipedia (http://en.wikipedia.org/wiki/Book_of_Enoch):

> The **Book of Enoch** (also **1 Enoch**) is an ancient Jewish religious work, ascribed to Enoch, the great-grandfather of Noah. It is not currently regarded as part of the Canon of Scripture as used by Jews, apart from the Beta Israel canon, nor by any Christian group, apart from the Ethiopian Orthodox Church and Eritrean Orthodox Church canon. . . .
>
> A short section of 1 Enoch (1En1:9) is quoted in the New Testament (Letter of Jude 1:14–5), and there it is attributed to "Enoch the Seventh from Adam" (1En60:8). It is argued that all the writers of the New Testament were familiar with it and were influenced by it in thought and diction.

A further summary of each chapter follows from http://www.earth-history.com/ Pseudepigrapha/Enoch/enoch-main.htm:

> From The Apocrypha and Pseudepigrapha of the Old Testament R.H. Charles Oxford: The Clarendon Press
>
> **Summary:**
>
> First Enoch may be divided into the following five major sections:
>
> 1. **The Book of the Watchers** (chs. 1–36). Enoch is a righteous man who has received heavenly visions. The book is a collection of revelations regarding divine judgment. It describes the rebellion of angels. The fallen angels, called "Watchers," have sexual intercourse with human women, who give birth to a race of wicked giants. The giants lay waste to the earth and humanity, and so become the occasion for the flood, in which they are destroyed. But once their demonic spirits are released from their dead bodies, these demons wreak havoc in the world until the end time of judgment.
>
> 2. **The Book of the Similitudes** (or Parables; chs. 37–71). Enoch again receives heavenly visions, which are interpreted by angels. The primary character of these revelations is the "son of man." Other titles employed to name this messiah figure are "the Chosen One" (the most common title), God's "Anointed One," and "the Righteous One." This heavenly being is God's agent for the final judgment and vindication of the righteous.

3. **The Book of Astronomical Writings** (or Heavenly Luminaries, chs. 72–82). Visions of heavenly and earthly occurrences advocate a 364-day solar calendar, as opposed to the controversial lunar calendar. Enoch describes to his son Methuselah his journey through the stars above the earth, guided by the angel Uriel.

4. **The Book of Dream Visions** (or Animal Apocalypse, chs. 83–90). Enoch recounts two visions to Methuselah. The first vision is of the sky falling and the earth undergoing cataclysmic disasters as a result. The second vision takes the form of an apocalyptic allegory describing the history of humanity from the creation of Adam to the final judgment. In it, humans are represented as animals and angels are represented as human beings. The apocalypse details the relationship of Jews with Gentiles and the end-time judgment.

5. **The Book of the Epistle of Enoch** (chs. 91–107). This epistle is written by Enoch for later generations. Righteousness and wickedness are contrasted throughout the letter in order to show that goodness and truth will be rewarded by God, but evil and sin will be punished by God. This sober eschatological prophecy admonishes readers about the final divine judgment.

Title: Also called the Ethiopic Apocalypse of Enoch

Sources: Attempts to explain some enigmatic passages from the book of Genesis. Influenced by the canonical books of Ezekiel, Jeremiah, and Daniel

Canonical Status: Old Testament Pseudepigrapha

Author: Anonymous Jews

Date: 250 BC–AD 50. The five books within First Enoch were apparently written at different times by different authors…

Original Language: Though written originally in either Aramaic or Hebrew, this book is fully extant only in ancient Ethiopic (Ge'ez) translation. Fragments exist in Latin, Greek, and Aramaic. Some fragments have been identified among the Dead Sea Scrolls.

Why is the Book of Genesis, likely written by Moses thousands of years ago in the Middle East, considered to be actually written by God, but the Book of Enoch, written by various Jewish writers thousands of years ago in the Middle East, considered to be just books written by Jewish writers thousands of years ago in the Middle East? Some suggest that either the book of Enoch or the book of Genesis had to be rejected as being part of the Bible because the two books could not satisfactorily be reconciled. Because God is not inconsistent, the major irreconcilable differences set forth in the books could not both be correct—but religious men made this comparison and decision for us and simply declared it to be so.

There are many other similar historical Judeo-Christian religious writings and books which were widely read and followed by various groups at the time that were ultimately rejected as part of what is now the "official" Bible. For example, "The Life of Adam and Eve" is a book which has a much more forgiving view of Eve portraying her more as being tricked by an evil Satan disguised as an angel of God, rather than simply being disobedient to God. And "The Book of Jubilee" explains that Adam and Eve's son, Cain, actually did commit incest with a younger sister in order to populate the world. When the Bible was officially canonized some 300 years after the life of Jesus, these books were rejected by a majority of then-existing church leaders, as were many other books that seemed too controversial or could not be readily reconciled with other books. Constantine, who organized the Nicene Conference to canonize the Bible, realized the importance of standardization of the text to promote unity in Rome.

[22] And Enoch walked with God after he begat Methuselah three hundred years, and begat sons and daughters:
[23] And all the days of Enoch were three hundred sixty and five years:
[24] And Enoch walked with God: and he was not; for God took him.
[25] And Methuselah lived an hundred eighty and seven years, and begat Lamech:
[26] And Methuselah lived after he begat Lamech seven hundred eighty and two years, and begat sons and daughters:
[27] And all the days of Methuselah were nine hundred sixty and nine years: and he died.
[28] And Lamech lived an hundred eighty and two years, and begat a son:
[29] And he called his name Noah, saying, This name shall comfort us concerning our work and toil of our hands, because of the ground which the LORD hath cursed.
[30] And Lamech lived after he begat Noah five hundred ninety and five years, and begat sons and daughters:
[31] And all the days of Lamech were seven hundred seventy and seven years: and he died.
[32] And Noah was five hundred years old: and Noah begat Shem, Ham, and Japheth.

This entire chapter shows the biological connection from Adam down to Noah and his sons. As we shall see, many pages in the Bible are painstakingly devoted to these ancestral lineages, so they must be there for important reasons. Showing the connection from Adam to Jesus is just part of the reason why showing this lineage is important. The lineage also reveals how Adam is traced through the house of David to Jesus (fulfilling a prophecy in the Bible about the Messiah). This ancestral connection is to Jesus's stepfather, Joseph, however, who was *not Jesus's biological father*. The only human DNA traceable in Jesus was that of His mother, Mary, not that of His stepfather, Joseph. Still, for Jesus to be the true Son of God, the Messiah, the Old Testament prophesy about Jesus being from the House of David had to be fulfilled.

It appears the sexism is so pronounced in the Bible, however, that Jesus being traced through His non-blood-related stepfather, Joseph, is simply overlooked; no one ever even tried to follow the ancestral line of Jesus's biological mother, Mary, which also would have ultimately led back to Noah and then to Adam (but perhaps not through David). Still, at least it would have actually been a true biological connection to Jesus, which is the whole point of ancestral lineages. It therefore seems ludicrous to devote so much time and effort recounting the biological ancestral lineage from Adam to Jesus only to have that biological connection not even actually be to Jesus, but only to Jesus's *unrelated* stepfather, Joseph! The connection is by marriage, not by blood—a human stepfather. If Joseph were actually Jesus's biological father, that would provide the direct biological link, but that would also undercut the whole notion of an immaculate conception, that Mary was a virgin, and that Jesus was not just a man but the promised Messiah.

These ancestral lines are also used to show that the earth must be around 6,000 or so years old. Calculating the age of the earth based on this lineage involves a lot of guesswork because not every generational transition says exactly how old someone was when the next generation was born as it does through verse 32. Still, reasonable approximations are made so literalist believers really have no choice but to believe that the earth and the universe are only about 6,000 years old. In light of various dating technologies, the age of (and light from) the stars, and the fossil record here on Earth, however, to say that the earth is only 6,000 years old is as silly a claim as that the earth is flat and rests at the center of the universe. No serious scientist believes any of these claims, as there is no credible evidence to support such claims. Indeed, all of the evidence points to the earth being much older than 6,000 years. Also, the earth is not at the center of the universe, unless the universe is infinite, in which case, *everything* in the universe would be, in a sense, at the "center," because the universe would be infinite in all directions, so everything and nothing would be at the (nonexistent) "center" simultaneously.

Notice also that people apparently used to live for an awfully long time. The longest current records of human longevity are only around 115–125 years old, and that is extremely rare. Could it really have been that the food was so much better back then, the air and water so much cleaner and purer, the planet so much less polluted, and the lifestyles so much more stress-free that the human body could typically live for 800 or even 900 years? Not only was that an astonishing biological and medical miracle, but men could also typically father children at well over 100 years old! Methuselah lived to be 969 years old and fathered a child when he was 187. Well done, Methuselah! Perhaps this is true and people literally did live and remain fertile that long, at least at a time near the beginning of creation, but if so, it sure makes a strong argument against polluting our environment and eating processed food, because now, even with the miracle of modern medicine, we can barely live, on average, into our 80s instead of living our 900s!

Chapter Sixty-Three

Giants, Violence, and Evil; Just Kill Everyone and Start All over

Genesis 6

[1] And it came to pass, when men began to multiply on the face of the earth, and daughters were born unto them,
[2] That the sons of God saw the daughters of men that they were fair; and they took them wives of all which they chose.

Who were these "sons of God"? From when and where did they come all of a sudden? Note that the non-Biblical Book of Enoch (referred to directly above) also spoke of these giants in a similar way (see "1. The Book of the Watchers"). It is not clear if these sons of God were angels, or some other type of divine beings (but isn't Jesus the only Son of God?), or just male super humans. It does not appear that they were mere human beings, however, as there is no lineage from Adam mentioned for them. It is interesting that they just appear completely out of nowhere without any explanation of how they fit into the creation story (although they are featured prominently in the Book of Enoch). Whoever these sons of God were, the verse implies that they may have raped the daughters of men, because it says the sons of God "took them wives of all which they chose." Unless every human daughter voluntarily consented to any and all sons of God who chose them for sex, this would have been rape.

[3] And the LORD said, My spirit shall not always strive with man, for that he also is flesh: yet his days shall be an hundred and twenty years.

At least limiting human beings to a top life expectancy of about 120 years here is a little more realistic and comports much closer to our current reality regarding human longevity. Perhaps the writer of Genesis, Moses, needed to supply a reasonable explanation even to readers of his day as to why the life expectancies of humans in his time were so dramatically lower than those of Methuselah and Noah.

[4] There were giants in the earth in those days; and also after that, when the sons of God came in unto the daughters of men, and they bare children to them, the same became mighty men which were of old, men of renown.

It is interesting that these stories are beginning to read a little like Greek mythology, and even fairytales, rather than as a literal reporting of actual events. It says "in those days" there were "giants," meaning that by the time this was written by Moses, this race of giants must have already died out. But again, when were these giants created, and were they human beings (just *very big* human beings), or were they a different species altogether that merely resembled human beings? Also, were giants the offspring of the "sons of God" and the daughter of men, or were the "mighty men" and "men of renown" the sons of the giants and the daughters of men (and how would that even work)?

As I read, I had to remind myself that it literally says "giants" here (and I guess we should not forget that "unicorns" are also mentioned in the Bible [Job 39:9]). Recall that unicorns and giants are common characters in children's stories. If we are to believe that these giants actually existed, however, of course we have yet another biblical "missing link" as there has been no legitimate discovery of fossils of giant humans found anywhere in the world (or of unicorns for that matter), unless by "giants," the passage means just very tall humans (like NBA professional basketball players?). So are we talking about 7-, 8-, or even 9-foot-tall human "giants" (which is at least within the realm of possibility as we know it)—remember that "Goliath" was the "giant" David fought and killed and he is reported to have been around 9-10 feet tall—or are we talking about 50-foot-tall giants who say things like "fe, fi, fo, fum, I smell the blood of an Englishman"? Again, I am not being sarcastic here merely for the sake of being sarcastic; instead, I am going by what the verse literally says: "There were *giants* in the earth in those days" (emphasis added). If God meant to communicate merely that there were very tall humans in those days by using the term "giants," why didn't He say so and make that clear, especially if He knew the term "giants" might someday cause obvious confusion and therefore result in a miscommunication of His true meaning?

The similarity to Greek mythology, in which Greek gods could have sex with humans and their offspring would be superheroes (such as Achilles and Perseus, who have one human and one god as parents), leads one to ask, are they both literal accounts, or both metaphorical accounts. Even more importantly, why is one obvious "mythology," and one is literal truth, when there is no proof to support either story/myth?

These offspring of the "sons of God" (whoever and whatever they were) and the daughters of men are referred to here as "mighty men" and "men of renown." What did they do? Why are they a part of the story? What significance did they have? Maybe these sons of God were angels, but why would angels have sex with human women, and why doesn't that happen anymore, if it ever did?

Although my literalist fundamentalist preacher father asserts, "If the Bible says there were giants back then, then there were giants back then, period;" even he feels a little compelled to explain why such fairytale-like stories exist in the Bible. His explanation for these more incredulous than usual stories in the Bible is that they only seem outlandish to us now because Satan, in an attempt to deceive and lead us astray, has over the years placed fairytale stories into the minds of human writers so they would write these ideas as fictional children's fairytales, and then someday, someone like me, who compares their similarity with what is written in the Bible, would be fooled into thinking that the Bible has fictional, fairytale-like stories rather than real accounts of actual events. It shows the power of Satan's negative campaigning and "fiction by mere association." The Devil is "awfully clever," my dad warns, so we have to be very careful here to not be easily deceived or tricked.

What I take from my father's explanation is that if a biblical story sounds fictional and like a fairytale, that can be taken as proof that these biblical stories are true. Why? Because we need to remember that the Devil is just trying to confuse and deceive us with copycat children's fairytales that we know to be fiction. It is a rather clever attempt to get us to mistakenly believe that the similar-sounding biblical stories must also be fiction because they sound so similar to fictional children's fairytale stories that we know to be pure fiction.

There are a lot of moving parts to that argument, however. In fact, there is an old metaphor that may apply. Someone once made an observation that an elephant was hiding in a little apple tree. A cynic said, "Impossible. I can't see any elephant hiding up in that little apple tree." But then the answer came, "Don't you understand that you can't see the elephant only because the elephant is *hiding* in the tree, so the fact that you can't see the elephant is proof that the elephant is hiding in the tree!" Accordingly, perhaps I cannot see the truth in the biblical stories of "giants" and "unicorns" and of gods (or "sons of God") having sex with daughters of human men, only because Satan has convinced writers of children's books (or writers of Greek mythology) to write obviously fictional fairytales that seem to be comparable to these biblical stories as a way of *hiding* the truth and the logical plausibility of the biblical stories. In light of that explanation, I don't know what is more clever, the alleged misdirection of Satan by planting biblical story ideas into the heads of writers of mythology and fairytales, or my dad's allegation of Satan's supposed misdirection plan as an explanation of the mythological nature of the biblical stories that are actually true.

With respect to there being "giants in those days," what about the fact that many organisms were much larger in the distant past and thus, perhaps humans were much larger too? For example, it is true that dinosaurs were "giant" animals compared to present-day animals (with the possible exceptions of blue whales and perhaps elephants). Even some insects were giant (dragonflies with 2-foot wingspans, for example) compared to the insects of today, and the same is true for certain plants. Maybe in a "purer," less-polluted environment, organisms could grow much bigger (and maybe live much longer) in the distant past than today. To the extent that reptiles grow all of their lives, if they lived extremely long lives that would explain why they would get so big. Certainly, such an explanation is plausible, but where is the evidence for giant humans? Where are the giant human skeletons (the "missing links")? Right now, the only "proof" is this unsupported assertion in the Bible that there were giants in those days.

There are also later accounts of giants in the Bible—entire societies of them—and these giants appear to be the 50-foot-tall kind:

[32] And they brought up an evil report of the land which they had searched unto the children of Israel, saying, The land, through which we have gone to search it, is a land that eateth up the inhabitants thereof; and all the people that we saw in it are men of a great stature.

[33] And there we saw the giants, the sons of Anak, which come of the giants: and we were in our own sight as grasshoppers, and so we were in their sight. (Numbers 13: 32–33)

If the human writers here were just "as grasshoppers," literally, that must mean these alleged giants were of the 50-foot-tall variety, not just very tall human "giants."

[5] And GOD saw that the wickedness of man was great in the earth, and that every imagination of the thoughts of his heart was only evil continually.
[6] And it repented the LORD that he had made man on the earth, and it grieved him at his heart.
[7] And the LORD said, I will destroy man whom I have created from the face of the earth; both man, and beast, and the creeping thing, and the fowls of the air; for it repenteth me that I have made them.

This seems to call into question whether God has any foresight at all. If God was regretful and grieved that He had created humans because humans would take such an evil turn and thus cause Him to want to destroy them all, why would, and did, God create humans in the first place? Did God not realize that this evil turn by humans would occur? Isn't it logically impossible to regret something one does if one knows exactly how it is all going to play out but does it anyway? Certainly, one cannot credibly claim surprise. We often say, "If I only knew then what I know now, I would have done it all so differently." But God did know then what He knew later; that is what being omniscient means. So either God is omniscient and the account of Him regretting the creation of humans is incorrect or this is a correct account and God cannot be omniscient, because if He were, He would not regret any course of action that He had taken— after all, He would have realized what was going to happen, before it ever happened. So shouldn't God have just started out by creating Noah and skipping all of the evil people who needed to be drowned? If God had done that, however, would Noah have been the one to eat the forbidden fruit and thereby introduce the knowledge of good and evil into the world? Maybe the flood would not have been necessary had God simply started out by creating Noah and the creatures on the ark as "the beginning."

Also, notice very early on in the Bible, by Chapter 6 of the 50 chapters of Genesis, God is already despondent with humankind and laments the wickedness of almost everyone on Earth, so He decides to kill all humans. While He was at it, He thought He might as well kill all of the other mammals and the reptiles, birds, insects, and plants on Earth, too, all because humans were choosing to do evil. Does that in any way seem fair to all of the innocent plant and animal life on Earth that had absolutely nothing to do with humans' moral choices? Was it rational, fair, and reasonable to punish not only the guilty but also the completely innocent? Doesn't this suggest the writers thought God was very capable of doing a great injustice? Why did all of these innocent animals and plants have to be killed off too? It wasn't the fault of animals or plants that humans were being evil, yet God killed everything—except fish and sea life, I suppose—in the great flood. After all, how does one drown a whale in the ocean, or fish in the seas, with a flood (unless it is by a world-wide mixture of all fresh and salt water, discussed later)? So, did sea life, because of their mere fortuity in living in water at the time (if they survived the mixing of salt and fresh water), escape God's wrath when He was destroying life on Earth? After all, the ocean is, in a sense, just a big, permanent "flood"—at least in the deep-sea trenches.

It is true that two of each kind of land animal would be saved by Noah's ark, thus avoiding their extinction, but how would that be fair to, say, an innocent deer that was not one of the lucky pairs of animals saved on the ark and instead was condemned to drown solely because human beings were choosing evil? Poor unsuspecting deer! Why was a flood even necessary to kill all of the evil humans? Why not simply kill all the evil people and leave all the innocent animals and plants, as well as any righteous human beings, alone? Wasn't God capable of using a sharp scalpel to kill only the evil human beings, or was He limited to using a big, blunt, great flood "ax" to kill everything on Earth except Noah and his family and two of every kind of animal? Why was there the need for this unnecessary step? Why not just kill *everything* and start all over with a second, entirely new, creation?

Chapter Sixty-Four

A Lifeboat of Hope; Not All Will Be Lost

[8] But Noah found grace in the eyes of the LORD.
[9] These are the generations of Noah: Noah was a just man and perfect in his generations, and Noah walked with God.
[10] And Noah begat three sons, Shem, Ham, and Japheth.
[11] The earth also was corrupt before God, and the earth was filled with violence.
[12] And God looked upon the earth, and, behold, it was corrupt; for all flesh had corrupted his way upon the earth.
[13] And God said unto Noah, The end of all flesh is come before me; for the earth is filled with violence through them; and, behold, I will destroy them with the earth.

Does this mean that Noah was righteous, just, and perfect and that is why he was saved, or was he saved because although he too was a sinner, God liked him more than other humans at the time? If it is that Noah was not evil or violent like all of the other humans, it seems odd that there would only be *one* human being in the world at the time, Noah, who was righteous. What about Noah's wife, their three sons, and their sons' wives? Were they all righteous, too, or were they just lucky that they happened to be related to Noah because God did not want to drown Noah's family members because Noah had found grace in God's eyes? How is it possible that Noah or any human would be found by God to be "righteous" when we are ALL sinners, subject to "Original Sin," bound for Hell, unless we are saved, as *"There is none righteous, no, not one."* Romans 3:10?

How reasonable was God's extremely violent reaction—killing almost everyone and everything on Earth—in these circumstances? Verses 11 and 13 say, the earth was filled with violence, so one of the reasons given for why God at this point decided to kill everyone (except Noah and his family) was because they were all violent, and violence is a serious sin. But I wonder just how many people were killed by the very worst, most evil, and most violent person in the world at the time during this violent period? Whatever that number was, it certainly must have been tiny in comparison to the total number of *all* existing humans, animals, and plants on the entire Earth at the time that God Himself would violently kill in the flood. God's reaction of using great violence to deal with the violence of humans seems hypocritical. For example, if a child hits his little brother, should the disappointed parent of the violent child beat that child senseless to show him that using violence against his little brother is not acceptable? Violence is bad if humans do it, but if God does it as a punishment, then it is OK (two wrongs make a right)? Is God above His own rules because He is God and therefore can do whatever He wants?

This is not to say that one in authority cannot punish a wrongdoer without running the risk of hypocrisy. It is true that in this example God used violence only on violent people, on wrongdoers, who were punished with a violent form of their own wrongdoing. It raises the familiar issues surrounding the death penalty used in the United States and a few other countries where people are put to death with the about same or even more frequency, such as China, Iran, and North Korea. Maybe we should be concerned with that kind of company, or maybe not, but if it is acceptable to punish a wrongdoer with the very same kind of wrongdoing they have perpetrated, why don't we do that in *all* criminal and sinful contexts? If someone physically assaults someone else, why doesn't the state hire a professional fighter to severely physically assault the wrongdoer as a form of perfect justice? Indeed, why not "an eye for an eye," or perhaps more fittingly, why not "a black eye for a black eye" or "a broken arm for a broken arm"? Better yet, if someone rapes a victim, then perhaps the state should hire a rapist to rape the guilty rapist. But if the state should not engage in such immoral or unsavory behavior as violently assaulting or raping those who assault or rape, then why is it not just as immoral and unsavory for the state to murder murderers? Regardless of the political issues surrounding the death penalty, if we generally expect the state to punish people *humanely*, or at the very least to not engage in cruel or unusual punishment, shouldn't we be able to expect at least that same amount of humaneness from God? And what about saving various extended family members here, such as Noah's cousins and uncles or the immediate family members of Noah's sons' wives? Was it simply "too bad" for them?

Chapter Sixty-Five

"We're Gonna Need a Bigger Boat"

[14] Make thee an ark of gopher wood; rooms shalt thou make in the ark, and shalt pitch it within and without with pitch.

[15] And this is the fashion which thou shalt make it of: The length of the ark shall be three hundred cubits, the breadth of it fifty cubits, and the height of it thirty cubits.

[16] A window shalt thou make to the ark, and in a cubit shalt thou finish it above; and the door of the ark shalt thou set in the side thereof; with lower, second, and third stories shalt thou make it.

[17] And, behold, I, even I, do bring a flood of waters upon the earth, to destroy all flesh, wherein is the breath of life, from under heaven; and every thing that is in the earth shall die.

[18] But with thee will I establish my covenant; and thou shalt come into the ark, thou, and thy sons, and thy wife, and thy sons' wives with thee.

[19] And of every living thing of all flesh, two of every sort shalt thou bring into the ark, to keep them alive with thee; they shall be male and female.

[20] Of fowls after their kind, and of cattle after their kind, of every creeping thing of the earth after his kind, two of every sort shall come unto thee, to keep them alive.

[21] And take thou unto thee of all food that is eaten, and thou shalt gather it to thee; and it shall be for food for thee, and for them.

[22] Thus did Noah; according to all that God commanded him, so did he.

It is an old, but still valid, skeptical question: how could this relatively small ark possibly have been big enough to store two of every kind of animal, bird, insect, and living creature on Earth? A cubit is supposed to be the length of a man's arm from the elbow to the tip of the middle finger. Obviously, that is not a consistent length. As a result, estimates vary, but a standard that has developed is that a cubit is 18–20 inches long. Using the longer measurement of 20 inches as a cubit, we find that the size of the ark, at most, was 500 feet x 83.3 feet x 50 feet (300 cubits x 20 inches = 6,000 inches ÷ 12 inches = 500 feet long by 50 cubits (83.3 feet) wide by 30 cubits (50 feet) high.

The ark was not even as big as a typical modern luxury cruise ship, and it was certainly not as high or wide. For example, the Carnival Cruise ship *Paradise* is listed at 855 feet long, so if it were just 145 feet longer, it would then be twice—*two times*—as long as the ark. And with its ten deck levels, the *Paradise* is 118 feet tall at the top pool deck, more than twice as high as the ark. At first glance, then, it is difficult to imagine that two of every type of creature in the entire world (including dinosaurs and all other now-extinct species) could fit and then survive for a year on something smaller than a modern cruise ship and insulated with pitch, apparently to keep it waterproof for a year.

Another issue that comes to mind when thinking about the literal plausibility of the ark saving all types of creatures is that there was only one small window in the ark for ventilation (a cubit across, so only 18–20 inches) because the entire ark had to be covered to keep all of the rain out. But how could one small window for the entire ark supply enough fresh air for all of those animals—especially for those down on deck 3? Also, if one visits a zoo, one might see the incredible amount of food that is required, as well as how much cleanup is necessary for all of the waste. Could only eight people really provide all of the adequate care for this many creatures for almost a year? Think how many people care for animals at just one zoo and then extrapolate that further to include the care that would be necessary for an entire ark of every species of animal in the world (including dinosaurs)—and enough fresh air coming through one little window for all of them. Consider also whether a big door on the side of the ark could have been constructed by Noah to keep water tight shut for almost a year with no leakage.

The really big issue here, however, is trying to determine just how many types of species there are, including all mammals, insects, birds, reptiles, etc. in the world. First, it is very difficult to come up with a precise number of species in the world. The estimated number of all species on Earth various from 3 million to 30 million. A recent *Time* article put it at 8.7 million (and if there were a male and female of each, that estimated number would double to17.4 million animals). I am not a scientist or biologist, and frankly, I have no idea how many species there are in the world, but would it be literally possible to collect a male and female of every type of creature in the world and then fit them all onto an ark smaller than most cruise ships? I found many estimates of the actual number of species on Earth. To be fair, most of them are water dwellers, but even the number of non-water dwellers is extremely high. The following list is typical:

Animals: estimated 3–30 million species
|—**Invertebrates:** 97% of all known species
|　`—+—**Sponges:** 10,000 species
|　　|—**Cnidarians:** 8,000–9,000 species
|　　|—**Molluscs:** 100,000 species
|　　|—**Platyhelminths:** 13,000 species
|　　|—**Nematodes:** 20,000+ species
|　　|—**Annelida:** 12,000 species
|　　—**Arthropods**
|　　　`—+—**Crustaceans:** 40,000 species
|　　　　|—**Insects:** 1–30 million+ species
|　　　　|—**Arachnids:** 75,500 species
|—**Vertebrates:** 3% of all known species
　　`—+—**Reptiles:** 7,984 species
　　　|—**Amphibians:** 5,400 species

|—**Birds:** 9,000–10,000 species
|—**Mammals:** 4,475–5,000 species
|—**Ray-Finned Fishes:** 23,500 species

It would be ludicrous to argue that the tens of thousands, or perhaps even millions, of non-water dweller species currently living on Earth, including insects and spiders, all somehow actually made it onto the ark (and then two of each, male and female). There also are a few types of animals that can reproduce asexually (aphids, cape bees, and turkeys, to name a few), so would there still have been a need for two of those kinds of animals? Was Moses even aware of such asexual-capable creatures when he wrote this part of Genesis?

It is also unclear whether literalists think that every type of dinosaur, and possibly all other extinct life-forms, were present on the ark too, but if so, then add whatever that number would be to the overall number of species on the ark. Keep in mind, though, that the overall number would be huge when one understands that more than 90% of all creatures that have ever existed on Earth are now extinct. Even so, they have to be added to the number on the ark unless they were already extinct by then. So, for instance, were there really two tyrannosaurus rexes, two brontosauruses, two mammoths, two stegosauruses, two pterodactyls, and two of each of all of the other thousands of various types of dinosaurs and countless other now-extinct animals on the ark? While we are at it, we should not forget about the two unicorns that also must have been on the ark (unless those two unicorns were gay, sterile, or extinct, and that is why they didn't make it)!

Whatever that very high total number of creatures that would have had to have been on the ark to account for the thousands or even millions of non-water dwelling species living on Earth today (and multiplied by a factor of nine if we include all of the extinct species that make up over 90% of all creatures that have ever existed), it obviously would have been far too many creatures to all fit crammed into a small cruise ship-sized ark—not to mention the challenges of all those various creatures actually being able to survive on the ark for close to a year. Accordingly, literalists concede that such a high number of species would simply be impossible to fit on the ark. Interestingly, literalists do not appear to make the argument that God somehow miraculously miniaturized all of the hundreds of thousands or millions of species down to a microscopic size as they got onto the ark so they could easily fit and then returned them to their original size as they got off the ark, although some argue that Noah loaded only baby or infant animals and as a result reduced their size somewhat. I suppose literalists at least could attempt to make the miniaturization argument, however, because remember, "with God, all things are possible," even apparently when it is not in any explicit text contained in the Bible.

Maybe God miniaturized all animals by giving Noah DNA test tubes containing the DNA codes and material of each creature and then that DNA was somehow reformulated into all of the species when Noah got off of the ark—a farfetched idea, to be sure, but at least it is a way that all species in the world could have fit. This type of miraculous "miniaturization" is not really the argument such literalists make; instead, although literalists do not admit it, their nonliteral, private-interpretation argument (which is made in an effort to save the story to still make plausible and logistical sense) is that perhaps only 5,000 to 10,000 actual "kinds" of animals were on the ark, and therefore, that much smaller number of general "kinds" of animals could have conceivably all fit on a small cruise ship-sized ark, even if tightly packed in. But why so few species on the ark if the world is now made up of so many more, perhaps millions more, actual species? Because according to the argument, not every single type of "variation" of creature had to be taken onboard the ark.

For example, take dogs, with over 400 genetically distinct breeds. Noah did not have two Chihuahuas, two greyhounds, two collies, two terriers, two poodles, two pit bulls, two Weiner dogs, two great Danes, two Doberman pinschers, two chows, two Labrador retrievers, two bloodhounds, two Pomeranians, and so on, on the ark. Instead, there was just one general male and female "dog" or "wolf," and from those two, all of these specific types canine "breeds" just *evolved* through natural selection and/or selective breeding—and the same for frogs, ants, spiders, bears, beetles, and everything else. Dogs and wolves and all of these breeds are still the same *species,* however, so the argument really goes even further and includes jackals, coyotes, and other wild canines. For example, there was only a single pair of "cats" on the ark, just some sort of common cat-like ancestor, from which came all lions, tigers, cougars, cheetahs, foxes, and bobcats, as well as housecats such as Siamese cats, Persian cats, and tabby cats.

In other words, not all species of animals were necessary on Noah's ark, given the fact that the specific varieties of all of these diverse life-forms currently in the world could have developed through, ironically, *a form of "evolution"* having taken place over just a few thousand years! Obviously, the text does not mention this anywhere in Genesis, but literalists must craft this kind of interpretive argument for the story to have any plausibility as a literal account. Of course, literalists would never admit that they need to partially rely on the theory of evolution to explain how Noah's ark holding all animals is possible. Instead of evolution, they call it mere adaptation, or perhaps, at most, "*micro*-evolution," as opposed to "*macro*-evolution." So, according to them, this micro-evolution is undeniably true and even helps to support the story by making the actual number of animal types small enough to logistically fit on Noah's ark. Thus evolution, or "micro-evolution," explains all of the later diversity and variety of life-forms (millions of species) within very general classes (or "kinds") of animals. "*Macro*-evolution," however, in which micro-evolutionary changes over hundreds of millions of years, instead of over just a few hundred years or even a few thousand years, could produce much more substantial change than just a husky and a Chihuahua from a common canine ancestor, or even a lion and a housecat from a common feline ancestor, is a flawed scientific theory concocted by atheistic scientists who hate God. Notwithstanding that charge against evolution, however, "micro-evolution" still helps to prove that the biblical story of Noah's ark is literally correct and plausible. So, to recap, the assertion is that hundreds of thousands or even millions of species have come from just 5,000–10,000 "general" species over a few thousand years. That seems like an awful lot of "micro-evolution" going on in a very short time, but thank God for evolution—

sorry, micro-evolution—although it is apparently *extremely fast-acting* micro-evolution to produce all of these varieties of animals in such a short time.

Genesis 7

[1] And the LORD said unto Noah, Come thou and all thy house into the ark; for thee have I seen righteous before me in this generation.
[2] Of every clean beast thou shalt take to thee by sevens, the male and his female: and of beasts that are not clean by two, the male and his female.
[3] Of fowls also of the air by sevens, the male and the female; to keep seed alive upon the face of all the earth.

As if there were any room to spare, there are now even more animals to add into the mix here, in light of verse 2 and verse 3, which say that all clean beasts and fowls (birds), Noah was to take not by twos but *by sevens*, both male and female. This conservatively means seven types of each bird, but it could also mean fourteen of each kind, because if there were seven male and female pairs, that would make a total of fourteen of each type of bird. Referring to the estimated number of species listed earlier, note that there are an estimated 9,000 to 10,000 species of birds in the world. So does this mean that Noah must have taken almost 70,000 birds on the ark, or even close to 140,000 birds? It is difficult to estimate the number of "clean beasts," but whatever that number would be, it also would have to be multiplied by seven, not just two. At some point, the story simply crumbles under the weight of its own logistical absurdity. The problem is that Moses basically had no idea how diverse all the species of creatures on the earth were when he wrote this story—he just assumed it would only be the limited number of animals in the ancient Middle East that he could see and was aware of, so that saving them all on a really big boat actually seemed plausible to him. The farce of literal plausibility grows as each kind of species of the world that was supposedly on the ark is considered, however.

For example, remember that in addition to saving all of the mammals, reptiles, amphibians, and birds, the ark also saved all of the *spiders and insects* of the world ("every creeping thing"). Literalist believers seriously advocating the plausibility of Noah's ark often overlook or simply ignore (conveniently, I might add) all of the spiders and insects that would have had to have been on the ark too. Perhaps it is because insects and spiders are so small; however, their small size, huge variety, and wide geographical distribution pose an even more vexing logistical problem for Noah than did those of the larger species. Did Noah really find all of the various spiders, worms, and insects of the world, two by two, and put them on the ark? For example, did an ant queen and a termite queen, along with a male ant and a male termite, dutifully march (or fly, run, walk, or crawl) into the ark together? What about two black widow spiders, two flies, two praying mantises, two ladybugs, two earthworms, two bedbugs, two ticks, two mosquitoes, two daddy-long legs, two wasps, two grasshoppers, two butterflies, two dragonflies, two trapdoor spiders, two wolf spiders, two bees, and on and on, each of which have many, many—perhaps thousands of—other varieties? And what about bacteria and viruses, microscopic life, and rare insects that live in only certain caves in the world or underground, or parasites of any type that can live only in certain other animals? How did all of these various types of life-forms get collected and then survive on the ark? Did Noah really supervise them all on the ark, making sure, for example, that there were tapeworm parasites existing in the intestines of certain host animals that were also on the ark?

If the sheer absurdity of the huge number of the various mammals, amphibians, reptiles, and birds all fitting and surviving on the ark did not make me completely doubt the literal story of Noah's ark, then the alleged inclusion of all of the types of insects and spiders on Earth did. And let's not even get started on the hundreds of thousands of different invertebrates (although again, admittedly, many of those species would live in the water, so many, I suppose, did not die in the flood or need to be taken on the ark—although there is no specific mention of this). Still, there are 75,000 species of arachnids (spiders) and 1–30 million species of insects on Earth, yet Noah really collected two of each and took care of them all on the ark for almost a year?

I guess literalists can attempt to trot out micro-evolution again, but hundreds of thousands and even millions of spider and insect species evolving from a much smaller plausible number of common-ancestor species of spiders and insects that could fit on the ark seems to rely too heavily on the power of micro-evolution in just a few thousand years. Even the most hardcore evolution supporters would not believe that this much evolutionary change of so many new and different species could have taken place in such a short time! It is funny to think that evolutionists would be telling creationists not to expect such unrealistic, really impossible, miracles from evolution (unless God miraculously sped up the process of evolution to use "miracle evolution").

Literalists are in a difficult position here—between a proverbial rock and a hard place. First, the Noah's ark story is simply impossible, given the astronomical number and variety of species on Earth, especially birds, spiders, and insects, all fitting on a small cruise ship-sized ark. Even more absurd is the fact that fundamentalist literalists—who decry evolution as heresy and as an incorrect theory full of holes that was concocted by atheistic scientists who hate God—then hypocritically rely on the theory of evolution to make this biblical story plausible! These literalists seem to believe that they can have it both ways when it comes to evolution, so for them, the evolution of species is simultaneously both true and false.

Not only that, but once all of the species of the world were all on the ark, how was Noah able to somehow keep all of these creatures alive and healthy in their cages—especially insects and spiders, in what I suppose must have been their little insect and spider cages—on the ark for almost a year? Many insects cannot even live for a year, so did Noah oversee their breeding during those months of caring for all of the creatures of the world on the ark with just eight human caretakers on board?

As if that were not enough to make one doubt the literal account of the story, how did Noah know what food to bring for each insect and spider and snake and bird and mammal to keep them fed and healthy for almost a year in this huge floating zoo? For example, 99% of what pandas eat is bamboo shoots. Did Noah know that, and if so, where did he get enough bamboo shoots to feed two pandas for a year? Were pandas even on the ark, or was there just a common bear-like ancestor from whom pandas, polar bears, grizzly bears, brown bears, black bears, koala bears, and all the rest, evolved? But wait, are panda bears and koala bears really even "bears," or are they more like kangaroos, wombats, opossums, wallabies, and other Australian marsupials? If they are members of the marsupial family, were koalas and pandas on the ark, or did they evolve too (sorry, *micro*-evolve) from a common marsupial-like ancestor—two of whom must have swam the ocean from Australia and then traveled across southern Asia and to the Middle East to board the ark?

How were all of the carnivorous animals fed if they only eat the meat from other animals? How many additional animals did Noah have to bring on the ark not to save for posterity but to serve as food for almost a year for the carnivores that were being saved from the flood? Did Noah also bring other insects for the main insects to eat? And why did God command Noah to bring seven of every type of clean animal, and seven of each type of bird, and only two of every type of unclean animal? Perhaps these additional numbers of clean animals (and extra birds) were to serve as the food during the year on the ark for Noah and for the rest of the carnivorous animals—but what about the food for every other animal, bird, insect, and reptile? How did Noah even know what to feed them—and when and how to feed them? How did he keep all of these creatures clean? Was each creature cooped up in a cage of some sort for almost a year, or did it ever get a chance to walk, run, fly, crawl, or move around in the fresh air and sunshine on the top deck? What about water-dependent amphibians and reptiles, like certain kinds of frogs and alligators? How did they survive for almost a year without being able to go into the water, unless Noah let them swim around the sides of the ark every once in a while? Again, if the story is literally true, there have to be some logical, plausible explanations for all of these types of questions—unless the standard stock answer is "because the Bible says so, 'nuff said."

Even larger logistical problems are present. How did species that live only on other continents, some separated by oceans, somehow get to the Middle East and dutifully march up and load themselves onto the ark, know exactly where to go and where to wait patiently, and live there for nearly a year while the ark floated until the flood waters receded? These concerns were mentioned earlier, but recall that polar bears and penguins would have to make it to the Middle East from the Artic and Antarctica, as would kangaroos and Tasmanian devils from Australia and Tasmania, coyotes and bison from North America, and elephants, lions, zebras, and giraffes from Africa. Also, on the island of Madagascar (a big island off of the southeastern coast of Africa), 70% of the mammals, 90% of the reptiles, and 99% of the amphibians are endemic only to Madagascar, but they too all somehow traveled to the Middle East and then travelled back again to Madagascar after the flood. But perhaps the oceans were much shallower back then such that there were landmasses bridging the world to the Middle East, making swimming an ocean unnecessary. Even if there were large oceans to cross, perhaps God simply transported the animals miraculously through the air. Remember, whenever there is a scientific impossibility or a logical implausibility in the Bible, there is a reliable, permanent miracle trump card that can always be played to address and explain away any inconsistency or implausibility.

For example, how did all of the animals in the entire world gather together without any of them killing one another for almost an entire year while being confined on a big boat? If the explanation for all of this is that it was simply a huge miracle of God, requiring God's extreme detailed intervention to make this tremendous logistical challenge possible down to the last detail, then why didn't God simply skip the whole enterprise and just create all of the innocent animals anew after all of the evil people and the animals of the Earth were destroyed by the great flood? If God was going to have to perform all of these really big miracles anyway, why did He even bother having Noah build the ark? Why didn't God simply suspend Noah and all the animals in a big magic bubble on the moon for almost a year until the big flood was over? Why should the magic bubble on the moon story be considered any more or less ridiculous and unrealistic than the Noah's ark story? Either story could be easily explained by the stock rationale "all things are possible with God" or "God could have done it"? If God created the entire universe, certainly, He could have created an ark *or* a big magic bubble on the moon. Why should those scenarios seem any more outlandish or implausible than the ark?

One final issue regarding the survivability of all of these animals once they got off of the ark would have been the complete lack of genetic diversity in their respective gene pools. This would have made it very difficult for them to survive after the ark, in any event. So if the story of Noah's ark is true, every species in the world would have had this dangerous lack of genetic diversity as there would have been only two animals for every species, or "kinds," in the world—and the offspring of each would have to inbreed with one another. But again, God must have temporarily eliminated this serious genetic problem, at least until the population of every species was built back up. At that later point, however, if a species' genetic diversity ever dwindled down again in the future, the lack of genetic diversity problems we now see would return for any and all endangered species (apparently, animal incest is neither a sin nor a problem).

Chapter Sixty-Six

Flood Doomsday, and Other Doomsdays to Come?

[4] For yet seven days, and I will cause it to rain upon the earth forty days and forty nights; and every living substance that I have made will I destroy from off the face of the earth.

A group of fundamentalist literalist Christians affiliated with Family Radio, led by Brother Harold Camping, recently interpreted this particular passage in the Bible in such a way as to support the extremely bold, and spectacularly wrong, conclusion that the world was going to end on May 21, 2011. The group heavily publicized their doomsday message, and, sadly, some true believers even spent all of their life savings on billboards and other advertising and made other related donations, believing that their money would no longer be necessary or valuable after May 21, 2011.The group claimed that this biblical verse in Genesis (7:4), combined with various other verses, led to the inescapable conclusion that God's judgment would be precisely on May 21, 2011, and that Jesus would return to judge the earth and all of humankind on that day.

Their reasoning went something like this: God originally gave humanity seven days' warning before He destroyed the world with a flood ("For yet seven days, and I will cause it to rain upon the earth forty days and forty nights"). But that was just the *first* explicit warning of God's judgment of humankind, which ended up in a worldwide flood of destruction (hence the need for Noah's ark). There was also a *second* warning to humankind that was implicit in that first explicit warning—but to see that second implicit warning, one must understand that when reading that God gave humanity seven days' warning explicitly in the first judgment, resulting in the flood, one should also interpret a day as being 1,000 years (recall II Peter 3:8: "But beloved be not ignorant of this one thing, that one day is with the Lord as a thousand years, and a thousand years as one day"). When one also interprets a day to be 1,000 years, one sees that God was also giving us a 7,000-year warning of the coming second judgment of humankind with a similar worldwide destruction (not with a flood but, as set forth in the Book of Revelation, with fire and war and Armageddon, etc.).

According to this interpretation, Noah's ark was built and completed 7,000 years ago, approximately in the year 4988 BC. I am not clear how they claim to know it was 4988 BC, but apparently, if they can calculate that the earth is 6,000 years old based on ancestral lineages in the Bible, they must believe they can also calculate those lineages to determine how old Noah was when he completed the ark. So they surmised that God not only gave an *explicit* seven-day warning to humanity that He would destroy the earth with a flood but simultaneously gave us an *implicit* 7,000-year warning of a second judgment of humankind. In other words, in 7 days, a flood was coming, and in 7,000 years, God would judge the world again in the final apocalyptic manner as set forth throughout the Book of Revelation—with that day of reckoning occurring exactly on May 21, 2011. Although 4988 BC to 2011 AD is a total of 6,999 years (4998 + 2011 = 6,999), according to their interpretation, we have to add one more year to account for the year 0 AD, so 2011 was really 7,000 years later, not 7,001.

First, it is incredible they claimed that they were doing a simple "plain-reading," literal interpretation of the Bible when they came up with this May 21, 2011 date, which was based on an implicit 7,000-year second warning based on the verse that a day to God is 1,000 years to us. They picked the month, date, and year and were even presumptuous enough to tell us the exact time of day Jesus would be returning—it was supposed to be at 6:00 p.m. as the hour transpired in each time zone on Earth. They further interpreted 6:00 p.m. as sundown, meaning that the "day" would end at that specific hour. They said God would judge the world in a twenty-four–hour wave of judgments starting in the South Pacific, Japan, and Australia, then going across Asia, then Europe and Africa, and then South and North America, ending in Alaska and Hawaii. It is interesting that God would follow our arbitrarily selected time zones, account for daylight savings time in the same manner, and agree that the international dateline in the Pacific Ocean was where daily time on Earth should begin. This all seems very far afield of some strict literal interpretation of the Bible.

Moreover, these believers seem to have completely disregarded the literal statement in Matthew 24:36, "But of that day and hour [when Jesus returns] knoweth no man, no, not the angels of heaven, but my Father only." That verse undercut the idea that they could know the time and date of His return would be at 6:00 p.m. on May 21, 2011. Matthew 24:36 also contains a curious assumption about Jesus's omniscience, or lack thereof. How is it that Jesus, as God, could not know something like the day and hour of His own return? Why would *only* God the Father know, if Jesus the Son and God the Father are both God? God doesn't know something—how is that supposed to even be possible?

The reason that many other Christians, who did not agree with Mr. Camping that Jesus would return on May 21, 2011, is because they believe that no one can know the day or the hour of Jesus's return. According to I Thessalonians 5:2 , "The day of the Lord so cometh as a thief in the night," which most other fundamentalist Christians interpret to mean that no one can predict Jesus's return precisely, although most believe that the end is coming soon, according to various other biblical prophesies. Still, it is interesting that the Family Radio Christian followers believed that they knew the day and the hour of Jesus's return when even Jesus Himself apparently does not know the day and the hour of His own return. Mr. Camping, the Family Radio leader, had also wrongly predicted that the world would end in 1994, and he had similarly vowed then that the Bible guaranteed it. So now that he has had to admit that he has been wrong twice, it is clear that his "literal," "objective," "plain-meaning" interpretations obviously were not the literal, objective, plain-meaning interpretations he claimed them to be, unless he now concedes biblical error. Although he now obviously has to admit his own error, anyone telling him he was in error before May 21, 2011, would have been, according to him, guilty of doubting God's Word.

A similar fundamentalist group also got the date of the end of the world wrong back in 1988, when they also claimed they were doing a strict literal analysis of what the Bible was saying about the end times. In 1987, they believed that the world was going to end in 1988 because according to Matthew24:1–40, during the end times, there will be many signs, "And as he [Jesus] sat upon the mount of Olives, the disciples came unto him privately, saying, Tell us, when shall these things be? and what shall be the sign of thy coming, and of the end of the world?" One of these key signs was that Israel would become a nation (which it did in 1948), and when that happened, that generation would not pass. These verses do not mention Israel by name; however, Israel is often referred to throughout the Bible as a fig tree, so they interpret verse 32–34 as saying that in the end times, Israel will again become a nation, and once it has become a nation, that generation will not pass:

> [32] Now learn a parable of the fig tree; When his branch is yet tender, and putteth forth leaves, ye know that summer is nigh:
> [33] So likewise ye, when ye shall see all these things, know that it is near, even at the doors.
> [34] Verily I say unto you, This generation shall not pass, till all these things be fulfilled.

They also interpret "generation" to mean forty years, but I have not been able to find any verse in the Bible that clearly states that a generation is forty years, or any specific amount of time, for that matter. Still, because Israel became a nation in 1948, and because the Bible says that after that point, this generation would not pass, that meant that the world would have to end by the year1988 (if a generation is forty years) or the Bible would be mistaken, and that could not be possible. I remember reading all of this in a pamphlet called "88 Reasons Why Jesus Will Return in 1988," which I guess now means that the Bible was literally wrong in 88 separate ways, because obviously, we are all still here and Jesus never came back—despite the alleged "88 reasons"—or perhaps their literal interpretation was not so literal or, heaven forbid, they were just flatly wrong.

The members of this group were not deterred by their embarrassing miscalculation. In fact, they still tried to salvage their predictions with additional amended predictions, so after 1988 had come and gone, they said Israel actually became a nation in 1967, after the Six-Day War, and not in 1948. That would mean the world was supposed to end in 2007, although some others thought that the Y2K bug in computers was a sign of the end times, even though that year 2000 calamity of a worldwide computer meltdown never came to pass, either. So after 2007 came and went, the group had to rethink it once again. It is very telling that various groups of people (and not just fundamentalist Christians) have been predicting the end of the world since the beginning of history. Many Christians have been predicting Jesus's return since Jesus left more than 2,000 years ago, and so far, they all have been embarrassingly wrong, despite their claimed literal interpretations of the plain meaning of various biblical passages.

Still, such expectant fundamentalists might warn us not to be so arrogant about predictions of the end of the world, for just as the people in Noah's time apparently didn't believe a flood was coming and suffered the judgment of drowning, we too might be horribly surprised. So even when a boy cries wolf, perhaps we should still listen? Maybe the Maya, despite not believing in Jesus, were nevertheless correct about the world supposedly ending on December 21, 2012, because that is when their very precise Mayan calendar ends—but would the Bible and fundamentalist Christians really follow the Mayan calendar from 500 years ago because of its apparent doomsday prediction? Unfortunately, we do not know much about the Maya because when the Christian conquistadors came to the New World, they burned all of the Mayan texts that told of their history and culture because the conquistadors believed God would judge them as heathen, satanic worshippers who believed in human sacrifice. Despite this, why does anyone assume 2012 is when the Maya thought the world would end? Perhaps that is simply when their calendar ends. Maybe some other unknown cycle or age of time might begin? I wonder if future historians discovering only scraps of our society might think that we were predicting the end of the world in the year 2000 because the computers that controlled our lives at that point did not register any year past the year 1999, at least before the year 2000. What ancient secret might they assume we believed about the supposed end of the world after 1999?

As long as various groups are making predictions, I have thought of a possible argument for fundamentalist Christians who have a penchant for interpreting passages from the Bible to predict the end of the world. My prediction ends up being a little further out into the future, but it still uses the same kind of interpretive logic and calculations that such fundamentalists have used in the past. Recall that a day to God is equal to 1,000 years to humans. There are 365 days in a year. That means if each day to God is equal to 1,000 human years, then 365 days, or one year, to God would actually equal 365,000 human years, so one year to God is 365,000 years to us. And if there are forty years in a generation and the generation from 1948 when Israel became a nation will not pass, then using God time, that would mean 365,000 human years x 40 God years = Jesus is not coming back anytime soon—that is, not for 14.6 million years from 1948, or, the year 14,601,948 to be exact!

Now I, of course, am not actually making that prediction, but I think my math and the math calculations based on my interpretations are at least as logical and plausible as these other predictions are, as far as predictions for the end of the world go, especially when creatively applying the idea that one day equals 1,000 years. I admit, however, that I cannot predict the end of the world with the same amount of precision as to choose which particular day of the month (and hour) it will be 14.6 million years from now when the world ends. The only troubling thing is that the Bible also predicted that Jesus would return and the world would end *within the lifetime of some of Jesus's disciples*, some 2,000 years ago: "Verily I say unto you, There be some standing here [Jesus' disciples], which shall not taste of death, till they see the Son of man coming in his kingdom" (Matthew 16:28). Of course, that did not come true, either, as the world continued well after Jesus's disciples all died nearly 2,000 years ago, so obviously, I must be interpreting this verse incorrectly and the true interpretation must be referring to something else—but again, the words literally say what the words literally say.

In fact, regarding that very point, C. S. Lewis once wrote, "The apocalyptic beliefs of the first Christians have been proved to be false. It is clear from the New Testament that they all expected the Second Coming in their own lifetime. And, worse still, they had a reason, and one which you will find very embarrassing. Their Master had told them so. He shared, and indeed created, their delusion. He said in so many words, 'this generation shall not pass till all these things be done.' And he was wrong. He clearly knew no more about the end of the world than anyone else. This is certainly the most embarrassing verse in the Bible" ("The World's Last Night," 1960, in *The Essential C.S. Lewis,* p. 385).

Perhaps the most troubling aspect about all of these predictions of doomsday is the utter arrogance of people who believe them. They assume that they know, and even worse, that the world will end before they do. They must say or think to themselves, "But we Christians are *so* special!" and therefore, when they are gone, there might as well not even be a world anymore; that is to say, when they leave, the party must be over. I guess not being arrogant also means that I must remain open to the fact that maybe the world will end during my lifetime, however, because how would I know either way? How does anyone really know, which is my overall point? I also don't know if there will be a sunrise tomorrow morning, *but* somehow, I think there will be a sunrise tomorrow, and therefore, I will live my life, and ultimately, my death, accordingly.

[5] And Noah did according unto all that the LORD commanded him.
[6] And Noah was six hundred years old when the flood of waters was upon the earth.
[7] And Noah went in, and his sons, and his wife, and his sons' wives with him, into the ark, because of the waters of the flood.
[8] Of clean beasts, and of beasts that are not clean, and of fowls, and of every thing that creepeth upon the earth,
[9] There went in two and two unto Noah into the ark, the male and the female, as God had commanded Noah.
[10] And it came to pass after seven days, that the waters of the flood were upon the earth.
[11] In the six hundredth year of Noah's life, in the second month, the seventeenth day of the month, the same day were all the fountains of the great deep broken up, and the windows of heaven were opened.

If the rain started on February 17 (in the second month, the seventeenth day of the month) wouldn't that mean that God's seven-day warning must have been made on February 10? If so, where did Mr. Harold Camping get May 21 as the date of the end? I can't quite figure it out, but Mr. Camping and his group must have had some reason for picking May 21 to make such a bold prediction. It must be that the calendars used in ancient times were somehow different from the modern calendar we use now (maybe because Julius Caesar and his son Augustus names were later added as months—July and August—making the ten-month calendar a twelve-month calendar, but those are after the second month, unless January is not the first month?). Undeterred, Mr. Camping has said there actually was a spiritual judgment on May 21, 2011 and the real death and destruction was supposed to be in October of 2011, which did not happen, either (as far as I know).

Chapter Sixty-Seven

How Much Water Does It Take to Flood an Earth?

[12] And the rain was upon the earth forty days and forty nights.

[13] In the selfsame day entered Noah, and Shem, and Ham, and Japheth, the sons of Noah, and Noah's wife, and the three wives of his sons with them, into the ark;

[14] They, and every beast after his kind, and all the cattle after their kind, and every creeping thing that creepeth upon the earth after his kind, and every fowl after his kind, every bird of every sort.

[15] And they went in unto Noah into the ark, two and two of all flesh, wherein is the breath of life.

[16] And they that went in, went in male and female of all flesh, as God had commanded him: and the LORD shut him in.

[17] And the flood was forty days upon the earth; and the waters increased, and bare up the ark, and it was lift up above the earth.

[18] And the waters prevailed, and were increased greatly upon the earth; and the ark went upon the face of the waters.

[19] And the waters prevailed exceedingly upon the earth; and all the high hills, that were under the whole heaven, were covered.

It takes a *lot* of water to have a worldwide flood, but it does not seem possible that a constant rain even for forty days and forty nights could provide anywhere near the volume of water required to inundate the entire Earth, including the very highest mountaintops, with floodwater so that every living substance on Earth was killed (unless it rained for 40,000 years, because a day to God is 1,000 years to us, but if that were the case, then Noah would have been almost 41,000 years old when he died—so that can't be right, but again, "all things are possible with God"). Flooding the world so the water would cover every mountaintop worldwide would take an awfully lot of water! For example, the Andes Mountains in South America along the Chilean Pacific coast essentially start at sea level near the Pacific Ocean and then rise up over 20,000 feet in altitude. That means that the entire Pacific Ocean, covering almost half of the Earth, would have to have risen more than 20,000 feet in just forty days and nights. Note that 20,000 feet ÷ 40 days = 500 feet of rain per day for forty straight days! Even if we require only half of that amount of rain to take into account the water displacement that would occur as the water rose above the lower landmasses, it would still be required to rain well over 250 feet every day, over every square inch of the world!

According to documented world weather reports, in July of 2005, in Mumbai, India, there was a twenty-four–hour rainfall of more than 1 meter, which is just over 3 feet, and this was said to be the world record for the most rain ever over a twenty-four–hour period in history. This is not to say that it is impossible to rain 250 feet per day instead of just three feet per day, in light of God being able to do anything, but literally, more than 250 feet per day is how much rain would have had to fall to flood the highest mountaintops on Earth—Mt. Everest in Nepal is over 29,000 feet (29,000 ÷ 40 days = 725 feet per day). Again, this does not take into account existing landmasses that would displace some of the water necessary to rise that high, but as the water got higher, there would be much less land to displace the water because there are very few mountains higher than 15,000 feet and even fewer higher than 20,000 feet. Of course, this assumes these mountain ranges existed 6,000 or so years ago, but virtually every geologist in the world states that most of them did exist then.

The only other explanation for all of that water would be to consider something in an often overlooked verse, verse 11: "the same day were all the *fountains of the great deep* broken up, and the windows of heaven were opened" (emphasis added). Maybe water inside the earth bubbling up, combined with rain, was enough to make the water rise hundreds of feet a day. If that is the explanation, however, why would God even bother having it rain? Whatever the water source, obviously, the water had to rise several hundred feet a day to completely cover every mountaintop in the world (more than 29,000 feet above sea level).

[20] Fifteen cubits upward did the waters prevail; and the mountains were covered.

The flood water rose only 15 cubits, and somehow, that amount of floodwater made it possible for water to cover the entire Earth, even the highest mountaintops? Recall that a cubit is only about 20 inches, so even if the waters rose 15 cubits that would mean that the water rose 15 cubits x 20 inches = 300 inches ÷ 12 inches = 25 feet. How could all of the mountains on the earth have been covered by floodwaters when those floodwaters rose by only some 25 feet? Newsflash: 25 feet does not come close to equaling 29,000 feet. Moses obviously did some seriously deficient and mistaken math here, or he simply could not measure or judge altitude very well—which still would be pretty elementary in this instance—or he just did not understand how high mountains rose above sea level and required the water level to rise to cover all mountains all over the world simultaneously.

Maybe we can forgive an ancient writer without a formal education in general science, geography, topography, or meteorology, but if God, not Moses, actually wrote the Bible, why would God be so mistaken about how high the waters had to rise to cover every mountaintop in the world if God is infallible and everything in the Bible is literally true? Perhaps there were no mountains at all in Noah's time, not even hills that were much over 25 feet in altitude? It would give new meaning to the notion that the earth was flat at one time, at least in a certain sense!

HOW MUCH WATER DOES IT TAKE TO FLOOD AN EARTH?

Perhaps the earth was entirely under water in the past, millions or billions of years ago. There is evidence that at one time, before mountain ranges were even created, at least part of the earth may have been under water, which can possibly explain fossilized seashells now found on mountaintops. Although there may be evidence of a "flood" millions or billions of years ago, the geological evidence of such a worldwide flood happening all at once is sketchy at best, and there is no evidence that a worldwide flood happened only some 4,500 years ago, because not all fossils found throughout the world were created at the exact time in history just after the alleged flood some 4,000–5,000 years ago.

There is always a pious answer to explain these logistical concerns. We can always just assume that it was a miracle requiring faith to explain how it could have rained so much that the entire Earth was flooded so much that the water could cover a 29,000-foot-high mountaintop (assuming Mt. Everest existed). We can always choose to believe that something that otherwise would be impossible nonetheless occurred because God said it occurred in the Bible. This is where it just takes faith in God. When there is an obvious mathematical mistake, however, such as water rising *only* 25 feet and still somehow flooding the entire Earth, even covering the highest mountaintops more than 29,000 feet high, such is a very serious and undeniable mistake that does not make logical sense, and no amount of faith in miracles can undo that clear mistake as written in Genesis.

For example, a cup of water that raises the amount of water by a tiny fraction of a millimeter in an otherwise empty swimming pool cannot be said to entirely fill up a 30,000-gallon pool! That would not be a miracle requiring faith; instead, it simply would be a mistake, an error. And faith alone cannot undo an undeniable written contradiction or an inescapable mistake in logic.

Of course, in trying to come up with something to salvage the claim, I suppose one could say that the water rose 25 feet above the ground, defying gravity, so that it would have been a 25-foot-thick cover of water above a valley floor, as well as a 25-foot-thick cover above a mountaintop (like a 25-foot-thick blanket of water all around the earth). Why not, when all things are possible with God? One would have to go that far in suspending logic, physics, and gravity so that a literal interpretation can still somehow make sense—either that or the text must be interpreted as meaning that the waters covered the highest mountaintop by 25 feet. So Mount Everest at over 29,000 feet was somehow underneath 25 feet of water, as were valleys all over the world? It is not clear whether the text literally means that, that there was a 25-foot-thick cover of water, or that God shrunk the earth so mountains somehow would be beneath 25 feet of water.

Chapter Sixty-Eight

Really? *Everything* Not on the Ark Died?

[21] And all flesh died that moved upon the earth, both of fowl, and of cattle, and of beast, and of every creeping thing that creepeth upon the earth, and every man:
[22] All in whose nostrils was the breath of life, of all that was in the dry land, died.
[23] And every living substance was destroyed which was upon the face of the ground, both man, and cattle, and the creeping things, and the fowl of the heaven; and they were destroyed from the earth: and Noah only remained alive, and they that were with him in the ark.
[24] And the waters prevailed upon the earth an hundred and fifty days.

Everything on Earth died, as "every living substance was destroyed," according to the Bible, but there had to have been some very important unstated exceptions here. For instance, complete death and destruction was not the case for all fish and sea life (there were no aquariums on the ark to save all of the fish), so obviously, they did not all die by being drowned in the worldwide flood—"all that was in the dry land, died." Even though all fish and water-dwelling life would not drown in a worldwide flood, such a flood might still have killed much sea life, nonetheless. This massive death would probably have happened because of the great mixing of salt water and a new vast amount of fresh (rain) water in a flood of these proportions. This is because the water in the world's vast oceans is saltwater but the water in rivers and lakes, as well as all rain water, is fresh (non-salt) water.

If there were a sudden influx of a massive amount of fresh water (rain) that mixed with existing ocean water (salt) due to a worldwide flood (enough to submerge a 29,000-foot mountain), the resulting fresh- and saltwater mix might have changed the pH, alkalinity, and other chemical balances in all of the waters to such a degree that it might have been "too salty" for fresh water fish while "not salty enough" for saltwater fish to survive. For example, when saltwater fish are placed in freshwater, they cannot adapt quickly enough to the change in salt concentration. Their cells flood in a sense, and sometimes even explode, because they do not have the ability to rid themselves of the excess water and the cells' chemicals are too diluted to function. The saltwater fish can rapidly die as their cells shut down.

Such a sudden imbalance in all water worldwide might have killed all, if not most, of the fish and other sea life at the time. Remember, freshwater would have had to have been more than 29,000 feet above sea level to cover Mt. Everest. Again, Moses was probably not considering such things because he did not know of such things at the time. Although he might have been able to distinguish between saltwater and freshwater, he might not have considered all of its biological implications if such a huge mixing of all waters worldwide were to have occurred. If certain fish or other sea life would have died, why were they not taken in aquariums on the ark? If mysterious water bubbled up from within the earth ("fountains of the deep"), who knows what kind of possible chemicals or other ingredients that water mix would have had? If the ark did float around at 30,000 feet above the preexisting sea level for a year, one wonders how cold it would have been, and how thin the air would have been; however, one might also suppose that all of the new water would have pushed all the atmosphere up and outward such that 30,000 feet above the preexisting sea level would have become the new, temporarily very high, "sea level."

There is an even more serious logistical problem here, however. What about all of the plant life on dry land before the flood, such as fruits, vegetables, trees, other plants, flowers, bushes, herbs, grasses, and basically everything that lived on the face of the earth (other than those creatures on the ark and, I suppose, seaweed)? If all of that plant life died in the flood ("every living substance was destroyed which was upon the face of the ground…[all] were destroyed"), how did all that plant life get restarted after the flood? How could there be a re-creation of all plants and trees if they did not have a Creator because God killed everything with the flood and did not recreate plants and trees just like He did not recreate all of the dead animals? It says, however, "all in whose nostrils was the breath of life, died (implying only land creatures?)." But plants still "breathe," and not every living creature has "nostrils." In any event, wouldn't most plants die if they were under water for almost a year?

Plants cannot reproduce if they are dead. Did God forget to tell Noah to also bring every type of tree, plant, flower, cactus, grass, onto the ark too, so that if the world were going to have plants on it *after* the great flood, then Noah had better bring each and every type of plant, shrub, grass, flower, and tree in the world with him on the ark? Would that requirement have been just a little too unrealistic and too farfetched for us to believe, even for staunch believers who say that with God, *all things are possible*? Imagine what that would have entailed: bring a redwood tree, an oak tree, an orange tree, a rose bush, a cactus, some ivy, some grapevines, a willow tree, some wheat, some pumpkin seeds, yams, lettuce, corn, potatoes, and cranberries (I am just thinking about Thanksgiving now), and even a carnivorous plant, a Venus flytrap (but one that would know how important it was not to eat the two flies on the ark, or even one of them!). There are more than 300,000 plant species in the world and between 10,000 and 100,000 tree species. Somehow, I don't think they all could have fit on the ark. Maybe God just buried all plant seeds in the earth so they could spring forth once the water dried up? Maybe…but the Bible doesn't say that.

If God did not bury all plant life for later, He must have recreated all plant life the same way He did during the third day of creation, but without telling us or mentioning His plant re-creation anywhere in the Bible. If all life on Earth died the way the Bible says it did in this great flood (even if some plants could survive under floodwater, the Bible says that *everything* was destroyed)—and there is no specific mention that God recreated all of the plant life anew—how did that plant life possibly begin (or "re-begin") after the flood? Was it mere "chance," or evolution—sorry, "micro-evolution"—in which all of the plant life now existing on Earth by some means "evolved" from seaweed and other sea plants? I do not think creationist literalists would say that all new plant life on Earth spontaneously began and/or evolved, or even that God simply recreated everything after the flood but then forgot to tell us that little piece of important trivia in the Bible—so where is this missing explanation in Genesis? Maybe God originally created super flood-resistant trees and vegetation that could withstand being under water for nearly a year and not die, even though modern plants and vegetation have apparently lost that ability. "The Lord works in mysterious ways." If He had created such super plants, however, why did God say "*everything* was destroyed" if it was not? And if we had flood-resistant plants, why didn't God also make temporary flood-resistant animals, all of whom could have been given temporary gills and could swim, and swim well, for months at a time without much food?

If God were just going to recreate all trees and other vegetation after the flood anyway, why did He even bother to have the flood? Why kill all the non-flood-resistant plants, only to have to recreate them, but go through the trouble of drowning all species of animal, except two of each kind in order to put them on an ark for nearly a year to save them and wait out the flood? Again, if God ended up having to recreate plant life, why didn't He just recreate all animal life too and then have the ark just for Noah and his family? Better yet, why didn't God just kill the hopelessly evil human beings (God could have just poisoned them, after all) and spare all of the completely innocent animals and plants on the planet from a destructive worldwide flood?

Chapter Sixty-Nine

"Rain, Rain, Go Away"...but How?

Genesis 8

[1] And God remembered Noah, and every living thing, and all the cattle that was with him in the ark: and God made a wind to pass over the earth, and the waters asswaged;
[2] The fountains also of the deep and the windows of heaven were stopped, and the rain from heaven was restrained;
[3] And the waters returned from off the earth continually: and after the end of the hundred and fifty days the waters were abated.

As the worldwide flood was winding down, where exactly did that massive amount of water go? The text says that a "wind asswaged" it. That seems to suggest that the water just dried up, which must mean that all of that extra water just evaporated. If that happened, the water would not have just disappeared, however, but would have eventually returned as rain in the water cycle, so this worldwide flood essentially would have been "permanent." If God actually created more water to flood the entire Earth, that water would have remained on Earth *in some form.* The problem is that Moses did not really understand what a flood actually is. A flood is not the creation of more water out of nothing, although it may seem that way.

With respect to a typical flood we now experience on Earth, we do not have new, additional water on Earth; instead, the water on Earth is constantly changing forms and locations around the earth, so we have a finite amount of water that keeps getting recycled and stored in the oceans, clouds, or polar ice caps or as snow, glaciers, and icebergs. If that were not the case, we would eventually run out of water (which is theoretically possible, but only if the sun heated up or cooled down so greatly that our atmosphere could no longer hold the evaporating water in the air).

The key is that a flood only seems like more water appearing from nowhere, especially after it rains, when the eventual drainage to rivers and oceans gets overwhelmed by the runoff, but a flood is not *more water* worldwide but simply more water *accumulating too quickly in one particular spot.* In a sense, a flood is really just a temporary water-distribution problem. The rain comes from moisture in clouds, which came from evaporated water, which came from liquid water previously someplace else on Earth. That is why we have dams and water-control systems to store water when it comes too quickly and to keep some spare water when it is not plentiful. When we can successfully regulate the water distribution, we can generally avoid floods (and droughts).

The great flood in Genesis was not a water accumulation and distribution problem in a particular place on Earth, however; instead, it was an alleged flooding of the entire Earth *all at once* requiring a massive amount of *new, additional* water worldwide. Where did all of that *new and additional* miraculously created water go after the great flood, then? I guess God created all of the new water, so He could make it all disappear too—the miracle trump card once again. Maybe God just created a big drain at the bottom of the ocean to suck up all of the extra water on the Earth ("the fountains of the great deep" again)? It does not say that in Genesis (it says only that the fountains stopped just as the rain stopped, not where all of that water went), but it doesn't say that God didn't have a big drain at the bottom of the ocean, so it's possible! That is not a literal interpretation of the express text, however; instead, that is adding to the text with private interpretation, which is supposed to be illegitimate.

[4] And the ark rested in the seventh month, on the seventeenth day of the month, upon the mountains of Ararat.
[5] And the waters decreased continually until the tenth month: in the tenth month, on the first day of the month, were the tops of the mountains seen.
[6] And it came to pass at the end of forty days, that Noah opened the window of the ark which he had made:
[7] And he sent forth a raven, which went forth to and fro, until the waters were dried up from off the earth.
[8] Also he sent forth a dove from him, to see if the waters were abated from off the face of the ground;
[9] But the dove found no rest for the sole of her foot, and she returned unto him into the ark, for the waters were on the face of the whole earth: then he put forth his hand, and took her, and pulled her in unto him into the ark.
[10] And he stayed yet other seven days; and again he sent forth the dove out of the ark;
[11] And the dove came in to him in the evening; and, lo, in her mouth was an olive leaf pluckt off: so Noah knew that the waters were abated from off the earth.

If God had just destroyed every living thing on Earth in the flood, where did this amazing new olive tree come from that the dove just happened to find alive and growing somewhere on dry land (that apparently had not existed some seven days earlier)? By the way, how big of an olive tree could it have possibly been? Remember, it could not have been a preexisting pre-flood tree, because the Bible said He killed everything in the flood; besides, an olive tree would die if it spent almost an entire year under water, so this would have had to have been a newly created olive tree, right? Was there enough time for that new olive tree to grow, even if God had buried olive tree seeds in the ground before the flood? Maybe when God recreated all the new plant life that He did not tell us about after the flood, He not only created new olive trees but also created new mature olive trees that were already established (like God created "mature" starlight from stars billions of light-years away that we can see from Earth, even though the universe was only created about 6,000 years ago).

[12] And he stayed yet other seven days; and sent forth the dove; which returned not again unto him any more.
[13] And it came to pass in the six hundredth and first year, in the first month, the first day of the month, the waters were dried up from off the earth: and Noah removed the covering of the ark, and looked, and, behold, the face of the ground was dry.
[14] And in the second month, on the seven and twentieth day of the month, was the earth dried.

Assuming that the dove found dry land and decided to stay there, and that is why he never returned to the ark, what food at that time could there have possibly been for him to eat to survive? None of this is explained. This seems to be a typical human oversight of a writer telling a mythical story, instead of an infallible God giving an accurate and historical account of actual events.

So Noah was required to wait around for the water to dry up or go away, but that would only happen with a water-distribution flood, not a worldwide flood in which the entire Earth would receive massive amounts of new, additional water. If God miraculously made all of that new, additional water on Earth just disappear, why did it take Him so long to make that water disappear? If it were a true miracle, God could have *immediately* removed all of that new, additional water from the Earth instead of making Noah wait around all of that extra time for the water to dry up or otherwise disappear. This biblical account makes it seem like the flood was a typical water-distribution problem in which the excess water has to dissipate and eventually be distributed to another area or even take on a new form (ice or evaporation) slowly over time, however—that is what is meant by the phrase stating that the flood waters receded.

Chapter Seventy

Being Fruitful and Multiplying…by Incest Again, as Well as Immediately Killing Many of the Animals Just Saved

[15] And God spake unto Noah, saying,
[16] Go forth of the ark, thou, and thy wife, and thy sons, and thy sons' wives with thee.
[17] Bring forth with thee every living thing that is with thee, of all flesh, both of fowl, and of cattle, and of every creeping thing that creepeth upon the earth; that they may breed abundantly in the earth, and be fruitful, and multiply upon the earth.
[18] And Noah went forth, and his sons, and his wife, and his sons' wives with him:
[19] Every beast, every creeping thing, and every fowl, and whatsoever creepeth upon the earth, after their kinds, went forth out of the ark.
[20] And Noah builded an altar unto the LORD; and took of every clean beast, and of every clean fowl, and offered burnt offerings on the altar.

Similar logistical problems involving getting every creature on the ark would have been present in reverse, getting every creature off of the ark. For starters, how did all of these creatures get back to their homelands *after* the flood—kangaroos back to Australia, penguins back to Antarctica, and so on—over oceans, especially after the flood, when the water presumably would still have been fairly high in the oceans as it was allegedly drying up? And why did the animals all leave at that point? Why didn't some of them stay and populate other regions of the earth, not just the regions from whence they came? And why did the ark end up resting on Mount Ararat, in Turkey, still very close to the location of the original launching of the ark in the Middle East? Wouldn't the tides, the wind, the currents, and the like for almost a year have made the ark travel at least a little further than that if it floated around all of that time? Why didn't it end up in Africa, East Asia, Europe, or even South America, for example?

Noah went to great lengths to save all of the animals from death by the great flood only to start immediately killing some of them and offering them to God as sacrifices once the ark hit dry land. Shouldn't those animals have bred and had offspring *before* Noah started killing certain animals that he had just saved from drowning? Of course, maybe these were just the leftover clean animals (which were brought by sevens, not just by twos) that were not eaten on the ark during the flood so they could now be sacrificed, as they were just for food (and sacrifices) anyway.

[21] And the LORD smelled a sweet savour; and the LORD said in his heart, I will not again curse the ground any more for man's sake; for the imagination of man's heart is evil from his youth; neither will I again smite any more every thing living, as I have done.
[22] While the earth remaineth, seedtime and harvest, and cold and heat, and summer and winter, and day and night shall not cease.

So, God first killed all mankind, except Noah and his family, because mankind was hopelessly evil and violent, but after God killed off all of humanity except Noah, He realized that mankind had been plagued with Original Sin from Adam and Eve and mankind is therefore evil and violent by his nature ("for the imagination of man's heart is evil from his youth"). After receiving a burnt offering of dead but clean animals that had just been saved on the ark, God once again appears to be sorry that He destroyed the Earth and vows never to do it again, at least not by a flood. Too bad for all of those dead humans who did not get to benefit from God's new way of conceptualizing the problem: that humanity does not need to be destroyed but instead needs a savior. It is better late than never, even if it is obviously too late for all those who had just drowned.

Finally, this ark, a ship that could weather a great storm and deluge of rain and float for months and months, was never built again on Earth by anyone such as explorers for thousands of years, so far as we know, until someone like Christopher Columbus finally was able to cross the Atlantic Ocean in 1492. Why didn't anyone else ever build a similar ark using the same technology and shipbuilding techniques used by Noah thousands of years earlier and use it to cross oceans and explore the world?

Genesis 9

[1] And God blessed Noah and his sons, and said unto them, Be fruitful, and multiply, and replenish the earth.

And here comes the return of that pesky incest problem again (as well as the lack of genetic diversity). We at least know that there are no other mysterious human beings on Earth at this point because they all have just been killed by the flood. Also, as with Adam and Eve, although the first generation would not be a product of incest because Adam and Eve were not related, just as Noah and his wife, and his sons and their wives, were not related, all subsequent generations immediately thereafter would have been products of incest. There is no escaping the fact that there must have been some sex between cousins, and perhaps with their aunts and uncles, to repopulate the earth. I suppose incest could have been avoided if one of Noah's sons had sex with one of his brother's wives, but even though that would not have been incest, it would be adultery, which is still a sin. So, God required either incest or adultery—some type of sexual sin—for the earth to be repopulated after the flood.

The Old Testament Book of Leviticus has many verses pointing out that incest is wrong and is a sin: Leviticus 18:6–18 contains a whole series of forbidden forms of incest with various relatives:

> [6] None of you shall approach to any that is near of kin to him, to uncover their nakedness: I am the LORD.
> [7] The nakedness of thy father, or the nakedness of thy mother, shalt thou not uncover: she is thy mother; thou shalt not uncover her nakedness.
> [8] The nakedness of thy father's wife shalt thou not uncover: it is thy father's nakedness.
> [9] The nakedness of thy sister, the daughter of thy father, or daughter of thy mother, whether she be born at home, or born abroad, even their nakedness thou shalt not uncover.
> [10] The nakedness of thy son's daughter, or of thy daughter's daughter, even their nakedness thou shalt not uncover: for theirs is thine own nakedness.
> [11] The nakedness of thy father's wife's daughter, begotten of thy father, she is thy sister, thou shalt not uncover her nakedness.
> [12] Thou shalt not uncover the nakedness of thy father's sister: she is thy father's near kinswoman.
> [13] Thou shalt not uncover the nakedness of thy mother's sister: for she is thy mother's near kinswoman.
> [14] Thou shalt not uncover the nakedness of thy father's brother, thou shalt not approach to his wife: she is thine aunt.
> [15] Thou shalt not uncover the nakedness of thy daughter in law: she is thy son's wife; thou shalt not uncover her nakedness.
> [16] Thou shalt not uncover the nakedness of thy brother's wife: it is thy brother's nakedness.
> [17] Thou shalt not uncover the nakedness of a woman and her daughter, neither shalt thou take her son's daughter, or her daughter's daughter, to uncover her nakedness; for they are her near kinswomen: it is wickedness.
> [18] Neither shalt thou take a wife to her sister, to vex her, to uncover her nakedness, beside the other in her life time.
> [19] Also thou shalt not approach unto a woman to uncover her nakedness, as long as she is put apart for her uncleanness.
> [20] Moreover thou shalt not lie carnally with thy neighbour's wife, to defile thyself with her."

Although this passage does not use the word "incest," it is implied by the phrase "uncover the nakedness" of a family member; however, if the passage is literally just saying that it would be a sin merely to see a family member naked, then surely, having sex with them would also be a sin, so these verses about incest being a sin ("it is wickedness") would cover not only the initial incest that had to take place to populate the world the first time (Adam and Eve and their children) but also that with Noah's family and his sons' wives the second time it became necessary to repopulate the world. However, perhaps it was okay for cousins to marry, a lack of genetic diversity notwithstanding.

Some Christian fundamentalists seem to lump incest, adultery, and homosexuality all up into one deviant triumvirate of sexual impropriety, which leads one to ask whether we should have laws prohibiting *all* of them. We outlaw incest for close family members, but not more distant relatives and we no longer outlaw adultery. And imagine a modern political campaign designed to pass a law outlawing sex during a woman's menstrual cycle! Although we used to outlaw homosexuality, we do so no longer, though many states still prohibit same-sex marriages—which is a particularly interesting and currently controversial area of the law.

Chapter Seventy-One

Pray Away the Gay to Save the Day?

Should Christian believers be religiously and legally opposed to same-sex marriages because in the Bible, homosexuality is considered a "sin"? Same-sex marriage is an issue that will be taken up by the US Supreme Court when it addresses California's controversial Proposition 8, which rendered same-sex marriages unconstitutional under the California state constitution, as well as when it addresses other cases involving similar state laws. The California case involves a federal issue because Proposition 8 itself is being challenged as unconstitutional (a state law, even a state constitution, may not violate the US Constitution). The case also follows an important legal issue about which there is much division in the country. The whole issue is controversial on many different fronts; for example, the old military policy of "don't ask don't tell" was repealed and the Justice Department, under the Obama Administration, no longer defends the constitutionality of the Defense of Marriage Act (DOMA) under which legal same-sex marriages in one state are not required to be recognized by states that prohibit same-sex marriage. In a sense, DOMA is similar to the pre-Civil War Fugitive Slave Act, under which slaves who physically made it into a free state had to be returned to their original slave state. The Fugitive Slave Act also supported the idea that free black citizens in the North would not still be considered free once they crossed over a border into a slave state. The constitutionality of DOMA likely will also be considered by the US Supreme Court.

These types of legal and political issues involve the very important constitutional issue of whether a state should be required to recognize the legal decrees of another state. Typically, under Article IV, Section 1 of the Full Faith and Credit Clause of the US Constitution, US states are required to recognize valid legal judgments from other states. Does that requirement apply to a same-sex marriage that is *legal* in one state but *illegal* in another state, though? In other words, which conflicting state law should be "in control"—that of the state that allows same-sex marriage, or that of state that makes same-sex marriage illegal? Although President Obama was the first president to ever personally support same-sex marriage, he still has left it up to the states to decide the issue as a matter of state law. An important question for Christian believers, both as a *religious* and a *political* matter, is whether they should necessarily be opposed to homosexuality and/or the legal recognition of same-sex marriages.

Many fundamentalist Christians believe that any person "choosing" to engage in "homosexual behavior" or the "gay lifestyle" would be engaging in an immoral sin against God. In support of this position, these believers point to a verse in the Old Testament, Leviticus 18:22, which says, "Thou shalt not lie with mankind, as with womankind: it is abomination." Later in Leviticus (20:13), it says, "If a man also lie with mankind, as he lieth with a woman, both of them have committed an abomination: they shall surely be put to death; their blood shall be upon them."

Because death would be an extremely harsh punishment for just being gay, it appears that even the most extreme believers do *not* think that gay people should legally be put to death in this country, although unfortunately, there are some.

If we take these verses literally, however, should we understand that God really teaches us that homosexuality is a sin, homosexuality should be criminalized, and homosexual offenders should be put to death? If so, perhaps there is much more common ground between the Bible and what many Christian fundamentalists would categorize as radical, Islamic Sharia law, which interestingly, some conservative state legislatures have already or are now trying to prohibit. These kinds of extreme Islamic pronouncements, with their very harsh punishments for certain consensual adult sexual activities, are sometimes viewed, even by Christian fundamentalists, as examples of oppressive Islamic religious zealotry, even though these same Christian believers apparently do not think such anti-gay views are so extreme or oppressive when they are set forth in the Bible—instead, they are simply "of God."

A very literal interpretation of these verses in Leviticus would be that although *male* homosexuality is considered a sin (an "abomination"); *female* homosexuality is not a sin, because lesbianism is completely ignored, at least by this text. Fundamentalist literalists, however, would maintain that it is *implied* that lesbianism should also be considered a sin, because God obviously would not unfairly discriminate, at least not *in favor* of women. Assuming that all male and female homosexuality should be considered a sin; does that necessarily mean that same-sex marriages should be legally prohibited? We should keep in mind that although Leviticus says a man lying with another man is an abomination, Leviticus 11:8–12 also says that eating shrimp and other types of unclean food is an abomination, and there is certainly no strong Christian political movement to make it a crime to eat such food:

> [8] Of their flesh shall ye not eat, and their carcase shall ye not touch; they are unclean to you.
> [9] These shall ye eat of all that are in the waters: whatsoever hath fins and scales in the waters, in the seas, and in the rivers, them shall ye eat.
> [10] And all that have not fins and scales in the seas, and in the rivers, of all that move in the waters, and of any living thing which is in the waters, they shall be an abomination unto you:
> [11] They shall be even an abomination unto you; ye shall not eat of their flesh, but ye shall have their carcases in abomination.
> [12] Whatsoever hath no fins nor scales in the waters, that shall be an abomination unto you.

The Westboro Baptist Church, among other very fringe hate groups against homosexuals, has a familiar mantra it uses at funerals and other protests: "God hates fags." In light of the verses in Leviticus about how eating shellfish and shrimp, like being gay, is an abomination, perhaps these churchgoing crusaders need to change their mantra to "God loves fags who hate shrimp."

Two important questions arise from these biblical passages and their interpretations about homosexuality and same sex-marriage:

> (1) Should society consider homosexuality to be a sin and prohibit same-sex marriages, even though there are many other similar pronouncements about various "sins" mentioned in the Bible against which we do *not* pass official legal prohibitions or deny certain legal rights? In other words, why should we have official laws against only *some* sins that are mentioned in the Bible but not against *all* sins that are mentioned in the Bible?

> (2) Is being a homosexual a choice, such that people choose to commit this sexual sin, or is a person just born with his or her sexuality? For example, if you are a heterosexual, ask yourself whether you chose to be heterosexual and to live a heterosexual lifestyle or whether you are simply heterosexual by nature, down to your core—that is, are heterosexuals just born that way? In either event, to what extent should it matter, spiritually and/or legally, whether a person either *chooses* to be gay or simply *is* gay?

Each of these two basic concerns is addressed in the several following chapters. The starting point for many Christians is that homosexuality is a sin. They also seem to think there is a cure for homosexuality—prayer; however, I don't think that they think prayer, powerful as it is, could work in reverse, that is, so we theoretically could just pray, and miraculously, a heterosexual could become homosexual. Putting aside that whole issue for the moment, the next assumption following is that same-sex marriage must also be a sin, and should be illegal, because God only recognizes heterosexual marriages between one man and one woman. Some believers therefore assume that they should oppose homosexuality and same-sex marriage not only as a *personal religious* matter but also as a *public legal* matter. We should remember, however, that we do not live in a theocracy in which *everything* in the Bible is enacted into our legal system in a "reverse Sharia law" manner.

For example, although a few of the Ten Commandments may overlap with some of our civil and criminal laws, most of the Ten Commandments do *not* overlap with our laws. In fact, if some of the Ten Commandments were codified into our law, they would actually *violate the US Constitution*. Consequently, they would be deemed *illegal* by our justice system. That should not mean that any Christian supporting our US Constitution necessarily should be thought of as opposing the Bible because they would be violating their personal beliefs by adhering to the requirements of the US Constitution. Again, this is because we do not live in a theocracy; instead, we live in a constitutional democracy, the way our founders intended when they originally wrote the Constitution.

It is instructive to consider what would happen if we passed laws solely because their principles might exist as religious pronouncements in the Bible. Some people might not oppose this codification of God's Law into man's law; after all, some Christians and some evangelical pastors say things like "Don't forget to take Jesus into the voting booth with you on Election Day!" What would it mean, though, to follow that advice and make illegal *all sins mentioned in the Bible*? Let's examine what would happen if we enacted laws based on each of the Ten Commandments in an attempt to legally apply to everyone in society these important biblical pronouncements against sin. Note that Exodus 20:1–17 setting forth the Ten Commandments will be considered in Chapters Thirty-One through Thirty-Nine that follow.

Chapter Seventy-Two

Commandment I

Exodus 20

[1] And God spake all these words, saying,
[2] I am the LORD thy God, which have brought thee out of the land of Egypt, out of the house of bondage.
[3] Thou shalt have no other gods before me.

First, it is interesting that this passage says, "And God spake all these words, saying" to introduce the Ten Commandments, as if to distinguish them in the text as a direct *quote* from God and not merely what Moses himself was writing about God and various other matters in the Bible. If God wrote *every word* of the Bible, as literal fundamentalists assert that He did, however, why does the Bible find it necessary here to qualify the Ten Commandments as coming *directly* from God as opposed to everything else that is allegedly directly written *solely* by God? If this were just for emphasis, God easily could have just emphasized that the Ten Commandments would be important direct words to live by to distinguish them from other passages in the Bible such as family lineages, historical statements, or stories from which to learn life lessons, and/or religious doctrine. This passage, however, says God directly wrote (or dictated) the commandments (as opposed to directly writing other parts), so isn't this phrase an admission that not every word of the Bible came *directly* from God?

If we were to enact this Commandment from God into law so it would be illegal to have any gods before the one true Christian God, then people could attend *only* Christian churches, thereby making it illegal to attend any non-Christian meeting that would fail to recognize Jesus as God (even though this Commandment is in the Old Testament, where God appears to be talking exclusively to Jewish people, commanding them to put Him first as He had freed them from slavery in Egypt, and so they owed Him this loyalty).

According to Christians, however, the God of the Old Testament is God the Father, God the Son, and God the Holy Spirit, the Holy Trinity, so the God of both the Old and the New Testaments *includes Jesus Christ as God.* As a result, a law prohibiting any other Gods would mean that only *Christian* churches would be legal. Thus, non-Christian gatherings would not be recognized under the law as legitimate houses of worship, so they would be denied the tax-exempt status that is available to Christian churches. As a result, anyone who did not believe that Jesus is the Messiah—the actual Son of God—would be violating this law. One cannot believe in just two-thirds of God and still be considered to believe in *all* of God. Obviously, modern Jews would disagree. Still, it is instructive and revealing that most Christians probably would *not* support such a Christian-God-Only law in American society, despite their own religious beliefs to not put any false gods above their own Christian God, because if there were a law that required people to have no other gods before the one true Christian God, that law would violate the 1st Amendment to the US Constitution.

Should that mean that Christian believers have a religious duty to oppose the 1st Amendment of the US Constitution because it would stand as a legal barrier to making the first of the Ten Commandments into one of our laws in society at large? Should Christian believers also think that our founders must have been a bunch of liberal, atheist progressives who hated God because they put the 1st Amendment into the US Constitution to allow US citizens to have other gods before the one true Christian God? Of course not; it just means that our founders were all too aware of the religious persecution in Europe and elsewhere and of the political danger in establishing an official state religion so people would not be free to exercise their own religious beliefs—*whatever* those beliefs might be. Instead, the 1st Amendment to our Constitution guarantees us the right to freely exercise our own religious beliefs, Christian or non-Christian. We simply cannot use our legal system to force those beliefs onto others, even if we strongly disagree with the beliefs of others, even if they deny that our God is God. So, even if a person denies that Jesus Christ is Lord, we should not have a law that prohibits those non-Christian beliefs. To do so would be using a kind of "reverse Sharia law" to force our Christian beliefs onto all others in society. That would be illegal, *un*-American, and unwise if we truly believe in our Constitution, our democracy, and all of our protected constitutional rights.

Chapter Seventy-Three

Commandment II

Exodus 20

[4] Thou shalt not make unto thee any graven image, or any likeness of any thing that is in heaven above, or that is in the earth beneath, or that is in the water under the earth:
[5] Thou shalt not bow down thyself to them, nor serve them: for I the LORD thy God am a jealous God, visiting the iniquity of the fathers upon the children unto the third and fourth generation of them that hate me;
[6] And shewing mercy unto thousands of them that love me, and keep my commandments.

Assume a state legislature passed a law prohibiting the wearing of any religious symbols or clothing except for crosses or other Christian symbols of the one true Christian God (even though the Bible says *not* to "make unto thee any graven image, or *any likeness of any thing that is in heaven above*" (emphasis added)), but does that include images of God, Jesus, or angels that are in Heaven above? If so, there go all of my mom's home religious shrines. Also, assume no allowance for any prayers to any gods but the one true Christian God. Finally, assume the purpose of this law would be to punish any society that does not worship *only God,* so that God would not get jealous. Supporters of this law might reason that anyone who wears any non-Christian religious symbols or clothing or who prays to any other god would be placing our society in danger because, as God tells us, He will not only punish guilty perpetrators but will also punish even people who are just close to the guilty perpetrators, such as an innocent daughters, granddaughters, or even great-granddaughters ("the third and fourth generation").

In addition to putting society at risk of suffering God's wrath, people violating the law might also be denying our society rich blessings from God because a jealous God might understandably withhold His blessings from our society. As a result, perhaps we should all have a legal *duty* to enact such a law to protect society and to punish those who would put our society in danger.

Again, however, the 1st Amendment to the US Constitution would not, and should not, allow any such law to stand under our 1st Amendment's principle of separation of church and state. The fact that such a law would be unconstitutional should not mean that Christians have some religious duty to oppose the 1st Amendment and even to seek to change it so we could then legally require the exclusive worship by everyone in society of the one true Christian God. Most Christians probably would oppose, or at least they *should* oppose, a law such as this, even if that law were to fully comport with the Second Commandment of the Bible not to worship any gods, or to put any false gods, before the one true Christian God.

Chapter Seventy-Four

Commandments III, IV, and V

Exodus 20

[7] Thou shalt not take the name of the LORD thy God in vain; for the LORD will not hold him guiltless that taketh his name in vain.

Again, the same 1st Amendment separation of church and state concerns would be present if a law prohibited taking the Lord's name in vain. Would such a law also include Allah's name, or would it not because Christians do not consider Allah to really be God? There might be some public contexts in which "swearing" (using offensive curse words) over the airwaves should not be allowed under our civil laws, but even in such cases, we currently have no laws prohibiting someone from yelling, "Jesus!" if they are angry. Imagine the reaction if we passed a law making it a crime to take Allah's name in vain—would there be any fundamentalist Christians asserting the 1st Amendment's separation of church and state to strike down such a law? Yes, and rightly so.

It is not that I am in favor of cursing or taking the Lord's name in vain in a very rude and disrespectful way as a personal matter, but I would oppose the enactment of a law to enforce that commandment as an official part of our legal system. It is just not the proper subject matter for a law in a pluralistic democratic republic that is *not* a theocracy such as the former Taliban-run Afghanistan.

Exodus 20

[8] Remember the sabbath day, to keep it holy.
[9] Six days shalt thou labour, and do all thy work:
[10] But the seventh day is the sabbath of the LORD thy God: in it thou shalt not do any work, thou, nor thy son, nor thy daughter, thy manservant, nor thy maidservant, nor thy cattle, nor thy stranger that is within thy gates:
[11] For in six days the LORD made heaven and earth, the sea, and all that in them is, and rested the seventh day: wherefore the LORD blessed the sabbath day, and hallowed it.

The same 1st Amendment separation of church and state concerns mentioned before probably should also prohibit us from enacting this commandment into law. Traditionally, however, there actually have been many "blue laws" in America requiring stores to be closed on Sundays. Many of those laws have now been held unconstitutional, or have been repealed, or remain on the books but are no longer enforced. Although some of them remain on the books and are enforced, the trend has been toward repeal or toward declaring them unconstitutional. The rationale for these laws often is suspect, such as a New Jersey law making the sale of cars on Sunday illegal but allowing for the sale of motorcycles on the same day, or closing brick-and-mortar stores on Sundays but not prohibiting all Internet sales on Sunday, or—my favorite—not being able to sell beer or hard alcohol on Sundays, which only seems to have had the effect of forcing people to stock up on their weekend alcohol stash on Fridays or Saturdays.

Even when we have tried to pass laws that indirectly support one of the Ten Commandments, it has not really worked out probably as it was intended, even if such laws were not directly unconstitutional. Maybe we should think of the Ten Commandments as instructions from God regarding our *personal* relationships with God, rather than forcing them—or at least most of them—onto other people through our legal system.

Exodus 20

[12] Honour thy father and thy mother: that thy days may be long upon the land which the LORD thy God giveth thee.

We also have no current laws that have tried to make the violation of this particular commandment a crime or the basis for a civil suit. Imagine someone being sued for dishonoring her parents by not calling or visiting them enough! Although I personally support the notion that we should honor our parents as a religious matter (and my mom and dad are worthy of honor, as I bet most people feel that way about their parents), it would be silly, as well as unrealistic public policy, to attempt to enact a law requiring citizens to honor their parents. Such a law probably would be struck down as "void for vagueness" because there are simply too many ways to define honoring one's parents to punish anyone for not honoring their parents. It is one thing to have the religious belief that we should generally try to honor our parents, but it is quite another thing to pass a law attempting to enforce that religious commandment on all citizens. The point, again, is that one should be able to simultaneously support a religious commandment to honor one's parents personally while still opposing any legal attempt to enact that religious commandment as an official law for all of society.

The Commandment also says that we should honor our parents so that our "days may be long," to live on the land that *God gave us,* although it appears that God was only talking here to the Jews, His chosen people. With that in mind, what if I honored my parents, but only because I wanted to live a long life—should that still count? If so, why would God reward that selfish calculation, and why did God give that as a reason to honor one's parents in the first place? Shouldn't one honor one's parents because it is the right thing to do and because someone loves their parents anyway and also loves God and wants to obey Him, *not* simply because one gets a longevity reward *in exchange* for doing so? This kind of selfish calculation goes to the ultimate question—do I believe in God because I really believe in Him, or is it just because I do not want to risk burning in Hell—kind of like having an eternal fire insurance policy?

Chapter Seventy-Five

Commandment VI

Exodus 20

[13] Thou shalt not kill.

We finally come to one of the Ten Commandments that most of us would agree should be enacted into an official law of society! Note, however, that we already are halfway through the Ten Commandments—which only underscores the point that we do not, and should not, enact *all* religious pronouncements in the Bible into official public, secular laws. Although laws not allowing stores to open on Sundays exist or have existed, there is not widespread agreement that those should be the law, at least not to the same extent that there is agreement that there should be a law making murder a crime. It is a simple point, but to the extent that we justify laws as necessary and/or reasonable, it should be because there are otherwise good legal, social, economic, and/or political reasons to do so. Just because something is in the Bible does not mean that there ought to be a corresponding public law to enforce it. Not *all* biblical pronouncements should be enacted into law. We do not pass laws just because something might be considered a sin in the Qur'an, either. In this instance of "thou shalt not kill," however, I agree that there are good secular political and legal reasons in addition to the religious and moral concerns to be opposed to murder and to make it a crime.

If we take this commandment as literally written, however, note that it states that we should not kill, period. It has no exceptions or degrees of possible justification. As stated earlier, certainly, there must be some kind of exceptions, such as self-defense, defense of others, killing in war if the war is "justified," killing as punishment (if the death penalty is justified), and others, but no such exceptions or limitations are mentioned here.

This makes one wonder about something like hunting, or even fishing—the killing of animals for sport. Are hunting and fishing sins because the Bible says we should not *kill*? Do Christian fundamentalist hunters who legally fight for their right to bear arms under our 2nd Amendment to the US Constitution think that the 2nd Amendment trumps their adherence to the literal words of the Sixth Commandment if they kill animals for mere sport with their constitutionally protected guns? Of course, "kill" may not mean, as a religious matter, that God does not want for us to kill insects in our homes or kill plants or kill germs, although it literally says, "Thou shalt not *kill*." If we go just by what it says here, then perhaps God actually does mean for us *not* to kill anything, ever. If that literal interpretation is not the correct interpretation of the word "kill," then what *should* be the correct interpretation? Does it mean only that we should not kill *humans*? If so, it does not say that specifically; it instead requires our own interpretation. Whatever "kill" may mean, it requires us to look deeper into the underlying meaning rather than just doing a superficial, literal interpretation of the actual words used in the text—but wouldn't that involve improper "private, subjective interpretation"? Is that bad, or is that in this instance good, given these circumstances?

Chapter Seventy-Six

God, Guns, and Gays: Does "No Killing" Also Mean "No Guns"?

Some conservative fundamentalists in the United States have lately been very motivated to vote in national elections by, among other things, the political issues surrounding "God, guns, and gays." With respect just to the "God and guns" part, in light of the staunch conservative resistance to "gun control" and the seemingly unwavering support for the 2nd Amendment right for private citizens to bear arms, I am curious whether fundamentalists really believe that Jesus would want for us all to have our own guns and to be willing to use them if necessary (whatever "if necessary" may mean). If Jesus would really want for us all to have guns, I wonder if fundamentalists also think that our society should become like that of the "wild, wild West," where people would carry guns in their holsters, ready to draw if anyone ever got out of line. Do fundamentalists really believe that there would be less gun violence in America if *everyone* carried around a loaded gun ready to use? For example, would the mass killings committed by the heavily-armed gunmen such as those in the Aurora, Colorado; Ft. Hood, Texas; Virginia Tech; Columbine High School, and Tucson, Arizona massacres have not occurred, or would have been mitigated, if the shooting victims in those incidents would have also had guns to shoot back at their attackers?

Somehow, arguing that Jesus wants for us all to carry guns around, maybe even in holsters, and be ready to draw seems rather farfetched, at best. I am unaware of any verse in the Bible supporting that proposition. So are we supposed to trust and believe in Jesus, but, in the event that our faith in God may not be enough to keep us safe, also be "packin' heat"—you know, just in case we need to shoot or threaten to shoot somebody? Fundamentalists who also believe we should all be able to carry guns must think that Jesus's teachings about turning the other cheek (Matthew 5:39), being meek (Ephesians 4:2), and loving your enemies (Matthew 5:44) are really just a bunch of "wimpy" liberal guidelines that have no place in the real world.

If owning guns is truly part of God's plan for our lives, why didn't Jesus, or any of His disciples, ever carry around swords for their own protection? After all, swords were the weaponry at that time in history. Even if Jesus wasn't armed Himself, because He is God and therefore didn't really need a sword to protect Himself, His disciples were not God, so why didn't they always carry arms for protection? Although Peter once drew a sword to protect Jesus, in Matthew 26:52, Jesus told Peter to put the sword down, and went on to say " . . . for all they that take the sword shall perish with the sword," which hardly seems like any kind of positive endorsement of bearing arms. If their protection was Jesus, such that their faith was enough to keep them safe, why isn't faith in Jesus enough for all of us in modern times? Why do we now also need arms if Jesus's disciples did not need arms? Can't God keep us safe?

Also, in 1787, when our founders wrote the 2nd Amendment as a part of the Bill of Rights to the US Constitution, the arms available were flintlock single-action muskets that were not capable of easily taking out an entire crowd the way modern firearms can, so this presents yet another interpretation problem. As technology progresses, why should we stop at swords or handguns? If there is a right to bear arms (ignoring for just a moment the part of the 2nd Amendment that talks about having a "well-regulated militia," suggesting that the right to bear arms may have been simply a way for the *states*, not just the *federal* government, to be able to maintain armed militias), why limit the *scope and power* of the arms to which we all have a personal constitutional right? In other words, where is the reasonable stopping point of the arms to which we are all entitled? This is a 2nd Amendment issue as well as a biblical issue. If Jesus thinks it is a good idea for me to have a gun, why wouldn't Jesus love the idea of me owning my own bazooka, my own rocket launcher, or my own tank? What about a flame-thrower? That would be cool. Or how about having my own remote-controlled predator drone? But maybe those kinds of weapons should be owned and operated *only* by, to use a 2nd Amendment term, a "well-regulated militia," so perhaps only military armies and police forces should have such arms, and not private citizens, who might get angry in a fight and use them mistakenly or irresponsibly, not to mention what an evil mad man might do. Do I have a right to any weapon, as long as I can carry it in my hands—is that what to "bear arms" means?

If not just professionals should bear these bigger arms and we all should bear any and all arms we prefer, then why not say that all of us should be able to own our own nuclear weapons? Although some people might exclaim, "Now that would be going too far," why would that be too far? Is it because certain arms would be *too* dangerous to allow private citizens to have pursuant to their 2nd Amendment right to bear arms? So, perhaps there is a constitutional right to bear arms, but only those arms that can easily kill "only" *a few* people at a time but if an arm can easily kill *a lot* of people all at once, there should be no right to bear such an arm because it would be "too dangerous." Should that be the meaningful stopping point for the types of arms that we have a right to bear, or should any citizen be allowed to own any arm, no matter what that arm might be, as it is very difficult to make a distinction between an arm that is "dangerous," as opposed to an arm that is "*too* dangerous"?

Of course, we can always go to the other extreme and just ban *all* guns in every situation, but if we do that, someone might say, "Alright, but if we outlaw all guns, then we have to outlaw all kitchen knives, too, because they can be used to kill someone, as well as all hammers, shovels, and baseball bats!" Such a sweeping law can't be right, however, as that would clearly go too far. So maybe there is something to the old pro-gun mantra, "Guns don't kill people, people do;" because often, people kill other people with whatever they can find, including their own bare hands. That argument makes a fair point, demonstrating that everything regarding the types of arms that citizens should be able to own is just a question of degree and of "acceptable" risk.

Drawing a distinction between acceptable and unacceptable risk may work well at the extremes—for example, we probably can and should risk private citizens owning knives (as there are many useful, nonlethal reasons to allow citizens to own knives), but it would be an unacceptable risk to allow private citizens to own their own nuclear weapons (after all, what would be the useful, nonlethal reason for having such a profoundly lethal weapon—perhaps to kill weeds…a *lot* of weeds?). If a person used a rocket launcher to take out a city block, killing hundreds of people, however, would we still say, "Rocket launchers don't kill people, people do"? Maybe, but rocket launchers sure make killing many people at once a whole lot easier, so perhaps citizens should not have such easy access to such powerful weapons—a "reasonable" right to bear some arms, but not really destructive military ones with thousands and thousands of rounds of ammunition.

Unfortunately, the overall point about the difficulty in attempting to draw a meaningful bright line of distinction inside of a spectrum of choices remains stubbornly apparent. The extreme example (kitchen knives versus nuclear weapons) presents a fairly easy call to make, but where do we draw a workable and meaningful dividing line? At what exact point do we cross over from arms for citizens that pose "acceptable risks" (knives) to arms for citizens that pose "unacceptable risks" (nukes)? A bright line of distinction is not defined in the Bible, nor is it defined in the US Constitution, and anyone trying to define that line would be engaging in his or her own private interpretation informed by his or her own subjective opinions and personal values.

Complicating this issue even further is that the precise amount of "acceptable risk" we should allow is probably a moving target (pun intended). Some would argue that as technology marches on and our armament capabilities advance accordingly, Jesus would want for us to "keep up with the times" by arming ourselves with the very same powerful modern weaponry with which criminals and terrorists are arming themselves. As a result, would that mean that we should have a "reasonable" right to bear arms *in light of the times and changing technological and historical circumstances*? If so, where does the Bible (or the US Constitution) specifically make such a claim? If it is merely implied, how are we to interpret such an implication in everyday situations? If there is such a verse in the Bible, implied or otherwise, aren't there far more verses in the Bible that would suggest that Jesus would *not* want all of His children to walk around fully armed, especially with the latest technological weapons and firepower, to be able to threaten or to actually harm or even kill each other?

Maybe it is very unfair to criticize the Bible's lack of a clear answer to a very modern problem (the right to bear arms), that is even further complicated by ever-changing technology, which fundamentally alters the very nature of available arms and weaponry. Moreover, although there are other modern contexts that the Bible does not address, that absence probably does not mean that the Bible should be considered antithetical to all things modern or that the Bible lacks modern applicability. I discount here negative things people have said in the past about what they think the Bible would say about all modern inventions, such as "If man were meant to fly, God would have given him wings," but there are more legitimate questions and concerns.

For example, the Bible does not say that we should all wear seatbelts in cars or wear sunscreen when exposed to the sun for long periods, even though we probably should generally do those things. I cannot think of any biblical verse that would suggest otherwise, despite the fact that seatbelts and sunscreen are not specifically mentioned or suggested in the Bible, given the historical context. Although some might say that if it is God's will that one has a car accident or gets skin cancer, then we should not to try to alter God's will with our technology, I can imagine Jesus telling His disciples to wear seatbelts if they were ever in cars or to wear sunscreen if they ever were to spend all day at the beach, much more easily than I can imagine Jesus telling His followers to always carry around loaded guns, ready to use—especially big guns with a lot of modern firepower to counter that of modern criminals and terrorists. Would Jesus reasonably limit His desire for us to own guns to our being able to carry around only *unloaded* guns, or would having to take precious time to load the guns violate our 2nd Amendment rights (and His plans for us) to be able to thwart crime or to protect ourselves in emergency circumstances? How about allowing guns but not silencers on guns because a silencer's only purpose is to conceal the use of a gun; would prohibiting silencers therefore be a reasonable limit on gun ownership that is not protected by the 2nd Amendment (or what Jesus would want)? So, is there a constitutional right to reasonable guns, or is there only a constitutional right to *loud* reasonable guns? What about children owning guns, mental patients owning guns, former felons owning guns, why are those regulations not considered to be violations of the 2nd Amendment right to bear arms? Would Jesus think those laws were unreasonable limitations? If criminals can wear bullet-proof vests, does that mean that we should have a right to buy armor-piercing, "hollow-point," "cop-killer" bullets? If so, where does it end? Is it really God's will that we engage in a citizens' arms race to possess ever more powerful weaponry?

I am not trying to be radically extreme and completely anti-gun here. I am not saying that Jesus would not believe in self-defense or hunting or target practice, necessarily, or even the ability to threaten someone with a gun in order to deter someone from committing violence. I admit that if my family were threatened, I would rather have a gun to protect them than not have a gun. God probably does approve of such uses of guns, I would imagine, but where does it specifically *say* that, *definitively,* in the Bible? Should my personal desire to have a gun if I am afraid be the standard we use to formulate overall gun policy in the United States? If the Bible either explicitly or implicitly suggests that God would so approve of guns, how and why is that not contradicted by other literal verses in the Bible about nonviolence?

This "Does Jesus really want me to have a gun?" issue seems to require a great deal of very involved, subjective private interpretation, and even pure conjecture, about what Jesus might think about Americans owning guns, or hand grenades, for that matter. How do we literally interpret Jesus's statements about peace in the Bible in light of this concern about the right to bear arms? Often, the very difficult thing about asking "What would Jesus do?" is that we have no idea what Jesus would do and we ought not to pretend like we do as a simple matter of literal interpretation of the Bible. What in the world Jesus would do in any number of certain specific, unique, and entirely modern circumstances cannot always definitively be discerned from biblical verses, so would anyone's guess here about Jesus's overall gun policy necessarily be better than anyone else's guess?

I admit that I do not know, and I do not think anyone else knows, either. Still, my personal guess is that Jesus probably does *not* want for us all to walk around with loaded, or even unloaded, guns. Besides, how safe would we really be if we all had guns pointed at one another? Does mutually assured destruction (MAD) work? MAD works if entire countries or nation-states, such as the United States and the old Soviet Union, are involved in détente, have a sufficient self-interested incentive to live, and are not willing to engage in a nuclear war for some political cause. In contrast, détente in which every citizen is fully armed personally would not work unless every single citizen is a rational actor with a greater self-interested incentive to live than to die, is not a sociopath, and is not subject to making a mistake or ever exercising bad or overly emotional judgment. That, however, seems highly unlikely, especially for more than 315 million Americans; indeed, if MAD did work, we never would have had a gun fight in the Old West or a duel anywhere else! People often assume that they would survive. Recall what the Romans eventually realized about themselves: "We came, we saw, we conquered, but in the end, the enemy was us." Or perhaps even more fitting, "if you live by the sword, you die by the sword" (as gun-owners are more likely to be harmed by guns than non-gun owners).

Assuming, just for a moment, that Jesus does *not* want for us all to have guns (not that He necessarily thinks that, but just assume for the moment, for the sake of this argument, that He does), should all Christians work to repeal the 2nd Amendment to the US Constitution because it would be contrary to the biblical teaching that not all citizens should have their own guns? I don't think so, even if that is what the Bible said. There may be good policy reasons to either limit gun ownership or not limit gun ownership, but we probably should separate our personal religious beliefs from our legal public policy choices. We should decide political and religious issues each within their own sphere, because, again, we do not live in a theocracy. What if the government ruled that churches have to teach both creation and evolution to "teach the controversy"? Fortunately, that would and should never happen, because we live in a constitutional democracy, with a constitutional right to freely and privately exercise our own religions. The government therefore should stay out of the church and the church should stay out of government, unless Sunday schools have to start teaching calculus, quantum theory, and even evolution, according to government proclamation.

Chapter Seventy-Seven

Do We Violate the Commandment of "Thou Shall Not Kill" by Allowing Abortion?

Technology allows yet another modern advancement that was not really known in biblical times—a safe, elective abortion. Many fundamentalist Christians believe that abortion should be criminalized. Abortion was illegal in most states in this country until 1973, when the US Supreme Court, in the famous *Roe v. Wade* decision, ruled that a woman's decision to abort her pregnancy, at least during the first trimester, is a guaranteed constitutional privacy right. The court therefore struck down any and all state laws criminalizing first-trimester abortions. The issue of abortion rights continues to be controversial and the subject of much angry political and ethical disagreement in the United States.

Legally, the issue has now become about how far and how extensively the government should be able to regulate abortion services, even if it cannot prohibit all of them outright, at least very early-term abortions. As with the 2nd Amendment right to bear arms, opponents try to regulate the exercise of the right, with the staunchest opponents attempting to regulate the right out of existence. Each court fight is often over the constitutional reach of such regulations.

Although there is widespread disagreement on whether abortion is murder, there is no disagreement that the killing of a human being that already has been born is murder. Some countries, and many US states, further criminalize the abortion of a viable fetus that is near birth, usually if it is done at some late stage in the last trimester of the pregnancy; however, very few countries, and no US states, legally consider an abortion to be murder if it is done fairly early in the pregnancy, well within the first trimester.

The reason many fundamentalist Christians, as well as various other religious groups, consider abortion to be murder is that they believe life begins at the moment of conception. They believe that a complete human life as we know it begins that instantaneous moment when the male sperm permeates the female egg and the process of cell division into a human being begins. A passage in the Bible that is sometimes quoted to support the notion that life begins at conception is Psalms 139:13–16:

> **[13]** For thou hast possessed my reins: thou hast covered me in my mother's womb.
> **[14]** I will praise thee; for I am fearfully and wonderfully made: marvellous are thy works; and that my soul knoweth right well.

[15] My substance was not hid from thee, when I was made in secret, and curiously wrought in the lowest parts of the earth.

[16] Thine eyes did see my substance, yet being unperfect; and in thy book all my members were written, which in continuance were fashioned, when as yet there was none of them.

Also, many Christians would argue that the passage in Exodus 21:22–25 (below) applies not only to infanticide (the killing of a viable late-term fetus, such as a person punching a pregnant woman in the stomach to harm or kill the fetus) but also to abortion done at *any time* during the pregnancy, by either someone committing a physical assault against a pregnant woman, or by the pregnant woman herself, so that both infanticide and abortion would be murder:

[22] If men strive, and hurt a woman with child, so that her fruit depart from her, and yet no mischief follow: he shall be surely punished, according as the woman's husband will lay upon him; and he shall pay as the judges determine.

[23] And if any mischief follow, then thou shalt give life for life,

[24] Eye for eye, tooth for tooth, hand for hand, foot for foot,

[25] Burning for burning, wound for wound, stripe for stripe.

The entirety of the abortion debate as a religious, historical, and public policy matter in this country is well beyond the scope of this book; however, I raise the debate here as an interpretive matter to question whether most Christian fundamentalists actually believe that life begins at the moment of conception and, as a result, that abortion is necessarily the equivalent of murder and should therefore be criminalized. Some fundamentalists, sincere as they are in that belief, do not appear to fully believe all of the related implications of their stated belief.

For example, shouldn't those fundamentalists who believe in the death penalty for premeditated murder also believe in the death penalty for both abortionist doctors *and* any pregnant mother who has chosen to have an abortion? If an abortion is truly a murder of a human being, then along with the abortionist murderer, isn't the pregnant woman also guilty of murder? Wouldn't all health care and/or hospital personnel participating in the abortion also be murder accomplices, and any supportive family and/or friends of the mother? Consider the full implications. Should a mother who wants to murder her child be able to hire a certain type of "hitman" (an abortionist) such that only the "hitman" and not the mother herself, is guilty of the murder? After all, she hired the hitman to commit the murder.

Many fundamentalists do not believe that the mothers of aborted fetuses should be punished so harshly or receive anything near the death penalty. Instead, they tend to focus only on making abortion itself as a medical procedure illegal so it should not be offered by hospitals and health clinics, and perhaps on making the abortionist doctors, at most, the ones who receive any criminal punishment. But if an abortion is really premeditated murder the same as the murder of a two-year-old child by its mother, who has made a premeditated decision to stab the child to death; shouldn't the mothers in both cases receive the same harsh criminal punishment for the same type of premeditated murder of a human life? What could justify this inconsistency in fundamentalist beliefs if they really believe that an abortion is truly the same as, say, the murder of a four year-old child?

An even a more curious inconsistency is when fundamentalists allow an abortion exception in cases of rape and incest. I can appreciate their Christian compassion and understanding for the mother in allowing such an exception, but it raises an important issue. If abortion is murder, then why should it be allowed simply based on the criminal decisions made by the fetus's father before the fetus was ever conceived? If a father raped and impregnated his fourteen-year-old daughter and when their resulting child was one year old, the mother-daughter decided to hire someone to stab their baby to death, would people who believe abortion is murder really say that stabbing a one-year-old to death should be allowed because the mother had been raped by her own father a year and nine months earlier and conceived the child as a result? Why should the method of conception matter so much? Why would it be murder to kill a child if that child's parents had consensual sex but *not* murder to kill a child if that child's father incestuously raped the child's mother? The fact that this inconsistency exists demonstrates that fundamentalists who allow for a rape or incest exception must not really believe their own argument that human life truly begins at conception. If they do believe that life begins at conception but still would allow for abortion in cases of rape or incest, at best, they would have a very seriously flawed, patently unfair, and wholly discriminatory sense of justice, in which it is OK to kill children whose fathers committed sexual crimes against their mothers before the children were ever conceived and born. Understandable compassion for the mother, sympathetic as it is, should not justify murder—should it?

In raising these inconsistencies in the rape/incest exception and the death penalty, it is very disturbing that some fundamentalist extremists would agree that there are indeed inconsistencies and therefore would conclude that they should take some rather extreme, but at least consistent, positions. For instance, they probably would conclude that (1) all pregnant mothers who have abortions should receive the death penalty, (2) abortionist doctors are nothing more than mass murders, and perhaps even (3) abortionist doctors should be hunted down and killed by "defenders" to protect the innocent human life that will be destroyed with every new abortion.

Such extremists actually believe that God would excuse their killing of these doctors in defense of human life, just like God would excuse a soldier fighting in a "just war" trying to resist an actual holocaust or genocide—in this case, the genocide of unborn children. For them, abortionists are evil murders who, just like Adolf Hitler in WWII, must be violently confronted and stopped. It is tragic that such extremists use this logic to justify bombing abortion clinics and killing abortionist doctors, rationalizing that such killing is justified because that is what God would have wanted them to do.

It is also ironic that they see themselves as totally justified religious heroes doing God's work, but they would see the likes of Osama bin Laden and the nineteen hijackers who flew planes into the World Trade Center and the Pentagon on 9/11 as despicable terrorists who kill in the name of their misguided religious beliefs. They see Jihadist terrorists as murderers, despite the terrorists' religious and political views that the "Great Satan," the United States, perpetrates cultural, economic, and militaristic imperialism that has led to the death and misery of many Muslims, who must be avenged as well as defended and protected in the future, in the name of Allah. Isn't it unfortunate when anyone—Christian or Muslim—uses his or her very passionate religious beliefs to justify such violent actions?

I believe that during a pregnancy, the fetus slowly crosses over from *potential* human life to *actual* human life. As such, it is not murder to abort human tissue that is closer to the conception side of the spectrum, where it is still merely *potential* human life. With every passing moment during a pregnancy, however, that fetus is transforming from potential human life over to actual human life, such that it would be murder to terminate a pregnancy much closer to the birth end of the spectrum because the killing of a prematurely born baby not technically in the womb still would be murder. If the moment of conception is an arbitrary point in time to assume that human life begins, so is the moment when the child passes through the birth canal. Instead of some precise instant in time—either conception or birth—I believe that the manner in which a conceived fetus becomes an actual human life is a much slower *process* that takes place over much of the earlier course of a pregnancy. I disagree that it is only at some precise and very brief moment in time, either just after conception or just after birth, that there is suddenly instant human life when there was no human life just a moment, a mere nanosecond, before.

I admit, however, that it is much easier to grapple with the ethical issues involved if we can simply select a precise moment in time when we consider human life to begin and say that anything before that moment in time is not murder but anything just after that moment in time is murder. Ease of administration should not be such a controlling factor in such a deep ethical issue, however. In fact, why not back up the precise moment life begins to even before conception? After all, human eggs and human sperm are also living human tissue, and some Christians say we are spirits that God recognized and was planning for entry into the world even *before* we were ever conceived (Jeremiah 1:5: "Before I [God] formed thee in the belly I knew thee; and before thou camest forth out of the womb I sanctified thee, and I ordained thee a prophet unto the nations").

So why is it not criminally negligent homicide every time a woman has her period instead of making sure that she gets pregnant according to her religious, life-giving duty? Indeed, would it be criminally negligent homicide if a man masturbates and his sperm dies, as he obviously has no intention of impregnating a female's egg pursuant to his religious, life-giving duty? In short, why is it not murder to purposefully let sperm and/or an unfertilized egg die instead of forming a human being? The Catholic Church and other strict literalists historically have opposed birth control, as well as certain sexual acts that are not sexual intercourse, even between heterosexual married couples, to avoid frustrating God's will and the entire, allegedly sole, reason for sex and marriage, in the first place—procreation.

Because the precise moment when live human tissue becomes human life complete with all attendant human rights is not definitive, as a matter of law, the government cannot and should not impose the religious views of some citizens regarding when life begins onto all other citizens as a matter of law. Instead, the government should leave that decision to us, individually, unless and until it becomes legally definitive that a fetus, at any and all stages in a pregnancy, is an actual human life equivalent to that of someone who has already been born. If some people believe that life begins at conception but others have a religious belief that our purpose in life is to procreate, such that if a man and woman do not always join their available eggs and sperm and their actions would thus be criminally negligent homicide, such religious beliefs should not be controlling on the rest of society. We should not pass a law making it illegal to fail to procreate, even though some people would subscribe to that as a personal religious belief.

Finally, although I may see the development of human life more as a slow and ever-changing developmental process over the course of a pregnancy instead of just as an instant moment in time (conception or birth), one could argue that those who believe that life begins at conception also believe that it is a similar process, albeit a much shorter one. For example, what would happen if we had the technology to perform abortions of human eggs at very precise moments in time that constitute very different stages of an egg's conception? Would an abortion of an egg be considered a murder if the sperm had penetrated the egg but no cell division had yet begun? What if the sperm had only begun to penetrate the egg's outer membrane but had not yet penetrated completely—if that partially impregnated egg were to be aborted at that point, would it be murder, or would it be just the removal of human tissue (potential human life, but not yet human life)? What if the sperm had merely *touched* the outside of the egg but had not yet begun to penetrate the egg's outer membrane at all, even though that sperm would do so shortly and would impregnate the egg if left alone? Would it be murder to abort that egg at that point, which would have been merely *touched* by the sperm at that moment? Would an egg touched by a sperm be human life, or would it at that point be only *potential* human life, where the process has just begun?

People who believe that life begins at conception and therefore think that they are necessarily united in that belief might have very different answers to these questions about the process of conception and at what precise moment in time in the process that human life begins, even though conception is a relatively short process. The ethical questions are the same whether the process is very short (the process of the sperm impregnating egg; conception) or much longer (the process of a fetus developing in the womb over the course of the pregnancy). Just as I do not believe that there is no human life at all and then suddenly, a mere instant after conception, there is human life, I do not believe that there is no human life at all and then, a mere instant later after birth, there is suddenly human life. It is very difficult to draw arbitrary lines in a spectrum or in an overall process of constant minute change and development, because a spectrum often is not really conducive to such arbitrary line drawing. That difficulty, however, does not justify the drawing of arbitrary lines to oversimplify the complicated ethical and even scientific and biological issues involved.

This idea brings us back full circle to considering whether we should necessarily enact all of the teachings set forth in the Bible into the secular laws of our society, so let's return to the "God and gays" part of the analysis regarding the legality of same-sex marriages and whether we should try to enact the Ten Commandments into public laws.

Chapter Seventy-Eight

Commandment VII

Exodus 20

[14] Thou shalt not commit adultery.

Christian fundamentalists probably would consider adultery to be as serious a sin as homosexuality, as both of these sins would constitute sex outside of marriage—at least religious heterosexual marriage—so they would consider both adultery and homosexuality to be *sexual* sins. The sin of adultery makes it into the Ten Commandments, however, whereas the sin of homosexuality does not, so maybe adultery is worse? Would the sin of homosexuality in a same-sex marriage still be interpreted as committing adultery because the homosexual people would be cheating on their "true" would-be opposite-sex spouses? It leads to the question of whether Christian fundamentalists would support a law making it a crime to commit adultery, even making convicted offenders exhibit a scarlet letter A, for adultery, perhaps tattooed on their foreheads, as punishment and ridicule for being adulterers. It would be a fitting punishment, as well as a great legal deterrent, so people would not cheat on their spouses. I think at this point in history, however, we might as a society say, "Been there, done that," and because it did not work out so well the first time for Puritans, maybe we should not have such a strict anti-adultery law now, even though in our spiritual home lives, we still might want to personally consider adultery to be a sin.

Perhaps the more fitting analogy would be to ask whether there should be a law against *divorced* heterosexuals being allowed to remarry because in the eyes of God, they *already* would be married to their original spouses and thus would be committing adultery. On people getting divorces (referred to as "putting away" one's spouse), the Bible states in Mark 10:11–12:

> [11] And he [Jesus] saith unto them, Whosoever shall put away his wife, and marry another, committeth adultery against her.
> [12] And if a woman shall put away her husband, and be married to another, she committeth adultery.

So if a state were to allow divorced heterosexuals to get remarried, wouldn't that state be supporting adultery and be "attacking" marriage? If we are really serious about legally "defending marriage," however, why not just make all divorces illegal? That would certainly "defend" marriage! Remember what God said about marriage: "What therefore God hath joined together, let no man put asunder" (Mark 10:9). Another way to interpret these verses is that only bigamy (being married to more than one spouse at a time) is sin. It, of course, all depends on what "putting away" means.

Assuming that people legally should be allowed to get divorces because to do so is not a sin, maybe there still should be a significant legal consequence for getting a divorce. Maybe we should defend marriage by providing that, if a person gets a divorce, that person cannot legally *re*-marry ever again, because that would be allowing someone to have two spouses in the eyes of God. Recall that divorced people would *already* be married in the eyes of the Lord, so if they were to get divorced and then remarried, that might be adultery, and the law should not condone such sinning! Such a law not allowing second marriages (unless a spouse dies) would be quite harsh, however—not to mention providing an awful incentive for people to have their spouses killed so they could legally get out of the marriage and still be able to remarry someday.

Should the commandment against adultery mean that we should not allow divorced people to remarry because they would be committing adultery? The Christian church leaders believed that for centuries—consider King Henry VIII, who worked hard to change that little rule. In a modern context, take, for example, the fact that I am married now but am divorced from my first wife. Also, my father, the pastor, has been married and divorced twice and is now married to his third wife. Neither of us thinks we are cheating on our first (or second) wives just because we got divorced and then remarried, however. Still, I could see some fundamentalists saying that we should only get *one* chance to be married and if we ruin it, that's it, there are no second chances to be married again. Instead, we all would just have to work it out with our one current spouse for life if we really want to be legally married.

Of course, I am not advocating for any public law that would prohibit divorces or that would prohibit divorced people from ever getting remarried, even if they would be laws "in defense of marriage." I am simply pointing out an inconsistency. Most Christian fundamentalists probably would not support a law making adultery a crime, or denying the right of divorced heterosexuals to legally marry other heterosexuals, despite the fact that adultery is considered a sin in the Bible. It is therefore inconsistent to *legally fight* against same-sex marriage because it is considered to be a sin in the Bible but to *not legally fight* against adultery, which is also considered to be a sin in the Bible.

We also should be very careful about what we ask for. If we take the position that, in order to be consistent, we should enact strict laws to make *all* biblical pronouncements into public legal provisions, that action would require us to enact some very objectionable and controversial policies. For example, in the Bible, adulterers (especially if the cheating spouse was a virgin) were actually stoned to death as a punishment, so they were put into pits where fellow citizens would throw stones at them until they were killed by the multiple relentless blows of the rocks or were eventually crushed to death by the totality of the stones (Deuteronomy 22:23–24):

> [23] If a damsel that is a virgin be betrothed unto an husband, and a man find her in the city, and lie with her;
> [24] Then ye shall bring them both out unto the gate of that city, and ye shall stone them with stones that they die; the damsel, because she cried not, being in the city; and the man, because he hath humbled his neighbour's wife: so thou shalt put away evil from among you.

Fortunately, no one today appears to be calling for a return to a legal justice system in which adulterers are actually stoned to death; however, if we are supposed to literally enact God's law into man's law so as to legally enforce the pronouncements in the Bible, there is an inconsistency here. Stoning someone to death, however, would violate the 8th Amendment to the US Constitution, which makes it unconstitutional for the state to engage in cruel and unusual punishment (assuming stoning would be considered cruel and unusual punishment, which I think it would be). So the US Constitution is at odds with the Bible again! Does that mean our founders were a bunch of liberal, God-hating, atheistic progressives because they wrote the 8th Amendment? Hardly; perhaps most instructive for Christians is the fact that Jesus challenged the stoning of a woman who was allegedly caught in the act of committing adultery:

> [3] And the scribes and Pharisees brought unto him [Jesus] a woman taken in adultery; and when they had set her in the midst,
> [4] They say unto him, Master, this woman was taken in adultery, in the very act.
> [5] Now Moses in the law commanded us, that such should be stoned: but what sayest thou?
> [6] This they said, tempting him, that they might have to accuse him. But Jesus stooped down, and with his finger wrote on the ground, as though he heard them not.
> [7] So when they continued asking him, he lifted up himself, and said unto them, He that is without sin among you, let him first cast a stone at her…
> [9] And they which heard it, being convicted by their own conscience, went out one by one, beginning at the eldest, even unto the last: and Jesus was left alone, and the woman standing in the midst. (John 8:3-9)

So the allegedly adulterous woman was not stoned. Perhaps it was because she never actually committed adultery, and that was why Jesus let her go, but the intriguing questions are (1) if she definitely had committed adultery, would Jesus have said she *should be stoned* because she deserved it, and (2) if so, does Jesus want His followers today also to enact laws that would require us to stone adulterers in the town square, and (3) if so, should we now be opposed to any law (like our 8th Amendment) making it unconstitutional to stone adulterers to death in modern society? On second thought, maybe Jesus meant that that we should not enact official public laws based on prohibiting actions that are considered to be sins in the Bible, largely because we are all sinners and therefore, by passing such laws, would be making all citizens criminals, to the extent they are all sinners, which we *all* are. Remember what Jesus said: "He that is without sin among you, let him first cast a stone at her."

Chapter Seventy-Nine

Commandments VIII and IX

Exodus 20

[15] Thou shalt not steal.

Here we have another commandment that most would agree should also be a public secular law, so we are two for eight thus far regarding the Ten Commandments (such that almost everyone would agree that murder and stealing should be criminalized by our laws). I agree that we should have public laws criminalizing murder and theft. In other words, society enacting a law to prohibit stealing makes good sense for secular, political and legal reasons, as well as religious reasons. Again, however, so far, there are only two out of eight Commandments that most people would agree should also be enacted into actual public laws, and six that should not be.

Obviously, atheists would also agree that there should be laws against theft and murder in society, but they would do so for reasons that have nothing to do with the fact that theft and murder are considered sins in the Bible, as well as in many other religious texts, for that matter. I assume that every society in all of the countries in the world prohibits theft and murder. Why would any government anywhere *not* prohibit theft and murder, even if they were not considered sins in the Bible? It is not like atheists support the "right" to be able to steal and murder and therefore argue that we should have no laws prohibiting theft and murder. One might wonder why there is not a commandment against the act of rape, a very violent sexual assault crime; certainly, rape is as bad a sin, or worse than, lying or not going to church on Sundays or being disrespectful to one's parents.

Exodus 20

[16] Thou shalt not bear false witness against thy neighbour.

Certain types of lies should be illegal—such as false advertising, lying in court (perjury), lying to police officers, defrauding investors, to name a few—but it would be silly to make other lies illegal, such as lying to friend that his shoes look good when they are in fact hideous, or lying that one watches only the news or the History Channel on TV, instead of soap operas and reality TV shows. In God's eyes, these are *all* lies and therefore are all sins, but that does not mean that they all should be illegal under our laws, so perhaps some of the commandment should be a part of our secular law, but certainly not in its entirety.

Most importantly, the reasons why only some lies should be illegal while others should not be illegal really have nothing to do with the fact that all lies violate God's law in the Bible. Instead, the reasons have everything to do with secular, legal, political, social, and economic concerns. In short, our laws should be enacted for legal reasons and not because they are either in or not in the Bible or any other religious text.

Perhaps this commandment not to bear false witness is limited, by literal interpretation, only to perjury—giving false-witness testimony in court—because it says not to "bear false witness." Also, it says not to do so "against one's neighbor." Still, it seems that a lie should be deemed a sin, regardless if the lie is in court, out on the street, against one's neighbor, or against anyone else in society. Should I be able to lie to someone who lives in France (and is therefore not my neighbor in a literal sense) and whom I am selling a camera to on the Internet? Am I being "too" literal in asking such a question? Maybe the commandment is stated this way because it is trying to distinguish between "serious" hurtful lies, and less-serious, innocuous "white" lies. Once we put that spin on the matter, however, doesn't it mean we are engaging in improper, personal, subjective interpretation of the text instead of strict literal interpretation? But how are we supposed to figure out what the commandment really means, and how far should we go in making a law enforcing the commandment on society at large?

Chapter Eighty

Commandment X

Exodus 20

[17] Thou shalt not covet thy neighbour's house, thou shalt not covet thy neighbour's wife, nor his manservant, nor his maidservant, nor his ox, nor his ass, nor any thing that is thy neighbour's.

Although this commandment equates human beings—a neighbor's wife, servants (slaves)—with animals and other possessory property, and is boldly sexist as it seems addressed only to men, this is still a pretty left-wing, socialist, communist radical commandment, in at least a certain sense, if we interpret it literally. Perhaps the Bible through this the commandment is instructing us to outlaw greedy, selfish, human systems like capitalism and property rights (except for a man's property rights over his wife, slaves and animals), because, as the Bible seems to suggest here, greed and envy are *not* good! All kidding aside, this is a great example of how conservative Christians, who would otherwise say that we should make God's law into man's law, make a completely different decision when it comes to "the rich." When Jesus says that we should part with all of our wealth and give it to the poor because our treasure is really in heaven, those teachings are somehow deemed as not intended by God to be taken literally. Parting with one's wealth and giving it all over to the poor must be completely voluntary, they would say, because Jesus does not expect us to pass socialistic laws that require such confiscatory wealth redistribution! Jesus is not a socialist, or a communist, Heaven forbid!

These very strong supporters of interpreting the Bible literally and making public laws out of those teachings suddenly seem to switch gears rather quickly and say things like "We cannot legislate morality" and as a result, "We shouldn't even try, even if it is in the Bible!" Thus, some biblical sins should also be legally prohibited (especially ones that a fundamentalist might *not* engage in—like homosexuality, if the fundamentalist is not really a closet homosexual), while other biblical sins should NOT also be prohibited (because a fundamentalist might engage in those sins, so it should be a personal religious matter—like greed and keeping all of one's wealth and money). When it comes to wealth, they seem to believe that a person's wealth is really not a gift from God but something entirely and completely earned, without anyone's help, even God's, and therefore that person should have no legal responsibility to share it with anyone else, especially some "lazy welfare cheats").

That seems quite duplicitous. These type of fundamentalists appear to believe that we should enforce the teachings of the Bible literally, and legally, *except* when Jesus says really outrageous liberal, radical, socialistic, wealth-redistribution kind of stuff, like telling us to sell everything we have and give it to the poor to be close to God, or that we must care for and love our fellow human beings more than ourselves and share what we have with them, or that we need to understand that it is virtually impossible for a rich man to enter Heaven unless he is willing to part with all of his wealth. Why is a strict literal interpretation of these kinds of teachings not warranted; and why shouldn't they be enacted into law? There is no ignoring the fact that Jesus reportedly said to sell everything and give it to the poor, so shouldn't we work to pass various laws that would enforce those social welfare concerns as laws in society? Why does that not legally rate with the passage in Leviticus about a man not lying with another man?

> [17] …Good Master, what shall I [the young rich man] do that I may inherit eternal life?
> [18] And Jesus said unto him, Why callest thou me good? there is none good but one, that is, God. (Mark 10:17–18)

Just as a quick interesting interpretation issue, it seems as though Jesus is *not* claiming here that He is God. Jesus is humble to be sure, but if He is God, why would He deny being God and make a distinction between Himself and God? Obviously Christians believe Jesus is God, but that is not what it literally says here. We know God cannot lie, so wasn't Jesus lying here if He is God but claims not to be God? If He is not lying here, is He really saying that He is *not* God? Why would Jesus admit that He was really not good if it were not true? In any event, Jesus then tells the man what the man must do to be saved:

> [19] Thou knowest the commandments, Do not commit adultery, Do not kill, Do not steal, Do not bear false witness, Defraud not, Honour thy father and mother.
> [20] And he answered and said unto him, Master, all these have I observed from my youth. (Mark 10:19–20)

So the young man wanting to be saved is saying to Jesus that he has indeed obeyed God's laws always and has followed all of God's commandments as instructed from his youth. Jesus says that such is not enough, so the young man wants to know *what else* he must do, and Jesus informs him that he still lacks something *very important* in his life that he needs to do:

> [21] Then Jesus…said unto him, One thing thou lackest: go thy way, sell whatsoever thou hast, and give to the poor, and thou shalt have treasure in heaven: and come, take up the cross, and follow me.
> [22] And he was sad at that saying, and went away grieved: for he had great possessions.
> [23] And Jesus looked round about, and saith unto his disciples, How hardly shall they that have riches enter into the kingdom of God!

[24] And the disciples were astonished at his words. But Jesus answereth again, and saith unto them, Children, how hard is it for them that trust in riches to enter into the kingdom of God!

[25] It is easier for a camel to go through the eye of a needle, than for a rich man to enter into the kingdom of God. (Mark 10:21–25)

Was this teaching by Jesus really just a big load of liberal, progressive class warfare and class-envy that culminated in an improper call for socialistic wealth redistribution from the hard-working rich down to the lazy, undeserving poor? Certain conservative Republicans seem to be as astonished as the disciples were that Jesus would make such statements about needing to give all of one's wealth to the poor. Could Jesus really have been serious about His teachings *as a legal and public policy matter*? If not, can we just ignore these teachings of Jesus as mere vague benevolent yearnings for our fellow human beings and yet still regard other religious teachings as things the government should pass into law?

It would appear that many seem to forget, or just ignore, the social and political context in which Jesus grew up in the very poor town of Nazareth. That context informed part of the reason for His teachings that seem to be based, at least in part, on the human suffering and injustice He likely witnessed during his life. Jesus grew up as an indigent laborer and carpenter in a poor family, under the very cruel and oppressive regime of the Roman occupation of Israel and Palestine. Jesus saw increasing urbanization and a growing working underclass subject to the oppression of the Roman occupation and control of Jewish lands and wealth through onerous taxes and confiscation of property where a political democracy was not known. Jesus also saw Jewish elders and priests who had to cut deals with the Romans to maintain their power in the temple and their privileged religious, political, and economic positions as long as they could help keep control of common Jews. Jesus would leave for the town of Capernaum, a poor fishing village, to launch a very different movement of forgiveness and salvation; it would be an entire new religion and belief system, as He took up the cause of John the Baptist. John the Baptist was at the time preaching in the wilderness and baptizing in the name of the coming Savior. John the Baptist was beheaded by the Romans just a few years before Jesus was crucified, for both of them represented a massive political, economic, and, most importantly, religious threat to the Romans and, to some extent, to the Jewish high priests who had privileged positions under the Romans (just like lords and viceroys under feudalism, or our own colonial system).

Jesus's advice to the rich man is quite radical and very demanding, but only if we take it *literally*. Because it is in the Bible, does it mean we should enact this wealth redistribution from the rich to the poor into actual law to be consistent with what it says in Leviticus about homosexuality and the implications for opposing same-sex marriage? It seems clear that Christian fundamentalists, especially politically conservative ones, would say a very resounding, *"No!"* Instead of enacting these particular wealth-redistribution teachings into law, these fundamentalists seem to believe that we should just think of Jesus's teachings here as mere voluntary guidelines of charity in our personal lives. Jesus is really nice, but, c'mon, He's God, and we are just humans; certainly, we should not be *legally required* to do such charitable things as a matter of law. Rather, we should be charitable only if we really want to do so in our personal lives and occasionally give to the charities of our own choosing (as long as we can also write those donations off as tax breaks, which of course, should be the law)—but it all has to be voluntary, not legally required.

OK, but does God really allow us to pick and choose this way between biblical teachings regarding what should be enforced officially as law and what is merely personal choice? I support that what is in the Bible should *all* be a personal religious matter and that if we enact any laws, even laws that I personally might favor, such as safety-net social-welfare laws for the poor, the sick, the elderly, single mothers and children, and so on, and universal health care, we should do so, but only if we can fully justify doing so on secular political, economic, social, and legal grounds, irrespective of whether they may be mentioned in the Bible. That is being consistent.

I am therefore not arguing that we should enact Jesus's teachings into law but *only* when they are liberal, and relegate His teachings to mere metaphors and voluntary guidelines that should *not* be enacted into law when they are conservative. If I were to argue that, such would be inconsistent. It is thus equally inconsistent when conservative Christian fundamentalists would support enacting biblical teachings into law, but *only* when those teachings are conservative, and then relegate biblical teachings to mere metaphors and guidelines that should *not* be enacted into law when those teachings are liberal. Still, what should we make of Jesus telling his followers that they must take care of Him in a social-welfare kind of manner just as they should take care of a complete stranger who is not Jesus?

> **[35]** [Jesus said] For I was an hungred, and ye gave me meat: I was thirsty, and ye gave me drink: I was a stranger, and ye took me in:
> **[36]** Naked, and ye clothed me: I was sick, and ye visited me: I was in prison, and ye came unto me.
> **[37]** Then shall the righteous answer him, saying, Lord, when saw we thee an hungred, and fed thee? or thirsty, and gave thee drink?
> **[38]** When saw we thee a stranger, and took thee in? or naked, and clothed thee?
> **[39]** Or when saw we thee sick, or in prison, and came unto thee?
> **[40]** And the King shall answer and say unto them, Verily I say unto you, *Inasmuch as ye have done it unto one of the least of these my brethren, ye have done it unto me.*
> **[41]** Then shall he say also unto them on the left hand, Depart from me, ye cursed, into everlasting fire, prepared for the devil and his angels:
> **[42]** For I was an hungred, and ye gave me no meat: I was thirsty, and ye gave me no drink:

[43] I was a stranger, and ye took me not in: naked, and ye clothed me not: sick, and in prison, and ye visited me not.

[44] Then shall they also answer him, saying, Lord, when saw we thee an hungred, or athirst, or a stranger, or naked, or sick, or in prison, and did not minister unto thee?

[45] Then shall he answer them, saying, Verily I say unto you, *Inasmuch as ye did it not to one of the least of these, ye did it not to me.*

[46] And these shall go away into everlasting punishment: but the righteous into life eternal. (emphasis added) (Matthew 25:35-46)

Jesus completely identifies with the poor here and commands His followers to treat the hungry, the thirsty, the immigrant, the sick, the naked, the imprisoned, the needy, and so on, as if Jesus Himself, God, were also in such need. Accordingly, if we are truly Christians, we should not ignore a stranger in need. Jesus teaches that if we ignore such people, we do so at our own eternal peril in Hell. This is a very serious matter; however, I wonder if Jesus would tell us that His teachings here are *not as important* as the passages in Leviticus about homosexuality. Does Jesus really want for us to engage in our own selective enforcement of biblical teachings into public law? Recall that the only time we ever see Jesus enraged with anger and engage in violent behavior in the Bible is when He witnessed the money changers in the church and those who were defiling the temple by selling animals for sacrifices in it as well:

[15] And they come to Jerusalem: and Jesus went into the temple, and began to cast out them that sold and bought in the temple, and overthrew the tables of the moneychangers, and the seats of them that sold doves;

[16] And would not suffer that any man should carry any vessel through the temple.

[17] And he taught, saying unto them, Is it not written, My house shall be called of all nations the house of prayer? but ye have made it a den of thieves.

[18] And the scribes and chief priests heard it, and sought how they might destroy him: for they feared him, because all the people was astonished at his doctrine.

[19] And when even was come, he went out of the city. (Mark 11:15–19)

Jesus seems to have a much bigger problem with capitalism than with socialism, as He turned over the tables of the money changers and animal sellers and kicked them all out. Why did He refer to what they were doing as making His house of prayer into a den of thieves? Why did Jesus equate what they were doing with thievery? Jesus also said, "Take heed, and beware of covetousness: for a man's life consisteth not in the abundance of the things which he possesseth" (Luke 12:15).

How far can we pursue this line of inquiry? Imagine if one were to suggest that our entire banking, financial lending, and credit system should be abolished because it is all based on a sin according to the Bible. There are certainly those who might welcome such a suggestion, such as the Occupy Wall Street folks of 2011, but can you imagine how some conservative Christians would label such people—communists or socialists committed to anarchy who want to destroy America—and that would be if they were being nice. Former presidential candidate and longtime conservative warrior Newt Gingrich suggested that the "hippie-looking" protesters should "take a bath" and then "get over it." I wonder if Newt Gingrich would have also told Jesus and His long-haired, sandal-wearing disciples to go take a bath and just get over it.

Still, the Bible calls the lending of money with interest—*any* amount of interest—usury. Under our current banking laws, however, the term "usury" has come to mean the lending of money with interest, but only when that interest rate *exceeds a certain amount*. For example, Merriam-Webster (http://www.merriam-webster.com/dictionary) defines "usury" as

> **1** archaic: interest, **2**: the lending of money with an interest charge for its use; especially: the lending of money at exorbitant interest rates. **3**: an unconscionable or exorbitant rate or amount of interest; specifically: interest in excess of a legal rate charged to a borrower for the use of money

The Bible makes no such exception or allowance, saying that *all* lending with *any* interest (not just high interest) is wrong and is called usury. That was the **1** "archaic" definition, whereas the modern definition came to be exorbitant interest (**2** and **3** above). Take these passages, for example:

> If thou lend money to any of my people that is poor by thee, thou shalt not be to him as an usurer, neither shalt thou lay upon him usury. (Exodus 22:25)

> Take thou no usury of him, or increase: but fear thy God; that thy brother may live with thee. (Leviticus 25:36)

> Thou shalt not give him thy money upon usury, nor lend him thy victuals for increase. (Leviticus 25:37)

> Thou shalt not lend upon usury to thy brother; usury of money, usury of victuals, usury of any thing that is lent upon usury. (Deuteronomy 23:19)

For 1,500 years, the Christian church completely banned the charging of interest—so was the church right or wrong for doing so for all of that time? Of course, by the 19th century, these restrictions on lending by Christians were no longer enforced or acknowledged, as the ban then began to morph into the present-day usage of "usury"—the charging of interest at an *excessively high rate* and thereby exploiting someone's financial need. In 1931, Pope Pius XI said, "The free market, of its own nature, concentrates power in those who are anti-social, in those who fight most violently and give least heed to their conscience."

The *only* exception in the Bible to the lending of money with interest as a sin is if one lends with interest *to a foreigner*! But this just raises another troubling aspect about the Bible. Apparently, the lending of money with interest is a sin, as it is "greedy," it represents "unearned" income (no labor, the money did the "work"), and it takes advantage of people in need of a loan. Even though lending is a sin, however, the Bible also says that it is perfectly fine to commit this sin against strangers and thereby discriminate against some of God's other children, so an act that is a sin is really only a sin when done against certain arbitrary groupings of human beings but perfectly fine when done against other arbitrary groupings of humans? Shouldn't sins be sins in all cases? Deuteronomy 23:20 states, "Unto a stranger thou mayest lend upon usury; but unto thy brother thou shalt not lend upon usury: that the LORD thy God may bless thee in all that thou settest thine hand to in the land whither thou goest to possess it."

There are other similar interesting financial issues in the Bible. Deuteronomy 15:1–11 orders the cancellation of all debts at the end of every seventh year:

[1] At the end of every seven years thou shalt make a release.

[2] And this is the manner of the release: Every creditor that lendeth ought unto his neighbour shall release it; he shall not exact it of his neighbour, or of his brother; because it is called the LORD's release.

[3] Of a foreigner thou mayest exact it again: but that which is thine with thy brother thine hand shall release;

[4] Save when there shall be no poor among you; for the LORD shall greatly bless thee in the land which the LORD thy God giveth thee for an inheritance to possess it:

[5] Only if thou carefully hearken unto the voice of the LORD thy God, to observe to do all these commandments which I command thee this day.

[6] For the LORD thy God blesseth thee, as he promised thee: and thou shalt lend unto many nations, but thou shalt not borrow; and thou shalt reign over many nations, but they shall not reign over thee.

[7] If there be among you a poor man of one of thy brethren within any of thy gates in thy land which the LORD thy God giveth thee, thou shalt not harden thine heart, nor shut thine hand from thy poor brother:

[8] But thou shalt open thine hand wide unto him, and shalt surely lend him sufficient for his need, in that which he wanteth.

[9] Beware that there be not a thought in thy wicked heart, saying, The seventh year, the year of release, is at hand; and thine eye be evil against thy poor brother, and thou givest him nought; and he cry unto the LORD against thee, and it be sin unto thee.

[10] Thou shalt surely give him, and thine heart shall not be grieved when thou givest unto him: because that for this thing the LORD thy God shall bless thee in all thy works, and in all that thou puttest thine hand unto.

> **[11]** For the poor shall never cease out of the land: therefore I command thee, saying, Thou shalt open thine hand wide unto thy brother, to thy poor, and to thy needy, in thy land.

This would be a great law if enacted, by the way, for my wife's bankruptcy law practice, as it would provide to her government guaranteed clients into the future! But I digress. God also said,

> **[19]** When thou cuttest down thine harvest in thy field, and hast forgot a sheaf in the field, thou shalt not go again to fetch it: it shall be for the stranger, for the fatherless, and for the widow: that the LORD thy God may bless thee in all the work of thine hands.
> **[20]** When thou beatest thine olive tree, thou shalt not go over the boughs again: it shall be for the stranger, for the fatherless, and for the widow.
> **[21]** When thou gatherest the grapes of thy vineyard, thou shalt not glean it afterward: it shall be for the stranger, for the fatherless, and for the widow" (Deuteronomy 24:19–21).

So, rich bankers, or any superrich people in America, should take heed of James 5:1–5, especially if it were to become law:

> **[1]** Go to now, ye rich men, weep and howl for your miseries that shall come upon you.
> **[2]** Your riches are corrupted, and your garments are motheaten.
> **[3]** Your gold and silver is cankered; and the rust of them shall be a witness against you, and shall eat your flesh as it were fire. Ye have heaped treasure together for the last days.
> **[4]** Behold, the hire of the labourers who have reaped down your fields, which is of you kept back by fraud, crieth: and the cries of them which have reaped are entered into the ears of the Lord of Sabbath.
> **[5]** Ye have lived in pleasure on the earth, and been wanton; ye have nourished your hearts, as in a day of slaughter."

Even if we enacted the Tenth Commandment, to not covet thy neighbor's property (including people) into law, how could we possibly enforce such a thought crime involving a person simply *wanting* something that someone else has, unless the government could somehow monitor our private thoughts so we could be punished every time we engage in greed, envy, or jealously?

It is interesting that in the Tenth Commandment, God is acknowledging the sins of jealously and envy. God apparently is above His own law, however, because jealousy is OK whenever God Himself covets the worshipers of other gods (see the First and Second Commandments). Our God is "a jealous God," as opposed to what I suppose would be a *more secure and mature* God who can handle rejection. But seriously, wouldn't our entire economic reward system of capitalism be greatly weakened if ambition, competition, and class envy for material wealth were prohibited by law as covetous, assuming that we could even enforce a law prohibiting this kind of thought crime?

The overall point here in contemplating any attempt to enact *all* of the Ten Commandments into law is very simple: Many religious pronouncements that appear in the Bible are things that we do not, and even should not, try to enact into law, despite the fact that these pronouncements appear in the Bible. It is therefore an inconsistent position to oppose homosexuality and same-sex marriage as a *legal or political* matter inside of a constitutional, pluralistic, and diverse modern democracy when there are so many other religious pronouncements in the Bible that are *not* also similarly enacted into law, even if we adhere to them as a personal religious matter.

For example, remember that the punishment for violation of any one of the Ten Commandments is death, as was done to a man who simply did not observe the Sabbath because he gathered sticks that day—God Himself commanded his death as punishment:

> [31] Because he hath despised the word of the LORD, and hath broken his commandment, that soul shall utterly be cut off; his iniquity shall be upon him.
> [32] And while the children of Israel were in the wilderness, they found a man that gathered sticks upon the sabbath day.
> [33] And they that found him gathering sticks brought him unto Moses and Aaron, and unto all the congregation.
> [34] And they put him in ward, because it was not declared what should be done to him.
> [35] And the LORD said unto Moses, The man shall be surely put to death: all the congregation shall stone him with stones without the camp.
> [36] And all the congregation brought him without the camp, and stoned him with stones, and he died; as the LORD commanded Moses. (Numbers 15:31-36)

Do any of us seriously think that biblical pronouncement ought to be the law—even though God Himself proclaimed this as the proper legal thing for the people to do against this man who violated the commandment? Christians consider the Sabbath now to be on Sundays, rather than Saturdays, because Jesus was resurrected on the "third day"—which would have been on a Sunday after being crucified on "Good Friday." Should we also stone professional football players for working on Sundays and making millions of dollars for their efforts? I doubt Tim Tebow, the NFL fundamentalist Christian quarterback, who prays every time he makes a touchdown, thinks that. I don't think even the most hardcore fundamentalist or follower of the Taliban would think that. If there really are such people, then we should fear them as well as pray for them (assuming God takes such requests). For many sins in the Bible—in fact, probably for most of them—there is no public outcry by fundamentalist literalist believers that we should enact a specific law to prohibit *every single* sin mentioned in the Bible as a legal matter in support of God.

In 2003, the US Supreme Court struck down laws making it a crime to be a homosexual in *Lawrence et al. v. Texas*, 539 US 558 (2003), overruling *Bowers v. Hardwick*, 478 US 186 (1986), which upheld a Georgia statute criminalizing sodomy. If it is wrong to have a law criminalizing *being* a homosexual, how can it be legal to deny those legitimate equal citizens their equal constitutional rights, such as the right to marry someone of their own choosing, and thus participate in society as equal citizens?

Chapter Eighty-One

Is Homosexuality a Choice, or Is It Just the Way a Person Is? Should It Even Matter?

I have often asked conservative Christian fundamentalists if they would be opposed to a law stating that only marriages between people of the *same race* would be legal but that *mixed-race* marriages would be illegal. I ask this to make a point about illegal discrimination when we legally deny people the right to get married based on their status (their race or sexual orientation) in relationship to one another (the race or sexual orientation of one's spouse). Most literalist believers agree that opposing mixed racial marriages as a legal matter would be unconstitutional discrimination based on status—race—but they make a significant distinction here between race and sexual orientation (or sexual preference).

Their rationale is as follows: "People cannot do anything about their race—they are just born that way—but people can and do *choose* to be gay, so homosexuality is not an immutable characteristic like race. Instead, it is a choice for which homosexuals should be responsible." Is that true? Do we really *choose* to whom we are, and are not, sexually attracted? Even if we do choose, should that matter, either legally or religiously?

It is helpful to draw on other examples of discrimination to compare and contrast. For instance, it is illegal to discriminate on the basis of one's religion, but people *choose* to follow or not follow certain religions, so one's religion is not a question of immutable genetics the way race is, but can still be the basis for illegal discrimination under Title VII of the Civil Rights Act of 1964. Thus, whether one "chooses" to be Jewish, Hindu, or atheist, the fact that it is a choice does not matter if improper religious discrimination has occurred. For example, if we discriminated against Quakers, should such discrimination be legal because Quakers "chose" to live the "Quaker lifestyle," which is unlike the immutable characteristics of race or gender (skin whitening/bleaching or transgender operations notwithstanding)?

Some people might argue, "Being a homosexual is a sin, but being Black is not!" OK, but such fundamentalists would also say that being an atheist (denying the divinity of God) is a sin, though atheists should still have the same constitutionally protected rights as religious/believer citizens.

What if we discriminated based on other areas of status that people "chose" to engage in—such as military service? Such discrimination against an active service member or a veteran would be illegal and could not be justified simply because that service member or veteran made a "choice" to serve in the military. The Uniformed Services Employment and Reemployment

Rights Act of 1994 (USERRA) is a federal statute that protects service members' and veterans' civilian employment rights. A fundamentalist might argue, "But serving in the military is not a sin!" Well, maybe, maybe not; it all depends on how literally one interprets the biblical commandment "thou shalt not kill," and how valid the argument of conscientious objectors is that killing is never justified, not even in war. Regardless, this is an example of an area in which we prohibit discrimination even if the thing against which we are discriminating is a choice.

That said, it is very interesting that many Christian fundamentalists make the argument that sexual orientation—be it homosexuality or heterosexuality—is all a matter of conscious choice. I once attended a debate between a liberal lawyer and a fundamentalist law professor on the issue of the constitutionality of same-sex marriage. The law professor argued that homosexuality should not be protected from discrimination because, although race is a protected immutable characteristic, that is not true for homosexuality, so it should therefore be legal to discriminate against homosexuals because they *choose* to be homosexual. During the question-and-answer period after the presentations of their arguments, I asked the professor whether he really believed his own argument about one's sexuality being a choice and, if he did, would he answer the following question for the audience: "Would you please share with us all of the various men in your life that you have been sexually attracted to, whom you have decided, or whom you have *chosen*, not to have sex with?" He either could not or would not name any man that he had ever been sexually attracted to during his lifetime whom he had chosen not to have sex with even though he may have wanted to. He then admitted that he had never once in his life ever been sexually attracted to a man. I pointed out that his admission about never having been attracted to another man in his lifetime might just prove the point that one's sexual attraction to any gender is not the conscious choice he seemed to be arguing it was—for either heterosexuals, like him, or for homosexuals.

I suppose sexuality can be a choice for bisexuals, who are, by definition, attracted to both men and women. Indeed, as Woody Allen once joked, "I am going to be a bisexual so that I can double my chances on Saturday night." Some gays, however, believe that bisexuals are not really bisexual but are instead homosexuals who are just not quite ready to admit that they are gay (it is more of a just "getting used to it" stage). I don't know about any of that, but I do know that as a heterosexual, I have never been sexually attracted to a man. Moreover, I never really consciously chose to be sexually attracted to women but just found that I was attracted to them. So I would think that it would be the same for a gay person, especially when it can be so incredibly difficult for some gay people to come to terms with being gay in our society. Often, they have to suffer horrible discrimination and homophobia, and they may risk the hurtful loss of relationships with certain judgmental family members and friends. As a result, it just doesn't seem like choosing one's sexual orientation would be such a flippant, inconsequential decision, like choosing between equally competing ice cream flavors. Many people likely would not choose to suffer such discrimination if it were not an innate part of who they are.

IS HOMOSEXUALITY A CHOICE, OR IS IT JUST THE WAY A PERSON IS?

Given this claim that sexual orientation is a choice, I would love to see where the Bible says that God created us all as bisexuals who are *equally sexually attracted* to both men and women and then we simply *choose* either to be evil and sin by being homosexual or to follow God and properly marry someone of the opposite sex. If you are heterosexual, try to imagine if you lived in a world where your attraction to the opposite sex were considered to be a sin and marrying another heterosexual was illegal and that being gay was actually the norm. Would you be able at that point to say, "Oh well, I guess I now will just have to be attracted to someone who is my same sex and fall in love with and marry them, because all I have to do is just reject my evil sexual desire for the opposite sex by praying about it until I am attracted to a homosexual and will want to marry and have sex with that homosexual like a normal person"?

Although I believe in miracles, that would be one that, I admit, my faith would be lacking in, no matter how hard I prayed, so if I lived in such a reversed world, where being heterosexual was considered the sin and marrying my wife would not be my legal right, I would at least want my fellow citizens, maybe even especially my fellow Christian citizens, to be a little bit more understanding of who I would be and why I would likely still want to be me. I would not want to have to live in shame or be considered a terrible sinner, and to have to hide who I was as a person. I would not want to have to sneak around with my female life partner. Perhaps most of all, as a believer in God, I would not want to believe that God made some horrible mistake when he made me.

I realize that we should not just say that because we may have certain biological urges, all such urges are justified and we do not have to control ourselves or take responsibility for our actions. For example, God made it so that I have to eat to survive, but if I went into a store and stole food, my innate biological desire and need to eat would not justify my theft of food (unless perhaps it were an emergency and I was dying of hunger, but it would still be theft). Also, as a heterosexual, although I may have a sexual attraction to women, it would still be adultery if I cheated with another woman, so I get that.

Here is the difference: There are certain *acceptable* ways that I can satisfy my biological urges, either to consume food or to have heterosexual sex, *without* those ways also being considered sins. For example, I can get a job, make money, pay for food at the store and then eat it—*sin free*. I can also justify my sexual urges by getting married to my wife and living with her and having sex with her—*sin free*.

As a result, for me, there is an available and acceptable way to legally "make it right" for me to be sexually attracted to my wife. My sexual attraction to my wife and my marriage to her are not wrong in the eyes of God or in the eyes of the law, but that is not true for gay people. How do they make their sexual urges right in the eyes of God or their marriages right in the eyes of the law of most states? Are gay people just supposed to suppress and/or "get over" their attraction somehow—maybe through extensive sexual psychological counseling? Must they become celibate homosexuals in order to follow God? I don't know that I would ever be able to just suppress or get over my sexual attraction to my wife—and even if it that were possible, I would hope that I never would get over that attraction and that she never would either. Most importantly, I would be angry if I could not legally marry my wife, even if the law would allow me the utterly offensive and ridiculous "consolation prize" of being able to marry another man who was homosexual.

I think same-sex marriage should be legal as a public-policy matter, regardless if it is classified as a sin in the Bible. After all, according to the Bible, it is also a sin to deny that God exists and to reject Jesus as our savior—which are, by the way, if you think about it, beliefs that attack or at least call into question the very heart of Christianity, the entire basis of the belief and the religion—yet I would strongly oppose any law outlawing non-Christian religions such as Judaism or Islam.

I realize that there are biblical verses that classify homosexuality as a sin, but I also know that there are other biblical verses saying that we should stone adulterers to death, and I certainly do not accept that biblical pronouncement as valid public policy, either; yet I also understand that Christian fundamentalists still have a 1st Amendment right, and a religious-faith right, to maintain their *personal* religious beliefs in light of how they personally interpret their beliefs, whether or not those beliefs may be supported by a religious text. Allowing same-sex marriage to take place legally between two people I do not know does not force me, or any other citizen, to accept homosexuality as a personal religious matter any more than allowing Jews to practice their religion by meeting in synagogues as legally allowed religious entities forces me to accept their belief that Jesus is not the Messiah.

Christian fundamentalist need not worry, however, because even if we as a society allow same-sex marriage legally, they can still believe that God will be standing at the Gates of Heaven in order to keep out all of those gays and lesbians and send them to Hell. If that is what one really wants to believe, one would and even should still have that right. The 1st Amendment protects that religious liberty right, and it is one of the reasons America is a great country.

It is helpful to ask someone who has personally had to address this issue all of his life, so after church one day, I was talking with a fellow parishioner who is gay. Our church, St. Francis, welcomes all people, regardless of whatever "sins" of which they may be guilty. We are taught not to judge any person (Matthew 7:1–2: "[1] Judge not, that ye be not judged. [2] For with what judgment ye judge, ye shall be judged: and with what measure ye mete, it shall be measured to you again"). We do not think it is right to judge or to make anyone feel unwelcome. None in my church judge me (at least I don't think they do), nor do they try to make me feel unwelcome, even though I am a sinner; so I try not to judge, because I have my own sins to worry about, believe me.

Although it seems clear to me that we should not, under our Constitution, legally discriminate against homosexuals when it comes to same-sex marriage, I nevertheless asked this gay fellow parishioner how he squares his homosexuality with what the Bible says about homosexuality in Leviticus, even though it is never mentioned in the New Testament by Jesus. He said that of course he has spiritually struggled with this issue and concern all of his life and had even been "kicked out" of many churches (apparently, that is what Jesus would have done—kicked him out of church too?), but after much soul-searching throughout the years, one day, he finally just came to the simple realization, *I am who I am. God made me, and God does not make trash. So, God did not make a mistake when He made me.*

Now that we have considered all ten Commandments and whether they should become public law, let's return to Genesis.

Chapter Eighty-Two

Post-Flood Life on Earth

Genesis 9

[2] And the fear of you and the dread of you shall be upon every beast of the earth, and upon every fowl of the air, upon all that moveth upon the earth, and upon all the fishes of the sea; into your hand are they delivered.

Why such a violent and adversarial relationship between humans and nature and animals? Does God really want us to treat animals this way and exercise arbitrary power of them? Why is respect and humility on the part of humans conspicuously absent here? Shouldn't we instead love and protect God's creatures? Is being kind to animals actually taking a controversial political position possibly at odds with the Bible?

[3] Every moving thing that liveth shall be meat for you; even as the green herb have I given you all things.
[4] But flesh with the life thereof, which is the blood thereof, shall ye not eat.

This is clearly contradictory, that every creature, except for those with blood, is food for humans. Does that mean we have to be vegetarians except for eating insects, spiders, shellfish, which do not have "blood?" There are many "clean" animals according to the Bible that we are allowed to eat, but those clean animals also have blood, so does that mean we can or cannot eat them?

[5] And surely your blood of your lives will I require; at the hand of every beast will I require it, and at the hand of man; at the hand of every man's brother will I require the life of man.
[6] Whoso sheddeth man's blood, by man shall his blood be shed: for in the image of God made he man.

These "shedding of blood" references I simply do not understand, as the meaning is not very clear. The cryptic language must be symbolic. Does it mean everyone will die and that if a person kills, that person will be killed? But we all die, so how does this add any meaningful information about which we are not currently aware?

Chapter Eighty-Three

"Yeah…Sorry about That"

[7] And you, be ye fruitful, and multiply; bring forth abundantly in the earth, and multiply therein.
[8] And God spake unto Noah, and to his sons with him, saying,
[9] And I, behold, I establish my covenant with you, and with your seed after you;
[10] And with every living creature that is with you, of the fowl, of the cattle, and of every beast of the earth with you; from all that go out of the ark, to every beast of the earth.
[11] And I will establish my covenant with you; neither shall all flesh be cut off any more by the waters of a flood; neither shall there any more be a flood to destroy the earth.
[12] And God said, This is the token of the covenant which I make between me and you and every living creature that is with you, for perpetual generations:
[13] I do set my bow in the cloud, and it shall be for a token of a covenant between me and the earth.
[14] And it shall come to pass, when I bring a cloud over the earth, that the bow shall be seen in the cloud:
[15] And I will remember my covenant, which is between me and you and every living creature of all flesh; and the waters shall no more become a flood to destroy all flesh.
[16] And the bow shall be in the cloud; and I will look upon it, that I may remember the everlasting covenant between God and every living creature of all flesh that is upon the earth.
[17] And God said unto Noah, This is the token of the covenant, which I have established between me and all flesh that is upon the earth.

God provided us with a beautiful and powerful symbol of His promise to never again destroy the Earth with a flood—a colorful rainbow in the clouds for all to see presumably every time after it rains—but why give us this symbol and make a covenant to never destroy the Earth again with a flood? If these evil humans who were drowned in the flood truly *deserved to die* because of their intolerable violence and evil, what was wrong with just giving them what they deserved—immediate worldwide death—and also giving us worldwide death if we ever were to act like them again? Was God wrong to do this in the first place, so afterward He had a guilty conscience?

Making a covenant and giving us a peace offering for doing something that was necessary and completely justified (the flood) seems misplaced. It also suggests that God was sorry for doing something so mean to us, and to the Earth, perhaps it was too mean. It is great that God would now have more compassion for us, but that would also mean that He did something wrong or regrettable for which he should now feel sorry and even try to "make up" for it by giving us some token, like a big bouquet of flowers. Because He is God, however, that symbolic bouquet of flowers would have to be spectacular and divine, such as a big beautiful rainbow in the sky that makes an appearance every time it rains (symbolic of the forty days and nights of rain). God says He will look at the rainbow so that He can remember His covenant with us—but would God otherwise forget His promise to us? Does God really need to be reminded of things that He might otherwise forget, like a celestial to-do list? How does an all-knowing God ever forget anything?

Of course, the scientific reason that rainbows appear after it rains really has nothing to do with the fact that it rains, per se, and everything to do with moisture particles being in the air which bend light rays that produce the colors of light spectrum, like when light passes through a glass prism and creates a multicolored design. That rainbow is a function of the glass prism bending the light rays slightly to create that effect. So, the question is, Did that scientific phenomenon of moisture particles in the air bending light rays like a big glass prism to produce a rainbow never occur *before* the flood? Was there ever a rainbow in the sky before God made the covenant to never destroy the earth again with a flood? Why would moisture particles not bend light rays to create a rainbow effect when light rays were passing through them at any time *before* the flood took place, assuming it briefly rained at least once before the flood ever took place?

Although God has made this covenant not to destroy the earth, God will destroy the earth again, according to Revelation, and there will be the eventual creation of a new Heaven and a new Earth—"And I saw a new heaven and a new earth: for the first heaven and the first earth were passed away; and there was no more sea" (Revelation 21:1)—so the rainbow promise made here in Genesis has a significant qualifying condition attached: God will not ever destroy the earth again—at least not by using a flood. That does not mean that God is not free under the covenant to use another means to destroy the earth in the future, however ("For, behold, I create new heavens and a new earth: and the former shall not be remembered, nor come into mind" (Isaiah 65:17) "[6] Whereby the world that then was, being overflowed with water, perished: [7] But the heavens and the earth, which are now, by the same word are kept in store, reserved unto fire against the day of judgment and perdition of ungodly men. (II Peter 3:6–7). So, here is some good legal advice: With any covenant, promise, guarantee, warranty, or contract, it is always very important to read the fine print to see what is actually promised—*and what is not.*

This story explaining where rainbows come from seems like an attempt to explain that which was not scientifically understood at the time. It reminds me of when we were kids and heard thunder and explained the phenomenon of thunder by either "God must be moving His furniture" or "God is bowling." Even then, however, as children, we somehow knew to take such explanations only *symbolically*, not *literally*.

Finally, if I spray a water hose toward the sun on a sunny day and I see the a rainbow, is that part of God's covenant with me to not destroy the earth with a flood ever again, or is that merely moisture particles bending light rays and thus producing a pretty image of colors on a sunny day with a water hose? Does the symbol of God's covenant count only when it actually rains and a rainbow appears way up in the sky, but not when moisture bends light rays in general?

Chapter Eighty-Four

Righteous Noah Has Some Post-Flood Issues

[18] And the sons of Noah, that went forth of the ark, were Shem, and Ham, and Japheth: and Ham is the father of Canaan.
[19] These are the three sons of Noah: and of them was the whole earth overspread.
[20] And Noah began to be an husbandman, and he planted a vineyard:
[21] And he drank of the wine, and was drunken; and he was uncovered within his tent.
[22] And Ham, the father of Canaan, saw the nakedness of his father, and told his two brethren without.

Recall that the Bible said earlier that Noah was righteous, just, and perfect, certainly not evil, and that is precisely why he and his family were saved on the ark and all of the other people perished in the flood. God was mad at all of the other evil people on the earth, but Noah was different from them, so he got to live. But that was then. Now, in this next chapter, Noah decided to establish and maintain a wine vineyard and apparently became a drunk, and a naked drunk at that! Did Noah change, or were the evil people just so much more evil than Noah that they all deserved to drown in the flood and Noah's sins were minor in comparison so he got to live, along with his family? But why would Noah find grace in God's eyes when he obviously had some issues with drunkenness and nakedness?

[23] And Shem and Japheth took a garment, and laid it upon both their shoulders, and went backward, and covered the nakedness of their father; and their faces were backward, and they saw not their father's nakedness.
[24] And Noah awoke from his wine, and knew what his younger son had done unto him.

What did his younger son do to him that was so bad? Did he force Noah to get drunk and take his clothes off? Does Noah take no personal responsibility for his own decisions? Ham just told Shem and Japeth about their father's drunken, naked condition, which was true, after all. And these other sons just tried to help Noah get through his hangover and to not embarrass him by looking at him while he was drunk and naked. So why didn't Noah thank all of them?

[25] And he said, Cursed be Canaan; a servant of servants shall he be unto his brethren.
[26] And he said, Blessed be the LORD God of Shem; and Canaan shall be his servant.
[27] God shall enlarge Japheth, and he shall dwell in the tents of Shem; and Canaan shall be his servant.

It seems like people are always getting unfairly blamed for things in the Bible, especially the completely innocent offspring of the guilty—but that appears to be OK, or at least acceptable standard operating procedure. In this instance, I do not understand what Noah's son, and his grandson, Canaan, did so badly to Noah that they now must be servants (slaves) from here on out (and again, why is slavery allowed and not a huge sin?). I realize that perhaps there is some hidden meaning here that is above me or that otherwise escapes me, but that is the problem—and the point—there should not be hidden meanings, or special meanings, that require years of study to divine, literally and figuratively, out of the plain meaning of the text. I would expect hidden meaning, ambiguity, and obfuscation, requiring the subjective interpretation of the writings of mere mortals (so to understand the true meanings, one would have to be in the club and know the secret handshake); but I would not expect such from the writings of God. I also wonder why God would use such precious limited room in the Bible to communicate His Word to all of humankind for all time but use that important limited space to recount these various mundane stories about petty jealousies or other such related matters that in the grand scheme of things do not really amount to a whole lot of significance that one would expect if the Supreme Being of the Universe had this one chance in time to communicate an official written record directly from Himself to humanity.

[28] And Noah lived after the flood three hundred and fifty years.
[29] And all the days of Noah were nine hundred and fifty years: and he died.

Chapter Eighty-Five

More Generations of People, and World Migration

Genesis 10

[1] Now these are the generations of the sons of Noah, Shem, Ham, and Japheth: and unto them were sons born after the flood.

[2] The sons of Japheth; Gomer, and Magog, and Madai, and Javan, and Tubal, and Meshech, and Tiras.

[3] And the sons of Gomer; Ashkenaz, and Riphath, and Togarmah.

[4] And the sons of Javan; Elishah, and Tarshish, Kittim, and Dodanim.

[5] By these were the isles of the Gentiles divided in their lands; every one after his tongue, after their families, in their nations.

[6] And the sons of Ham; Cush, and Mizraim, and Phut, and Canaan.

[7] And the sons of Cush; Seba, and Havilah, and Sabtah, and Raamah, and Sabtecha: and the sons of Raamah; Sheba, and Dedan.

[8] And Cush begat Nimrod: he began to be a mighty one in the earth.

[9] He was a mighty hunter before the LORD: wherefore it is said, Even as Nimrod the mighty hunter before the LORD.

[10] And the beginning of his kingdom was Babel, and Erech, and Accad, and Calneh, in the land of Shinar.

[11] Out of that land went forth Asshur, and builded Nineveh, and the city Rehoboth, and Calah,

[12] And Resen between Nineveh and Calah: the same is a great city.

[13] And Mizraim begat Ludim, and Anamim, and Lehabim, and Naphtuhim,

[14] And Pathrusim, and Casluhim, (out of whom came Philistim,) and Caphtorim.

[15] And Canaan begat Sidon his firstborn, and Heth,

[16] And the Jebusite, and the Amorite, and the Girgasite,

[17] And the Hivite, and the Arkite, and the Sinite,

[18] And the Arvadite, and the Zemarite, and the Hamathite: and afterward were the families of the Canaanites spread abroad.

[19] And the border of the Canaanites was from Sidon, as thou comest to Gerar, unto Gaza; as thou goest, unto Sodom, and Gomorrah, and Admah, and Zeboim, even unto Lasha.

[20] These are the sons of Ham, after their families, after their tongues, in their countries, and in their nations.

[21] Unto Shem also, the father of all the children of Eber, the brother of Japheth the elder, even to him were children born.

[22] The children of Shem; Elam, and Asshur, and Arphaxad, and Lud, and Aram.

[23] And the children of Aram; Uz, and Hul, and Gether, and Mash.

[24] And Arphaxad begat Salah; and Salah begat Eber.

[25] And unto Eber were born two sons: the name of one was Peleg; for in his days was the earth divided; and his brother's name was Joktan.

[26] And Joktan begat Almodad, and Sheleph, and Hazar-maveth, and Jerah,

[27] And Hadoram, and Uzal, and Diklah,

[28] And Obal, and Abimael, and Sheba,

[29] And Ophir, and Havilah, and Jobab: all these were the sons of Joktan.

[30] And their dwelling was from Mesha, as thou goest unto Sephar a mount of the east.

[31] These are the sons of Shem, after their families, after their tongues, in their lands, after their nations.

[32] These are the families of the sons of Noah, after their generations, in their nations: and by these were the nations divided in the earth after the flood.

This entire chapter, Chapter 10, is another long lineage of various families and tribes and their geographies. It explains how the world was populated and how different nations emerged from these great migrations of various peoples in what appears to be very early human history. It is interesting to note how the world was populated, how that population physically spread, and how different languages developed among different groups of people.

Even before considering the many languages that grew out of this migration, how about considering the races of people that must have developed and that now account for all of the racial diversity in the world? Starting with Adam and Eve—what race were they? Some believers in the United States and Europe assume that they must have been white and somehow, all other races and ethnicities in the world developed from them; exactly how or why that would be the case is not explained or even considered. Perhaps Adam and Eve were a race that we do not even have today, some sort of common ancestral race out of which we all developed and evolved (but only micro-evolved).

As it turns out, Adam and Eve's race is not that critical anyway, because every race that had developed from them died in the great flood; therefore, only Noah's race, and the race of the members of his family (his wife, his three sons, and their three wives), is all that matters because all races currently on Earth have to have developed from these eight people who allegedly repopulated the world just a few thousand years ago. It is not clear what the race of Noah, his wife, and their three sons was, nor is it clear what the race of the sons' three wives was. I suppose the wives all could have been different races at that point, but how would those races develop in less than a couple of thousands of years between Adam and Noah? We would have to believe that all races and ethnicities ultimately came from Adam and Eve, but, in reality, all races and ethnicities would have had to come from Noah and his family, within a very short time.

If all ethnicities *did* descend from Noah's family, some of his family members must have migrated north through Asia and become Russian, while others did not go quite so far north and became Chinese, Japanese, Korean, and Vietnamese, while others migrated only to Southern Asia and became Indian, Pakistani, and Afghani while still others migrated to Africa and became Kenyan, Zulu, and Sudanese, still others migrated to Europe and became English, Italian, Spanish, and French, and somehow, others migrated over oceans (long before Christopher Columbus) and became Native Americans (throughout North, South, and Central America) and still others to Australia and Polynesia, becoming Aborigines or Samoans or Hawaiians. All of this happened in just a matter of a few thousand years of micro-evolution, adaptation, which, remember, is possible though Darwinian evolution is not.

During that time, all of the cultural, ethnic, and racial diversity we see today—African, Asian, Southern Asian, white European, Arabic, Persian, Latin, Native American, and so on—must have developed. Also, everyone except for a certain group who remained in the Middle East in and around Israel and still believed in the one true God of Abraham, the God of the Bible, must have lost their religion and belief in the real God during this time and started believing in all of these other false Gods and religions that have existed in the world and now exist. Even early white Europeans seemed to have lost their religion and belief in the God of Abraham and did not get back on track until they were later re-exposed to the one true religion and the Bible.

In reality, it seems rather farfetched to assume that all of this racial and ethnic diversity could develop so distinctly in such a short time. Of course, the world about which Moses was aware (the Middle East) may not have had as much racial diversity, so he apparently did not find it necessary to explain such human physical variety—God did not have to change everyone's race suddenly to somehow explain how all of these racial differences could exist if we all came from Adam and Eve and, really, from Noah and his family. It makes one wonder if Moses was fully aware of all of the racial and ethnic diversity that existed in the world at the time he wrote Genesis. Was he fully aware of the Chinese, of Native Americans, of Eskimos, of Africans, of Incas, of Spaniards, of New Zealander Maori, of Australian Aborigines, and many others? Why no explanation at all of how all of the various races and ethnicities developed? *Why* are there different races? And which race is "in God's image"?

Regardless of the differing races and how they developed, there were also new languages among various peoples. Who created these different languages? Was it God, or was it humans, and how long did it take to create and/or develop all of these languages? This issue is important, because in the following chapter of Genesis, Chapter 11, a specific story appears as an attempt to fully explain how all of the languages in the world were suddenly created by God. Again, it makes one wonder why there is no similar explanation for all of the *races* of people when there is an explanation for the *languages* of people. The Tower of Babel story in Chapter 11 explains the rise of languages of people, but we are simply left with micro-evolution as our implicit explanation for all of the races of people, even though the development of physical races seems like it would be more involved and take a much longer time to micro-evolve than would the development of new and different languages; but now on to Chapter 11's explanation.

Chapter Eighty-Six

The Mother of All Skyscrapers, and the Creation of Instant New Languages

Genesis 11

[1] And the whole earth was of one language, and of one speech.

This chapter begins by proclaiming that all humans on Earth were speaking only one common language at that time and had been doing so apparently since the time of Adam and Eve. Presumably, it had been the same language of Adam and Eve, Noah, and all of their descendants up to that point, but how could that possibly have been true, when there *already* were people who had started to speak different languages at an *earlier* point in history, as told in Chapter 10? Recall that Chapter 10 says that after Noah's time, people began to leave together in different groups according to their own tongues (Genesis 10:5: "divided in their lands; every one after his tongue, after their families, in their nations"—and this statement is repeated for various other general groupings of peoples, see Genesis 10:20 and 31), so the notion that later, somehow, "the whole earth was of one language, and of one speech" directly contradicts what is revealed in Chapter 10 about different people migrating to different lands ("every one after his tongue, after their families"). In short, how could different languages *already* have existed on Earth if *later,* there is but "one language" on the entire Earth?

This oversight might be small, and even understandable, for a human writer (to err is human), but not so much for an *infallible, inerrant* God, if God is the one who actually wrote this passage. The only way this could possibly even make sense is if humans first naturally developed other languages (as set forth in Chapter 10), then somehow all began speaking one common language again (as set forth in Chapter 11), even though by that time, humans were supposedly all scattered throughout the earth "in their nations." That unlikely "miracle" of everyone on Earth all *later* starting to speak just one common language again from many different languages is what one would have to believe for this story not to contradict and cast doubt on what was said in Chapter 10. Perhaps Chapter 11 should be reordered and really come *before* Chapter 10. Of course, perhaps Chapter 11 is just a flashback, like we often see in books, motion pictures, and television programs.

Chapter Eighty-Seven

Of Linguistic Realities and Credible Threats of an Unauthorized Invasion of Heaven

[2] And it came to pass, as they journeyed from the east, that they found a plain in the land of Shinar; and they dwelt there.

[3] And they said one to another, Go to, let us make brick, and burn them thoroughly. And they had brick for stone, and slime had they for morter.

[4] And they said, Go to, let us build us a city and a tower, whose top may reach unto heaven; and let us make us a name, lest we be scattered abroad upon the face of the whole earth.

[5] And the LORD came down to see the city and the tower, which the children of men builded.

[6] And the LORD said, Behold, the people is one, and they have all one language; and this they begin to do: and now nothing will be restrained from them, which they have imagined to do.

[7] Go to, let us go down, and there confound their language, that they may not understand one another's speech.

[8] So the LORD scattered them abroad from thence upon the face of all the earth: and they left off to build the city.

[9] Therefore is the name of it called Babel; because the LORD did there confound the language of all the earth: and from thence did the LORD scatter them abroad upon the face of all the earth.

I am certainly no linguist, but I do know that human languages are not static and somehow frozen in time. Instead, languages are living, in the sense that they are used every day, and there are slight linguistic changes made in use and meaning that, over long periods of time, can and do turn into significant linguistic changes, such that new meanings and even new words are created, and eventually even new languages can develop therefrom, while other languages might die out from non-use or obsolescence. It is also fairly easy to trace how certain languages were developed from earlier ancestral languages over time. Also, current languages can, and often do, overlap with one another with certain root words that often have been borrowed from still yet other languages. Just consider the Latin roots of words present in many Western languages. Consequently, languages slowly develop over time, and even now, they are still in a slow and constant process of being created and recreated (An excellent, yet still fairly rudimentary primer quite helpful in explaining such linguistic change is available at http://www.ling. upenn.edu/courses/Fall_2003/ling001/language_change.html).

All of this gradual development and very subtle but constant change suggests that new languages build and transform very slowly over time and that linguistic reality therefore tends to cast significant doubt on the notion that God simply snapped His fingers and in an instant, a few workers on the Tower of Babel began speaking, say, Chinese, and therefore could not be understood by other workers who suddenly began speaking Spanish, while still others suddenly began speaking all other manner of different, yet perfectly formed, new languages such as Dutch, Arabic, Samoan, Russian, Navajo Athabaskan, Latin, Portuguese, Zulu, Japanese, Hindi, English, Bengali, Thai, Serbian, Slovak, Korean, Bulgarian, Yucatan Maya, Swahili, and others. Indeed, in just the Central American country of Guatemala, there are at least 22 different languages spoken just by indigenous Mayan descendants. Was it really necessary for God to create 22 indigenous Mayan languages for the people who would come to inhabit Guatemala in order to thoroughly confuse tower builders in the Middle East thousands of years ago? If all such languages were abruptly created at the Tower of Babel, what language was the "original" language that Adam and Eve spoke in the Garden of Eden, and/or that Noah and his family spoke; and is/are that/those languages still spoken?

If someone does not understand how languages slowly change and develop over time, that person probably would think that it would be necessary to explain why we have so many languages on Earth. The existence of different languages becomes difficult to explain if Adam and Eve started speaking only one common human language. Where would these other world languages have possibly come from? Consequently, if Moses, the writer of Genesis, did not understand how languages evolve over time, he would have wondered how there possibly could have been more than the one language in the world beyond that which Adam and Eve (and Noah) would have passed down to all of their descendants. How could the existence of these many other languages possibly be explained if Adam and Eve (and Noah) spoke only one original language, and we all learn and speak only the language of our parents? From the above source, consider the following:

> Generation by generation, pronunciations evolve, new words are borrowed or invented, the meaning of old words drifts, and morphology develops or decays. The rate of change varies, but whether the changes are faster or slower, they build up until the "mother tongue" becomes arbitrarily distant and different. After a thousand years, the original and new languages will not be mutually intelligible. After ten thousand years, the relationship will be essentially indistinguishable from chance relationships between historically unrelated languages.

For a simple example of this slow change in language, compare the Early Modern English of the verses in Genesis of the King James Version of the Bible that we read (not to mention the almost unintelligible older English versions) to how the English language is currently spoken today in the United States. There has definitely been a perceptible change, or evolution, in the English language in just a few hundred years. We clearly no longer speak the way the King

James Bible is written. Whole words and categories of words have been jettisoned from the English language since then, and thousands of new words, perhaps even more, have been created, while many definitions have changed, as well as new formulations of acceptable grammar and syntax have been formed. So, languages are undeniably living and are constantly changing and evolving, both the written words and how they are spoken. From the same source:

> **The analogy with evolution via natural selection**
> Darwin himself, in developing the concept of evolution of species via natural selection, made an analogy to the evolution of languages. For the analogy to hold, we need a pool of individuals with variable traits, a process of replication creating new individuals whose traits depend on those of their "parents", and a set of environmental processes that result in differential success in replication for different traits.

There appears to be no understanding whatsoever by Moses in his writing of this particular portion of Genesis that languages were, and still are, alive and continually changing and adapting. In some ways, we currently might even see how languages might be evolving into more shared word languages as the Internet and global travel and communication allow us to have more and more exposure to each other's languages and key words (although we certainly have not become so technologically connected that we now have one common worldwide language—perhaps math and/or computer code would be the closest things to a world language).

Moses was not a linguist, nor a globalist, however, so he of course had no exposure to such things. From his limited point of view, the only plausible way to explain why different languages existed in the world where from his point of view there should logically be only one language (that of Adam and Eve, and/or of Noah) was that God must have magically created all of the different languages out of thin air at some point for some apparent necessary reason—such as overly ambitious people trying to sneak their way into Heaven by building a great tower to the sky because that is where Heaven is. Apparently, if we just had a tall enough ladder, we could get to Heaven, "way up there," although a ladder many miles high probably would have been a bit unrealistic—after all, a ladder could fall over, but that problem could possibly be solved if we had a big solid tower using building technology from more than 5,000 years ago!

So, putting aside for the moment the significant linguistic misunderstandings of language development, consider the even more preposterous reason why God would have even found it necessary to frustrate the laughable building efforts of these particularly ill-informed humans who made the ridiculous decision to build a most absurd tower to Heaven in the first place. Wouldn't the realities of the limits of ancient tower-construction techniques have taken care of any alleged credible threat of intruders actually being able to crash the gates of Heaven, not to mention the sheer vastness of outer space, and the lack of oxygen in the stratosphere, that also would have constituted an impenetrable barrier to getting into wherever Heaven is located, and thus not even require God's intervention? Could we extrapolate and argue that is the same reason why God blew up the Challenger and later the Columbia space shuttles, because we were developing space craft that one day might allow us to illegitimately crash the gates of Heaven and enter improperly?

The fact that God apparently found it necessary to frustrate these outlandish efforts thousands of years ago to build a tower to Heaven that was doomed to failure anyway suggests that this tower was conceived of at the time to be a *credible threat and a realistic concern* and therefore had to be stopped by God's divine intervention. But if God wrote this story and actually took the actions attributed to Him and God is omniscient, God obviously would have known that such a tower was nothing more than the ignorant folly of some very poorly educated builder-engineers who clearly would not have posed any kind of credible threat whatsoever. God therefore obviously would not have found it necessary to do something as drastic as creating all of the new and different languages of the world to thwart this ludicrous effort to gain improper entry into Heaven, but recall Chapter 11, Verse 6, in which God seemed to actually fear that these particular humans were mounting a serious threat, a threat that He found necessary to defend against, "and now nothing will be restrained from them, which they have imagined to do."

According to the story, there was a great, immediate "confounding of language" by God to thwart the construction of the tower, and that was the end of it—problem solved? For being such ambitious builders who sought to bypass God and build their own tower to Heaven, these builders sure folded quickly and just gave up at the first sign of trouble. It makes one wonder why God didn't just whip up a little earthquake when the tower got to be about two miles high (by the way, we haven't, and probably couldn't, build a two-mile-high tower even today) and then watch these easily discouraged builders quit and all go home when their tower came tumbling down (unless they were constructing one of those modern earthquake-proof towers like the ones in San Francisco)? Seriously, though, why, for example, once the new languages were created, didn't these builders simply continue with their efforts to build the tower, if that was what they really had wanted to do? And why would they even need to communicate through language at that point to complete the construction of the tower that was well underway?

Once the tower was planned and the construction had already begun, it seems like continuing to build the tower would have been simple, this new language barrier issue notwithstanding. The building plans were already done, one would assume. Couldn't the workers have continued loading stone on top of stone or whatever they were doing to build this doomed-to-failure tower, anyway? People certainly can communicate visually and employ a simple sign language of sorts, so the building tasks necessary to continue constructing the tower could have been sufficiently acted out, like a simple game of charades. In fact, try acting out for a moment the continuation of loading stone blocks and connecting them with mortar without speaking. It seems like it would be fairly simple to demonstrate the necessary task visually, especially once the tower-building process already had begun. The plans were already made (did they have blueprints?), and they had begun building while they still could communicate using one common language before the languages suddenly all were changed.

What does this suggest about the portrayal of God in this story when God apparently found it necessary to deal with the Tower of Babel as a *credible threat*? It shows that whoever actually wrote this story did not understand the limits of ancient building engineering, how vast the universe is, and that Heaven does not simply exist "way up in the sky" where humans can access it if they can just build a large enough tower or even a really great rocket ship. A god who actually created our universe obviously would have understood these limitations and undoubtedly would not have taken this threat seriously or have found it necessary to come up with a way to thwart this rather silly and inane tower-building scheme to Heaven.

Consider how the creation of all of these new and different languages ended up eventually requiring multiple language to language biblical translations that are now fraught with errors and definitional ambiguities. Why would God take the completely unnecessary action of creating such languages in order to frustrate the building of the Tower of Babel, when such was not even a credible threat, and when that action would later cause some obfuscation of God's Holy Word to humanity? Why make modern-day preachers feel that they must consult various language translation dictionaries to obtain allegedly correct or at least more reliable word definitions just to understand the Bible, especially when thwarting an obviously impossible invasion attempt of heaven thousands of years ago was doomed to failure anyway? Does that really sound like the divine work and the godlike thought process of the Supreme Being of our universe?

Chapter Eighty-Eight

What about a Futuristic Symbolic Tower of Babel?

It might be that in the future, we humans will again attempt to use technology in an effort to circumvent God, not merely by constructing some tower (or even a super rocket starship) to gain improper entrance into Heaven, as if it is a physical space in our universe, but instead by using biotech in an attempt to someday achieve a form of immortality and thereby cheat our own inevitable deaths. First, start by considering the current sophisticated computer hardware and software programs that can use artificial intelligence and algorithms to play, and even beat, human grandmaster chess champions as well as solve the most intricate math problems, performing millions of calculations in a second, which is far superior to what any human brain can do (consider Watson, the computer that managed to beat the top former human champions on the quiz show *Jeopardy,* applying sophisticated artificial intelligence). These computing feats, which are commonplace today, would have been considered impossible science fiction even just a few decades ago.

Assuming a steady and ever-growing trajectory of continuing computer advancement, what if artificial intelligence and supercomputing continue to progress exponentially into the future? Might we someday be able to replicate an all-embracing data map and formulate a comprehensive information processing software system that could mimic the entire information-processing system of the human mind? After all, the human brain is just a super-sophisticated electronic and chemical circuitry processor that processes all incoming information and can store and retrieve much of that information and, most importantly, can learn and then apply that existing information to new situations and contexts according to a most complex system of thoughts and ideas (highly complex algorithms, programming, and decisional flow charts?). So, what if the entire thought-processing system of a particular human mind could be captured, mapped, copied, transferred, and stored so it could exist virtually as software somewhere inside of a computer and do so in a way that would entirely replicate the manner in which a human mind exists and functions inside of a human brain and human body? Such may not be impossibly complex at some point in the future. As Stephen Hawking recently said, "I regard the brain as a computer which will stop working when its components fail. There is no heaven or afterlife for broken down computers; that is a fairy story for people afraid of the dark."

If a person's entire mind were fully captured, stored, and transferred to a computer software program that data-mapped software system could exist long after the biological person after whom it was created died. Conceivably, every person could have their own mind "applications" (the ultimate "Mind Apps" of their entire minds and all of their memory data) that could exist forever, or as long as the software program and the computer hard drive housing that software could exist. But could such a Mind App actually contain *all* of the data memory that a particular human mind now has as stored memory? Moreover, could that Mind App then learn, remember, reason, and even feel and express emotions the same way the human mind can because the Mind App could fully replicate that mind's *entire* information-processing system? Could the Mind App develop the ability to actually care about anything? If this could be accomplished technologically, the mind of a person could *live on, indefinitely,* in the form of a computer program. The computer program would have to capture and fully replicate human psychology and personality, which admittedly might be impossible for us to fully conceive of now but it might not be impossible for future generations of thinkers and scientists.

Even if the biological human were to die, if his or her entire mind previously had been fully downloaded to his or her own Mind App, would that person really have died, if his or her entire mental essence continued to exist in a computer? Indeed, would the deceased biological person actually at that point *become* the Mind App, much like a caterpillar becomes a butterfly? Would the Mind App continue to have that person's personality and learn the same way the person learned during his or her lifetime and then add to that existing knowledge and memory database? It sounds like a really good episode of *Star Trek*, but think about the way a description of a modern heart or liver transplant would have sounded to a person 300 years ago. Science fiction has a way of becoming science reality. If a heart transplant is possible, and if an artificial heart can be manufactured and then implanted into someone and function as a real heart, why not have the equivalent of a "brain/mind transplant" or an "artificial brain/artificial intelligence implant," which would be a full copy that could exactly mimic the real thing, the entire human mind of an existing person?

If so, what if we could have mind-mapped, say, Leonardo da Vinci, Albert Einstein, or even Steve Jobs, before they had died; even today, what if we could mind-map Stephen Hawking or astrophysicist Neil DeGrasse Tyson? How posterity would benefit from having their minds live on forever in a software computer program, constantly learning and adding to their knowledge and databases, which formulate who they are and what during their lifetimes essentially made them them! The program could use the existing algorithms that formulate how their minds work in a way that would allow the program to continually process new information as them, without possibly ever having to eat, sleep, rest, or do any other mortal or biological function.

Think about the implications. Suppose one's biological parents were to die. If those parents had been mind-mapped before they had died, their child could go to that computer program (like one might visit a grave) and ask his or her "parents" for advice about life and actually receive that advice, that accumulated "wisdom" of his or her parents, even though those parents' physical bodies were dead, but would those parents *really* be dead? True, the computer program might not really be them, but that program would be a complete interactive copy of their minds that would still be "alive" in the sense that the minds still would be able to make connections between incoming data and absorb it into the existing database/memory that is the essence of everything that those parents were when they were alive. Recall the scene in the first Superman movie in which Superman (Christopher Reeves) visits his ice cavern and is able to talk to a computer program of his the dead parents and ask their advice (or the computer's rendition of their advice) about his feelings of love for his girlfriend, Lois Lane (Margot Kidder).

Moreover, the computer program could "learn" about new information, such as the graduation of a great-granddaughter, and then "react" to it in an interactive way by actually "caring," and perhaps even "feeling" some actual pride, even though the "real" great-grandparents' bodies would be gone. Even more interesting, would a current physically alive human being still love his or her "dead" parents, which would still be living, as the program, and still talking to their child? But perhaps the most interesting question is, Would the computer program actually love someone, or would the program merely be intellectually mimicking the thought processes and series of decision options of the past parents that would provide only the illusion of actually loving their child? That is, would the computer-program parents still love their child the same way the biological mother and father did when they were physically alive?

Going to visit a grave and having to access to the memory of the deceased person would become a whole new activity if one could access what would be a complete interactive computer program of the entire mind of a loved one, with whom that person could still have a conversation. The parents' Mind App could answer their children's current questions, and those answers would be exactly what those parents would have told their children if the parents were still alive! Imagine what Leonardo da Vinci's mind would think about modern space travel, television, and cell phones if his mind were still with us, existing as interactive software. What would Albert Einstein's mind think about the Internet, global warming/climate change, and the string theory in physics? What would Carl Sagan's mind have been able to think about...well, whatever might be unimaginable today but will probably be very commonplace 500 years in the future?

Remember, however, the final step to immortality would still need to be taken, because a *biotech* solution to immortality would also involve a *biological* regeneration of cloned tissue to create a live cloned human body of the person. That is, what if we were also to develop cloning of the human genome and full physical DNA mapping, so not only the live person's brain is captured and replicated on a computer through sophisticated software but that person is also physically mapped so his or her body can continually be cloned to recreate that same physical body down to the last cell in the future? If that would be possible, we would simply have to somehow implant the Mind App of that person into his or her cloned physical body—and voila! If we could do that, we would get to live forever as immortals and cheat death, especially if the software of our minds would be continually learning and adding to our existing knowledge databases so we could remember everything forever and access it instantly, and we could constantly replace our cloned human tissues so we could always get new trade-in bodies forever. One's intelligence would be limited only by the amount of space that one's program has available and by how fancy and fast one's algorithms and data-processing systems are.

So, instead of a brain in a body that eventually dies, I could have a total software program of my entire mind, including who I am, complete with all my thoughts, memory, ideas, emotions, and creativity, existing entirely in the form of a digital database, algorithms, artificial intelligence, and super information-processing systems. Not only that, I could also have a tangible, physical body that I could continually trade in for a brand new version, forever. Although any current cloned physical biological body would eventually die, it would not matter as long as that body could continually be cloned. I could always have access to my body, at whatever age I would want. Before I (or really just my current body) would die, the software of my mind could be copied and transferred for placement into a brand-new cloned body so I could literally live forever. My Mind App could be continually inserted into a freshly cloned body every few years, and that replacement process could be continued forever. Perhaps I could always have a cloned body or set of bodies growing and developing in different stages, literally lying in wait for me to tap as my new body when the current one dies—kind of like a bench of replacement athletic ballplayers (literally without any brains, but open to be wired with my copied Mind App) just waiting for the chance to "get into the game," with my ever-growing mind and experiences, as the perpetual me forever.

But why stop there? Various software and bio upgrades probably would become possible, so why not clone my latest new body with the genes of an Olympic athlete, a movie star, or even just a very healthy person? Even more intriguing would be the possibility of mental software upgrades. Because my particular mental Mind App algorithms would be rather deficient when compared to Einstein's superior math and physics algorithms, I would have no need to accept my intellectual inferiority, because maybe some of his fancier superior algorithms could simply be downloaded from his Mind App and uploaded to mine! In fact, as long as we are doing that, I could not only be physically and mentally immortal but could also obtain all the knowledge of every human being that has ever been mind mapped—a true marketplace of ideas where I get to download and upload *everything*—all accumulated knowledge—talk about a *real* "Tree of the Knowledge of Good and Evil"! I could not only now *access* the "forbidden fruit" of entire Internet, I would *be* the entire Internet—eat your heart out Al Gore—and whatever else is available as downloadable software and data. How is that for complete equality and a communistic connection to the entire human species collective? We would all be equally knowledgeable and literally have equal thought access to everything that is currently known, and beyond! I am wildly exaggerating, of course, just to get someone like former Fox TV commentator Glenn Beck to scream, "See, I told you, America! I was right; these atheist progressives want to control your mind and destroy your freedom and individuality under the guise of equality!" In this regard, however, perhaps such hyper paranoia would be right (for once). Glenn Beck had better warn everyone that the Evil Empire US federal government in the future wants to completely control all of our minds!

As with the opening of any Pandora's box, there would be new issues, as well as some old issues in new forms. Imagine the privacy concerns involved in accessing and downloading all of the private thoughts, ideas, and data of one's entire mind. Try to contemplate the full extent of identity theft that would become quite literal in every sense of the word. Deleting someone's Mind App would become the equivalent of murder, so that our immortality would be only as good as the data backup tapes and disaster recovery systems available to restore our deleted data. So abortion might not be murder, but deleting the computer program that is someone would be?

What about our more intangible human factors, such as competitiveness, drive, envy, love, kindness, empathy, and jealousy? Would those continue to exist, or would we be tempted to delete certain "irrational" or "undesirable" algorithms? If we were to delete such algorithms, might the idealistic equality of shared Mind Apps end up becoming a curse of manufactured *sameness*, coupled with a complete and rather tragic loss of human diversity and individuality? Could the "evil government" (even though it is a democracy) then have access to and thereby control all of our thoughts and even technologically override actual memories with false, computer-generated memories, as apparent evidence of wrongdoing once there is computer access to all of our individual Mind Apps?

These new types of legal issues are fascinating to think about—who or what should have possession, custody, or control, or even access to our Mind Apps? If a person has nothing to hide, what would be the problem with allowing the government to have access? Would there be nothing to fear from the government as long as we had nothing to hide? Couldn't the government stop all crime and terrorism because it would literally know what everyone would be thinking (and plotting and planning) at all times—security ultimately wins out over privacy? It would be the loss of freedom and individuality and the beginning of a super police state, in control of everything, even our minds, literally. Consider the chilling proclamation from the Police State (in the voice of James Earl Jones as Darth Vadar): "Resistance is futile, for you must succumb to the unrelenting will of the superior socialist collective!" I am not sure if that quote is from a movie or a book or if I just made it up or somehow added to it, but whatever its source, it sounds so menacing, in a scary sci-fi sort of way, that I just couldn't resist.

Also, if I were to get sued in this future world, would I have to turn over my Mind App so the other side could research my database memory to see if I am liable or not, guilty or not? Legally, the factual investigation for evidence in a case is called discovery, and the exchange of electronically stored information is called e-discovery (for electronic-discovery). Wouldn't a Mind App of a person be the ultimate electronic document containing everything (all conceivable information and data about that person and all of his or her affairs) even remotely relevant to the legal dispute at hand? But which information, even if relevant to a legal case, would nonetheless be privileged and confidential, and how long would it take to review and to fully consider the entirety of one's knowledge and memory to determine what should and should not be legally relevant and not privileged in a particular case and therefore should be disclosed? I suppose a Mind App program would be fully searchable by other types of search-and-retrieve programs.

As far as trials in courtrooms, forget testifying in court anymore and trying to cross-examine witnesses and then having juries guess if they are lying or telling the truth, because having access to a witness's entire mind as searchable software would be the ultimate lie-detector test. It would be like cross-examining someone, only we would not have to wait for a formulated answer and a possible lie; we could directly access the answer, and everything else about the person, and have access to everything the person has ever even thought. As a result, would all possible objections be effectively overruled, unless the information sought is irrelevant or otherwise privileged for some reason? Imagine parents having access to everything their children have ever thought. Would spouses who say they trust one another be so trusting as to turn over every thought they have ever had to one another? We may want to be careful here about what we ask for.

If someone could plant "evidence" (false memories) in an undetectable way into the witness's Mind App and thereby frame someone with false mental applications in a most convincing way, we would have a huge problem. If the evidence tampering would be detectable in the Mind App, perhaps the new expert witnesses would become Mind App forensic experts who could discover such tampering (but who also might be able to do some Mind App tampering of their own). Perhaps there would be very revealing metadata showing exactly who accessed the Mind App and how they manipulated the data, if that data itself could not be manipulated.

Something else to consider would be how much a Mind App would cost and if it would be available only for the rich, and, if so, how fair that would be. Should Mind Apps be made available to poor people, assuming there are still poor people in the future (I do not know why there would not be, unless we start taking very seriously Jesus's teachings about fully caring for the poor)? Will we still be arguing over whether the rich should be forced by the government to subsidize the poor, especially when the poor work for the rich? Finally, would this very expensive "immortality" made possible by the Mind App and cloned body become a guaranteed constitutional right, or would it be a privilege only for those who could afford it? Would the promise of "life, liberty, and the pursuit of happiness" become "immortality (for either you or a copy of you), liberty (to the extent such is allowed by the government collective), and happiness (as long as there is an App or a fancy algorithm for that), all of which has to be economically affordable before it is widely accessible"?

In any event, if an entire interactive mind could exist as me in a computer program forever, constantly learning and growing and adding to its database, and a cloned physical body would always be available, just like one can always buy a new car (if one could afford it, which again raises the issue of the gap between the immortality haves and the immortality have-nots), would we, for all intents and purposes, become immortal? Would we become like gods? Could two cloned bodies with the Mind Apps of two former people in them not only live forever but also reproduce by creating a new "clone" that would be a mixture of the DNA of the two clones, and have a new, clean hard drive for a new Mind App that would borrow algorithms from each of the two "parent" Mind Apps?

But wait, isn't this essentially what we already have now, assuming God created us and gave us minds, DNA, and the ability to procreate? Yes, except for the fact that we eventually die, whereas the Mind Apps and the cloned bodies would get to exist forever. That's the difference between mortality and seeming immortality.

Even if all of this were possible and all of this outlandish science fiction could somehow become science reality—it still would bring us right back to the two fundamental questions we humans started with and have always had: Is there a God? And do we have souls? After I die, would my soul be me, or would my cloned body and my downloaded Mind App be me, or would there now actually be two of me? One me might be my soul—the "real" me that still has to answer to God—while the other me might be the sophisticated interactive copy and biological clone of me that would still be existing here on Earth even after the "real" me is gone. But maybe the two of me could be united so *both* of me would be just me. Perhaps that could be accomplished in the following manner: first, what if the immortal software copy of me were made *before* I died, and then what if that copy of me—the full copy of my entire mind—were used to overwrite my current brain inside of my physical body right now, so that my current mind would become just a copy of my Mind App, which then could be copied once again and transferred into my new cloned body, at which point authorities could then terminate (kill?) my original physical body. Now would I (whoever or whatever that truly is), my true essence, have become the immortal Mind App, or would I have died when my mind (my physical brain) was overwritten with a copy of my own mind—my Mind App? It is difficult to fully conceptualize, but think about a document file that is copied on a computer and then that copy is immediately used to overwrite the original document file—*once that is done, would the original have now just become a copy of the copy*? If not, and there still would be two distinct documents, would they be two originals or two copies, and would any distinction between such an original and such a copy now have become entirely meaningless?

It is interesting to think about how I might fear that a Mind App replica of my mind existing as interactive software inside of a biological clone of my physical body might become and actually *be* me in place of the "real me," who is walking around for now in this temporary physical body. So there might be two of me competing as me—the "immortal" biological clone of me implanted with my Mind App AND the original "mortal" me that will eventually die as a biological organism. Might the original me become worried that the clone-app of me could legally (or otherwise—say, in the eyes of God) take my place as me, or at least be the parallel me, but I would not be "immortal," only the clone-App copy of me would be immortal. Would only the real, mortal, me retain my original soul, as my soul would literally have been lost in translation over to the clone-App copy of me, or would the clone-App copy of me now really also possess my soul, especially if the clone App copy of me had been used to overwrite my original self while I was still alive?

As advanced and puzzlingly difficult such a conceptualization of the problem of dual souls might be given such advanced technology, it may not be much beyond what some indigenous people on Earth first thought when they encountered the new technology of photography and even videotape used by more technologically advanced explorers. There are accounts (or at least folklore) that people from certain indigenous tribes did not want their photograph taken because they feared that the photographs would capture and "steal" their souls—after all, the photo technology captures one's image, and an even more advanced video camera can "capture" how one actually looks, moves, sounds, and talks. After someone dies, that person's children can still access a video of that person and see and hear that person as if that person is still alive, but the video is not really that person. In short, a copy of me is not me, but perhaps those indigenous people who feared the photo or video camera were on to something in at least a certain sense, even if we can now contemplate much more sophisticated technology like a Mind App and fully cloned bodies that are not mere passive recordings but actual interactive software that can learn.

Remember, in the context of a Mind App and a cloned body, we would have more than just a *passive* recording of light and sound waves emanating from a person at a certain point in time and captured in photo or video. Instead, we would have a fully *interactive* database Mind App that would replicate everything that would constitute a person's entire mind. It seems like such an app might be thought to capture one's soul because what am I, besides, or in addition to, my mind, other than my biological body (but we can all agree that my body is not my soul but just a temporary biological vehicle for me that will eventually expire)? So, do we have souls that transcend the essence of our entire minds and thought processes, and is there a God who created us with those souls? Even if there is such a thing as a soul and we each have one, will science nevertheless one day be able to replicate that soul or, better yet, even to create a soul?

It is strange to me that one of the reasons I believe in God is that I do not want this life to be all there is and I quite like the idea of being immortal, especially the part about never having to say the ultimate good-bye to a loved one, or to the universe, for that matter, yet the idea of creating a Mind App for my mind that can be stored and transferred forever and even be implanted into biological clones of my body, although amazing and incredible, in the end, somehow still seems deficient to me and perhaps not even desirable. Imagine the nerve of me to be so picky as to the type of immortality that I am willing to accept!

Maybe the final step would be to convince me that my Mind App would be the real me and that the brain, the mind, and the biological body that constitute who and what I now am are nothing more than a temporary vehicle until I can be fully transferred into a software program in a cloned body that can exist forever. Could I ever be convinced that my Mind App is not just a *copy* of me but actually *is* me? At that point, I would have to be able to consider the brain and body that I was born with to be nothing more than just human tissue that, like shed skin, would no longer be the true, core essence of me but just a shell of me because I truly would have become my clone-Mind App.

WHAT ABOUT A FUTURISTIC SYMBOLIC TOWER OF BABEL?

If so, immortality would be possible, and it would be great, although there also might be something to the notion of not overstaying one's welcome here on Earth. Perhaps we should simply muster enough class to take a final bow and then be willing to fade off of the stage, so to the extent there might be any real possible immortality left in life, perhaps it exists only in how we are remembered by others and how we get some of it in the form of our children—and in our own human posterity. Perhaps that's as good as it will ever get, Mind Apps and cloned bodies notwithstanding. The reality might be that any immortality on Earth could never really be anything more than our own children and the next generation, anyway. I know that when I look into my two young sons' eyes and I see all the hope and promise they represent and I also realize that with every passing moment, it is profoundly becoming "their turn" in life—that is still pretty good, even though my mortality awaits! Still, I am thankful for just that as a gift, even if it is but a very temporary gift.

So perhaps the story of the Tower of Babel is really just a huge lesson about how even if the people could have built that impossible tower to Heaven, they would not have gained *true entrance* into Heaven anyway but only entrance into a cold, dark outer space. Therefore, even if we somehow, someday, develop the technology to capture a human mind in a Mind App where one's mind can live forever and can be transplanted into one's own cloned body every so often, forever, that still might not be the kind of immortality that we would be searching for, because it would not be "real"—whatever that may be.

I would just have to decide at that time whether I would cross that Mind App-clone bridge if I ever came to it. It is interesting to think about whether I would or could be immortal or whether, at most, only a copy of me could or would be immortal, because that distinction would affect my decision. If only a cyber-clone copy of me would be immortal, then I suppose that I would be very jealous of my copied cyber-clones' immortality. If that copy of me would be anything like the original me, and I guess we are assuming a big "yes" to that one, then, although I could not say for sure, I bet the cloned copy version of me would likewise be jealous of my soul (assuming I would retain it) and of the fact that I, "the real thing," was here first.

I would have to ask him, my Mind-App clone, if he would be jealous—and if I did so right now as a result of considering my own question, the answer would be this: although he cannot say for sure and does not really even know why, the Mind App clone of me would be jealous of my soul, despite his Mind App-clone immortality. But he also would say, "Maybe you were here before me, but remember that I'll be here long after you are gone." Perhaps that is a good thing for him, or maybe all it means is that he just gets left behind.

If we really want to talk about a true test of faith, however, consider this: How would you choose if you either could be immortal on Earth, in the form of a Mind App and a new cloned body forever, or you could elect to die on Earth to free your soul so your spirit could enter Heaven and you could be with God forever? Would you have enough faith in God and in having a soul that lives on to take that gamble, or would you instead opt for the sure thing here on Earth—an immortal Mind App-clone version of yourself that might just be you and that gets to exist forever? Maybe you could hedge your bets and do both without having to choose, but would that really count as true *faith?* Does true faith require taking that ultimate risk?

Chapter Eighty-Nine

What Are We Going to Do When We Finally Discover That There Is Other Life in the Universe?

It is amazing to me that the possibility of other life existing in the universe is still considered much of an open question when one contemplates the astronomical (pun intended) odds at work here. How reasonable is it to assume that in this unbelievably vast universe of ours, there is no life whatsoever besides what we have here on Earth? How absurdly myopic, and even silly, that seems in terms of what qualifies as reasonable speculation on our part. What will our descendants hundreds or even thousands of years from now think of us and our most unenlightened assumptions about our own alleged self-importance in this universe? Until we find it, however, we cannot say for sure.

I am not necessarily talking about little green men or UFOs containing human-like grays that for some strange reason would have evolved with the exact same physical characteristics as humans—two arms, two legs, two hands, two feet, a head, a face, two eyes, a nose, a mouth, lungs, a heart, a digestive system, blood, and so on, unless they are human beings from our own future who can engage in time travel and have come back in time, and have evolved to be very thin humanoids with big heads, and so we must look like short muscular gorilla-like primates compared to them, much like we probably would think early humanoids millions of years ago would appear compared to us now. Of course, maybe UFOs themselves are just spacecraft from aliens, just like we send out our own unmanned spacecraft and space probes with computers and special motors on board that possibly would be UFOs to other worlds. Interesting as all that may be, I am instead wondering about other life in forms that we may not even be able to imagine at this point—*and consider the possible mistakes* we might make, much like those by the Native Americans who had never seen a horse until they encountered a Spanish soldier riding a horse and thought it was all one God-like creature, or those by natives who constructed idols of airplanes the first time they ever saw an airplane in the sky.

It follows that it would be wise of fundamentalist believers to at least consider the possibility extraterrestrial life, and also what such a discovery would mean for their belief in the literal God of the Bible. Would discovering other life in the universe drastically change their religious beliefs, perhaps making them doubt the Bible because the Bible appears to completely ignore the possibility of life anywhere else? Or would fundamentalists instead try to reinterpret the text of the Bible to somehow argue that the Bible actually acknowledges, and maybe even has predicted, the discovery of other life in the universe?

Another response might be to doubt the discovery of other life as just an evil trick of Satan or of atheist scientists who must hate God. But wait. How can atheist scientists simultaneously hate God *and* not believe in Him? If they actually hate Him, then aren't they unwittingly admitting that also He exists? Perhaps believers will say that although the Bible does not clearly state that there is extraterrestrial life in the universe, neither does the Bible definitively state that there is *not* extraterrestrial life and thus, the Bible is not wrong. Or maybe after all the dust would settle, they would just nonchalantly say, "So what? The discovery of life on other planets does not mean that God does not exist."

Whatever their particular reaction may be, the reaction of humanity is sure to be quite profound. Our discovery of life on other planets, or in other parts of the universe, would represent an incredible paradigm shift in our entire concept of the universe and of our place and insignificance in it. Such a discovery would be profound for religion because it would show that the universe is not just some vast wasteland without any importance. All of a sudden, it would seem like the God of the Bible would be, quite literally, very local, insular, and quite unaware of our significant surroundings instead of being truly universal as the omniscient, omnipotent Creator of the entire universe, who ignores all life in the universe except us. Look at all of the variety of life God allegedly created just on this planet (and only we matter—that life was put here just for us)!

Imagine, if we can, what we don't know. What if life as we know it currently on Earth did not include plants and trees and vegetation but only mammals, birds, insects, and fish, and then we discovered plants existing on some other planet? At first, we might not even recognize those plants as life-forms because they would be so different—we probably would ask, Is it really even alive if it cannot move around or think about anything or if it has no consciousness? Maybe streams of energy or conglomerations of gases are actual entities or life-forms of some sort that we may not at first even be able to recognize as such.

Moreover, if the life-forms we discovered were advanced, and if we could somehow actually communicate with other beings that we could even recognize as other beings, how interesting would it be to compare and contrast everything, and anything, with them? Would they have anything resembling political or social systems, religion, science, games, history, physics, economics, emotions, love, empathy, justice, logic, mathematics, fears, dreams, psychology, children, pets, senses of humor, and other things, that might even remotely resemble what we have and what we care about in any way? And what would be just insanely different about them and literally out-of-this-world distinct about them from everything and anything we might have ever been able to imagine heretofore?

How amazing and fascinating it all would be. Such a discovery would require huge adjustments to a dogmatic, literal interpretation of God, as did the discoveries that the earth is not flat; that we revolve around the sun; that we are not at the center of the universe; that organisms adapt, change, and evolve (or at least micro-evolve); that psychological diseases or psychiatric disorders are not all simply a function of demonic possession; or that weather events have scientific, meteorological causes rather than just being the result of angering some weather god, perhaps for not sacrificing a person or animal in some elaborate ritual.

Of course, the scientific paradigm shift would be enormous. That's why I also wonder to what extent there would be a similar momentous shift in religious thinking. Would such a discovery somehow be incorporated into religion, or would the "alleged" discovery be rejected as an evil trick (perhaps as a government conspiracy designed to scare us into submission)? Would people think it was the end of the world (like we do whenever there are lots of natural disasters), or would they think it was the dawn of an entirely new age of possibility, or would it merely be just another really interesting scientific discovery, albeit a huge scientific discovery? Would we assume that God must have created that life too?

If we do not take the Bible so literally—like it is an accurate recipe book or an unvarnished historical scientific journal of the universe that was actually written by God—perhaps we could conceive of God in such a way that the discovery of life on other planets would not make a continued religious belief in the literal God of the Bible seem so naïve. To still believe in God, despite life being discovered on other planets, we would need to not be so beholden to certain Bronze Age beliefs stemming from a dogmatic interpretation of an ancient text written by ancient men employing ancient ideas about ancient history.

Obviously, I am not referring to life in other parts of the universe as being the inhabitants of Heaven or Hell or other spiritual or mystical constructs but instead as real, tangible life-forms. Of course, we have not yet discovered other life in the Universe, and, so, really, who knows for sure if there is, or is not, other life in the Universe? Although we have to be open to the possibility that there is no life anywhere else in the Universe, because we still have not yet found any; with the sextillions of stars and trillions of galaxies in the Universe, with countless planets, many of which are very Earth-like in their structure, position, and make-up, it seems astoundingly narrow-minded and blindly insular to assume that the life-forms here on Earth are all alone as life-forms in the entire universe. Time and space are so vast, however, that perhaps other life has existed somewhere in the universe in the past, but is now extinct; or once we become extinct, other life in the universe will develop—all so far away in time and space that we would never know about it.

So far, the reality is that we have made no such discovery, and I suppose it is unlikely that such a discovery will be made for sure anytime soon. Still, I would be very nervous if my religion required me to bet against it. I look at the incredible diversity of life-forms just here on Earth and wonder how it could be possible that life does not also exist in unimaginably fantastic forms, on countless other planets, throughout the universe. Various types of insects sure look like what "space aliens" might look like. It seems insufferably arrogant and incredibly self-absorbed to think that only we are here and the entire universe is just all about us.

I think the discovery of other life in the universe is inevitable. Maybe it will be soon, or maybe it will be far off into the future, but I would hate to think that it would mean that much, if not all, of my religious construct of God would have to come crumbling down because scientifically unaware and uneducated men thousands of years ago in the Middle East either could not or did not conceive of such a discovery when they wrote about the universe in the Bible, to the extent that they even wrote about the universe or had even the slightest idea how incredibly vast it is.

Chapter Ninety

More Genealogy Charts of Various Super-Old Jews

[10] These are the generations of Shem: Shem was an hundred years old, and begat Arphaxad two years after the flood:

[11] And Shem lived after he begat Arphaxad five hundred years, and begat sons and daughters.

[12] And Arphaxad lived five and thirty years, and begat Salah:

[13] And Arphaxad lived after he begat Salah four hundred and three years, and begat sons and daughters.

[14] And Salah lived thirty years, and begat Eber:

[15] And Salah lived after he begat Eber four hundred and three years, and begat sons and daughters.

[16] And Eber lived four and thirty years, and begat Peleg:

[17] And Eber lived after he begat Peleg four hundred and thirty years, and begat sons and daughters.

[18] And Peleg lived thirty years, and begat Reu:

[19] And Peleg lived after he begat Reu two hundred and nine years, and begat sons and daughters.

[20] And Reu lived two and thirty years, and begat Serug:

[21] And Reu lived after he begat Serug two hundred and seven years, and begat sons and daughters.

[22] And Serug lived thirty years, and begat Nahor:

[23] And Serug lived after he begat Nahor two hundred years, and begat sons and daughters.

[24] And Nahor lived nine and twenty years, and begat Terah:

[25] And Nahor lived after he begat Terah an hundred and nineteen years, and begat sons and daughters.

[26] And Terah lived seventy years, and begat Abram, Nahor, and Haran.

[27] Now these are the generations of Terah: Terah begat Abram, Nahor, and Haran; and Haran begat Lot.

[28] And Haran died before his father Terah in the land of his nativity, in Ur of the Chaldees.

[29] And Abram and Nahor took them wives: the name of Abram's wife was Sarai; and the name of Nahor's wife, Milcah, the daughter of Haran, the father of Milcah, and the father of Iscah.

[30] But Sarai was barren; she had no child.

[31] And Terah took Abram his son, and Lot the son of Haran his son's son, and Sarai his daughter in law, his son Abram's wife; and they went forth with them from Ur of the Chaldees, to go into the land of Canaan; and they came unto Haran, and dwelt there.
[32] And the days of Terah were two hundred and five years: and Terah died in Haran.

I suppose it is a fitting, although certainly an anticlimactic, way to end this exploration of the first eleven chapters of the text of Genesis with yet another typical detailed family lineage of A begetting B, who begat C and then lived for X number of years. Interestingly, it picks up with Noah's son, Shem's generations. What possible significant relevance do these lineages have, as there is more information provided in them than would allow for simply marking the passage of years or tracing the ancestral line from Adam to Noah to Abraham, through the house of David, and then finally to Jesus's step-father, Joseph (while completely ignoring the line of Jesus's mother, Mary, who was the source of 100% of all the human DNA in Jesus). If the purpose of these lineages is not to show the relatively short time the universe and the earth have been here—a mere 6,000 to 10,000 years or so, despite all the scientific evidence to the contrary—one does wonder why God would use all of this valuable communication space in the Bible simply to trace this rather mundane, and mere chart-like information of these particular people in history in the Middle East.

Chapter Ninety-One

But What if I Am Wrong?

Perhaps this is a good place to ponder what effect the text of the first 11 chapters of Genesis might have on the issue of faith, either because of or in spite of the text of the first eleven chapter of the Bible—which is the topic for Part Four, which follows. Before moving on to Part Four, however, I include here the text of one last letter that I wrote to my father years ago. It actually relates to a concern that a believer might have for an atheist. In fact, Richard Dawkins, the famed atheist and scientist-author, at a lecture on atheism and religion, was once asked by a believer in the audience about the possible consequences of his atheism regarding eternity. The believer asked him, "What if you're wrong?"—implying that Dawkins would be bound for Hell and an eternity to be spent in pain and torment, whereas if the believer was wrong, then it would not be nearly as risky for her because she would simply die, just like the atheist and everyone else, and that would be the end of it. So the implication of her question was, Isn't it taking a monumentally stupid risk to be an atheist in the event that you are wrong?

Dawkins's reply to the question was simple but powerful: "well, what if you're wrong!" He put the question right back to her by asking her to consider any and all of the seemingly endless possibilities of beliefs and myths about various gods and the cosmos—indeed, what if when a fundamentalist Christian is being judged at the gates of Heaven, Allah and Muhammad show up, and unfortunately for the believer, they are very angry? The implication is that, in reality, the risks for both a believer and an atheist are almost identical. This is known as Pascal's Wager, which rhetorically postulates why, as a matter of game theory, it makes rational sense to believe in God. I have always thought that if one does not *really* believe in God but is simply hedging one's bets by believing, that kind of a faith somehow should not count as a legitimate, genuine faith in God anyway. If it does, then we allow for God just scaring and intimidating us into professing faith in Him and letting us into Heaven, but only because of His colossal potential threat against us, which He fully intends to implement if we do not comply.

My father once made this same argument to me, in an attempt to show me, "mathematically," why one should believe in God. It rested on the assumption that there would be at least a 50-50 chance that my dad or an atheist was either correct or incorrect about his belief or non-belief in God. I disagreed with the reasoning of Pascal's Wager, because, again, we would be reducing God to mere fire insurance as a way of escaping Hell if a mere strategic game-theory maneuver would be the only reason we would believe in God. I also disagreed with my dad's math that there is a 50% chance that he is right about his beliefs and a 50% chance that an atheist would be right about his non-beliefs. My letter to him follows:

THE 50/50 PERCENTAGE ISSUE WITH THE HYPOTHETICAL ATHEIST

*Dad, I return to this issue because I want you to understand why I believe so strongly that you were mistaken when we discussed it. Frankly, I could not understand your tenacious resistance to this point, but I realized that perhaps you did not understand my point (which is probably my fault for failing to explain it adequately). Thus, it is a rather **small** point, but I still want you to at least understand my argument.*

*It is important to note at the outset that my problem with your position was more of a **mathematical** one, and not so much of a **theological** one, although the motivation to believe in God seems like it should be more positive than simply being intimidated into believing— "believe that I am a loving God so that I do not have to torture you forever." But at least the math issue I think is clear, as opposed to more typical disagreements about esoteric matters of theological interpretation.*

Beginning with your initial statement, you stated that whenever you speak to an atheist, you always concede to him that there is a 50% chance that he may be right and, as a result, that both of you, along with the rest of humanity, will simply die and that will be the end of your existence because there would be no after life. However, in fairness to your concession to him, you further point out that there is also a 50% chance that you may be right about the existence of Jesus/God and the plan of salvation, and, as a result, when the two of you die, you will go to Heaven and he (the atheist, and all others who think like him and who reject Jesus) will spend eternity in Hell.

*Your underlying rationale for making this comparative/contrasting type of argument is to demonstrate that even if an atheist is right about there being no afterlife, he or she really has "nothing to lose" by being a Christian (because we will all just die anyway). But if you are right, that person would go to Hell and thus would have **everything to lose** by being an atheist (and you would go to Heaven and thus would have **everything to gain** by being a Christian). Accordingly, when all is said and done, the underlying mathematical odds are all clearly in favor of being a Christian, given the comparative risks of being incorrect. In short, why do atheists take this huge risk, especially when such is not necessary? Actually, your argument is an old argument first made by the philosopher Pascal, who agrees with you. This argument is referred to as "Pascal's Wager." In any event, I understand what you (and Pascal) are saying here, as the following diagram demonstrates:*

IF DAD IS CORRECT:	DAD GOES TO HEAVEN (ETERNAL BLISS); ATHEIST GOES TO HELL (ETERNAL PAIN)	50% POSSIBILITY IT IS TRUE
IF THE ATHEIST IS CORRECT:	BOTH DAD AND ATHEIST SIMPLY DIE (THERE WOULD BE NO HEAVEN, HELL, OR AFTERLIFE FOR EITHER OF THEM)	50% POSSIBILITY IT IS TRUE

However, **and this is where we got into trouble,** I then qualified this simple, but correct, model with the observation that this 50/50 proposition remains valid only if you and the atheist are **the only two people on earth who have ever thought about, and have the only two arguments regarding, the afterlife** (and assuming each of your opinions is entitled to equal weight, which is a huge assumption, but in fairness and for the sake of argument, let's make that assumption). I stated that once you **add** the theologies of others who have **competing** conceptions about the afterlife, then the 50/50 percentage model, as a matter of logic and math, **necessarily** changes (as long as each human being's view remains entitled to equal weight, which, admittedly, is a huge assumption).

Although there still may be a 50% chance that the atheist is correct about there being no afterlife, it is incorrect for you to argue that there is also a 50% chance that **your particular conception of the afterlife** is the **correct AND ONLY conception of the afterlife** such that there is a corresponding 50% chance that you will go to Heaven and the atheist, to Hell. In other words, perhaps there still might be a general 50% chance that there is **an** afterlife (and a 50% chance that there is not), which I grant you for the sake of argument; but there is **not** a corresponding 50% chance that **your particular conception** about the afterlife is the **only** correct one, whereby you can argue to the atheist that there is a 50% chance that you, Dad Galves, will necessarily go to Heaven and the atheist will necessarily go to Hell simply because there may be a 50% chance of **an** afterlife **of some kind**.

The "qualified" diagram below takes this point into account. This is all I was trying to say when I made my observation in the first place that the 50/50 percentage **changes** once the issue is no longer posed **exclusively** between you and the atheist.

THERE IS AN AFTER LIFE **OF SOME KIND**	(1) Dad is correct about it	(2) Buddhist is correct about it	(3) Muslim is correct about it	(4) Catholic bishop is correct about it	(5) Native American is correct about it	(6)	etc.	= 50% POSSIBIL ITY
ATHEIST IS CORRECT (no afterlife)								= 50% POSSIBIL ITY

The numbers [(1), (2), (3), etc.] in the above diagram represent various groups of individuals who all agree that there is indeed an afterlife (your point) of some kind but who also *disagree (my point): (1) on what that afterlife is and which deity is the one true deity, (2) on how to get to enjoy that afterlife (presumably getting to go to Heaven and not being sent to Hell), and (3) on which among them is going to Heaven and who is going to Hell, or some other spiritual construct of the afterlife.*

*For example, (1) you, (2) a Buddhist monk, (3) a member of Islam, (4) a Catholic bishop, (5) a Native American medicine man, and (6) a Hindu (into the thousands of different religions and sects) all may believe there is indeed **an** afterlife (hence the original 50% chance that there is an afterlife, with which I agree), but they do **not** agree that you, Dad Galves, as a Baptist preacher, are necessarily going to Heaven just because there is **some kind of afterlife** and they will all be going to Hell, along with the atheist, but only you and everyone who agrees with you will be going to Heaven.*

*In reality, the 50% chance that there is some kind of afterlife needs to be **further divided** among the competing individuals who believe that there is an afterlife (but only for those who believe **just like them**). Indeed, many of those who believe there is an afterlife also believe that **you** and everyone who agrees with you are going to Hell (or something or somewhere akin to it) exactly because you, along with the atheist, are a "non-believer" and "infidel" of **their** religion (and vice versa).*

*Thus, as I said before, I believe that you must amend your statement to the hypothetical atheist and reduce your percentage of possibly being correct to something along the order of perhaps 1% (assuming there are only 50 religions competing with yours, which is quite low; in reality, it should be reduced by the huge numbers of belief systems that are different than yours) for the proposition that you, Dad Galves, will go to Heaven and the atheist will go to Hell. You cannot correctly hold on to the proposition that there is a 50% chance that you are going to go to Heaven simply because there may be a 50% chance that there may be **some kind of an afterlife.** According to some, even if there is an afterlife, you still would be going to Hell, because as far as they are concerned, you would be no different than any other "atheist" who does not believe in their god—the only "true" god.*

*To the extent there are groups of atheists or agnostics who may believe differently among themselves as to how we all got here (i.e., evolution, a "Big Bang" theory, space aliens are just having an interesting "experiment," we are being overly egotistical in even theorizing that any of us could ever even know, etc.), those are all disagreements about where humankind **may have come from** but not disagreements as to where we **might be going after we die**—there seems to be complete agreement among atheists on that point: NOWHERE, or, among agnostics: WE DON'T KNOW. So perhaps their 50% does not need to be subdivided because they do not believe anyone is going to Hell, because for them, there is no Hell or Heaven to go to.*

As a result, all atheists, no matter how diverse or downright "crazy" you may think their cosmology is, still all agree with each other on one thing: that everyone will simply die and there will be no afterlife for anyone, no exceptions, and what we do on Earth does not matter, at least not in any ultimate sense. The diagram below represents that view:

THERE IS AN AFTERLIFE **OF** **SOME** **KIND**	(1) Dad is correct about it	(2) Buddhist is correct about it	(3) Muslim is correct about it	(4) Catholic bishop is correct about it	(5) Native American is correct about it	(6)	etc.	= 50% POSSIBILITY
ATHEIST IS CORRECT (no afterlife)	Atheist (1); Atheist (2); Atheist (3); Atheist (4); Atheist (5); etc. These atheists still **all agree** on the idea that there is no afterlife, and, most importantly for our purposes, they do **not disagree** on the ultimate implications of this belief, unlike those directly above, who believe there is an afterlife of some kind but disagree on which among them will get to enter "Heaven" and which of them is destined for "Hell."							= 50% POSSIBILITY

*Logically, you really cannot have competing conceptions of a **non-**afterlife **of any consequence.** No atheist believes any another atheist is **not** going to be any less [or more] dead than they are, with no place for their nonexistent soul to go, anyway.*

*Thus, it is not necessary to **further subdivide** the 50% chance that there is no afterlife because atheists all **agree** on the proposition that there is no afterlife. If they believed otherwise, then they would move to the general 50% category that believes there is an afterlife of some kind. Again, that 50% chance of a non-afterlife is **opposite** to the 50% chance that there is some kind of afterlife because those who may agree there is an afterlife (generally most every religion on earth) also **disagree**, among other things, on which of them are going to go to "Heaven" and which of them may be "misguided" and bound for "Hell."*

*As a result, your particular conception (Baptist, fundamentalist Christianity) is only **one among many**, and therefore, the percentage chance of your being correct about your necessarily going to Heaven has to correspondingly be reduced when you introduce others into the mix, besides you and the atheist—which, again, has been my point all along. I apologize for being so repetitive, but I wanted to take a few different stabs at the issue from slightly different directions. It is really a very simple mathematical observation, but obviously a difficult one to explain. Again, my disagreement with you on this point is a matter of math and logic, not of theology, but I believe the point of contention is, nonetheless, irrefutable.*

Chapter Ninety-Two

Conclusion to Part Three

At this point, the first 11 books of Genesis have been analyzed and considered, the creation stories are complete, and later biblical history of humanity (at least in the Middle East) begins. I had planned to continue to go through all 50 chapters of Genesis, but the analysis and commentary up to this point are far too long now to complete all 50 chapters in a single book. This juncture is a fitting place to proceed to Part Four, a shorter part of the book, which comes full circle to the very general topic with which I started—do I believe in God and, if so, why?

It is with a heavy heart, however, that I close Part Three by revealing an unfortunate personal development that occurred during the middle stages of writing this book. As I was writing the book, I thought my dad should have a draft of the book so he would not totally be blindsided by it when and if it ever got published. I had written him letters before over the years (see above), but this book is something he views as the ultimate disrespectful "letter" to him, though I contend that it is not. In fact, I greatly thank my dad for all of the past discussions we have ever had, because I appreciate his perspective. I think he is very smart, and wow, has it ever given us something to talk about over the years, but the book is not all about him. After all, I do have my own ideas and questions about religion, the Bible, and God, from my perspective, and I wanted to share them in this book.

Before I gave him an earlier draft of the book, my dad and I already had exchanged some heated words about the Arizona immigration bill passed in 2010 (most of which has been struck down by the US Supreme Court) and the general politics of US immigration policy. It was really more of a political debate between us than a religious one. In that debate, I could not believe that my dad could be so callous and uncaring for immigrant families that have come to this country because we lure them with low-paying jobs. Similarly, he could not believe that I didn't want to arrest them all as law breakers and deport them and their families back to Mexico, especially because I am a professor of law, who is supposed to believe in upholding the law.

Of course, it is not that I support "breaking the law," but I did think it was very mean-spirited to refer to them as "illegals," and even "criminals," who should all be rounded up and deported without regard to splitting up families or to considering why they were here in the first place—to supply exploitable cheap labor that many Americans are not willing to do. I argued that rounding them up, as well as making Latino-looking people, including US citizens, produce their papers if they are ever legally detained, seems unrealistic and, to some extent, unconstitutional. It is, of course, a difficult, multifaceted, and highly nuanced policy problem, but these people are not just like illegal cattle that we have to deal with (and take advantage of).

I guess it became a little too offensive when I stated to my dad that I did not believe that Jesus would be so uncaring about these human beings just because they came from the wrong side of the border and were here without proper documentation. I quoted the verse about Jesus wanting us to see the Jesus in every stranger we meet, which I argued includes even an undocumented worker/illegal alien. All my dad could say was that they were illegal drug smugglers who wanted to sneak across the border to have babies and to take advantage of our welfare system. In my emotional indignation, my judgment faltered and I made a terrible mistake. I said to my father that instead of acting like Jesus, he was acting like an asshole. It was a mistake, and I should not have said that.

Obviously at that time, I could not see that, no matter what my dad was advocating, I was actually the one who clearly was acting like the asshole for even saying that, to my own father, no less. Although I was quoting Jesus about being kind to strangers, I am sure that Jesus was not too proud of me at that moment, when I was being unkind to my own dad and certainly not honoring my father as the one of the Ten Commandments commands. It was wrong of me, it was hypocritical of me, and I shouldn't have said it, obviously, and I am sorry. I should have known better. It is a struggle to control our passion—at least it is for me.

The next week, I drove, with my two boys, down to San Diego from Sacramento (about an 8 or 9-hour drive) to see my dad and so my boys and I could attend his church in person on Father's Day to surprise him and so that I could apologize to him face to face. He was distant about us being there but cordial enough and even acknowledged our presence in front of the people in his church; however, he told me from the pulpit that he had to leave town right after church ended so we could not stay and visit with him. People were around, and he said he had to leave, and then he hastily said good-bye to us, so we could not really talk, but he told me and the boys that he would call us and we could talk then. We had surprised him, and it was true that his trip out of town right after church had already been planned. I wanted to respect his wishes and let him call when, and if, he was ready to accept my apology when we could talk privately. I felt OK about it because I at least had shown up to see him on Father's Day in his church as a show of respect and to demonstrate that I was sorry for what I had said to him and that I wanted to talk about it.

Unfortunately, I never heard from him again, and it became clear that he did not want to talk to either me or to my boys. After he got a copy of an early draft of the book, I called him to try to apologize again, and although I did apologize, it was simply too late; the damage had been done; it was not a pleasant conversation. In short, I had crossed the line, and I was not to be forgiven. Not surprisingly, the early draft of the book certainly did not help. It has been over two years. I miss talking to him; I even miss arguing with him; plus, he's my dad.

Calling my dad a bad name in a disrespectful way and daring to write this book, asking the questions I have, which call into doubt many of his beliefs, but not all of his beliefs, have together been far too much of a personal affront to him. It is now simply too late. I was going to write to him yet another long letter reminding him about the story of the prodigal son in the Bible and say that there was a biblical lesson here about a wayward son asking for and receiving forgiveness from his father, but my dad was, and is, in no mood for my arguments, analogies, another letter, or my references to the Bible about anything I may think about it, not to mention this book.

I guess some things just cannot be forgiven. Of course, I am glad Jesus does not see it that way when we ask for forgiveness from Him, unless what I have done truly is an unpardonable sin—the blasphemy of the Holy Spirit. We make mistakes, we are human, and we have to take responsibility for our mistakes. We can ask for forgiveness, but of course we cannot *demand forgiveness* from anyone. Jesus may have forgiven me, but my dad still has not—but that is my dad's right. There is no automatic right to demand and receive forgiveness from another human being; it doesn't work that way.

The situation has also been very disappointing for me because I was actually very excited to let my dad know that I am not an atheist, even if I cannot quite agree with his very literal, fundamentalist interpretations of the Bible and his personal views about God—that despite everything, I still believe in God. My dad was not impressed, however. Although we certainly had risen above such disagreements and different perspectives in the past, this time was different. Although my dad has made mistakes in the past as a father, as I have as a son, mistakes for which we both have apologized, this time was different; I am disappointed that the gulf between us has seemingly become insurmountable.

Nonetheless, my wife, our two sons, and I remain hopeful that one day, my dad will let us back into his life and that "one day" will be sometime soon, as we are all getting older and the boys are growing up so fast. I especially feel bad because my two boys had nothing to do with it; they are just my sons, and it is not their fault they happen to have me as their perhaps overly argumentative and petulant father. Nevertheless, I still believe in the goodness of my dad's heart, and I give him the benefit of the doubt. His great qualities as a person far outweigh any of his bad, and most of all, I apologize again for offending him. I apologize for calling him a bad word; but I guess I cannot go so far as to also apologize for writing this book, or for seeing the world and the universe the way I do.

Now for Part Four …At this point, just exactly what do I think about God, the Bible, and my own faith? Is it possible to be a nonbeliever in some literal interpretation of the Bible yet still somehow believe in God? I think so…

PART FOUR

THE PARADOX OF FAITH AND RATIONALITY

It was the best of times, it was the worst of times, it was the age of wisdom, it was the age of foolishness, it was the epoch of belief, it was the epoch of incredulity, it was the season of Light, it was the season of Darkness, it was the spring of hope, it was the winter of despair, we had everything before us, we had nothing before us, we were all going direct to heaven, we were all going direct the other way—in short, the period was so far like the present period, that some of its noisiest authorities insisted on its being received, for good or for evil, in the superlative degree of comparison only.

—Charles Dickens, *A Tale of Two Cities*

Chapter Ninety-Three

Belief without Proof? Based on What?

Because I claim to believe in God, or a Supreme Being, I can imagine a very incredulous and quite disappointed Richard Dawkins, the famous author and atheist, saying to me, "Fred, given all of what you have written in your book about Genesis, how can you intellectually still believe in God? What form of logic or rationale could you possibly be using in order to come to that most unsupportable conclusion? In short, why are you not an atheist? Did you not read or fully understand your own book, especially Parts Two and Three?"

These are fair questions. They are questions that permeate my conscience and for which I still search for answers. The truth is, I don't know how, or even why, I believe in God, but I do. Perhaps it is because of a fear that there is nothing more than this life, coupled with a delusion that we are these supremely important beings with metaphysical spirits that get to live forever at the center of an epic battle in the universe between the forces of good and evil. The truth is that I do not have a good, logical, evidence-based rationale for my belief. Instead, my belief is almost entirely intuitive and emotional. If I were judging a debate between atheists and believers, the atheists would win because what fundamentalists offer as proof that God exists and that the Bible is literally true is not proof at all. In fact, it is laughable as "proof" because it is similar to arguing that there is proof that Greek mythology is true or that any religion is true. Most importantly in terms of faith, if there were actually verifiable scientific proof that God exists, there really would not be any need for our faith in God, because He would exist purely as a matter of undeniable demonstrative logic—the same way we need no faith to know that the Pacific Ocean exists.

We cannot say that God exists purely as a matter of undeniable logic, however, so I reject the arguments of fundamentalists who think that only they know God and know what I must do and not do to know God too. I also reject their very judgmental and narrow concept of God and their assumption that God wrote every word of the Bible. I do so because if God did actually write the Bible, He would not have made *any* mistakes or contradictions in it. Also, God would not now require believers to perform tremendous mental gymnastics to rationalize all of the mistakes, inconsistencies, and contradictions the Bible contains. I therefore reject the intellectually weak effort to assert that the Bible makes logical sense as a book written by an omniscient and infallible God.

So, my belief in God is not in the literal portrayal of Him as set forth in the Bible. Although my belief in God might be a great contradiction, it is for me more of an enigma, inside of an apparent contradiction, circumscribed by a mystical connection to something that is infinitely more grandiose than what has been written in the Bible. The Bible was written by various authors thousands of years ago, and it has since been interpreted and reinterpreted in many different ways by many different people with many different agendas. Thus, trite as it may sound, God is truly a mystery found within contradictory information, so, to limit the definition of God to the writings of certain men who lived in one part of the ancient world is, to my mind, a moronic oversimplification of God.

Grappling with these issues has been quite an intellectual and spiritual challenge for me, as well as a personally revealing journey. I started out as a believer but was still quite skeptical of a literal interpretation of the Bible, or of any text, for that matter. At that time, though, I had never attempted to read the Bible word for word, cover to cover. I had read only bits and parts and listened to what other people had said about it. I had tried to take it seriously in a very general way and then, maybe subconsciously, convince myself that it all must be true. I saw that much of the Bible was metaphorical, yet I believed it was still divinely inspired, if not the actual Word of God. As I first began fully reading Genesis with an open mind, hoping to get a general or even personal message from God, however, the stories became more and more incredulous. As I thought seriously about what I was reading, trying to deepen my understanding and strengthen my faith, I became troubled with the Bible as a basis for my belief. My faith at that point seemed like a huge rationalization for all of the problematic aspects and contradictions I was noticing.

Reading the Bible as a true and literal statement of what God is actually made me feel further away from God, not closer. It made me feel as if I were reading a mere caricature of God—a fairytale depiction, complete with a white robe, a long white beard, and a loud, booming Cecil B. DeMille-produced voice. Once I really tried to take the text of the Bible seriously and literally, the stories began to seem like preposterous historical accounts of events. I did not doubt that God would possess the power to do the things He is portrayed as doing in the Bible, but it seemed unreasonable that God actually would say and do many of those things. I wondered how any intelligent, thinking person could just ignore science and logic and accept that this is how God would actually think, talk, and act. If the Supreme Being of the universe were going to use some old books to communicate with all of humanity for all time, it seemed like those books would read very differently.

This thinking was all still very unsettling for me, however. It reminded me of the famous quote by Friedrich Nietzsche:

> God is dead. God remains dead. And we have killed him. How shall we comfort ourselves, the murderers of all murderers? What was holiest and mightiest of all that the world has yet owned has bled to death under our knives: who will wipe this blood off us? What water is there for us to clean ourselves? What festivals of atonement, what sacred games shall we have to invent? Is not the greatness of this deed too great for us? Must we ourselves not become gods simply to appear worthy of it?"

BELIEF WITHOUT PROOF? BASED ON WHAT?

As I continued through the entire Bible, however, a curious thing began to happen. I started to feel that I was unfairly judging God based on the various implausible stories and dubious assertions in the Bible. Not only did this seem unfair to God, but I began to feel a bit defensive about God, thinking that perhaps the errors and shortsightedness contained in the Bible should be attributed not to God but to the people, many of whom were desert shepherds, of the Middle East, who had written about God so long ago. It seemed like the authors were just trying to pass off their own opinions about God as objective truths, as if those assertions had been written by God Himself.

As such, what a perfectly unassailable defense the biblical writers had created for themselves—casting their own *subjective* opinions about God as the *actual* Word of God. It meant that the writers would never have to defend their ideas as their own if they could just define them as God's, thus allowing them to decree that anyone criticizing their writings would be attacking God in blasphemy. Of course, I do not think they consciously conspired to lie about the Bible being the Word of God when they really knew it was just their own words, but that assertion still seemed to be where they had ended up.

As always, however, turnabout is fair play, so some might accuse me of attacking the Bible, and even of engaging in blasphemy and then supplying a rival text to the Bible by writing this book. But I hardly think that is what I am doing. For one thing, I am certainly not claiming that God actually wrote this book instead of me! Quite the opposite, I admit that my book is a collection of my own subjective thoughts, opinions, questions, and ideas, as well as those borrowed from other mere humans like me. I also admit that I have a certain point of view and that what I have written can reasonably be interpreted in many ways.

Unless I have a competing Bible, according to the logic of those believers who require a religious text as a foundation for religion, I have no ability and no right to question or to challenge biblical authors. Nevertheless, the lack of a rival text does not mean that the Bible (or any other religious text) must be true simply by default. Moreover, if the written text from God is the basis of belief and the source of what is known to be true about God, then how were people able to come to know God before writing was invented in 3,700 BC in Mesopotamia and before the ability even to read became commonplace? Is literacy a requirement of faith and salvation? Also, because it took thousands of years to complete the Bible as a literary work, and even longer for it to have pervasive availability worldwide, were those alive in the interim provided by God with only part of His message or denied all of it if they could not read? What if they did not have a copy of it? What if they had a copy, but not one in their own language?

What Bible did Adam, Noah, Moses, or David ever read, and how did they come to accept Jesus as their savior if they did not even know of Jesus, as Jesus would not come to Earth until thousands of years thereafter to die for their sins? Before they had Jesus as a savior, these Jewish forebears killed and burned animals and that sacrifice supposedly "washed away" their sins, or at least postponed their sins for a year or so. They believed this was because such sacrifice symbolically represented the blood of Jesus, the Messiah, who eventually would wash away their sins forever. But why kill an animal in a barbaric ritual to symbolize God's great love for us? Who started that sacrament? Why imitate the murderous sacrifices of virgins who got thrown into volcanoes to appease some volcano god? Hundreds of other such questions led to the overarching one: If God could create the universe, why couldn't He create his own official Bible *without* any writing assistance from any human being? Was God powerless to write, produce, copy, and distribute His own book all by Himself? Is it right to think that God actually needed help from humans to write the Bible?

Chapter Ninety-Four

"Objection, Your Honor!"...Isn't the Bible All Just Hearsay?

What is "hearsay"? If I tell you that I saw a ghost, that would ***not*** be hearsay, because you could ask me any skeptical question you may have about my claim of seeing a ghost and then decide whether you believe me based on how well, or not so well, I am able to address your skeptical questions and concerns. It might be a tall order to convince you that I saw a ghost, but at least you can *directly* assess my credibility on the issue. What if I instead told you that a friend of mine told me that she saw a ghost and I think that you ought to believe her? To believe that she really saw a ghost, you not only would have to believe my account of what she allegedly told me, but also, more importantly, you would have to believe that what she told me was the truth. Your belief in the existence and appearance of a ghost would be based on the hearsay statement of my friend, although you could not directly question my friend about it (assume for our purposes here that she is now gone).

In a court of law, not only would that hearsay usually be considered unreliable evidence, it would also be inadmissible, so it would be prohibited from even being considered by a jury. It does not matter if those statements are oral or if they are written down in some text; they would be inadmissible, in either event. Accordingly, I admit that my skepticism of any text containing hearsay is a function of my being a legal academic. My training as a law professor who also happens to teach an evidence course in law school, coupled with my experience as a lawyer and a coauthor of an evidence textbook, leads me to the inescapable conclusion that the Bible is entirely a hearsay document when being used to prove the truth of the matter asserted therein.

Let's look at another example of hearsay. Assume that a witness in a legal dispute dies before the trial but that, before dying, that person had written a long letter stating what he or she allegedly knew about the case. That letter, like the Bible, would be a hearsay document. In fact, that witness to the dispute would not really even be a witness at that point because that person (who actually would be an out-of-court declarant, but not an in-court witness) would not be available to testify, and be subject to cross-examination, so the earlier assertions that the person (the declarant) would have made about the dispute in his or her letter would be hearsay. That is what the Bible is—a document containing all of the hearsay assertions of now dead-and-gone authors (declarants), like Moses, who wrote the Book of Genesis if asserting the truth of what they wrote.

The Bible also often contains hearsay within hearsay, in which the writer/declarant is someone who is reporting what someone else, another declarant, had said or written before—in the previous example, it would be that a friend told me, that a friend told her, that he had seen a ghost. Although hearsay, as well as hearsay within hearsay, is generally inadmissible in a court of law, there are numerous exceptions. Those exceptions do not mean that the hearsay is to be considered true; instead, the hearsay is just admissible and can be *considered* by a jury, like any other evidence, to be either true or false. Still, the basic idea is that witnesses should have direct knowledge about which they can testify and be subject to cross-examination in court. With respect to the Bible, however, obviously, that is not possible because all of the authors/declarants of the Bible have been dead for thousands of years now.

Additional hearsay probably was created as handwritten copies of the Bible were made and various translations occurred through the ages, where these changes were made by scribes and translators. If so, then there were even more declarants—the scribes and translators—who made either accidental or purposeful transcribing and/or translation errors or even intentional transcribing or translation changes. So not only is there hearsay by the original writers of the Bible (like Moses), which may reduce the reliability of the information contained within the Bible, but other early methods of reproduction are potential further "levels of hearsay" that may have reduced its reliability even further. For example, the first mass production of the Bible occurred in Catholic monasteries. At each of these monasteries, a group of Catholic friars would sit down in a room and transcribe the Bible by hand. There is some evidence that if there was a part of the gospel with which they disagreed or that they thought was poorly written in the copy they were using for reproduction, they would change it, thinking they were somehow making it "better" or more "consistent" or more in line with God's true words and intentions.

Moreover, because many of the Bibles were part of the same method of reproduction, there was a high probability that each copy a friar possessed was slightly different from the others because of slight human error. Thus, it was quite possible, before the printing press, that twenty friars could transcribe twenty copies of the Bible resulting in twenty slightly different copies of the Bible. In short, because each friar could make his own copy and interpretation, he may have added yet another layer of hearsay. More reliable attempts at standardization only occurred with printing presses.

Consider the hearsay statement in Genesis 1:1—"In the beginning, God created the heaven and the earth." First, the writer/declarant, Moses, is not here today to be a live witness to testify and to be subject to cross-examination about what he knew, saw, and heard, so all of what he wrote in this verse is Moses's hearsay statement. Indeed, the Bible is entirely a hearsay document in that general sense—and that is just the first level of the hearsay in this example. Next, notice that Moses had no direct personal knowledge of God creating Heaven and Earth because, of course, Moses could not have been there to witness any of that. Adam, the alleged first human, had not even been created at that point, so no human being could have witnessed creation actually taking place. Accordingly, asserting that God created Heaven and Earth is a hearsay statement of which no human has personal direct knowledge. The verse also contains two huge implied assertions, or assumptions: (1) that Heaven is an actual place and (2) that there exists a

God. Although these assumptions are technically not hearsay because they are only *implied* assertions in the statement that God created the heaven and the earth—that is, they are not *express* assertions in that statement (at least not in this verse); that God created Heaven is the express assertion—the *existence* of both Heaven and God still represent wholly unsupported assumptions, that is, implied assertions, within the verse with no independent evidence to support them.

Additionally, it is unclear exactly who told Moses that God created Heaven and Earth. If another human being told Moses, that statement to Moses would be another level of hearsay, but again, whoever told Moses also would not have any personal knowledge of creation because no human being could have been there to witness creation taking place. The law of evidence also generally requires a witness to have personal knowledge, because we want to hear only from people who actually have witnessed something—in fact, that is why they are called witnesses.

If God Himself was the one who told Moses directly that He had created the heaven and the earth, assuming that hearing "internal voices" from God even counts as evidence of real statements, that too would represent yet another level of hearsay because that would be God's assertion to Moses (one level of hearsay from a declarant), which Moses then reasserted to us in written form in Genesis (a second level of hearsay from a second declarant). Even if we could somehow cross-examine God (the first declarant) and actually get His answers to these questions, we could not cross-examine Moses (the second declarant), as Moses is now dead and dead witnesses are legally incompetent as witnesses.

Asking such questions as these, of course, often offends fundamentalist believers, who will quote key words from the Bible that tend to show that such questions are probably offensive to God:

> [1] Then the LORD answered…and said, [2] Who is this that darkeneth counsel by words without knowledge? [3] Gird up now thy loins like a man; for I will demand of thee, and answer thou me. [4] Where wast thou when I laid the foundations of the earth? declare, if thou hast understanding. [5] Who hath laid the measures thereof, if thou knowest? or who hath stretched the line upon it? [6] Whereupon are the foundations thereof fastened? or who laid the corner stone thereof; [7] When the morning stars sang together, and all the sons of God shouted for joy? (Job 38:1–7).

Some believers might attempt to attack my position by asking me where was I when God laid down the foundations of the earth. Of course, I was not there, and I certainly was not alive to witness it; I admit that, as well as the fact that I do not have complete understanding of the cosmos. But my point is simply to ask that same where-were-you question, in reverse, about biblical authors. Thus, where was the human author who wrote Genesis 1:1 when God "laid the foundations of the earth" at creation? That would be the same place I was—not there, and not alive to witness it, and so the hearsay concern does not rest with what God Himself directly said or did; instead, the hearsay concern rests with the reliability of the mere humans who were biblical authors (including translators and transcribers) that have asserted in various writings recorded in various versions of the Bible what God allegedly said or did.

If it is offensive on my part even to suggest that, as a legal definitional matter, the Bible is just hearsay from all of the various human authors of the Bible, should I equally be offended if someone were also to say that my book is just hearsay of its mere human author (me)? What if I asserted that God wanted me to write this book and that God specifically told me to write this book one night two years ago in a dream? If a fundamentalist were at all skeptical of my claims of divine inspiration about God's direction for me to write this book, could I then rightly accuse that person of attacking God's word as blasphemy for doubting what God had said to me? Isn't that the height of presumptuousness? Whether I claim that God told me certain things that I wrote in a book and now assert to be the truth, or whether Moses claimed that God told him certain things that he wrote in a book and later asserted to be the truth, both of our books would still be, by definition, hearsay documents.

If the Bible is hearsay, that would mean that the faith God asks of us, as defined by fundamentalists, requires faith not only in the version of God put forward in the Bible but also in the humans who wrote those assertions about God in the Bible, as well as in those humans interpreting those written words. That does not necessarily mean that the Bible is not true—not at all—but it does mean that the Bible is hearsay if used to promote what is written therein as the truth. The Bible contains the assertions of the writers who wrote about God, and sometimes the assertions of others who told the authors something about God—but in every case, the assertions are all hearsay statements. Whether they were written or oral statements, they were still assertions that were intended as a communication to a listener and then to a reader.

Of course, the Bible did not have to be written using human beings as direct or indirect scribes. According to the book of Exodus, and as dramatically depicted the movie *The Ten Commandments*, God used fire to write the Ten Commandments on stone tablets Himself. So why didn't God use fire to write *everything* in the Bible on stone tablets? The Bible also says that God spoke directly to Adam and Eve and many other biblical figures. If direct oral communication from God is possible without using a human mouthpiece, why wasn't direct written communication from God employed for the Bible, without using a human scribe? Why did God communicate His important messages to humanity using the very indirect and often unreliable method of hearsay when God had no difficulty talking directly to people in the past? Why involve imperfect humans in the writing and translation of the Bible, a book so monumentally important and containing God's personal message to us all, instead of using nothing more than the perfect hand of God to write the Bible? And while He was at it, why did He not write it perfectly without any translation errors in every language on Earth, both at the time and in the future? This leads to the larger question of whether the Bible would have been written exactly as it is now if God were to have used fire to write it all on stone tablets *by Himself.*

Chapter Ninety-Five

Does God Really Want Us to Rely on All of This Hearsay?

Let's further explore the hearsay concern. Ask any trial lawyer in America what hearsay is, and he or she will tell you that it is something like "an out-of-court statement made by a declarant that is related in court by a witness and being used to prove the truth of the matter asserted by the declarant" or something a bit shorter, such as, "it is what someone (a witness) says that someone else (a declarant) has said out of court about something to be proven in court." Another example in context would help to further clarify these legal definitions of hearsay.

Suppose that I am a witness in a traffic accident case and I testify, "I saw that the light was green for the plaintiff as she drove through the intersection." That statement would *not* be hearsay because the truth of what I am saying is based on my personal knowledge and can be tested in court by cross-examining me right then before a jury that could assess my credibility. Now suppose that I testify, "Lisa told me [or Lisa wrote to me in a letter] that she saw that the light was green for the plaintiff as the plaintiff drove through the intersection." That would be hearsay if the plaintiff's lawyer were using Lisa's out-of-court assertion (what I said that Lisa said or wrote to me) to prove that the light was green for the plaintiff as the plaintiff drove through that intersection. In contrast, if Lisa took the stand herself and testified directly about what she saw and didn't see, her testimony would not be hearsay. We could test her assertions directly through cross-examination. Of course, if Lisa were now dead and therefore could not testify in court herself, we could never know directly from her.

Note that the truth of what Lisa said is not based on my personal knowledge; all I know is what Lisa either said or wrote to me as her assertion. Thus, the truth of what Lisa has asserted (that the light was green for the plaintiff) cannot be tested in court by the cross-examination of Lisa right then in front of a jury that can assess her credibility based on how she might answer. To believe that the light was green for the plaintiff as the plaintiff went through the intersection would be nothing more than a complete leap of faith, a speculative guess, based solely on what I claimed that Lisa had said or had written to me. Generally, that would be inadmissible in a court of law because we want to hear directly from the people with *actual* knowledge about the issue in dispute, especially when the matter at hand is important. We want to hear it "straight from the horse's mouth." Whether I saw it or not, we certainly wouldn't want my personal interpretation of what I think (1) Lisa meant, (2) possibly meant, (3) must have meant, or (4) should have meant when she said or wrote to me what she allegedly saw regarding the accident.

This hearsay problem is compounded by more hearsay if I then wrote what Lisa said to me in a letter and that letter was introduced in court without me, because my whereabouts at the time of the trial also would be unknown and therefore I could not testify in court either. The letter would now contain my written hearsay assertions (one hearsay level with me as a declarant) about Lisa's verbal or written assertions made to me (yet another hearsay level with Lisa as another declarant). Such hearsay, and hearsay within hearsay, is generally inadmissible in court.

Like so many times when it comes to the law, there are numerous exceptions. Still, as a basic rule of evidence, hearsay is generally inadmissible in a court of law because it is considered to be *unreliable evidence*. We believe that our American justice system is so important that we should not be making legal decisions about the guilt or liability of a person based on mere hearsay. Thus, on that basic level alone, I am skeptical of the hearsay that makes up the Bible. The Bible is not necessarily, therefore, what God has said; instead, it is what men have said that God has said, or what others have written that others have said that God has said. What we are being asked to believe is only what those men thought God meant for us to believe was the actual Word of God. Indeed, in the New Testament, for example, the first four books are called the Gospels "According to" Matthew, Mark, Luke, or John; they are according to human authors and are *not* said to be "according to God." Also, there are many letters—personally written letters—that were written by the Apostle Paul to various groups of early Christian churches (the Galatians, the Thessalonians, and the Philippians, for example) included as books of the New Testament. These were letters that are admittedly written by Paul to specific people, and as such, they are all Paul's hearsay.

Some Bibles are marketed and sold as special red-letter editions, meaning that all of the words of Jesus in the New Testament are printed in red ink so a reader knows the exact words that Jesus supposedly spoke, as direct quotes, at least according to the writers. But if God directly wrote *all* of the Bible, not just some of it, and Jesus *is* God, then logically, shouldn't the *entire* Bible be printed in red ink? If not, doesn't that demonstrate that all of the *non*–red-letter words are *not* those of God but are instead just the words of the men who actually wrote the words used in the Bible? Moreover, even the red-letter words of Jesus are, in reality, just what the New Testament human authors have asserted that Jesus allegedly said directly. To be consistent, how much of the Bible should be printed, perhaps in blue ink for the direct words of God the Father (like the Ten Commandments or discussions with Adam and Eve in the Garden of Eden), and how many letters should be printed in perhaps yellow ink for the direct words of the Holy Ghost, assuming the Holy Ghost ever said anything that is a direct quote?

Even if that were done, many of the words contained in the Bible still would not be in any special color at all because there is not even a claim that those words (for example, geographical descriptions or family relationships, or descriptions of wars or various other incidents) would be the direct words of God or any one member of the Holy Trinity. Any words printed in red, blue, or yellow ink would still be whatever the human writer/declarant (who was not God Himself) penned them to be (except for the actual stone tablets on which God wrote the Ten

Commandments with fire), even if God allegedly inspired the human writers, in which case, maybe those words could be printed in green ink to signify non-direct quotes but words allegedly divinely inspired by Jesus, God the Father, or the Holy Ghost. Again, however, all of the Bible is hearsay as admittedly second- and third-hand information written by human authors.

Hearsay is not any more reliable because it was written a very long time ago by some religious people in the Middle East. It is still hearsay, just extremely *old* hearsay. Some might point to certain exceptions to the hearsay rule, however. For example, if someone is describing an event as it occurs, that is called a present-sense impression, and it is admissible. The assumption is that people do not have time to lie about something as they are describing it while or immediately after it occurs. Similarly, if a person under the stress of a startling event makes a statement about that startling event, it would be admissible as an excited utterance. The assumption is that people do not lie when they are under such stress. They could still be lying, of course, but at least we will now allow the jury to hear what they allegedly said because it is thought to be at least a bit more reliable.

There are plenty of other of these kinds of exceptions and thus many examples in the Bible that would fall within the exceptions to the rule against hearsay and thus would allow the biblical hearsay to be considered as evidence in court. For example, if a blind man exclaimed, "I once was blind, but now I can see!" such would be both a present-sense impression and an excited utterance of the cured blind man declarant, but that exception would not cover the hearsay of the biblical human writer declarant of the incident, because it would apply only to the hearsay statement of the now cured blind man but not to the writer. Remember also that the gospels were written several decades after Jesus's time. These writings, at that much later date, would still constitute hearsay, and exceptions such as the present-sense impression and the excited utterance would be inapplicable to them, even if they would be applicable to the hearsay-within-hearsay statements of the non-writer declarants (such as the cured blind man) when they made those particular hearsay statements.

Of course, the Bible is not on trial here, and this is not a court of law. Still, it is interesting that courts of law generally find hearsay to be so unreliable that we have an entire rule prohibiting the jury from even considering hearsay, yet we base our entire Christian doctrine on the hearsay contained in the Bible. Although foreign court systems often allow hearsay, they consider it to be very weak evidence; these countries just do not exclude hearsay from consideration at the outset as in the US.

There are a couple of other exceptions to the hearsay rule in the US that I have not discussed under which the Bible might possibly fit, but the fact that the hearsay in the Bible would be admissible in court under such exceptions does not equate to the Bible being true; it only means that the hearsay statements could be considered by the jury. In considering that hearsay, the jurors could still find that hearsay as not credible or reliable enough upon which to base their verdict.

For example, there is an exception for "ancient documents" (documents more than twenty years old, such as property deeds) because someone is probably not going to forge and then wait twenty years to act on it (although there would still be an incentive to rely on a religious document into the future). There is another exception for a "learned treatise" so an expert witness physician, for example, could refer to basic medical or anatomy books, which are entirely factual and scientific, testable, and largely empirical and certainly not spiritual and supernatural. Still, those possible exceptions would not change the fact that, at its core, the Bible is entirely hearsay. For that matter, so is the Qur'an, as well as all other religious texts, so if the Bible is not hearsay, then neither is the Qur'an, and if the Bible is hearsay but possibly could fall within the ancient-documents or learned-treatise exceptions, so could the Qur'an. As such, the same arguments really could be made for any and all religious ancient-document or learned-treatise texts.

It is revealing that both Christian and Muslim fundamentalists probably would agree that any religious text other than their own would be unreliable hearsay but their own particular religious text would not be unreliable hearsay or, at the very least, their own text would nicely fit into an exception in a way that any and all other religious texts would not. As far as the ancient-document exception goes, keep in mind that a twenty-one–year-old *National Enquirer* article may qualify as an exception to the hearsay rule under the ancient-document exception, and that obviously would not necessarily mean that the article should be taken as true.

Recall that we are not talking about proving the ultimate truth but only about whether we would *consider* a book to be admissible in court for the jury to consider as an exhibit. The point is that hearsay is often considered to be so unreliable that it not only should be discounted by jurors as unreliable when they are weighing the evidence but should never even reach the jury's consideration—meaning that we should not even waste the jury's time with it. Hearsay is thought to lack so much credibility and believability by our legal system that it is usually inadmissible so the jury cannot even consider it as evidence. Hearsay does not necessarily make something a lie or untrue, but it is not considered as reliable as the direct testimony from a witness with personal knowledge about an incident. Still, there are numerous exceptions.

Whether the Bible would be inadmissible hearsay or would fit within an exception to the hearsay rule, can't we just say that the Bible must be true because so many people from so many countries for so many centuries have believed that it is the authentic Word of God? Along these lines, there is a residual exception or sort of a catchall exception to the hearsay rule for anything that has other indicia of reliability. Perhaps the Bible, as well as any other religious text, could fit within that general exception, but the reliability would have to be based on faith and/or on the fact that so many other people throughout time have considered it to be true (keep in mind, however, that many people *not* believing it to be true would not necessarily render it untrue). Mob psychology does not necessarily override hearsay concerns, nor should it. No matter what people may believe (or not believe) about the Bible, the hearsay assertions of biblical authors are still just their opinions and personal interpretations about God and other matters. Remember that at one time, most people believed that the world was flat—and that didn't make it so. The Bible therefore remains what God *allegedly* said or wrote to us all, according to the assertions of the human writers of the Bible. As a result, my skepticism is with these written hearsay assertions by ancient human beings in the Middle East, and not with God.

Simply doubting other human beings, however, is by itself no answer, either. That other people do not know something does not mean I do. If I am skeptical about what others have written about God, then all I am left with is my own thoughts and feelings on the subject. Although I would not purposefully lie to myself about God, I am also equally skeptical about my own beliefs and perceptions of God as authoritative for others. If I am skeptical of fallible human authors telling me who and what God is in a book or through sermons about passages in the Bible, why should I, also being a fallible human being myself, escape my own skepticism?

The difference between me and most other fundamentalist believers, however, whether they staunchly believe in God or whether they are hardcore atheists, is that I am at least willing to admit that I do not know for sure if the Bible is actually the Word of God or not. It might be that the Bible was divinely inspired but only some of it is accurate while much of it could have been inadvertently compromised by the people who wrote it. I admit that this shortcoming is a possibility, but even with that admission, my faith in God can be as strong as that of someone who refuses to question the Bible at all. Perhaps my faith, then, unorthodox as it may be, is even stronger than theirs.

Chapter Ninety-Six

Can I Worship God, without also Having to Worship the Bible?

I realize this concern might be quite controversial and provocative, especially to fundamentalists who no doubt would cite John 1:1–3: "**[1]** In the beginning was the Word, and the Word was with God, and the Word was God. **[2]** The same was in the beginning with God. **[3]** All things were made by him; and without him was not any thing made that was made." But let me clarify my point. My problem is not with what would be God's Word. Instead, my problem is in trying to figure out what is definitively God's Word in the Bible and what are man's words as mere hearsay assertions of humans who are allegedly speaking and writing for God in the Bible.

There are many levels of subjectivity that cannot be overcome simply by appealing to a written text that one claims one can objectively interpret. First, all we have are competing subjective opinions of what the text means and how it should apply to our lives. Again, consider any US Supreme Court opinion in which nine justices, the most learned jurists in the land, often cannot agree on what the supposed objective text of the US Constitution means. Next, those subjective personal opinions are not magically elevated into absolute truths just because they are written in a text. For example, are any of my opinions in this book any more objective or true simply because I have written them instead of just stating them orally? Aren't my written ideas still just my subjective opinions, regardless of how they have been expressed, orally or in writing? Moreover, hearsay is generally unreliable, regardless of whether it is written in a text or repeated by word of mouth. Finally, even assuming that what has been written in a text is the objective truth, we can still have huge disagreements over what that text implies because each of our own subjective interpretations about what the text actually means.

Something I have learned and try to teach in law school, is to always consider the source. If God wrote every word of the Bible Himself the same way Shakespeare wrote *Othello*, as fundamentalists allege, assuming that Shakespeare actually wrote *Othello*, wouldn't the definitive message of God Himself addressed to all human beings clearly be a work befitting the omniscient, omnipotent, and infallible supreme being of the universe? Wouldn't God be incapable of writing any error, making any contradiction, or writing any ambiguity even slightly lacking in clarity? If the Bible contains some serious, or even not-so-serious, errors, contradictions, or ambiguities, then perhaps those deficiencies would indicate that it is actually the work of some human beings. This seems reasonable, because people cannot write in an all-knowing, all-powerful, omniscient, omnipotent, and infallible way, as they are none of those things. In short, a written work necessarily reveals something about its author(s), one way or another.

So, if I doubt or question something written in the Bible, I am not necessarily doubting or questioning God Himself. Rather, I am questioning the people who wrote the text of the Bible, as well as their followers and interpreters—this is an immense difference. It is not enough if the people who actually wrote the Bible, or those following them all of these years afterward, merely assert, "God really wrote this, not me, nor any human being, so if you doubt what is written here, you do not just doubt me, you actually doubt God."

Why doesn't God just skip the hearsay and audibly talk to us the way He talked to Adam and Eve—when there was no guessing involved in determining what God was saying to them? There was no guessing when God made pronouncements to them, and no guessing as to who was talking to them when Satan supposedly tempted them with the forbidden fruit. When I pray, I cannot ever hear any audible voice that is really that of God answering. I am unaware of anyone who claims that God actually speaks *audibly* to them the way that He spoke to Adam and Eve—and if He does, I would love to hear a tape recording of it!

People who claim God speaks to them personally and explicitly are reminiscent of people who claim to be abducted by space aliens but never seem to be able to produce any tangible, credible evidence of it—no real artifact taken from the spacecraft, and certainly no videophone recording of the event. Instead, all they have are their own marvelous verbal tales of abduction. It is also interesting that alleged abductees often relay very similar descriptions of their abductors and that their abductors often mirror the appearance of human beings, with two eyes, two arms, and two legs, and standing upright with a head, fingers, and so on. It doesn't seem reasonable that such aliens from a vastly different part of the universe, and presumably a very distinct environment, would have the same organs and appendages that humans do. Perhaps even more interesting is that we humans often similarly describe our gods in ways that mirror us, in that our Gods can be angry, vengeful, or jealous, and often can take human form, sitting in heaven, having children, doling out justice, and so on. The fact that we describe our gods as like us in certain respects might indicate that we are doing our best to imagine something of which we have no knowledge and hence use the characteristics for human life that we already know in order to create an accessible and understandable construct of God.

Chapter Ninety-Seven

Getting Beyond the Hearsay in the Bible: What About Direct Access to God through Prayer?

How should we regard prayer, and more specifically, the power of prayer? After all, according to Matthew 21:22, Jesus said, "And all things, whatsoever ye shall ask in prayer believing, ye shall receive." If I pray to God about something I need to do or something that I feel, I can at least see a legitimate *personal* purpose for such a prayer, as it is just between God and me. Whether my prayer would be clearly and definitively answered by God, like a reply to an e-mail message, is another story. I am fascinated by the external things about which people pray, however. For example, before a football game, some players will pray—but why? Certainly, God would not take sides in the football game, would He? And would God actually care who won a particular football game? So first, would God be fair, and second, would God even care?

Similarly, if two alley cats get into a fight, would which cat won be a function of God's will? Would God take sides in that catfight? Would God even care? If not, could God be persuaded to care if I prayed really hard for one cat to win? If it were God's will that one particular cat was to win this catfight, could my diligent prayers for the *other* cat to win actually change God's will and thus change God's intended outcome of the catfight? Some people might say that God would care more about a football game involving human beings than He would about the outcome of a cat fight, but why? Wouldn't we just be assuming how God feels about such things based on our own personal values? Does God care more about football games than about cats, or does God care more about the welfare of living things (cats) than about the outcome of mere football games? Indeed, does God answer such prayers? Is it God's will that one beauty pageant contestant wins the crown over another, depending upon who has prayed the hardest?

It depends on how literally we take the Bible. According to Matthew 7:7–11, Jesus said:

> [7] Ask, and it shall be given you, seek, and ye shall find; knock, and it shall be opened unto you;
> [8] For everyone asketh receiveth; and he that seeketh findeth; and to him that knocketh it shall be opened.
> [9] Or what man is there of you, whom if his son ask for bread, will he give him a stone?
> [10]Or if he ask a fish, will he give him a serpent?

> **[11]** If ye then, being evil, know how to give good gifts unto your children, how much more shall your Father which is in heaven give good things to them that ask him?

Many religious coaches and players probably realize that their football games might not rate as a legitimate or good thing for which to pray or to ask for God's special intervention and that to do so might even be considered cheating in a certain sense; however, many players and coaches might say that they do not ask for victory, but only for God to keep the players safe. Although God may not care who wins some football game, God might take an interest in ensuring that the players are not injured during their game, so even if a "safety prayer" is more of a legitimate prayer topic than is a request for victory in a football game, an even more important question emerges: Why would God ever change *His preexisting will* just because a prayer is prayed? Does God have a plan, or doesn't He? Indeed, when we talk about the power of prayer, exactly whose power are we referring to—God's power to control events as God, or our own power to change God's will through our humble, but apparently sometimes quite powerful, prayer requests?

What if God's will is that a particular player must break an ankle, perhaps as punishment for some sins that he previously has committed and thus, praying for an injury-free game would actually run counter to God's overall plan? Maybe there are many unforeseen consequences that would create a domino effect of occurrences that run counter to God's plan. For example, perhaps a player would die in a car accident on the way to a football game the following week. As a result, God might need to allow this player to break his ankle in the game this week as a way to keep him from playing and thus driving to the game next week, therefore avoiding the fatal car accident.

As faithful, prayerful people console a depressed player who suffered a broken ankle in the football game, they might understandably wonder why God would allow his ankle to have been broken when they had dutifully prayed for God to keep all of the players safe (they asked but did not receive). A pastor, assuming that God must have had a reason, might say that the ankle injury was God's will and that God possibly even kept the player alive by breaking his ankle to make him avoid a fatal car accident: "God was watching out for him in a way that we did not even realize!" Well, maybe, though it seems like an all-powerful God would be a little more resourceful than that, in that God could ensure the player's life still would be saved without having to break his ankle in the game the previous week just to avoid the fatal car accident the following week. Is micromanaging the affairs of billions of human beings this way and playing through various alternative scenarios what God does daily?

I realize that perhaps my example of winning a football game as a trivial prayer request is not so trivial for some people who might take football very seriously. For example, there is an old joke that in some parts of the country, people strongly believe in "faith, family, freedom, and football—and not necessarily in that order!" Still, many believers in the power of prayer probably would agree that we should not ask for God's intervention in providing a victory in a game, so it must be that certain prayers constitute "improper" requests. For instance, I assume that God would not be too pleased if I prayed for God to seriously harm someone I do not like and of whom I am jealous. I guess one can always just say that God answers prayer but that we may not always be able to see *how* He answers. Still, if we ask but do not receive, then what Jesus said is literally not true. Instead, it requires more personal interpretation of what Jesus must have "really" meant.

As a very public example of these issues, consider Tim Tebow, the former Denver Broncos quarterback, who led the Broncos to many exciting come-from-behind victories in 2011, and impressively so. First, I admire his athletic ability and the strong leadership of his team that year. I also admire his underdog status and how he overcame his athletic critics. There is no doubt that Tebow is an impressive young man who helped the Broncos to win, but, in fairness to other individuals, we shouldn't forget that the Denver defensive players also helped the team to win, as did all of the other players on the team, as well as all of the coaches. Football is not just a one-man show and never has been. It is a team sport, after all.

That said, what should we think about the fact that after scoring a touchdown, Tebow would get down on one knee and pray to Jesus, apparently thanking Jesus for allowing him to score that touchdown, or praying for whatever else one would pray for in front of 75,000 screaming fans and a live television football audience? It appears that Tebow believed that when he scored, God actually had allowed, or even had wanted, the players on the opposing teams to miss their tackles, fail to execute their defensive assignments, let him score, and maybe even lose the game, because God must really have been a Denver Broncos fan that year. Apparently, (1) God does care who wins football games; (2) God is actually responsible for how well (or poorly) each of the players play; and (3) God is invariably on the side of a player who publically prays—witness the many "miraculous" comeback victories of the Broncos and Tim Tebow!

Of course, supporters of Tim Tebow, and his public show of faith that year, would argue that any losses or mistakes on the field that Tebow made would be completely irrelevant to this discussion and that noting any of them would just be a cynical attempt to trivialize God's power. Still, does all of this mean that the Broncos being in the 2012 Super Bowl obviously was not God's will? Some might argue that even though the Broncos ultimately did not win in the 2012 Super Bowl, or even make it that far, such does not prove that God does not exist and that the power of prayer is not real. That statement certainly is correct; however, it also means that had the Broncos gone to and won the 2012 Super Bowl, such would *not* have proved that God exists and that the power of prayer is real, either—at least if we are going to be consistent.

Reportedly, Tim Tebow said that when he prayed to God after a touchdown, he was simply glorifying God, not himself, but was Tebow really just "giving all of the glory to God," as he claimed when he prayed so publically, and none of the glory to himself? Or did Tebow, and fellow worshippers and others, really glorify Tebow himself for his "brave" decision to make such a public showing of his faith to demonstrate to everyone his very public—yet somehow still very humble—worship of God? Maybe Tebow and all of his religious fans should have gotten out their Bibles and read Matthew 6:5–6 and then have had the courage to ponder whether these words should be interpreted literally:

> [5] And when thou prayest, thou shall not be as the hypocrites are: for they love to pray standing in the synagogues and in the corners of the streets, that they may be seen of men. Verily I say unto you, They have their reward.
> [6] But thou, when thou prayest, enter into thy closet, and when thou hast shut thy door, pray to thy Father which is in secret; and thy father which seeth in secret shall reward thee openly.

If Tebow privately prays to God in order to thank God, that appears to be OK, according to this command, but if so, then why did Tebow thank God so *publically* for all to see? Is God's ego so fragile that He really needs us to make these very public displays for Him, or are such displays really more about us and our own egos, celebrating how humble we really must be for publically acknowledging God in this way?

Perhaps there is an argument, as there always is, that could explain away these pretty clear biblical words advising us to pray in private, not in public, and justify engaging in a very showy public prayer the likes of which probably were never imagined in Jesus's time. But if there is an argument that could explain away this command, such an interpretive argument would simply make my more general point about how literal interpretation is open to almost whatever we want it to be. Nonetheless, coming up with such a justificatory argument would demand some awfully impressive maneuvering, even for a very talented professional football player like Tebow, to dance around the above-quoted words from the Book of Matthew.

With respect to properly thanking someone for making the touchdown, how about just thanking one's fellow players and coaches without parading one's faith and calling attention to oneself in the process? I realize other NFL players often act ridiculous in the end zone, wildly calling attention to their actions and clearly engaging in their own form of self-aggrandizement, but they are not attempting to recast their actions as anything but their own personal and team glory. Perhaps all players should just give the ball to the referee after they score and then celebrate and thank their fellow players and coaches, but Tebow's end-zone prayers seemed to go a bit beyond that. Indeed, Tebow may have been making a religious and even political point by his football field prayers and seemed to be taking advantage of a very public stage to do it.

To what extent do our political ideologies, however, motivate and inform our reactions to Tim Tebow's end-zone displays? Would the support of Christian conservatives and the critique by certain liberals of Tebow completely change if Tebow, instead of praying to thank Jesus, had prayed to thank Allah for allowing him to score the touchdown? Would liberals then support a diverse religious minority's right to express his religion publically while conservatives criticized him for thanking the same God the "9/11 hijacker terrorists prayed to"?

It is fascinating (and revealing) to witness the inconsistency from people on all political sides when we mix politics and religion. For example, compare political conservatives' reactions to the personal views of another entertainment group—the Dixie Chicks, the country-pop singers from Texas with a strong country fan base. Recall a few years ago how the Dixie Chicks started saying at concerts that they were ashamed of the US war in Iraq, how much they disagreed with it, and how they wanted to distance themselves from fellow Texan and then President George W. Bush? What did many conservatives generally have to say to the Dixie Chicks then? They told them to just "*Shut up and sing!*" Imagine the nerve if someone were to have told Tebow to just "*shut up and play football*" during the 2011 season. Of course, if Tebow were praying to Allah after scoring a touchdown, I bet many conservatives might have told him to do just that: "shut up and play football, boy!"—and they likely would have done so out loud if not under their breaths.

Just to be clear, I am *not* saying that Tebow should have just "shut up and played football." I would not be so presumptuous. In fact, I would oppose the NFL forcing him not to pray after a touchdown if he so chooses. The NFL hardly limits the end-zone antics of players as it is, so Tebow should not be singled out with any kind of anti-religious ban. My only concern is this: Is God Himself (assuming He wrote the Bible) possibly advising against end-zone prayers in the Book of Matthew by implying, "If you really want to pray, great, then pray, but if you do so, do so without calling so much public attention to yourself in the process, unlike the hypocrites." so instead of "shut up and play," perhaps it should be "when you pray, shut up."

Whether Tebow is a good guy, whether other athletes do similar things at sporting events, whether Tebow gives unselfishly to charities, whether Tebow has a compelling life story, and so on, or whether I am an argumentative troublemaker for even raising this issue—all of these issues are irrelevant and miss the point of asking whether we should not publically pray according to instructions that are right out of the Bible (Matthew 6:5–6). I have merely cited those words here and asked if Tebow might not be following those biblical instructions when he publically prays after scoring a touchdown. I am not the one saying how one should pray and how one should not pray—Jesus, in the Book of Matthew, allegedly said how we should and should not do that. Maybe that biblical language is wrong or inapplicable, or maybe Jesus really did not say that. If one admits that that language is wrong or inapplicable, or that Jesus really didn't say it, think about what one would be admitting—that the Bible is wrong, or that otherwise clear, applicable instructions in the Bible about how to pray and how not to pray in public are now somehow inapplicable or are not really the words of Jesus.

Tim Tebow is an impressive young man who certainly seems sincere and he appears to be trying to do the right thing in all moral aspects of his life. I certainly give him a lot of credit in that regard. Because of that, I wonder if Tebow ever objected to people referring to the sacred act of prayer as "Tebowing" instead of "praying". When fans referred to prayer as "Tebowing," was that still really just Tebow "giving all of the glory to God," even though Tebow's name had been elevated in that significant way? Finally, consider the old question: If a tree fell in the forest, would it make a sound if no one were there to hear it? Before answering that question, answer this: If a football player prayed to thank God for allowing him to make a touchdown, would that thankful prayer not register with God in a meaningful way unless there were a stadium full of people and a national television audience there to witness it?

I must admit, however, that I have engaged in various similar forms of "Tebowing" myself. As a child, I used to pray the Catholic Rosary (a rosary is a chain of beads attached to a crucifix in which each bead represents a Catholic prayer for one to pray). I would dutifully pray one Our Father bead for every ten Hail Mary beads of the rosary—which could take a long time to accomplish for a young boy just before going to bed. But that was nothing. My grandmother showed me what it meant to seriously pray one day when my family all drove from my hometown of Pueblo, Colorado, up to the Mother Cabrini Shrine located on the side of a mountain near Golden, Colorado (a two-hour drive one way). There are 373 steps up to the Sacred Heart Statue of Jesus of the Mother Cabrini Shrine. I was a very young boy at the time, but I remember that my grandmother prayed an Our Father or a Hail Mary for every step up the shrine, all the way to the top! It literally took her all day to do it. That takes commitment and discipline to pray one repetitive prayer right after another like that for several hours at one time! I was impressed, as were many people visiting the Shrine that day.

Although I never asked her, I wonder what my grandmother would have thought about the instructions in the Bible about not praying in public and about Jesus's additional instructional words about avoiding prayers that are said (chanted?) in such a repetitive rote-memory sort of way (Matthew 6:7: "But when ye pray, use not vain repetitions, as the heathen do: for they think that they shall be heard for their much speaking"). I guess if I question Tim Tebow, then I had better be able to look in the mirror, as well as question my own beloved and dearly departed grandmother—but knowing my grandmother, she would have gone to confession about it immediately if there were even a hint that it might have been wrong for her to pray that way (so publically and so repetitively). If she had, however, the officiating confessional priest might have just told her that she would be forgiven, as long as she prayed ten Our Fathers and one Hail Mary. How's that for irony? Still, he probably would not have told her to pray on a public stage.

I have an even more fundamental concern, however, for Tim Tebow, my grandma, myself, and everyone else: Should we *ever* pray to God expecting Him to change His will based on our personal prayer requests? Is it true that God can be lobbied like some bought-and-paid-for politician? What if God has allowed someone to be stricken with cancer because it is time for that person to die but there are people praying for that person, appealing to God on that person's behalf? Would those appeals to God convince Him to allow the person to live and beat cancer as a miracle of God? What about a poor, unpopular woman who has no family or friends to advocate or pray for her—would God just let her die? Would God tell her, "I could have and I even would have saved your life, but nobody asked me to save you, so, too bad, I will now let you die"?

I have heard many times that God has a plan, that God's will is what God will do. But maybe that's not true. Perhaps God is just making it all up as He goes along, completely open to suggestions and always taking last-minute requests. That doesn't seem quite right for an all-powerful God, however. That is why I think prayers often enable us to feel like we have power in a powerless situation. They give us hope in what might otherwise be hopeless situations. Praying to God allows us to feel somewhat in control at times when we really have no control at all, so even though we cannot personally perform miracles, the act of praying allows us to feel that we sometimes can get to the same result—that we can be responsible for miraculous events if we just pray hard enough and somehow can convince God to do something that we obviously cannot do ourselves. Just like a rooster's morning "cock-a-doodle-doo" is not responsible for the sunrise, however, our prayers may be just as unlikely to be responsible for the way events unfold in reality.

For example, what would fundamentalist Christians say about the effectiveness of a Native American rain dance that might not also be said about their own power of prayer? If a Native American medicine man performed a rain dance and then it rained, would fundamentalists dutifully have to admit that such was proof of the power of the rain dance? If it did not rain, even after a vigorous rain dance, and the Native American explained that it was simply because he had not danced hard enough or long enough, how understanding of that rationalization would a fundamentalist be? What if it did not rain and the Native American explained that it must be the will of the rain gods to have a continued drought and we therefore must accept their will for it not to rain? Would such explanations be accepted by fundamentalists, or would they instead be quickly dismissed as weak religious superstitions and pagan rationalizations, no matter the result?

What if a meteorologist explained to the medicine man that rain is actually the result of atmospheric conditions related to precipitation, humidity, and high- and low-pressure systems that have nothing to do with humans dancing or failing to dance, because the actual reason for rain can be scientifically explained? Would the medicine man simply accuse the scientist of being an atheist who hates the Great Spirit, Mother Earth, and the rain gods? Would that scientist be guilty of disrespecting the faith of the medicine man, and would the rain gods therefore punish the meteorologist for his lack of faith? Would any Christian arguments calling into question a "misguided" and "uninformed" rain dance of a Native American who may "not know any better" completely and immediately change if it were the pastor of their own church who had prayed for rain and the rain had then fallen—because the pastor, unlike the Native American medicine man, can actually ask and receive from a supernatural god? If so, what would be the logical, evidence-based, provable difference between the two?

Chapter Ninety-Eight

What about Competing Prayer Requests of the Faithful?

Suppose that two neighbors who both faithfully love God happen to be voting in a very important upcoming political election. Assume further that they each support a different candidate. Each neighbor believes that his candidate is a very good person and that his candidate's opponent is a bad choice because that opponent has very bad views on the issue of, say, immigration. One candidate believes that we should secure our borders first and that only *after* we do that can we think about comprehensive immigration reform. In contrast, the other candidate thinks we should *start* with comprehensive immigration reform, not securing the border first but instead dealing with the entire issue all at once. Each neighbor believes that it would be better for America's security and economy if his particular candidate got elected. As a result, both neighbors begin to pray in earnest asking God to make sure that *their* respective candidates win for the sake of America and for the sake of America's future immigration policy.

Assume that both neighbors work very hard supporting their candidates; however, recall that they are also equally faithful. Both believe in the power of prayer, and both believe that God answers prayer, so the question is, Would either prayer, either appeal directly to God to intervene in the election, actually affect the outcome of the election? If so, would God answer yes to the prayer of the more righteous neighbor and no to the "less Godly" neighbor? What if God thinks one candidate is great on the immigration issue but also would be a horrible choice regarding many other issues? How would God answer the immigration prayer, if at all, in those circumstances? What if God thinks that candidate A should be elected instead of candidate B? Would God actually *change* His mind and allow candidate B to win instead, provided one of the neighbors really had prayed hard for candidate B (at least harder than the neighbor praying for candidate A)? Would it also depend on how many other people had prayed for candidate A to win and how many had prayed for candidate "B to win?

Maybe God should just hold an election to see how many prayers candidate A receives and how many prayers candidate B receives, because, after all, perhaps God shouldn't be "fixing" elections—how undemocratic (and un-American) that would be of Him! The silly nature of these questions, as well as how ludicrous any attempt at an answer would be, illustrates my point. Is God in control and dictating His will as God, or is He simply running a representative democracy and taking requests? If God believes in democracy for us, would He defer to the democratic will of the people in certain situations, or would He instead insist upon His own will and change the result of an otherwise fair election regardless of the democratic will of the people?

Of course, in our political system of democracy, the policy is "one person, one vote," a principle established by the Supreme Court in *Reynolds v. Sims*, 377 U.S. 533, 84 S. Ct. 1362, 12 L. Ed. 2d 506 (1964). The Supreme Court held that a state's apportionment plan for seats in its state legislature had to be based on population so that the voting power of each voter is equal. In God's system, however, a more righteous person's prayer might be worth more than a less righteous person's prayer (Romans 3:23: "For all have sinned, and come short of the glory of God"), so wouldn't an all-powerful God just veto all prayers anyway, as none of us is truly worthy or righteous (Romans 3:10: "There is none righteous, no, not one.") and simply follow His own intended will? After all, God is God, and His will is *His* will, not ours. If God is constantly changing His mind based on prayers, then God's will is not really God's will but more of God's first rough draft.

If you really think about it, prayers such as the ones that ask God to do something simply because we ask are either disrespectfully blasphemous or completely superfluous and ineffectual in achieving the intended result (other than making us feel better). Such a prayer seems blasphemous because it is quite arrogant to assume that we can influence God and can convince Him to change His mind based, potentially, on an entirely selfish human desire. Of course, how made up can God's mind be if we can convince Him to change it with a prayer? If we do not have this kind of pull with the Supreme Being of the universe, our prayers are superfluous and ineffectual because God is going to do whatever He is going to do anyway!

This calls into question, by the way, why Jesus ever prayed. There are numerous accounts in the Bible of Jesus praying to God (Matthew 11:25–26, Luke 10:21, and John 11:41–42, for example), but, literally, wouldn't that mean that Jesus was just talking to Himself? I guess it is OK for one to talk to oneself—I talk to myself sometimes. Maybe we talk to ourselves all of the time whenever we think about anything. Still, although I think and talk to myself, I would not consider what I do to be a prayer that I pray to myself. Jesus prayed to God the Father, but did God the Father ever pray to Jesus, and does either of them ever pray to the Holy Ghost? If so, wouldn't they all *already* know what the prayer is before it is prayed? Maybe Jesus's praying was just to teach us that we should pray, but again, pray for what—for God to change His plans, or to make up His apparently very un–made-up mind?

Chapter Ninety-Nine

Does It Ever Make Any Sense to Pray?

Don't get me wrong, I still pray to God, and when I do, it usually makes me feel better. But I try not to ask for external things or results; all I do is ask for strength and understanding from God (and, like Jesus, perhaps, from myself) to try to be a better person in general. Although Jesus was already perfect, I am not. Anyway, I try to get God's help or guidance in working on all of my many failings and shortcomings as a human being. Prayers other than this kind seem either arrogant or useless.

I remember hearing about televangelist Pat Robertson praying on a particular occasion for God to save the Virginia Beach area from a hurricane that was headed right for it (as well as to avoid Hurricane Gloria in 1985 and Hurricane Felix in 1995). Powerless to change the weather on their own, Robertson and his followers apparently prayed to God about it. They prayed very hard for God to deliver them from the devastation of these hurricanes—and it may have worked! The hurricanes missed the area but created problems in other areas. Those unfortunate people in those other areas apparently had not prayed hard enough for the hurricanes not to hit them and to stay on course to hit Virginia Beach and maybe even Pat Robertson's church instead (God's original plan?).

I have an idea: How about using the power of prayer to ask God to stop all hurricanes, earthquakes, tornados, tsunamis, blizzards, and other extreme inclement weather phenomena from ever harming anyone again? Would God ever answer that prayer? Perhaps I am going too far here, because it may be God's will for these severe weather events to occur. Maybe the occasional earthquake or tornado lets people know that God is still the boss. So, the foregoing leads to this conclusion: Pray for good weather, unless bad weather is God's will, and if bad weather is God's will, then pray for acceptance of God's will, unless you can get God to change His will through prayer for good weather.

Another type of prayer that is particularly interesting is the type of prayer where someone just prays for God's will. Even the Lord's Prayer (Matthew 6:9–13) has the line "…Thy will be done on earth as it is in heaven…" but think about why we would ask God to do whatever He is going to do anyway. Such a prayer might go something as follows (although obviously, someone actually praying for God's will would not state it quite this way, but still, try to think what it would mean to pray for God's will, in what ends up being a very absurd and pointless request):

> God, I pray that You will allow your Will to be done, because if I did not pray
> this prayer, You might not do what You are planning to do. This prayer might
> therefore convince You, or at least remind You, to do whatever You were

planning to do anyway. Perhaps You really do not need for me to pray this prayer, but somehow it makes me feel relevant and important to ask You do what You are going to do anyway. That way, when You do whatever You are going to do, then I can still claim that You have answered my prayer for You to do Your own will. Thank you. Amen.

What am I missing about the purpose and value of praying for God's will? Would a person praying for God's will be praying for God to stay focused, to not get sidetracked with other prayer requests that might make Him veer off course or forget what He is planning to do ("Stay on target, God, and pay attention")? Does God need us to pray that prayer? Does it show much respect for Him?

Still, if a loved one were dying and a friend told me that he or she was praying for my loved one, I would not reject that prayer. I would not tell my friend, "God is going to do whatever God is going to do anyway, so don't even bother praying. Your useless prayer would be arrogant, as it would assume that God is just bumbling along, open to mere random requests and our human lobbying efforts." No, I wouldn't say that. Instead, I would appreciate my friend's love, concern, and hope. And I, too, would pray for my loved one, because after getting them all the earthly care I possibly could and after exhausting all of my efforts to help, I would still hope that my loved one would live. And even though my prayer might be arrogant, in a sense, because it assumes that I have pull with God or that God doesn't have a plan and is simply open to my requests; still, that prayer would represent all that I would have left to give to my loved one. And so, I would pray for them.

In truth, I would stand on my head at that point if I thought it might help, but I guess that's the point—is praying as useless as standing on one's head as far as actually affecting God's intended outcome? Still, somehow, praying would make me feel better than standing on my head, so I would pray, and I would welcome the prayers of others.

I have faced this particular dire situation many times in my life, as has anyone who has been on Earth long enough to endure the death of a family member or friend. Most recently, my uncle George (my mother's brother) passed away after a very long battle with emphysema. He smoked nearly all his life, so it was a gift that he made it all the way to the age of 84. He was in the nursing home hospital during the final days of his life, and I was able to visit with him along with his son, my cousin, Eric; my aunt Ginny; and my mom when I flew back to my hometown, Pueblo, as the end of his life was near.

As Uncle George lay there, barely able to speak, or even breathe, all we could do was be with him in the room, talk to him, and be relieved when he raised his fist to acknowledge what we were saying. George was a great musician and a very talented artist, and I had enjoyed listening to him and talking politics with him ever since I was a young boy. I even enjoyed arguing with him occasionally. When I became a lawyer, he would always ask me interesting questions about the law. He loved to think and to speak his mind, and so it was especially difficult for me to see him so frail, old, and struggling mightily for a small breath as he would try desperately to speak.

At that point, we were all helpless and the situation was hopeless; it would be only a very short time before he would be gone. The end-of-life care group, hospice, came and made him more comfortable as the end approached. We were thankful for their care and concern and support. All we could do was occasionally complain to the nurses about making sure they did not put any unnecessary stress on George whenever they would come to change his bedding and had to move him a bit—it was all we had left to offer, as well as our prayers. The nurses were gracious and listened to our many suggestions, but we all knew what was happening and what was about to happen.

George would sleep much of the time, slowly slipping in and out of consciousness. We said our good-byes one night, and the next day, he died. It is difficult to see how our prayers could have possibly helped, but I guess somehow they made us feel better because they represented hope in a hopeless situation. They made us feel a little less sad and a little less helpless in what was a very sad and helpless situation. Our prayers also represented basic human kindness and empathy for George. Prayers allow us to show kindness and empathy, even for strangers among us with whom we share our humanity.

Along those lines, I note the passing of the indelible author and commentator Christopher Hitchens, who died of cancer. I highly respected and greatly admired Mr. Hitchens's intelligence, wisdom, and insights, and I think he has made a marvelous contribution to human thought on many levels. Hitchens was an atheist, yet I agreed with him on many issues, even though I ultimately still believe in God. If I ever would have had the pleasure to meet him, I am sure he would have provided me with a most interesting intellectual chastisement for my faith. I look up to great thinkers like him. That is why I find it so unfortunate, and even shameful, that some self-proclaimed believers in God had the nerve and cruelty to mock Christopher Hitchens as he battled cancer. They seemed to delight in the fact that he was human, that he was mortal, and that he, like all of us, would pass. Jerry Falwell died of a heart attack in his office, so did that mean Allah struck him down as a liar and as a charlatan infidel? We can disagree with Jerry Falwell, or with Christopher Hitchens, but in either case, we should not assume that their deaths were any more punishments than our own deaths will be when we die, no matter what we may believe or not believe.

We are humans. We live, we get ailments, and eventually, we die—all of us. We should therefore celebrate that we even get to be here, and we should respect anyone and everyone who has ever been here or is still here now. We need not respect all that a given person has chosen to do in life, of course, because we all have the right to disagree with the choices that others make, but we should at least respect the fact that that person was and is here on Earth, sharing the human experience with us. So I salute you, Christopher Hitchens, just as I have saluted my family members, high school friends, and others who have since passed. You will be fondly remembered, Mr. Hitchens, and highly respected and celebrated by many people in many ways that you may not have ever even realized.

Of course, there is no shortage of stories about miraculous healings of those afflicted by various ailments and diseases that are all allegedly the result of prayer and divine intervention by God. For example, there are many anecdotes from all over the world in which someone was close to death but faithful people prayed for them and then God miraculously healed them—at least for a while. Stories often include someone with terminal cancer whose cancer simply disappeared, someone with severe back pain that suddenly vanished; or someone with a tumor that went into remission without medical explanation. In all of these situations, the power of prayer is credited. Sometimes faith healing or the laying on of hands is credited, where a preacher puts his hand on a sick person's forehead, says a quick prayer, and then pushes that person over and they are healed. It is as though the electricity of God flowed through the faith healer. The sick person, believing in the healing by God, then makes a recovery.

Often, however, it is not mentioned when a person is sick, prayed for, and touched on the head by a faith healer but then dies anyway. Such is not recorded as a statistical loss or as a story about the *lack* of the power of prayer. Instead, that person's death, as well as all of the ineffectual prayers for that person, are together just accepted as God's will, not as a *failure* of the power of prayer. In fact, by definition, whatever happens—death or healing—is accepted as God's will when it occurs, so if the person remains alive after prayers for healing, then it is proof that God answers prayer, but if the person dies even after prayers for healing, then his or her death obviously was God's will, and so now we need to pray for acceptance and understanding of God's will. Even though God did not save my Uncle George pursuant to all of our prayers, George did get to live longer than most emphysema sufferers, and so some would say that our prayers were actually answered in that he got to live longer than most in his situation. I suppose every cloud has a silver lining: He got to live a long and full life even before we started praying for him, but if he would have lived even longer, would we have been tempted to credit our prayers? I guess it all depends on how you look at it.

Similarly, if someone is ill but survives, even though no one ever prayed for that person, his or her survival is not counted against the power of prayer, either. Often, there are perfectly logical and scientific medical reasons why some people with ailments are able to survive and even completely recover from their illnesses while others succumb and eventually die. To the extent there appears to be a miraculous healing, there are also accounts that some such healings might simply be psychosomatic. For example, some people with cancerous tumors are told that a faith healer can literally reach into their bodies and pull out their cancerous tumors. The faith healer performs an elaborate ritual and pulls out what appears to be a bloody mass of tissue from the person's body right in front of his or her eyes. The healer, using sleight of hand, a magician's trick, actually pulls the bloody tissue from out of his sleeve. Because the sick person is so desperate and wants to live so badly, there can be a psychological effect in which the mind convinces the body that it has been healed, so the body puts up more of a fight and the person therefore actually can live longer, at least for a while. It makes sense. Humans are very resilient creatures, and the power of our minds and our incredible wills is one of the reasons we have been able to survive, reproduce, and pass along those strong survival genes to later generations.

The human mind is very powerful, but it can be tricked. There are accounts of people who still have terrible phantom pains from severed limbs long after those limbs are gone. The brain has difficulty processing the fact that a limb is gone, so the brain gives off a residual pain feeling to let the person know that something is wrong with the severed limb; however, a form of pain therapy can be done with a person who, for example, lost a hand severed at the wrist. The patient originally feels pain not from the severed portion of the wrist but from the entire missing hand. The doctor gives the patient a mirror to place near his severed hand that reflects the image of the person's *other* hand to make it look as though the missing hand is still there. "Miraculously," the residual phantom pain disappears as the person's brain, apparently subconsciously, registers that the hand is not missing because deep in the brain, the reflection makes the missing hand appear to be there.

In terms of faith-healing prayers, it would be much more impressive to me, and much more noteworthy as proof of the divine supernatural intervention of God, if a person who had both legs amputated after a horrible accident could be prayed for and then right there, in front of all of our eyes, that person could grow a pair of new legs and then immediately use them to begin walking. It would also be helpful if there were a legitimate videotape of God miraculously making the legs spontaneously grow while the person was being fully monitored in a doctor's office. That way, the supernatural growth of these new instant legs, grown by God to replace the amputated legs could be officially documented. Such an event would be a miracle that even the likes of atheists Sam Harris or Christopher Hitchens would have to acknowledge as remarkable.

But why hasn't such a miracle ever happened, such that amputated limbs have actually grown back because someone prayed to God for new limbs, and why hasn't that miracle ever been documented? Would that be too much to ask of the power of prayer? If this question seems sarcastic, my next question is, Why should it be considered a sarcastic question? It is only a sarcastic question if we all know deep down that our prayers could *never* convince God to create new limbs for an amputee and so we shouldn't even ask. "God just doesn't do that; do not mock God!" someone might say. But I am not mocking God, because growing new limbs for an amputee shouldn't be an impossible prayer request, should it? Aren't we taught that all things are possible with God? Seriously, if God can create the entire universe, why can't God answer prayers to create new limbs for amputees? (For more on this, see http://whywont godhealamputees.com/.)

Are there no believers out there at all who have enough faith in God even to *attempt* to pray for an amputee to grow new limbs? The fact that believers never pray for such things is revealing in and of itself. But why stop there if one truly believes in the power of prayer? What about exhuming from a coffin a deceased person who has been dead for more than thirty years, so all that is left of the body is a skeleton? Why not start praying for God to grow new tissue, skin, muscle, flesh, eyes, and working organs, and then restart and revive the brain and bring the person back to life right before our eyes? Why does no believer have enough faith to pray that prayer and fully expect for God to answer? Why has God never answered such a prayer so the entire regeneration process from a skeleton back to a full live person was documented?

Jesus reportedly raised Lazarus from the dead (John 1:43–44:"[43]…[Jesus] cried with a loud voice, Lazarus, come forth. [44] And he that was dead came forth, bound hand and foot with graveclothes: and his face was bound about with a napkin. Jesus saith unto them, Loose him, and let him go"), but Lazarus was no skeleton at that point in need of growing new flesh and tissue and organs. Besides, Lazarus merely could have been in a coma (according to the scripture, he had been "dead" for only four days), and then awakened so that people might have mistakenly thought that Lazarus had come back to life, if we believe the hearsay accounts of that biblical story. Jesus just commanded him to "come forth," however, not necessarily to come back to life from being dead. Note that there are horrible fairly modern accounts of people in comas who are pronounced dead and who are buried alive in coffins only to later awake and then to eventually suffocate.

Finally, prayer can be thought of as a very humble way to give all decision-making power in one's life over to God, which also takes a great deal of faith in God. I have often heard some Christians say that they have made real messes of their lives because they were in control instead of God. They are advised by pastors or others to let go—indeed, to "let go and let God," not to worry as long as "the Lord is on board." But again, what does that mean, and how literal should we take such spiritual advice? How much faith do we really have to completely "let go and let God?" Somehow, if I were driving my car home on a windy mountain road and I wanted to humble myself to God and give to Him my decision-making power and control over all aspects of my life, I still probably should not *literally* let go of the steering wheel and let God drive—but would that be because I lack faith? Would even the most faithful fundamentalist Christian ever let go of a steering wheel and simply trust God to take control and operate the vehicle? Again, that should not be considered such a sarcastic question if we truly believe the literal advice to let go and let God control our lives. At what precise point does such spiritual and religious advice cease to be literal and become only figurative?

If Faith Must Rely on Proof, Then Is Faith Really "Faith"?

If prayers could produce actual accounts of amputees growing new limbs or of skeletons regenerating new tissue and coming back to life as the people they were before, or, for that matter, if God were to open the heavens and clearly reveal Himself as the one true God of the universe and tell us all directly to believe in Him because He is real…well, then there would be no need for faith. If that were to happen, I suppose even atheists would believe in God, just the same way they believe that there is a sun that gives off light and warmth. It is *easy* and fully rational to believe that the sun exists when we can document the sun's light, warmth, and existence, so again, there would be no need for our faith if the experience of God were completely self-evident.

This conception of faith posits that God will only grant prayers that can also be explained by other simultaneous phenomena so that we are always provided with a choice, at every turn, whether to believe in God based on faith alone, or to *not* believe in God because there is a perfectly logical alternative explanation. When faced with these differing choices—the work of God or another logical explanation—we get to choose. Do we trust God, or do we trust only our eyes? By definition, faith is belief in things not seen, so it misses the mark to think that faith must be proved by the things we see, because if that were the case, faith and rationality would morph into the very same thing.

This is at the core of the mistake that I think both fundamentalists and atheists make. Like doubting Thomases, fundamentalists believe in God only because they think they can see God and that there is thus rational proof supporting their beliefs, like believing in the existence of the sun. But faith that the sun exists is not much of a leap of faith at all. It takes no guts to believe in something when reason, logic, and evidence fully support one's belief. In comparison, I think the mistake that atheists make is that they cannot conceive of anything at all *but* the rational; they believe that if something cannot be rationally explained, it simply does not and cannot exist. As a result, they can poke holes in the alleged evidence-based "rationale" of fundamentalists (which is not hard to do), after which, for them, there is no *reason* to believe and the entire inquiry is over.

Paradoxically, then, I think both atheists and fundamentalists over rely on the rational and the logical (at least from their own points of view). Fundamentalists believe in God, but only because they think that it is entirely rational to believe in Him, while atheists do not believe in

God because they think it is entirely *not* rational to believe in Him. In both cases, however, rationality is the foundation of their belief or of their non-belief.

This all puts me in the most enviable position of arguing for complete irrationality and the wholesale absence of logic and evidence as the foundation for my beliefs! By the way, I just love to say things that can be easily ripped out of context and then later used against me because they seem so outrageous, but the juxtaposition of faith and reason, faith being separate from reason, is at the heart of the faith-reason paradox. That *is* the paradox of faith and reason. One shouldn't believe merely because it makes rational sense to do so. If one believes, one should believe *in spite* of the fact that it does *not* make rational sense to do so—at least not provable, definitive sense that requires no leap of faith at all. Besides, true faith involves believing in the sense of being truly committed to a way of life or to a larger mystical and spiritual connection, not just that something exists as a matter of scientific logic. After all, Satan and his angels/demons believe that God *exists*, yet they are still bound for Hell. (See James 2:19–20: "**[19]** Thou believest that there is one God; thou doest well: the devils also believe, and tremble. **[20]** But wilt thou know, O vain man, that faith without works is dead?"

So, belief also involves commitment, even to things unseen. Again, it is easy to believe when it all makes sense in a rational way (I believe that the sun exists, I can prove it, and therefore I believe—big deal), and it is easy not to believe when it does not make sense in a rational way (I do not believe that the Earth is flat, because there is definitive proof that it is actually round—big deal [although that actually was a big deal just a few hundred years ago!]). True faith is not called for in either of these situations, however, because simple rationality is enough by itself to explain the beliefs, so it is in that sense that I maintain that faith is something different from and beyond rationality—faith *without* proof. Faith is also where one must keep open to the distinct possibility that one just might be wrong, so it is much like being a trapeze artist "flying without a safety net" of rationality. That is what faith is to me—and it even takes some faith (and irrationality) on my part to admit what it is.

Whatever faith or belief might be or should be, why does so much consequence seem to turn on it according to most religious constructs? In other words, why is there such extreme eternal reward or eternal punishment associated with belief according to these religious constructs? I wonder why God would find it so necessary to torture us forever in Hell simply because we do not believe in something that has no rational definitive proof, and why He would allow us to live forever in the paradise of Heaven simply because we chose to believe in something that has no rational definitive proof (fundamentalists' intellectually suspect arguments notwithstanding). Why should there be such monumental consequences bestowed upon us where either scientific rationality is punished so very severely (Hell forever) or unsupported rationality is rewarded so spectacularly (Heaven forever)? Is that really fair? Or rational? Or appropriate?

Does it seem fair to reward fundamentalists who do not even have faith in this sense, given that they believe based on their delusional ideas that there is absolute and definitive proof of an unseen God that exists? What about others who believe in a God but have a very different concept of God that may be contrary to what is written in the Bible about the Christian God— how fair is it that they must burn in Hell forever for having faith but not choosing the "right" God in which to have faith? And what about those who have never even heard of the God of the Bible or of Jesus in their entire lives and must burn in Hell forever if they are not saved by Jesus before they die? What about those who simply cannot get beyond their own rationality, which cannot allow them to elevate superstition up to and beyond the level of scientific rationality? How fair and understanding is God in such circumstances? Does God really say, "too bad" for such people, and "to Hell with them," literally?

Are we not allowed to expect fairness—or at least our concept of fairness—from God because our concept of fairness may be different from God's concept of fairness? If we cannot expect for God to be fair as we know it, how would one know for sure that even if one follows the fundamentalists' plan of salvation down to the last letter, God might not still send them to Hell? Would God obviously not do that because He is not unfair? How do we know that our concept of fairness—defined in this context as living up to a written promise that is relied upon—is also necessarily God's concept of fairness? Once we allow for the possibility that God's concept of fairness can be different from our own, then God can do anything that we consider to be unfair because it very well might still be fair in God's universe and according to His higher rules. Of course, this assumes there is even a common human idea of fairness, which seems awfully dubious when life (and lawsuits and courtrooms) are full of disputes in which people cannot agree on what is fair.

Still, in the law, there is a constitutional concept known as procedural due process. In this process, generally the government—the legal system—must give citizens (1) notice of a lawsuit or criminal charges against them and (2) an opportunity to be heard (as in a trial) *before* the government can deprive a person of life, liberty, or property. But how can a person who has never even heard of Jesus Christ, the Bible, or the plan of salvation, be said to have received proper and fair notice and the opportunity in life to either accept or reject God before that person dies? If it is unfair not to give a person proper (or even any) notice according to a rather basic legal human standard, why would God sink below that standard and judge someone who in life never received notice and an opportunity to accept or reject God? Even if there were technical notice given, what if that notice seemed illogical or implausible such that a person might reasonably not take it seriously?

With all of this in mind, is it fair to be required to burn in Hell forever all because a series of remarkable stories in an ancient book about supernatural events seemed implausible to someone in light of modern science, logic, rationality, and evidence? And is it fair for someone to get to enjoy Heaven forever all because these remarkable stories about supernatural events seemed plausible to that person *despite* the contrary doubts raised by science, logic, rationality, and evidence? I have difficulty seeing how any of that can possibly be considered fair, or even mature, and in seeing how a loving, rational, omnipotent, and omniscient Supreme Being of the universe could be so unfair and immature. God just seems like He would be so much greater and far beyond that. I cannot prove it, of course; I have no evidence. I merely have *faith* that whatever God may be, He would not be that small, narrow, shallow, and unfair.

Coincidence and the Correlation-versus-Causation Question; Another Personal Experience

I have asked myself, *Don't I even have one logical, evidence-based reason why I believe in God?* Although my belief in God, admittedly, is almost entirely intuitive and emotional, the closest thing to a rational reason I have for believing in God would be experiences that have happened to me at different times throughout my life. I have noticed certain eerie coincidences in my life, many of which appear to have at least an ostensible connection to spiritual matters. Maybe those constitute the "reasons" I believe in God. I realize that mere coincidences are not proof and, in fact, are often the basis for patently incorrect and false conclusions. For example, if I wore a blue t-shirt and I got an A on a test, would that *prove* that wearing a blue t-shirt will result in my receiving an A on an upcoming test? No, because mere correlation does not equal causation. Coincidences are not *necessarily* proof of anything.

Still, sometimes I think that not all situations are mere coincidence, even though I remain open to the notion that they might be. It is possible that what appears to be mere coincidence is actually God's will expressing itself in our lives. For example, as a general matter, whenever I can possibly avoid sinning, my life seems to be happier, more centered, and more peaceful. When I engage in more sinning, however, my life tends to have more turmoil and more controversy, and I seem to have less peace. Some would call it karma. Other people might call it staying out of trouble. For me, it just seems like, for whatever reason, "you get what you give" in the universe, and "you reap what you sow." (See Galatians 6:7–8: "[7] Be not deceived; God is not mocked: for whatsoever a man soweth, that shall he also reap. [8] For he that soweth to his flesh shall of the flesh reap corruption; but he that soweth to the Spirit shall of the Spirit reap life everlasting.") That connection between moral and immoral actions and consequences seems very real and true for me, and not only as a general matter, but also very specifically.

For instance, I have a very vivid memory of something that happened to me once when I was in college that convinced me that God was real and was very involved specifically in my life, even though it might have been nothing more than a random coincidence. I therefore would not hold this out as proof to others that God exists, but at least at the time (and even sometimes now), it seemed liked *proof* to me.

First, a little college background to set up the context in which this incident occurred: Recall that my mother and father divorced when I was five and that I lived with my mother, along with my older sister and brother, as I was growing up. My mom did not graduate from high school, so her earning power was very limited, and after the divorce, she found herself having to raise and support three kids as a saleswoman at Goodwill, St. Vincent De Paul, and then various other clothing stores, as well as earning money from babysitting and cleaning houses.

My dad paid a total of $110 per month as child support for the three of us kids (although this seems like a shockingly low amount, remember that these were 1966–1979 dollars). My mom agreed to this so the divorce would not force us to leave the house that we had lived in before the divorce. My dad's child support payments were used to pay the house payment, with the proviso that when I turned 18 (because I was the youngest), my mom would have to sell the house and move out, and then my parents would split the proceeds from the equity. For the most part, my dad paid, although there were times when he would be late and there were threats of foreclosure. Still, my mom and my dad always got it together and paid and we never lost the house. In addition to providing a place for us to live, the house was an investment for them. My mom had to pay all other expenses for us (which ended up being more than $110 per month), and she never received a return on that investment, at least not in strict economic terms.

Going back even further, my mom and dad got married when my mom was still in high school and my dad had just graduated. My dad started out by making pistons in a piston factory, and after a few years, he wanted a better-paying job, so he convinced a credit union to hire him as a loan officer. He worked very hard and did well, and from there, he eventually landed a job in the US Labor Department. He worked there for several years before becoming a full-time pastor of a church. We had a relationship with him off and on over the years, and less so after he remarried, but he still tried to be there for us in difficult circumstances. My brother, sister, and I were able to live in the house that our parents provided for us during our childhoods after the divorce. Both of my parents worked very hard to make ends meet, and at times, my mom, sister, brother, and I also received assistance from the federal and state governments (food stamps, free-lunch programs, welfare assistance, Aid to Families with Dependent Children, and so on.), as well some personal aid from additional family and friends.

To this day, I am very grateful to my parents for all of their efforts to support us and for the help from others that we received during my childhood. I am also grateful to the taxpayer strangers who funded various government programs that not only helped to feed us but also later made it possible for me to get financial aid to go to college and then to law school. If that was "liberal wealth-redistribution socialism," as some would claim it to be, well then I say thank God for that "socialism" and for those governmental officials and taxpayers who provided support to me and my family as I was growing up. Because of that support, along with the assistance of others, we were saved from very dire economic circumstances and I was able to get educated and eventually become a lawyer.

When I was in college, I was on financial aid, and as part of the financial aid package, I was granted a work-study job—I got to work at the college gym, checking IDs. I played football and ran track while in college (and in high school), and that was why I decided to go to college in the first place—the football and track coach at Colorado College, Frank Flood, convinced me in high school that I should try to go to college and that he would help me do it. Early on, Coach Flood began letting me work in his coach's office in the gym. I worked there every night from 6:00 pm to 10:00 pm to make sure, as he said, "there were no fires in the building, and to make sure there were no other general problems," because if there were, it was my job to be there to call campus security. I always thought that job was important. I guess I actually thought that, somehow, no one else could or would call campus security if there were ever such a problem (as if there were actually a major threat of a fire in that big concrete El Pomar sports building). I didn't realize it at the time, but Coach Flood was just watching out for me and giving a kid like me a break in the hopes that I would complete college and then have choices and options in my life. He knew that although I was not prepared to go to college, I was still willing to try.

Back in high school, starting my freshman year, I had been put into a vocational graphic arts program and had been taught how to run a printing press. During my junior and senior years, I had only a class or two because most of the time, I went to my printing job and got high school credit for it. Making money for me and my mom while getting high school credit for it seemed like a great arrangement at the time, even if it was not the best preparation for college work. Of course, Coach Flood knew all of this. That is why he gave me the job in college and watched out for me while I was there. There were no windows in his office, and there were certainly no computers or the Internet back then; he was very clear about telling me that I could not use the telephone. I asked him, "Well then what am I supposed to do for four hours every night, other than just check the building every once in a while for a fire or something"? He said, "Stay out of trouble! And because our insurance says that someone has to be here at night, that is why we are hiring you; I know it will be boring just sitting here all night, but you can always bring your books in here and study . . . if you want." Maybe there are people who are angels, or at least people who just act like angels, in our lives.

I was thankful for that job and to be able to play sports and go to a very good four-year liberal arts college. Few in my family ever had that opportunity. My mom and brother really did not have the chance to finish high school. Although my sister eventually finished high school and even took some college classes, she was never able to complete college. Life and various unfortunate and even unfair circumstances made it virtually impossible for them to pursue college or any type of graduate school. Thus, college was a fantastic opportunity for someone like me. I had a small opening, and I knew I had better take it.

But I needed money. Financial aid did not cover everything, so every penny was accounted for. One night at the gym, several non-student guests wanted to use the athletic building. Although students always got in free, all guests had to pay. That night, those guests paid with a $20.00 bill, and I was on my honor to turn in the money and account for the visitors who had signed in as guests, but I had a great idea—if I were to erase where they had signed in as guests, because they had used a pencil, I could keep the $20.00 and use the money to go on a date at the movies.

All I needed was a friend to lend me his car. I made some quick calls and arrangements, even though I was not supposed to use the phone. Although my friend let me borrow his car, he told me there was no gas in it, so I would need money to fill up the car and pay for the movie—and $20.00 extra would just about cover it. And so, my many rationalizations to "take" (I should say steal) the money began to freely flow from my perceived victimhood: *No one would miss it*, I thought, and *I need the money very badly, more than the college does*!

Obviously, I knew that it would be stealing from the coach and from Colorado College—people who were just trying to help me by giving me this special supervisor job with trust and responsibility, but that night, I continued to rationalize. Indeed, now I argued that it seemed like a waste of money that I was paid just to watch the building, and if the college could afford that, then the college certainly would never miss the $20.00 that would make such a huge difference to me. I also started to wonder whether the school was just exploiting me for cheap labor so they did not have to hire a much more expensive security guard to watch for problems that almost never occurred. Moreover, the college really did not expect to make any real money off of non-student guests anyway, because the price for admission for non-student guests was really just a way to deter non-students from using the sports facilities. There was no attempt to actually make any profit by the college as a regular, for-profit sports gym business, so the purpose was only to charge the money as a deterrent, not to depend on it as a business concern. At about the same time, I started to realize that perhaps I should go to law school, because by the end of the night, I had thoroughly convinced myself that I really was doing the college a favor by taking that $20.00 so the college would not have to worry about it! In short, I found it easy to steal the money as part of my overall plan that night to borrow a car and arrange a date after I got off of work.

I am sorry to say that even though Coach Flood and Colorado College had given me a chance to get an education and to play sports, and though they had provided me with financial aid to pay for it all and even had given me that special job to earn some extra money while I was there, I decided to steal the $20.00 anyway. I stole it, rationalizing that I should not have to feel so poor all of time. Not only was it stealing, but it was the worst kind of unappreciative stealing. Justifying the theft because I didn't appreciate the generosity of the entity I was stealing from seemed worse than just stealing in general.

It was fairly late when I got off work that night, past 10:00 PM, so I had to hurry to get the car, fill it up, pick up my date, and make it to the late showing of the movie. I got the car, went to the gas station, and filled up, but when I went to pay for the $11.00 of gas, my $20.00 was gone! I simply could not find it anywhere. I desperately searched the entire car and my pockets. I retraced my steps, but I just could not find the money, even though I had had it in the car just before I put in the gas. It was a disaster. The 7-11 gas station clerk was not happy and said he was going to call the police if I did not pay. I could not call my date, although even if I could have called her, I didn't have any money to take her to the movie.

I remember sitting on the ground of the 7-11 minimart feeling dejected. Life seemed so unfair. What a loser I was. Amazingly, I had lost the money that I had stolen so perfectly. I was just sitting there on the curb by a pay phone, trying to think of who I could call to help me. Did I dare call Coach Flood (collect) and ask him to give me some money? I chuckled to myself, "The nerve of some people!" I finally prayed and asked God to forgive me, not only for stealing the $20.00 but also for not appreciating the lucky break that I had been given to go to a fancy college with financial aid, receive an education, and get to play sports, all at other people's expense—and all because they thought it was a worthwhile endeavor to give someone like me a chance. I also thought about how anytime anyone ever criticized me, I would accuse them of being racist, classist, or both because I had grown up poor, yet there I was, stealing from those who were trying to help me and still acting like they owed me something.

I felt horrible and guilty, as I should have, and so I shamefully walked back to the car, thinking about what I could do next. Maybe I could convince the 7-11 clerk to give me a break? He was in no mood, and it seemed like he actually deserved more of a break than I had in getting to go to college on someone else's dime. When it seemed most hopeless, however, as I got into the car and looked down on the car seat, right there in plain sight was the $20.00! It was just lying there. *What the hell? Are you kidding me?* No way, I had searched the car through and through, but it was not there, and now, all of a sudden, it was there! Even now as I write, I can remember how simultaneously ashamed and thankful I was to see that $20.00. At that moment, somehow, I knew God was real and had taught me a very dramatic lesson. I walked over to the clerk, and he looked at me like I was some dumb college kid, which I was, but at least I had become a little wiser that night. It was too late by then to go to a movie, so I apologized to my date for being late when I finally showed up, and we just went to eat. The next day, I paid back the $20.00 by borrowing $15.00 to pay it, and then I paid back that $15.00 right when I got paid. I also thanked God for teaching me a lesson, for putting people like Coach Flood in my life, and for providing me the wonderful opportunity to go to college.

So what is the point of this story? Does it prove that God exists and that He created the universe and that the story of Noah's ark must really be true? No, it doesn't prove anything. An atheist also could have learned the exact same lesson that I did about how stealing is wrong, and maybe the atheist could have even learned the lesson without actually having to steal from well-meaning people just trying to help him. Still, the story is indicative of what I think we are faced with in life: maybe it is God at work in our lives, or perhaps it is just something else and we get to choose what we think it is. For example, maybe the $20.00 going missing right then was my own psychological construct, which I subconsciously used to ease the guilt I felt for stealing the money. Then I could still have a loving God allow me to miraculously find the money (and still use it, by the way, that very night) and then pay it back later. I got my way, and I no longer had to feel guilty about it, and all was forgiven. When I admitted to Coach Flood what I had done, he simply said, "To tell you the truth, Fred, I'm just happy that you haven't stolen a whole lot more stuff out of here than that...so far!" What a good person he was—an angel without wings!

Somehow, it hurt much worse that he wasn't mad at me and that he let it all go with only a joke and the sincere and important hope that I would do much better than that in my life.

So, perhaps my story has nothing to do with God's divine intervention. Instead, maybe I am just a hopelessly absentminded professor. Even today, my wife and kids actually make bets on how long it will be before I lose a new pair of sunglasses—on which I am no longer allowed to spend more than $10.00 because I always lose them, as well as my wallet, my keys, my phone, and my watch. My secretary every so often has to let me into my office whenever I manage to lock myself out. That is how absentminded I am. Maybe all it proves is that ever since college, I have been absentminded, but I now remember this particular story about misplacing something just because I have attached so much spiritual significance to it. In contrast, whenever I lose my keys and then later find them in the dryer, I do not think God has taken time out of His busy schedule to teach me yet another absentmindedness lesson or to possibly attempt to save me from a potential fatal car crash because my trip is delayed until I find the keys. So is the loss and rediscovery of the stolen $20.00 just a coincidence, or was there actually a force in the universe, like God, at work in my life? My story can be evidence that God was working in my life; but it also can be that I just subconsciously lost and then found the money on purpose, or even that I simply lost it and then found it, but decided to attach further personal spiritual meaning and importance to it.

In law, this correlation-versus-causation dichotomy is often an important source of information to analyze. For example, assume that children in a city who live near a local uranium mill have a 20% higher rate of cancer than do children who do not live near the uranium mill. Does their higher cancer rate necessarily prove that the uranium mill has caused the rate of childhood cancers to increase, or could that higher cancer rate of children living near the mill have been caused by completely unrelated factors, as many cancers can have a multitude of possible causes? Perhaps the families living next to the mill were lower income and did not have good access to healthcare, good nutrition, and/or good exercise, and therefore, the higher incidence of cancer was caused by these particular factors that had nothing to do with living near the mill. If the uranium mill were found liable, it would have to be because the mill actually caused the children's cancer. There would have to be some causal nexus between the mill and the cancer, even if it was a combination of various factors. If the uranium mill were not found liable, it would be because the location of the uranium mill merely *correlated* with the nearby children's higher cancer rates—those children just happened to live close by. Without more than a simple correlation, the mill would not be liable. Maybe the correlation would be enough and cross over into causation, however, if the children had radiation poisoning, because that circumstantial evidence would be more powerful and more direct as uranium definitely produces radiation, while it may only cause certain types of cancer that might also have many other plausible causes.

Although the defendant uranium mill would not be liable if the plaintiff children could not prove that the mill caused the higher rates of cancer, that result might be reversed if we switched the burden of proof and put it on the uranium mill. Based on the correlation of the higher incidence rate of cancer among children living closer to the mill, the law might then require the mill to prove that the higher cancer rates were *not* a function of the children living close to the mill. If the burden were switched this way, the mill might not be able to satisfy that negative burden. In simpler terms, it would be the equivalent of saying, "The children may not be able to prove that the cancer was caused by the mill, but given the correlation of higher cancer rates of children living close to the mill, the mill cannot now prove that the cancer was *not* caused by the mill." In close cases, the side that ends up with the burden of proof often loses the case.

Another stark example of correlation, and *not* causation, follows. Assume that in professional football, every time a team from the American Football Conference (AFC) wins the Super Bowl, the stock market *rises* the next day, but that every time a team from the National Football Conference (NFC) wins the Super Bowl, the stock market *falls* the next day. One would be hard pressed to argue for any causation between which pro team from which NFL conference won the Super Bowl and why stock prices rose or fell the next day, even though there would be an undeniable coincidence of events that could be correlated with one another. I suppose football teams in certain cities winning the Super Bowl possibly might have a certain causal economic effect in that city that can result in either a general stock market increase or decrease, but that would be a different cause than the mere arbitrary grouping that the teams belonged to, the NFC or the AFC, so perhaps there could be causation lurking in what appears to be mere correlation.

In my story, stealing the $20.00, losing it, and then finding it after asking for forgiveness formed an eerie set of coincidences, but was there actual causation, or was it merely correlation? Could that be the nature of the test that God often gives us in life? Is it foolish to argue that as a matter of logic, the incident can be *only* causation or *only* correlation, because the truth is that it can be *either*? Complicating the matter is that sometimes, things have happened to me that are very unpleasant and appear to be purely random. They have blindsided me out of nowhere, with no apparent connection to anything I had done. This can be true for other people, as sometimes, bad things happen to good people. This makes it difficult, if not impossible, to say that what has happened always must have been deserved. What about a baby, or a five-year old, who suffers a horrible, painful disease? What about a young child who dies a painful death when murdered by a sexual predator? What about an aborted fetus, whom some people believe is a child with a soul? Are we to assume all of those children (even fetuses) did something so bad that God was fairly and justly paying them back for all of their horrible sins? Is that fair and just in a way that our minds, with their limited sense of justice, just cannot understand?

That is also why I continue to wonder whether God exists. Perhaps we believe because the stories of our lives are better, more interesting, and more meaningful if there is a god out there, we all get to live forever, and all of what we do matters on a spiritual level because, in the end, good can ultimately triumph over evil. Somehow, that seems better and more significant, than us just being organisms, albeit interesting and complex ones, who live out our lives in which the events involved are nothing more than a haphazard occurrence of chance incidents —meaning that we are not part of some grand plan authored by God.

Things aren't necessarily true just because they would make for a better story, however. On a very simplistic level, our existence in the universe is like a great, wonderful movie that we never want to end. We just cannot seem to accept the fact that this movie called life has a very final ending, but believing in God changes all of that. It means that we get to live on, that life is not over and will never be over because we get to be forever with God in Paradise! Perhaps we developed that belief/delusion as a survival mechanism to give meaning to our lives, especially in difficult times when we might have just given up, thinking that life really doesn't matter anyway. If we do not have hope, then we might despair to such a degree that our very survival would be compromised.

Chapter One-Hundred-Two

Where Do We Go from Here? Toward Understanding a Progression of God, from the Simple to the Complex

Maybe God is not as simplistic as He is often made out to be in the Bible. My brother suggested an excellent thought experiment in this regard. He asked what would happen if we could somehow get all of the following writers and biblical figures together in a room and ask them to describe God in their own words: (1) Abraham describing God in Genesis; (2) Moses describing God in Exodus; (3) David describing God in the section known as the writings, which is the middle part of the Old Testament; (4) Isaiah describing God in the section known as the prophets, the latter part of the Old Testament; (5) Jesus describing God (the Father, not just Himself) in the Gospels at the beginning of the New Testament; and (6) John describing God in the last book of the Bible, Revelation. What if they each described their various personal understandings of and individual experiences with God? If they were to remain true to their writings or quotations, what we would get? After some initial agreement on many of the basics, we probably would get a rather heated argument as their interesting discussion developed.

For example, Abraham is remembered as the friend of God. His experience (the revelation of God) at the beginning of the Bible is described very simply as God being "three men standing outside of his tent" (Genesis 18:1–3). In Genesis 18:3–16, God makes a prediction about Abraham and Sarah (his wife) having a child when they are both very old, and Sarah laughs at the prediction because of their old age ("and the lord appeared unto him (Abraham)…and he sat in the door of the tent in the heat of the day") Later, when the Israelites were about to be invaded and the leadership of Israel gathered to appeal to God for His help in the matter (II Chronicles 20:1–13), they acknowledged, "art thou not our God, who didst not drive out the inhabitants of this land…and gave it to the seed of Abraham thy friend forever" (verse 7). There are, of course, more details concerning Abraham's relationship with God, but it is a relatively simple and literal relationship, especially at first.

Moses, in comparison, experienced a passionate God who was very dramatic, vengeful, and jealous and who appeared and acted in spectacular ways. For example, in Exodus 20:5, God says, "Thou shalt not bow down thyself to them [other gods] for I the lord thy God am a jealous God." Also see Exodus 3:2–6, for Moses's burning-bush revelation of God:

> [2] And the angel of the LORD appeared unto him in a flame of fire out of the midst of a bush: and he looked, and, behold, the bush burned with fire, and the bush was not consumed.
>
> [3] And Moses said, I will now turn aside, and see this great sight, why the bush is not burnt.
>
> [4] And when the LORD saw that he turned aside to see, God called unto him out of the midst of the bush, and said, Moses, Moses. And he said, Here am I.
>
> [5] And he said, Draw not nigh hither: put off thy shoes from off thy feet, for the place whereon thou standest is holy ground.
>
> [6] Moreover he said, I am the God of thy father, the God of Abraham, the God of Isaac, and the God of Jacob. And Moses hid his face; for he was afraid to look upon God.

God is seen by Moses in many instances as an almost theatrical God with super powers who creates fear (similar to the frightful way the Wizard of Oz is first portrayed to Dorothy), as in Exodus 19:16–25:

> [16] And it came to pass on the third day in the morning, that there were thunders and lightnings, and a thick cloud upon the mount, and the voice of the trumpet exceeding loud; so that all the people that was in the camp trembled.

Again, it is an interesting aside that there are clear grammatical mistakes, even in the original Middle English in which the King James Version of the Bible was written; why would God have allowed that to happen to His word … "all the people that *was* in the camp…"?

> [17] And Moses brought forth the people out of the camp to meet with God; and they stood at the nether part of the mount.
>
> [18] And Mount Sinai was altogether on a smoke, because the LORD descended upon it in fire: and the smoke thereof ascended as the smoke of a furnace, and the whole mount quaked greatly.
>
> [19] And when the voice of the trumpet sounded long, and waxed louder and louder, Moses spake, and God answered him by a voice…
>
> [21] And the LORD said unto Moses, Go down, charge the people, lest they break through unto the LORD to gaze, and many of them perish…
>
> [24] And the LORD said unto him, Away, get thee down, and thou shalt come up, thou, and Aaron with thee: but let not the priests and the people break through to come up unto the LORD, lest he break forth upon them.
>
> [25] So Moses went down unto the people, and spake unto them.

To David, God was more of a political advisor, in that God helped David by giving him instructions on how to create a successful monarchy. King David was the first king of Israel. Technically, Saul was first king of Israel, but not as a practical matter, because David was the true king in the eyes of the people, the prophets, and possibly even God. (See II Samuel 5:2–3, 10-13, where God makes David the king of Israel (apparently with the fringe benefits of more concubines and wives.)

> [2] Also in time past, when Saul was king over us, thou [David] wast he that leddest out and broughtest in Israel: and the LORD said to thee, Thou shalt feed my people Israel, and thou shalt be a captain over Israel.
> [3] So all the elders of Israel came to the king to Hebron; and king David made a league with them in Hebron before the LORD: and they anointed David king over Israel…
> [10] And David went on, and grew great, and the LORD God of hosts was with him…
> [12] And David perceived that the LORD had established him king over Israel, and that he had exalted his kingdom for his people Israel's sake.
> [13] And David took him more concubines and wives out of Jerusalem, after he was come from Hebron: and there were yet sons and daughters born to David.
> (II Samuel 5:2–3, 10–13)

It is interesting that taking multiple wives and even having concubines apparently is not seen here as violating the commandment against committing adultery. It appears politicians have been engaging in this kind of behavior for a very long time; nevertheless, it doesn't seem like God should give King David a pass if consistency is important. In any event, God is portrayed here as the ultimate political advisor and even as a secret political weapon. See II Samuel 5:17–23, where God takes sides in a war and advises David about one of his national war campaigns:

> [17] But when the Philistines heard that they had anointed David king over Israel, all the Philistines came up to seek David; and David heard of it, and went down to the hold.
> [18] The Philistines also came and spread themselves in the valley of Rephaim.
> [19] And David inquired of the LORD, saying, Shall I go up to the Philistines? wilt thou deliver them into mine hand? And the LORD said unto David, Go up: for I will doubtless deliver the Philistines into thine hand.
> [20] And David came to Baal-perazim, and David smote them there, and said, The LORD hath broken forth upon mine enemies before me, as the breach of waters. Therefore he called the name of that place Baal-perazim.
> [21] And there they left their images, and David and his men burned them.
> [22] And the Philistines came up yet again, and spread themselves in the valley of Rephaim.
> [23] And when David inquired of the LORD, he said, Thou shalt not go up; but fetch a compass behind them, and come upon them over against the mulberry trees.

To Isaiah and the prophets, God is manifested in many varied ways ranging from quite magnificent productions to the simple "still small voice." God is also seen as something more complex than just a manifestation of the elements of the earth or as any inclement weather events (I Kings 19:11–14)—as a more spiritually symbolic and less literal god:

> [11] And he said, Go forth, and stand upon the mount before the LORD. And, behold, the LORD passed by, and a great and strong wind rent the mountains, and brake in pieces the rocks before the LORD; but the LORD was not in the wind: and after the wind an earthquake; but the LORD was not in the earthquake:
> [12] And after the earthquake a fire; but the LORD was not in the fire: and after the fire a still small voice.
> [13] And it was so, when Elijah heard it, that he wrapped his face in his mantle, and went out, and stood in the entering in of the cave. And, behold, there came a voice unto him, and said, What doest thou here, Elijah?
> [14] And he said, I have been very jealous for the LORD God of hosts: because the children of Israel have forsaken thy covenant, thrown down thine altars, and slain thy prophets with the sword; and I, even I only, am left; and they seek my life, to take it away.

To Jesus, God was the quintessential father. Although Jesus is said to be the literal Son of God and therefore obviously would view God as His Father, we are supposed to view God the Father as our Father, too, as we are also God's children. There are several instances in the book of Matthew alone where Jesus refers to God as *His* Father, in a special and unique way beyond that which God the Father is our spiritual father as well:

> Not every one that saith unto me, Lord, Lord, shall enter into the kingdom of heaven; but he that doeth the will of my Father which is in heaven. (Matthew 7:21)

> But whosoever shall deny me before men, him will I also deny before my Father which is in heaven. (Matthew 10:33)

> [25] At that time Jesus answered and said, I thank thee, O Father, Lord of heaven and earth, because thou hast hid these things from the wise and prudent, and hast revealed them unto babes.
> [26] Even so, Father: for so it seemed good in thy sight.
> [27] All things are delivered unto me of my Father: and no man knoweth the Son, but the Father; neither knoweth any man the Father, save the Son, and he to whomsoever the Son will reveal him. (Matthew 11:25–27)

Finally, to John, God was "seven spirits sitting on seven thrones with seven eyes gone out into the world" (Revelation 4:5–5:14). This particular vision of God is much more complex and detailed and, frankly, much more confusing than the others. What is interesting is that just before this vision in Chapters 4 and 5, in Chapters 2 and 3 *seven churches* are addressed that started out doing well, but eventually, God says that He "has something against them." In other words, these churches seem to have started off correctly but then have fallen short in some other area. The prescribed remedy for them was to hear what the spirit (one of the "seven spirits gone out into the world") is saying specifically to them, not to the wicked or sinners or nonbelievers, but to the *churches*. Because the church is falling short and God Himself "has something against them," God advises them to go a step further and engage Him in spirit.

Of course, all of these various writings to which I refer may be interpreted in any number of different ways, especially because the language used seems so convoluted and heavily symbolic. It is very easy to quickly get lost in the weeds here, in the very difficult-to-understand text. On one level, pointing out that the Bible can be used to come up with various interpretations loosely based on the text is precisely the point of citing these textual passages—to expose by example the extremely open-ended nature of the text and the creative interpretation of it. No doubt there would be fundamentalists, or other literalists, who would say that my interpretation is misguided and completely off the mark (before they would then start to disagree with one another on their own various doctrines and biblical interpretations); however, that really only makes my overall point about how difficult, if not impossible, it is to have just one authoritative interpretation of the Bible. Still, these passages suggest at least a possible interpretation in which spiritual development, progression, and even change are fully contemplated and symbolically represented.

So, putting these passages all together, one might say that at the beginning of the Bible, God is described as "three men standing outside Abraham's tent" (a relatively simple symbolic, or perhaps even literal, construct) but that by the end, God has become "seven spirits on seven thrones with seven eyes gone out into the world," whatever that imagery might mean. Whatever this description from Revelation may now mean, or whatever it was intended to mean, if we can even now figure that out for sure, it clearly is a much more complex and far more symbolic conceptualization of God than as merely Abraham's friend.

This progression from the simple to the complex, is a theme that is also clear in the book of Hebrews. Hebrews 1:1 begins "God …in diverse manners spake in times past unto the fathers by the prophets," but later, in verse 2, "hath in these last days spoken unto us by his son." God apparently has a history of changing the way he communicates to humans. The author of Hebrews then goes on for several verses about how and why this *new* type of communication is better. In verse 4, he compares this new "son speaking" communication as being better than that of the angels. Whoever wrote Hebrews (its authorship seems unclear and is the subject of much debate) also compares this new type of "son speaking" communication to the type of communication given through Moses and explains why it is now so much better (see Hebrews 3:1–6).

Then, in Hebrews 5:10, the author introduces a very deep subject concerning a "new" and "eternal" priesthood modeled not after the order of the Levites but after the order of Melchisedec (Hebrews 7:11–12: "For the priesthood being changed, there is made of necessity a change also of the law"). Apparently, God has a history of changing not only the priesthood but also the law. It appears, then, that God is possibly much more flexible and open-minded than we have been led to believe.

Beginning in Hebrews 5:11 and through 6:3 is the turning point that starts the spiritual maturation process. God scolds the churches for not understanding important matters like the priesthood after the order of Melchisedec, and he basically calls them immature and likens them to babies who can only digest milk when they should be able to handle solid food (Hebrews 5:10–14; 6:1–3):

> **Chapter 5**
> [10] Called of God an high priest after the order of Melchisedec.
> [11] Of whom we have many things to say, and hard to be uttered, seeing ye are dull of hearing.
> [12] For when for the time ye ought to be teachers, ye have need that one teach you again which be the first principles of the oracles of God; and are become such as have need of milk, and not of strong meat.
> [13] For every one that useth milk is unskilful in the word of righteousness: for he is a babe.
> [14] But strong meat belongeth to them that are of full age, even those who by reason of use have their senses exercised to discern both good and evil.
> **Chapter 6**
> [1] Therefore leaving the principles of the doctrine of Christ, let us go on unto perfection; not laying again the foundation of repentance from dead works, and of faith toward God,
> [2] Of the doctrine of baptisms, and of laying on of hands, and of resurrection of the dead, and of eternal judgment.
> [3] And this will we do, if God permit.

We see that the prescription suggested for maturation is set forth in Hebrews 6:1–3. In verse 1 ("therefore leaving the doctrine of the principles of Christ let us go on unto perfection"), it is interesting that to "go on" to perfection and maturity, one should leave the principles of the doctrine of Christ. Also in verse 1 ("not laying again the foundation of repentance from dead works and of faith toward God"), we are being instructed to go beyond repentance of our sins, of "dead works," and, amazingly, of faith toward God to mature. Verse 2 mentions all the things that present-day Christianity emphasizes ("of the doctrine of baptisms, and of laying on of hands, and of resurrection of the dead, and of eternal judgment"). It is not that these principles are wrong in some manner, but just that we should venture and develop beyond them. Thus, the book of Hebrews can be seen as a call to maturity. Its basic underlying theme, its foundation, is found at the very beginning. God has changed the way He is speaking, and we should open up and listen to what He is saying, in the same way that the seven churches in Revelation are admonished to "hear what the spirit is saying."

In many ways, this book I have written can be seen as being in line with this very general theme of engaging in a changing and developing spiritual journey. The only way to change one's position and make progress is to honestly question where one is currently with respect toward an understanding of God, unless one already knows everything and is somehow completely right about everything. Perhaps we need to open up and, in effect, leave the first principles of our own understanding and move on to maturity, possibly even taking a position based on God's up-to-date manner of communicating.

Accordingly, there appears to be a possible progression of the description of God from the simple to the more complex. If the principal figures in the Bible were preachers, priests, or pastors living today, they might find themselves embroiled in some serious disagreement as to who God is, what His purpose is, and how humans should now experience Him. Why would there be these differences among them when they are all purportedly authors, or at least principle figures, of the same book containing writings about the "same" God? Should it be all that surprising when we now have so many different religious sects of Christianity conceiving of God and the Bible in so many distinct and even profoundly different ways when the authors of the Bible do not even seem to have a unified vision of God? Think about the profound differences noted at the beginning of this book among and between Catholics, Evangelicals, Mormons, Lutherans, Jehovah's Witnesses, Assemblies of God, Baptists, Presbyterians, Pentecostals, Orthodox Christians, Church of Christ members, and so many more. It is not that traditional literalists are necessarily contradictory, but there still are significant differences that can be very difficult, if not impossible, to reconcile. What are we to make of this apparent progression of God regarding either how the Judeo-Christian God revealed Himself to humankind as a whole over a long period of time or how humans in the Judeo-Christian tradition began to conceptualize God during all of that time?

Although this revelation covers a period of thousands of years chronologically and is meant for humankind in general, it might also represent an individual's potential experience chronologically during his or her *own* lifetime over perhaps 70 or 80 years. In other words, although the length of time involved may be quite different, the principle of development from the simple to the complex over time might be the same. That is, within one's own lifetime, there could be a progressive revelation of God, beginning in a relatively simple way, such as three men who are standing outside Abraham's tent, and then moving to John's more complex construct, "seven spirits on seven thrones with seven eyes gone out into the world."

This development from the simple to the complex involves change, and the only way to create change is to start by questioning. With that in mind, this book has been an attempt to open the door to some challenging yet honest questioning that allows a possible change in positions needed to go from a simple understanding of the Judeo-Christian God and a "simple theology" to the "seven spirits sitting on seven thrones with seven eyes gone out into the world." The more complex notion of God envisioned by John implies a deeper, more complex, and more metaphorical and symbolic revelation.

Hopefully, more than just raising various and detailed questions about literal pronouncements in Genesis and throughout the Bible, this book has the potential to help foster a deep state of wonder about God and all things spiritual in the reader and to cause the kind of inquiry that fosters the ongoing desire necessary to progress from the simple to the more complex. Without this type of questioning, the individual gets caught in the Procrustean trap of dogma and theology that cannot allow the next unveiling of God, and one can therefore easily get stuck in the dogma and doctrine of "religion," in which the Bible is reduced to God's alleged codebook of dos and do nots, used by religious experts and leaders to tell the rest of us how to live, and how to die.

Let me repeat that I am not saying that anyone else's interpretation is necessarily wrong and that mine is necessarily right. In fact, I am being very honest about the notion that my interpretation of the Bible is just that—*my* personal interpretation, which might be right, might be wrong, or might be somewhere in between—but in any event it is what it is because there is no such thing as a pure, literal interpretation. Indeed, I have sought to demonstrate in this book that any dogmatic claim of a supposed strict literal interpretation is just another form of someone's personal interpretation. I have sought to expose the narrow-mindedness of seriously arguing that only one's own interpretation of the Bible is the "correct" interpretation and that anyone who may have a different interpretation of the Bible is incorrect and must be defying God's true intentions, so I am clearly not saying that I am the sole true, self-appointed expert who knows what God must have meant, because I am doing nothing more than attempting to reasonably interpret what God allegedly has said!

Although there are many different *types* of religion on the surface, I often see only two types. First, there is the type of religion that has evolved in response to our social, political, and cultural development, not to mention in response to our numerous superstitions that have been manifested as various fears during our existence on Earth. Second, there is a type of religion that is continuously being revealed, or at least understood, on a less superficial and more mysterious and spiritual level. It is helpful to compare and contrast the two types. For example, the type of religion that first evolved with our worship of the sun filled a basic need and pacified certain human fears. Also, various natural phenomena (such as lightning, thunder, floods, hurricanes, and famine) each became a God of sorts, such that early humans worshiped each of them. This type of religion evolved over time. As a result of making progress scientifically, we lost the need to worship the sun for its life-giving qualities and instead began to understand the sun on a more natural, cosmological, and astronomical level.

As a result, we now understand how photosynthesis works and how we get energy and life support from the sun, so we do no not see the sun as a metaphysical deity itself bestowing life upon us (or as a Great Queen Bee Protector as bees might believe) but as a scientific, natural phenomenon. Over time, the religious understanding of the sun (Apollo) became obsolete and gave way to advancements in science. This change in understanding also meant that our deities had to evolve into more symbolic and metaphysical forms. This, in turn, has led to deeper arguments over theology and *positions* instead of natural phenomena. As our scientific understanding of the world around us has developed, it has meant that we have had to make adjustments in our theology. Just ask the Catholic Church, which excommunicated scientists as recently as a few hundred years ago for daring to speak the heresy that the earth was not at the center of the universe and that the earth revolved around the sun with other planets in our solar system. Indeed, look at the raging debates over religion that have taken place throughout the past century and currently over evolution, the age of the earth, dinosaur fossils, and whether dinosaurs and humans inhabited the earth at the same time—evil atheist scientists at work again!

The unfortunate formula of dogmatic fundamentalists seems to be the following:

> (1) Take a position, usually based on fear of judgment, a lack of understanding, or a need to make sense of a very complex universe, and believe in human beings' unique and extremely elevated importance in it.

> (2) Next, make a powerful unwavering stand by creating unquestionable dogma with unassailable textual support, as interpreted by those with power and or influence, no matter what the *facts* are—and then insulate that stand by believing that God is on one's side and anyone who disagrees must be under Satan's evil influence.

> (3) *Never* dare to question or challenge that dogma or sourcebook of dogma in any way, shape, or form, because to do so is to doubt God and to lack faith, and to sow seeds of confusion and discord.

> (4) Finally, be damned or ostracized if you dare to seriously question or challenge that dogma, its subjective interpretation, or those who espouse it (as I have in this book), who or whatever they might be.

It is not that this type of dogmatic understanding of God and religion is necessarily wrong, because it may nonetheless, on a certain level, help one to see some very limited *parts* of God that at least are easily understood. Unless one can make an honest and in-depth inquiry by raising serious questions, however, one cannot, in effect, make progress into a possible deeper understanding. Perhaps most importantly, one might miss out on a deeper revelation of God, to the extent there really is such a revelation to have.

In other words, we may understand at a certain level the God of Abraham, Moses, David, etc., but unless we can honestly question *our own* understanding and *our own* personal experiences with God, we might get stuck into not allowing ourselves the necessary questioning that creates the progress needed to see and understand any deeper revelation. The inevitable result is that we might become trapped in a religion that is simply evolving according to the particular fears and superstitions and basic needs of humankind at any particular stage of our overall awareness in history and in life. The type of God that is needed at this moment will evolve and come to the forefront as the particular need requires. This is how, I believe, religion as we know it has until this point *evolved*.

In order to mature beyond a dogmatic conceptualization of God according to a doctrinaire and allegedly literal and objective interpretation of Him, I have personally challenged any believer from any faith to read this book with an open mind and heart and to see whether and how God might speak and reveal Himself further, if at all. To do so would be to welcome an understanding that is outside of, and in spite of, any particular packaged belief system that has evolved for the safety, comfort, and security of a structured, systematized theology. Such personal inquiry may serve as a catalyst for one to move further along one's own spiritual quest. We might then just happen to stumble upon one of the seven spirits with seven eyes gone out into the world and as a result become rescued from our own preconceived belief system(s) and truly find a living, active, and loving God.

Of course, I must still be open to the critique often made by atheists that our superstitions are what create a need for a god to explain the universe to us on a simple and accessible level. That need may be developed and become more complex, and even grow more sophisticated over time, as I have just suggested in this Chapter; but in the end, maybe the search I am suggesting is also still just more complex superstitions in search of an elusive god, in what is another delusional attempt to explain the complexity of the universe. So instead of there being two kinds of religion, maybe everything is really the same religion, based entirely on fear of the unknown and a need for a spiritual answer that calms that fear and makes the unknown not so intimidating. Still, we should always be trying to progress in our understanding of science and religion, whether or not there is any ultimate reconciliation of the two. If there is, I submit that it will not and cannot be found simply in pretending to literally interpret an ancient text without adding one's own interpretations and subjective opinions about what the text really means. God, if there is a god, certainly is also found, perhaps even more so, beyond any ancient text.

I realize that such a journey is scary, in the sense that it calls for one to literally think outside the religious box and traditional constructs that we have created over time. It also means that some people might use such a personal spiritual journey as a convenient excuse to just make up whatever newfangled religion they want. I guess that is one's prerogative, and it is an ever-present danger. We all have choices to make, and we can proceed in good faith or in bad faith. In law, some would argue that, like judicial activism, this kind of journey invites judges to make up their own laws instead of applying the written laws we already have. That is certainly a risk—where each of us just creates our own personal little dogmatic religion—and there is significant validity in being gravely concerned about that problematic risk.

The other problem is that going on a personal quest to seek God that transcends traditional religion and dogma may just invite hopeless confusion, which can be discomforting and ultimately frustrating if one can never make sense of anything. That particular concern reminds me of the allegory of the cave from Plato's *Republic*. People who live their entire lives in a metaphorical cave—a cave of familiarity, comfort, and lack of exploration—so they never venture out to see the sun, the flowers, the mountains, the oceans, and the sky, the complexity that makes up our world, can become completely pacified with staying in their cave and never really exploring or living in the world. They can become, as the song says, "comfortably numb," because their cave represents all of what they know and understand, and so for them, "ignorance is bliss." The outside world may be beautiful, but it is also scary and can be awfully dangerous, and so one might decide never to venture out because the world can be very confusing and intimidating in a way that a familiar cave may not be.

Even though the outside world may be scary, and even confusing, however, life might be better lived outside of the comfort zone of one's own placated, self-imposed, metaphorical cave. True, living life outside of the cave may not be better if one ventures out and, immediately upon stepping outside, is crushed by a boulder, viciously attacked by a bear, or exposed to the elements with no safe shelter. Nevertheless, that is no reason to live life in the cave and never take the chance to endeavor beyond. Perhaps the possibility of harm should be taken simply as a cautionary tale to help one realize that life is interesting, dangerous, and, in any event, still worth venturing and living outside of the cave. As Henry David Thoreau once said,

> I went to the woods because I wished to live deliberately, to front only the essential facts of life, and see if I could not learn what it had to teach, and not, when I came to die, discover that I had not lived. I did not wish to live what was not life, living is so dear; nor did I wish to practise resignation, unless it was quite necessary. I wanted to live deep and suck out all the marrow of life, to live so sturdily and Spartan-like as to put to rout all that was not life, to cut a broad swath and shave close, to drive life into a corner, and reduce it to its lowest terms. (Henry David Thoreau, *Walden: Or, Life in the Woods*)

In a certain sense, it is rational not to believe in God, I concede that much. But if we choose to believe in God, we need to ask whether it would be fair to God for us to believe that He would be an indignant tyrant demanding unwavering uncritical simplistic adherence to ancient writings of men from the Middle East; and if we fail to comply with such demands, that He would then send us to burn in Hell, forever, no matter how reasonable or logical our questions or wonderment may be. It certainly appears from the Bible that God can be both loving and wrathful, but can He also be reasonable and fair; can He be a friend, rather than an enemy, of science, logic, evidence, and rationality? We should hope so for the Supreme Being of the universe. Thus, we should not be so fearful of a traditional and doctrinal concept of a God that we do not dare to "step out of our cave" in order to ask some hard and honest questions about who God is, and how we might come to know the real Him beyond what others may have written and thought about Him so long ago. We should instead use our minds—the minds that God gave us—to seek Him out, and then to trust that He will not be angry or judgmental merely because we are trying to make sense of our spirituality inside of the fascinating and complex universe and world in which we live.

Chapter One-Hundred-Three

Conclusion

Although I have come to the end of this book, it seems silly to call this the conclusion, as my questions just seem to go on and on; and I certainly have provided no definitive doctrinal answers. I have been able to make, however, at least what I hope are some interesting and helpful observations about God, faith, religion, and the problems with a proclaimed literal interpretation of the Bible, to the extent that any kind of a literal interpretation is even possible. Insofar as I believe in God, I have what is, admittedly, an intuitive, emotional, and even irrational belief in Him. Still, it is a very sincere belief, whatever "God" even really means.

Of course, there may be no definitive answers to any of our questions because life may be just like a giant test—and how could it be a true test if we were given all of the answers beforehand? Perhaps there should be more to our spiritual lives than just a literal and mechanical application of an ancient codebook written in cryptic, storybook form. Looking beyond rudimentary elements like this—which often leads to more and even deeper questions—reminds me of Albert Einstein's scientific journey in physics, when he counter intuitively noted that the more he learned about physics, the more he realized how much he did not know and how much more there must be to physics than was known at the time.

Although my personal search may go on as my life goes on and my questions may even go on forever, the reality is that this book cannot—my penchant to be longwinded notwithstanding (as this very sentence exemplifies). Given that reality-imposed constraint, I offer two parting thoughts. The first is a very old and venerable Catholic prayer, and the second is a short quote from the Bible, which is, after all, perhaps a very fitting way to end the book.

I offer the following prayer not only for believers, who may recognize some of the religious values contained therein, but also for atheists, agnostics, and others, who at least will likely appreciate the philosophical, humanistic, and universal values set forth therein, irrespective of the obvious religious connotations.

The Prayer of St. Francis

Lord, make me an instrument of your Peace.

Where there is hatred, let me sow love.
Where there is injury, pardon.
Where there is discord, union.
Where there is doubt, faith.
Where there is darkness, light.
And where there is sadness, joy.

O Master, grant that I may not so much
seek to be consoled, as to console;
to be understood, as to understand;
to be loved, as to love.
For it is in giving, that we receive.
It is in pardoning, that we are pardoned.
And it is in dying, that we are born to eternal life.

Amen

A Final Biblical Quote

After all that I have said and considered in this book about the problematic literal interpretation of the first 11 chapters of the book of Genesis, and after all that I have criticized about the Bible and have questioned about its lack of objectivity, and the fact that there is not, nor can there be, just one literal interpretation of it, as well as my concerns about the fallibility of its authors and all of the various people who actually wrote the hearsay contained in the Bible, and after all of the open-minded critique of my own faith, a faith which admittedly is not based on logic, science, rationality, or evidence-based reasoning but only upon my own blind intuition, all of which has caused me to seriously wonder what it may all mean, if anything... I now end the book with a very simple and comforting biblical quote:

"Be still, and know that I am God" (Psalms 46:10).

Well...OK. I will; but, to be continued.